POSTCOLONIAL APPROACHES TO THE EUROPEAN MIDDLE AGES

This collection of original essays is dedicated to the intersections between medieval and postcolonial studies. Ranging across a variety of academic disciplines, from art history to cartography, and from Anglo-Saxon to Arabic studies, this volume highlights the connections between medieval and postcolonial studies by exploring a theme common to both areas of study: translation as a mechanism of and metaphor for cultures in contact, confrontation, and competition. Drawing upon the widespread medieval trope of *translatio studii et imperii* (the translation of culture and empire), this collection engages the concept of translation from its most narrow, lexicographic sense, to the broader applications of its literal meaning, "to carry across." It carries the multilingual, multicultural realities of medieval studies to postcolonial analyses of the coercive and subversive powers of cultural translation, offering a set of case studies of translation as the transfer of language, culture, and power.

DEANNE WILLIAMS is Associate Professor of English at York University, Toronto. She is the author of *The French Fetish from Chaucer to Shakespeare* (Cambridge, 2004).

ANANYA JAHANARA KABIR is Lecturer in the School of English at University of Leeds, UK. She is the author of *Paradise, Death and Doomsday in Anglo-Saxon England* (Cambridge, 2001) and is currently working on post-partition cultural politics in South Asia.

CAMBRIDGE STUDIES IN MEDIEVAL LITERATURE

General editor
Alastair Minnis, *University of York*

Editorial board
Zygmunt G. Barański, *University of Cambridge*
Christopher C. Baswell, *University of California, Los Angeles*
John Burrow, *University of Bristol*
Mary Carruthers, *New York University*
Rita Copeland, *University of Pennsylvania*
Simon Gaunt, *King's College, London*
Steven Kruger, *City University of New York*
Nigel Palmer, *University of Oxford*
Winthrop Wetherbee, *Cornell University*
Jocelyn Wogan-Browne, *Fordham University*

This series of critical books seeks to cover the whole area of literature written in the major medieval languages – the main European vernaculars, and medieval Latin and Greek – during the period c. 1100–1500. Its chief aim is to publish and stimulate fresh scholarship and criticism on medieval literature, special emphasis being placed on understanding major works of poetry, prose, and drama in relation to the contemporary culture and learning which fostered them.

Recent titles in the series
Margaret Clunies Ross *Old Icelandic Literature and Society*
Donald Maddox *Fictions of Identity in Medieval France*
Rita Copeland *Pedagogy, Intellectuals and Dissent in the Later Middle Ages: Lollardy and Ideas of Learning*
Kantik Ghosh *The Wycliffite Heresy: Authority and the Interpretation of Texts*
Mary C. Erler *Women, Reading, and Piety in Late Medieval England*
D. H. Green *The Beginnings of Medieval Romance: Fact and Fiction, 1150–1220*
J. A. Burrow *Gestures and Looks in Medieval Narrative*
Ardis Butterfield *Poetry and Music in Medieval France: From Jean Renart to Guillaume de Machaut*
Emily Steiner *Documentary Culture and the Making of Medieval English Literature*
William E. Burgwinkle *Sodomy, Masculinity and Law in Medieval Literature*
Nick Havely *Dante and the Franciscans: Poverty and the Papacy in the Commedia*
Siegfried Wenzel *Latin Sermon Collections from Later Medieval England*

A complete list of titles in the series can be found at the end of the volume.

POSTCOLONIAL APPROACHES TO THE EUROPEAN MIDDLE AGES

Translating Cultures

Edited by

ANANYA JAHANARA KABIR

University of Leeds

and

DEANNE WILLIAMS

York University

CAMBRIDGE
UNIVERSITY PRESS

CAMBRIDGE UNIVERSITY PRESS
Cambridge, New York, Melbourne, Madrid, Cape Town, Singapore, São Paulo, Delhi

Cambridge University Press
The Edinburgh Building, Cambridge CB2 8RU, UK

Published in the United States of America by Cambridge University Press, New York

www.cambridge.org
Information on this title: www.cambridge.org/9780521827317

First published 2005

A catalogue record for this publication is available from the British Library

Library of Congress Cataloguing in Publication data
Postcolonial approaches to the European Middle Ages: translating cultures / edited by Ananya
Jahanara Kabir and Deanne Williams.
p.   cm. – (Cambridge studies in medieval literature 54)
Includes bibliographical references and index.
ISBN 0 521 82731 0
1. Literature, Medieval – History and criticism.   I. Kabir, Ananya Jahanara, 1970–
II. Williams, Deanne.   III. Series.
PN681.P55   2005
809′.02 – dc22   2004051852

ISBN 978-0-521-82731-7 hardback

Transferred to digital printing 2008

Contents

Contents

Illustrations

Acknowledgments

This book shows how continuities as well as disjunctions in time and space are crucial in conceptualizing historical processes. When we arrived at Oxford from Toronto and Calcutta to embark on our careers in medieval literature, we did not realize that we were, perhaps, post-colonial medievalists *avant la lettre*. What did strike us both then was the sudden expansion of spatial and temporal horizons that our new life entailed. This sense of wonder has sustained us, even as it has itself been sustained, during our subsequent intellectual journeys, parallel and intertwined. This collection of essays can be seen as its tangible avatar.

The collection was conceived through fruitful conversations during spring 2000; the many splendors (including gastronomic) of the Bay Area provided key inspiration. We would like to thank John Niles at the English Department, UC Berkeley, and the John Sias Dissertation Fellowship at Stanford University, for giving us the opportunity to be in (roughly) the same place at the same time. Seth Lerer and Ato Quayson encouraged this project from the very beginning, and we are grateful to them for their assistance.

We would also like to thank Alastair Minnis for welcoming this collection into his series, Linda Bree, our Cambridge editor, for her endless patience and goodwill, and our contributors for their enthusiastic participation in this long-term, long-distance relationship. The collection as a whole benefited greatly from the insightful comments of anonymous readers for the Press, and from the inspiration and insight of the participants and organizers of the "Orientalism before 1600" conference, which took place at Trinity College, Cambridge, in June 2001. Trinity College, Cambridge, the Centre for History and Economics at King's College, Cambridge, the University of Leeds, York University, the University of Toronto, the Social Sciences and Humanities Research Council of Canada, the Huntington Library, and the Folger Shakespeare Library provided us with financial support and ideal environments for completing various stages of the project.

We acknowledge with gratitude and pleasure the encouragement, advice, and support of our friends Amartya Sen and Emma Rothschild, Montu Saxena, James Simpson, David Dumville, Alfred Hiatt, and Simon Palfrey, and our teachers and mentors at Oxford: Helen Cooper, Malcolm Godden, Douglas Gray, Rohini Jayatilaka, Heather O'Donoghue, and Eric Stanley. Andreas Bücker, Magnus Marsden and Priya Natarajan opened up their Cambridge homes to Ananya, often at short notice, during her year spent in Geneva. Very special thanks are due to the Kabirs at Calcutta and the Dasguptas at Delhi for their kind hospitality, and to our wonderful partners, Mrinal Dasgupta and Terry Goldie, for their good humor, great wisdom, and endless indulgence. Finally, we would like to record our profound debt to the late Edward Said, from whose intellectual and political achievements we, along with so many others, draw continuing inspiration.

This book is dedicated to our mothers, Mary Chesney and Khairan Ara Kabir, and to the institution that brought us together, our alma mater, Lady Margaret Hall, Oxford.

Contributors

Suzanne Conklin Akbari is Associate Professor of English and Medieval Studies at the University of Toronto. Her work, which focuses on the intersection of literary and intellectual history, includes *Seeing through the Veil: Medieval Allegory and Optical Theory* (University of Toronto Press, 2004) and *Idols in the East: European Representations of Islam and the Orient, 1100–1450* (University of Pennsylvania Press, forthcoming).

Roland Greene is Professor of English and Comparative Literature and Head of the Division of Literatures, Cultures, and Languages at Stanford University. His most recent book is *Unrequited Conquests* (University of Chicago Press, 1999). Greene is also the author of *Post-Petrarchism: Origins and Innovations of the Western Lyric Sequence* (Princeton, 1991) and the editor, with Elizabeth Fowler, of *The Project of Prose in Early Modern Europe and the New World* (Cambridge University Press, 1997).

James G. Harper, Assistant Professor of Art History at the University of Oregon, received his PhD from the University of Pennsylvania in 1998. He is the Rush Kress Fellow at Villa I Tatti, the Harvard University Center for Italian Renaissance Studies, 2003–4. He is currently editing a volume of essays entitled *The Turk and Islam in the Western Eye (1453–1750)*.

Alfred Hiatt is a Lecturer in the School of English, and a member of the Centre for Medieval Studies at the University of Leeds. He is the author of *The Making of Medieval Forgeries: False Documents in Fifteenth-Century England* (British Library, 2003).

Nicholas Howe is Professor of English at the University of California, Berkeley. He is the author of *The Old English Catalogue Poems*

(Copenhagen, 1985), *Migration and Mythmaking in Anglo-Saxon England* (Yale University Press, 1989), and *Across an Inland Sea: Writing in Place from Buffalo to Berlin* (Princeton University Press, 2003). He is currently at work on two books: *Writing the Map of Anglo-Saxon England* and *The Yale Guide to Old English Literature*.

Ananya Jahanara Kabir is Lecturer in Postcolonial Literatures at the School of English, and a member of the Centre of Medieval Studies at the University of Leeds. She is the author of *Paradise, Death and Doomsday in Anglo-Saxon Literature* (Cambridge University Press, 2001). She is currently working on a study of imperial medievalism and researching literary responses to political conflict in Kashmir.

Seth Lerer is the Avalon Foundation Professor in Humanities and Professor of English and Comparative Literature at Stanford University. His most recent book is *Error and the Academic Self: The Scholarly Imagination, Medieval to Modern* (Columbia University Press, 2003).

Ato Quayson is Director of the African Studies Centre, Lecturer in English and Fellow of Pembroke College, University of Cambridge. His publications include *Strategic Transformations in Nigerian Writing* (Indiana University Press and James Currey, 1997), *Postcolonialism: Theory, Practice or Process* (Polity, 2000), *Relocating Postcolonialism* with David Theo Goldberg (Blackwell, 2002) and *Calibrations: Reading for the Social* (Minnesota University Press, 2003). He is currently working on a comparative study of representations of physical disability in world literature.

Michelle R. Warren is Associate Professor of French and Director of Graduate Studies at the University of Miami. She is the author of *History on the Edge: Excalibur and the Borders of Britain, 1100-1300* (Minnesota University Press, 2000) and co-editor of *Postcolonial Moves: Medieval through Modern* (Palgrave Macmillan, 2003) and *Arts of Calculation: Quantifying Thought in Early Modern Europe* (Palgrave Macmillan, forthcoming).

Deanne Williams is Associate Professor of English at York University, Toronto. She is the author of *The French Fetish from Chaucer to Shakespeare* (Cambridge University Press, 2004).

Introduction: a return to wonder

Ananya Jahanara Kabir and Deanne Williams

> Wonder is the first of all the passions.
> René Descartes, *The Passions of the Soul*

Any list of "wonderful" medieval European artifacts would have, somewhere near the top, the *Très riches heures* of Jean, duc de Berry, illuminated by the Limbourg brothers. One of the most famous examples of medieval manuscript illumination, the *Très riches heures* languished in obscurity until it was purchased by the Musée Condé at Chantilly in 1856. Initially received as an exotic curiosity and celebrated as one of the *primitifs françaises*, the manuscript was regarded in terms typically applied to artifacts of Africa or the Far Pacific. Now it is celebrated as a rare and precious art object: so rare that the Musée Condé has decided to remove it entirely from public exhibition and even private scholarly viewing.[1] The history of the manuscript's reception highlights the extent to which modernity casts the medieval past as a "foreign country," aligning it with the binaries of East and West, Europe and abroad. Nevertheless, even as the Middle Ages came to occupy the position of the "dark continent" for post-Enlightenment Europe, its alterity is capable of generating an aura that emanates especially from its material culture. We call this aura "wonder."

By juxtaposing East and West, and past and present, readers of the *Très riches heures* imposed the preoccupations of modernity on a hapless past, its object. Their response exemplifies how the medieval past can be colonized, like a distant continent, to further the interests of modernity, and anticipates the common ground that medieval and postcolonial scholars have found in recent years. As postcolonial scholars have sought to dismantle the notions of modernity upon which colonialism was predicated, medievalists have, in turn, challenged the binaries of medieval and modern (or early modern) that bracket off the Middle Ages, and keep it as exotic and foreign – and also as domitable – as any orientalist fantasy. As critiques of colonialism work in tandem with critiques of modernity, medieval studies and postcolonial studies have sought to undermine a series of western myths of origin, history, identity, and temporality. Our collection joins this evolving trajectory.

At the same time, by characterizing the manuscript as one of the great medieval "wonders," we participate in a resurgence of scholarly interest in the marvels, the prodigies, and the wonders of the Middle Ages, as well as the Renaissance. As Caroline Walker Bynum puts it, wonder takes place "when the specificity, the novelty, the awe-fulness, of what our sources render up bowls us over with its complexity and its significance."[2] Wonder has become a catchphrase for a scholarly response to medieval alterity that seeks neither to accommodate it to the priorities of the present, nor to bracket it off as irredeemably alien and different. Stephen Greenblatt distinguishes wonder from historical and scholarly resonance by defining it as "the power of the displayed object to stop the viewer in his or her tracks, to convey an arresting sense of uniqueness, to evoke an exalted attention."[3] However, this sense of an arresting encounter, and of the shock of the new and different, is often lost when the sister processes of orientalism and medievalization are demystified and deracinated. As Greenblatt asks, "How is it possible, in a time of disorientation, hatred of the other and possessiveness, to keep the capacity for wonder from being poisoned?"[4]

To answer this question, we turn to the *Très riches heures* (Fig. 1). The manuscript generates wonder by participating in a conflation of time and space that seems, at first glance, to share much with its nineteenth-century classification as *primitif*. This conflation of cultures, and of past and present, is also the manuscript's theme. Described by Erich Auerbach as "providential time" (in contrast to the linearity of modern conceptions of time), the temporalities of medieval Christianity produce similar juxtapositions through a triadic fascination with the past (the Old Testament), the present (the birth of Christ), and the hopeful future (the New Jerusalem).[5] Thus, the Limbourg brothers' depictions of the life and surroundings of early fifteenth-century inhabitants of the French countryside share space with spectacular renderings of the most sacred

1 The Meeting of the Magi, *Les très riches heures de Jean, duc de Berry*, fol. 51, v.

moments, such as the Annunciation, or St. John on Patmos. The artists, a trio of brothers displaced from Germany, take pains to emphasize the messianic qualities of Christ by depicting his acceptance by a variety of cultures. This cross-cultural, even ecumenical aspect of Christianity is present in the depiction of the Exaltation of the Cross, which presents the Byzantine emperor Heraclius with a multiracial set of companions, and in the Nativity scene, where Jesus' visitors possess a variety of skin tones. Yet such charming anachronisms and apparent inclusiveness cannot be detached from stereotypes that highlight difference. The Revealing of the True Cross uses the pointed hat typically used to designate a Jew, which functioned as a kind of visual shorthand for medieval anti-Semitism.

The illumination of the Meeting of the Magi that appears on our cover illustrates our concept of "wonder" even as it highlights its problems.[6] On their way to visit the baby Jesus at Bethlehem, the three Magi meet at a crossroads, on which is erected an elaborately Gothic Montjoie: one of the sites, marked by crusaders, from which Jerusalem could be seen. In the background, Jerusalem is figured as medieval Paris, complete with Sainte-Chapelle and Notre Dame. In the foreground, the gorgeously embellished Magi and their entourages flow like three rivers from three different directions, coming to a conclusive stop at the Montjoie. Just to the left of its spires nestles the Star of David. As the Magi, of Zoroastrian faith and Eastern origins, witness the unfolding of a new religion, this focal conjunction of star and spire subsumes a variety of human times and places within the eternal and the providential. As a vantage point for crusaders seeking out Jerusalem, the Montjoie conflates the Magi's pilgrimage to seek out the Christ Child in Bethlehem, with the battlecry "Montjoie!" used by medieval knights in the *Chanson de Roland* during their manifold encounters with the demonized "pagans." Architecture and performative speech acts thus draw the ostensible timelessness of biblical typology into the world of the crusades: a conflict whose repercussions continue to be felt today. The Parisian edifices of Sainte-Chapelle and Notre Dame mask the extent to which the site of revelation segues into contested territory: a battleground between "Europe" and "Orient," East and West, Christian and Jew and Muslim. As the Star of David beckons to the Magi, we are reminded of the centrality of encounters with difference to

Christian mythology. Simultaneously, the appropriation of Jerusalem for Paris recalls the more recent invocations, by both George W. Bush and Osama bin Laden, of the "clash of civilizations" and the medieval crusades.

Nevertheless, the star itself radiates alternative interpretative strategies. It is a signifier that King Herod, who throws down the prophetic books in denial, reads very differently from the Magi, for whom it provides direction and meaning. Likewise, the illumination's depiction of cross-cultural contact can be read in a diametrically opposite way. With their crowns and turbaned followers, in embroidered silks and satins, and accessorized with damascene scimitars, the Magi reflect the movement and appropriation of culture from the Byzantine East to the Latin West. The fifteenth-century vision of luxury that they embody visually echoes the increasing characterization, in the commentaries of the Church Fathers, of the Magi as mysterious Others. The Magi, figures of Zoroastrian learning, are thus layered with contemporary Oriental significations of Saracens and Ottomans. This shift at the level of exegesis took place in the context of Western Europe's increasingly frequent encounters with "the Orient," through the crusades, trade and pilgrimage routes, and in the contact zones of the Outremer, Sicily, and Spain.

The work of Edward Said provides us with a ready framework for theorizing the reconceptualization of the Magi in accordance with emerging Western systems of knowledge that sought to define, and to control, "the East."[7] Yet the historical context in which it took place is very different from the post-Enlightenment world of European imperialism that produced Orientalism. Prior to the age of European expansion, the balance of power between Western Europe and "the Orient," and the European admiration for – and appropriation of – the non-European, makes the Magi of the *Très riches heures* bearers of what Lisa Jardine dubs "worldly goods."[8] As an artifact, the *Très riches heures* is itself crowded with sumptuous objects – luxury textiles, gemstones, damascene swords, hunting dogs, thoroughbred horses. By attending to the "social life" of these things, we complicate both the Magi's Othering and their role as proto-crusaders, even as that role, in turn, is blurred by the coexistence of Jerusalem as a site of crusade and pilgrimage.[9]

The multivalent Magi, who signal both spiritual rebirth *and* commodity culture, invite us to read Jerusalem, too, as a site that accommodates conquest, appropriation, and bloodshed with travel, pilgrimage, and cross-cultural encounter. Returning to Greenblatt's question of recuperation, we propose a return to wonder, and an effort to keep it from being poisoned, by reading the Meeting of the Magi as a translated artifact. The Limbourgs translate luxurious commodities from East to West, and from physicality to representation, and from the fifteenth century back to the time of the birth of Christ, illustrating ostensible geographic and temporal oppositions while, at the same time, enacting the inextricable embeddedness of cultural contact. As animal hide is translated into illuminated book, the artistic process of illumination likewise brings together European parchment with gold, lapis lazuli, and vermilion imported from the East. If the experience of viewing this illumination produces wonder and rapture (in its literal sense of being borne away, upwards), then translation itself may be viewed as a kind of transcendence. And transcendence, itself, speaks with two tongues: on the one hand, it moves toward the erasure of difference, and on the other, it moves away from pernicious distinctions and toward incorporation as well as variegation.

Postcolonial Approaches to the European Middle Ages: Translating Cultures develops this variegated, seemingly contradictory, understanding of translation as a mechanism of and metaphor for cultures in contact, confrontation, and competition, but also as a means of rehabilitating wonder. Translation is often seen as a metaphor for postcolonial writing itself, with the literal act of translation embodying the asymmetrical power relations and violence of different colonialisms.[10] The father of Orientalism, William Jones, has been accused of sanitizing "odorous" native realities within his translation of the Sanskrit classic *Abhijnanasakuntalam*; yet the same Jones, while voyaging out to India, eagerly sniffed the sea air and marveled "that India lay before us, and Persia on our left, whilst a breeze from Arabia blew nearly on our stern."[11] Taking a cue from the affective and symbiotic relationship between Jones and his own physical, temporal and linguistic translations, we reengage what many perceive to be "the shameful history of translation" by examining different aspects of medieval European culture through the lens of postcolonial studies.[12] Our multiple uses of translation foreground the intersections between medieval and postcolonial studies while at the same time suggesting some recuperative measures that we consider useful for both disciplines.

Highlighting the interactions between colonial representation and postcolonial resistance, Maria Tymoczko points out: "translation is paradoxically the means by which difference is perceived, preserved, projected and proscribed."[13] The essays in this volume illustrate these paradoxes by drawing upon the widespread medieval trope of *translatio imperii et studii*. They thereby engage the concept of translation from its most narrow, lexicographic sense, to the wider applications of its literal meaning, "to carry across." Translating between postcolonial and medieval studies, as well as between disciplinary boundaries, including classical and vernacular literatures, historiography and biography, they carry across the multilingual, multicultural realities of medieval studies to postcolonial analyses of the coercive and subversive powers of cultural translation.

By offering case studies of translation as the transfer of language, culture, and power, we make available to postcolonial scholars a rigorous historicization of their own insights. At the same time, our essays actively acknowledge and respond to a sense of wonder. Even though it is evoked by material artifacts such as maps, monuments, and paintings, rather than natural or geographical phenomena, this experience is in many ways comparable to the Romantic sublime. As David Hume observes, in *An Enquiry Concerning Human Understanding*:

> The imagination of man is naturally sublime, delighted with whatever is remote and extraordinary, and running, without control, into the most distant parts of space and time in order to avoid the objects, which custom has rendered familiar to it.[14]

In Immanuel Kant's theory of the sublime, which moves more closely to the awesome and the unrepresentable, this uncontrolled "running" toward the remote – whether spatial or temporal – emerges even more clearly as the active desire for and engagement with Otherness.[15] However, we differentiate wonder from the sublime by foregrounding the acts of decentering the ego that can occur at precisely the moment of experiencing wonder. Joseph Bédier encountering the *Chanson de Roland* for the first time under a mango tree in his tropical island home of Réunion, medieval cartographers inventively and imaginatively reorienting Roman maps, a twenty-first-century scholar marveling at an Anglo-Saxon church built from a Roman ruin and nestled in the postmodern urban sprawl of contemporary provincial Britain: our essays reveal these and other responses to the past not as cynical acts of appropriation or suppression, but as cultural encounters signaling immersion, even negation of the self, engagement, and wonder.

The chapters in this volume thus engage forms of translation that accommodate and express wonder at the newness that enters the world through the act of cultural dialogue. Like many others, we draw our inspiration from Walter Benjamin's sense of translation, which he defines as "a somewhat provisional way of coming to terms with the foreignness of language."[16] Yet the awkwardness and alienation that define Benjamin's "The task of the translator" also contain glimpses of nostalgia for the premodern. Referring to the interlinear glosses that appear in medieval religious manuscripts, he declares, "The interlinear version of the scripture is the prototype or ideal of all translation."[17] Images of medieval icons and early modern portraits also seem to underscore his statement that "the language of the translation envelops its content like a royal robe with ample folds."[18] For all its high-modernist longing for the purity and essence that exists "between the lines," Benjamin's account of translation mines the Middle Ages for images that convey a sense of the coexistence of difference. The temporal distance between medieval and modern, and the inaccuracies in appraisals of the past that occur as a result, thus accompany and illuminate the linguistic problematics of "translation" and "original." Interestingly, this nostalgia for the Middle Ages reappears in current discussions of postcolonial translation: Tymoczko invokes the physical translation of medieval saints' relics in her discussion of the utility of translation as a metaphor for postcoloniality, while Harish Trivedi and Susan Bassnett declare that "medieval writers and/or translators were not too troubled by [the] phantasm" of the high-status original text.[19] In this way, the Middle Ages contributes to, and even enables, a process of centering and displacement that complicates the equation of translation and wonder: its role in these discussions of translation invites a reconsideration of the role of historical nostalgia as a force that generates empathy and recognition, as well as wonder.

Trivedi and Bassnett's turn to the Middle Ages supplements their argument about the mutual implication of authorship, copyright, and the emergence of print culture: an argument that relies on Benedict Anderson's account of nationalism.[20] Medievalists have repeatedly intervened into this supposed rupture between the medieval and the modern in Anderson's construction of modernity exposing the reproduction of these paradigms in the work of Homi Bhabha and others. These interventions have produced a series of critiques of the constructs of nationhood and national identity, as well as of the ideologies of colonialism itself.[21] Yet in deconstructing the binary between medieval and modern, it is not enough, as Ruth Evans points out, to rest on analogy: "while the situation of medieval vernacular writers was analogous to that of modern postcolonial writers confronting the cultural hegemony of English (and other colonial languages), this confrontation cannot be represented straightforwardly as English playing the David to Latin's Goliath."[22] Rather than lamenting the "abiding historical trauma" of medievalism, the essays in this volume advocate not only the problematics of engaging with history, but also its potential.[23]

This collection works alongside and expands upon recent scholarship dedicated to the intersections between medieval and postcolonial studies. Jeffrey Jerome Cohen's *The Postcolonial Middle Ages*, the first collection on the subject, uses medieval, and mostly English, culture to present a variety of engagements with and critiques of Said's *Orientalism*, justifying its Anglophone remit with reference to the Anglophone domination of postcolonial theory.[24] A more recent volume on the subject, *Postcolonial Moves: Medieval to Modern*, presents a wider geographical field of vision, and focuses specifically upon the task of dismantling the ultimately teleological periodization of European history from the standpoint of medieval studies.[25] The dual critiques of colonialism and modernity are fruitfully reflected in essays that present a series of juxtapositions of medieval and modern texts, revealing a modernity that is persistently haunted by the medieval past. Attentiveness to historical difference characterizes the work of medievalists who have convincingly intervened into those new master-narratives of difference and rupture, while avoiding the danger of conflating intellectual and historiographical paradigms with the lived experience of oppression that lurks in the call to "decolonize" the Middle Ages.[26]

While our collection draws inspiration from these parallel enterprises, its emphasis on translation calls attention to material and linguistic as well as theoretical details, and to the texts and artifacts in themselves. The requisite scholarly training of medievalists, which notoriously saddles us with linguistic training as well as paleography and codicology, leaves us particularly eager and willing to engage with the demands of the archive and the manuscript. However, the particular consideration these essays give to buildings and maps, paintings and statues, philology and biography, moves the discussion of medieval postcolonialism, or postcolonial medieval studies, into different arenas of translation. As Bruce Holsinger warns, "in a number of ways the presumptive belatedness of medieval studies in relation to postcolonialism threatens to be counted among what Louise Fradenburg calls 'those modes of self-marginalization' that medieval studies enjoys perpetrating against itself."[27] This collection does not merely inflict the postcolonial on the medieval (or vice versa). Rather, it highlights the connections between the two by exploring a theme common to both medieval and postcolonial studies: translation as a mechanism of and metaphor for cultures in contact, confrontation, and competition. It reconsiders the role of historical nostalgia as a force that generates empathy and recognition, as well as wonder. It reveals how cultural relationships in the Middle Ages can be viewed through the filter of translation-as-wonder, and shows how the idea of the Middle Ages itself is the product of ceaseless decenterings, displacements, and translations.

Many themes resonate throughout the collection: the legacy of Rome, the "idea" of the Middle Ages, the politics of cultural identity, the prehistory of Orientalism, the impulse toward genealogy, and the power of memory. However, we have grouped the essays in this volume in order to reflect a past, a present, and a future. The first group, "The afterlife of Rome," calls attention to ancient Rome as an antecedent to imperialism in modernity, and charts a series of "postcolonial" responses to it in the Middle Ages. The second section, "Orientalism before 1600," examines medieval representations of cultural difference, and reveals the fluidity of identifications of self and Other that proliferate in a period that precedes European domination. The third, entitled "Memory and nostalgia," reveals how the medieval past signified and was deliberately manipulated in colonial as well as postcolonial contexts, from India to France to the New World.

"The afterlife of Rome" highlights the relationship between the Middle Ages, late antiquity, and imperial Rome. With the spreading nexus between capitalism and globalization in a post-Cold War world, evocations of America as Empire in popular as well as academic discourses have become commonplace. The Roman Empire has reemerged as a historical and political predecessor to contemporary neo-imperialism: from the Hollywood extravaganza *Gladiator* to Michael Hardt and Antonio Negri's recent work of radical political philosophy, *Empire*. Yet discourses about the primacy of Rome invariably invoke some aspect of the Middle Ages as a regressive space of "anti-Empire" to be fetishized and infantilized as non-civic, non-democratic, and non-modern. Thus, the fertile culture of late antiquity becomes, in *Gladiator*, the chaotic border between classical imperial order and medieval Gothic disorder, represented by the contrast between the armored phalanxes of the Roman army and the long-haired, club-wielding masses of the Germanic hordes it encounters.

The revisionist, anti-imperial approach of Hardt and Negri discards the image of the chaotic early Middle Ages in exchange for a Christian Middle Ages that challenges imperial might.[28] Their opening discussion of Empire as world order concludes by invoking "the birth of Christianity in Europe and its expansion during the decline of the Roman Empire," a "chiliastic project [that] offered an absolute alternative to the spirit of imperial right – a new ontological basis." Although they use this analogy to seek out "an ontological basis of antagonism – with Empire, but also against and beyond Empire," Hardt and Negri gloss over the intense political struggles within early Christianity, seamlessly conflating the several centuries between Christianity's birth and its expansion (not to mention geographical distance between Near East and Europe).[29] Such space-clearing moves romanticize the Middle Ages in ways that undermine rather than highlight its "radicality," posing serious intellectual challenges to an otherwise laudable counter-imperialist philosophy.

The chapters in this section historicize the much invoked binary between Rome and the Middle Ages by focusing on the material culture that was left behind: buildings, floors, roads, maps. Different phases of the Middle Ages then appear differently "postcolonial" when situated in relationship to Rome, and the very idea of postcoloniality emerges as imbued with more imperial and colonial legacies than the "post" would suggest. Together, these essays offer new challenges to postcolonialists and postmodernists who continue to see the Middle Ages as modernity's other, as well as to medievalists who place the Middle Ages at the beginning of European historical teleology.

Nicholas Howe's chapter, "Anglo-Saxon England and the postcolonial void," clears theoretical space for the interpretation of Anglo-Saxon England as the postcolony of the Roman Empire by reading architectural and textual traces of Roman material culture as the haunting of the Anglo-Saxon imagination by the Roman colonial past. The *spolia* that litter the physical landscape of England are translated into the Latin textual witnesses of Gildas and Bede as well as the Old English poems *The Wanderer* and *The Ruin*. This "line of memorial transmission" traverses the historiographic void between the departure of the Romans and the Saxon Advent, as well as between the two languages of Anglo-Saxon England. The continuing legibility of those *spolia*, ensured by the monastic use of Latin, signals the reconnection of the postcolony of the Roman *imperium* to the new empire of Latin Christianity that continues to be centered on Rome, though with a transformed significance. Anglo-Saxon England thus emerges out of the postcolonial void by critically scrutinizing its relationship to Empire, albeit not without a sense of eerie melancholy. The material and memorial overlap of imperial and Christian Rome, Roman Britain, and Anglo-Saxon England both complicates the simplistic application of postcolonial theory to the period and calls for greater recognition, by postcolonialists, of the coexistence of colonial and postcolonial structures, in a manner analogous to the assimilation of former British colonies into the "Commonwealth."

Alfred Hiatt's chapter, "Mapping the ends of empire," examines a similar overlap of colonial and postcolonial discursive practices through medieval mapping practices. By reworking the traditions of classical geography, medieval maps are both "enablers of colonial vision and colonialism's detritus." Hiatt proposes that we view medieval maps not through "binaries of preservation and innovation," but instead through the processes of translation. As Isidore of Seville and Orosius, key sources for medieval geography, grapple with Roman modes of spatial

organization and representation at the very moment of empire's dis-
solution, they participate in the *translatio studii* of classical knowledge
to the medieval period; simultaneously, they assume a postcolonial status. Hiatt proceeds to chart the changes in mapping practices from
the twelfth century onwards, engaging cartographic evidence for the
intertwining of commerce, pilgrimage, and occupation that occurred
under the rubric of the crusades. The changing representations of the
Holy Land demonstrate how maps, crucial in the formation of Roman
imperial discourses, lived on as colonial formations after the colony.
By reminding us of the continuing contested cartography of Palestine,
predicated on imperial redrawing of boundaries prior to decolonization,
Hiatt urges us "to rethink the post in postcolonialism." By emphasizing
that "narratives of curiosity, accident, and imagination also make maps,
not only histories of contestation and encounter," he also recuperates
the wonder that the collection, as a whole, emphasizes in postcolonial
readings of medieval artifacts.

Themes of translation, recuperation, and Rome's legacy to postcolonial Europe recur in Seth Lerer's "'On fagne flor': the postcolonial *Beowulf*, from Heorot to Heaney." Lerer reads the "fagne flor"
(stained/marked floor) of Heorot, the great hall in *Beowulf*, as a tessellated floor of the Roman past. Through Seamus Heaney's recent translation of *Beowulf*, he magnifies the contemporary postcolonial resonances
of a vernacular present set on an ancient relic. Feuds and pyres of *Beowulf*
emerge as a layer of the "modern scarred political body" that includes
Heaney's Northern Ireland. However, the memory of Roman magnificence, inscribed through the Latin and Old English equivalents of
wonder (*mirabilis/wrætlic*), rescues *Beowulf* from melancholia. Through
the reclaimed nexus between Anglo-Saxon England and imperial Rome,
Heaney transcends his own (post)colonial relationship to England. The
translator's "illumination by philology" leads to a postcolonial sublime
effected through the vernacularizing of that magnificence, epitomized
in Heaney's renaming of Heorot as "bawn." Through an Irish word that
connotes simultaneously simple barn and grand castle, Heorot becomes
a hybrid structure, "part native settlement, part foreign imposition,"
just as Howe's reading of the church of St. John at Escomb, built upon
a Roman arch, physicalizes translation in the form of historical syncretism and cultural assimilation. The Irishness of Heaney's *Beowulf*

makes philology reverberate not with the desire for pure origins – and its concomitant associations with empire and colony – but with the joy of the contaminated and stained.

Themes of syncretism, assimilation, and cultural encounter return with the second section, "Orientalism before 1600," that takes its name from a conference held at Trinity College, Cambridge, in July, 2001.[30] Said's widely influential *Orientalism* demonstrates the extent to which European colonization of the East from the Enlightenment through the nineteenth century was produced by discursive practices of ordering and shaping the world. Somewhat like the legacy of the Roman Empire, the success of *Orientalism* may be measured in the overwhelming number of responses to it (many of them critical): its East–West binaries, its Foucauldian focus on western forms of knowledge, and its analysis of discourses, as opposed to, say, psychological formations or economic structures.[31] Early modern cultural historians such as Lisa Jardine, Jerry Brotton, Nabil Matar, Daniel Vitkus, Jyotsna Singh, and Andrew Hadfield have offered a series of critiques of Said, and uncovered material evidence that reveals a multiplicity of responses and engagements between East and West. As a whole, their work reveals a complex of western attitudes to the East and in particular to Islam, and of eastern responses to the west, that are, variously, envious and pragmatic, condescending and admiring, eager to convert and eager to emulate, and, very often, charged with wonder.[32] This body of evidence, as Jardine and Brotton conclude, allows us to "circumvent an account of the marginalized, exoticized, dangerous East within Renaissance studies as not only politically unhelpful but also historically inaccurate."[33]

Within medieval studies, however, the response to *Orientalism* remains somewhat more binaristic. Some medievalists have critiqued Said's emphasis upon spatial and geographical distinctions of East and West at the expense of time and history, as, on the one hand, re-affirming the timelessness of the East–West binary, and, on the other, producing an image of the medieval as either antecedent or Other to this modern framework.[34] Others have engaged with Said by locating, particularly in the literature of the crusades and in the genre of romance, a kind of prehistory of Orientalist paradigms. The chapters in "Orientalism before 1600" contribute an alternative perspective. Rather than critiquing postcolonialists' attitudes toward temporality and ideas about the Middle Ages, or elaborating Said's existing binaristic structures, they locate numerous examples of western self-identifications and representations as, in a variety of ways, "Eastern." These essays demonstrate the fluidity and porousness of cultural paradigms in the Middle Ages, locating processes of identity-formation that move between and among alternate and competing perspectives and definitions of cultural difference.

The tangled routes of cultural transmission crisscrossing antiquity and the Middle Ages, and bringing together Persia, Byzantium, Greece, and Rome, provide complex antecedents for Saidean Orientalism. In "Alexander in the Orient: bodies and boundaries in the *Roman de toute chevalerie*," Suzanne Conklin Akbari examines the multiple westward turns embodied in a twelfth-century Anglo-Norman romance of Alexander, a member of the Alexander corpus that provided the Middle Ages with a vast template of "Oriental wonders." Akbari complements Hiatt's discussion of the medieval recycling of late antique geography by focusing on Orosius' quadripartite sequence of *translatio imperii* (from Babylon to Rome via Macedonia and Carthage). Although the text does not engage with western geographical extremities, it makes a series of movements west that illustrate multiple significations of "the West." Alexander's conduct on the battlefield with the Persian king Darius and in the bedroom with the Oriental queen Candace, makes him a mediator between the familiar space of home and the exotic terrain abroad. Whereas the Roman describes unsettling locations where identity is contingent and danger close at hand, the return of the narrative to the West anticipates the medieval vernacularization of Latinate culture through the enactment of *translatio imperii*, as well as the early modern cultural ascendancy of Western Europe.

Deanne Williams observes, in "Gower's monster," that some aspects of the Middle Ages have proved more amenable to "postcolonization" than others. Taking an unlikely candidate, the medieval English poet John Gower, Williams examines the ways in which his work, with its royal dedicatees and learned frames of reference, has been considered inhospitable by medievalists who are eager to recuperate and celebrate the "Other" Middle Ages. Polyglot, elite, and (as some argue) politically conservative, Gower is frequently associated with the structures and hierarchies of a Middle Ages that previous generations of medievalists found consoling, and that medievalists today are more willing to demonize. However, Gower's fascination with the biblical figure of Nebuchadnezzar, the king of Babylon from the book of Daniel who is transformed into a beast and exiled to the wilderness, complicates our understanding of this author. It constitutes a direct engagement with the questions of civility and barbarism that medieval English culture was contending with, as it was developing a distinct identity in conversation with the Latin and French cultures that dominated in the aftermath of Roman colonization and Norman Conquest. Williams shows how Gower uses Nebuchadnezzar's monstrous form to reclaim, even celebrate, an English reputation for barbarism. A figure for acts of translation and interpretation, as well as for wondrous revelation, Nebuchadnezzar sheds light on Gower's authorial identity as well as on the literary culture of late medieval England.

As "Gower's monster" concerns an English identification with Nebuchadnezzar, the king of Babylon, James Harper's chapter, "Turks as Trojans; Trojans as Turks: visual imagery of the Trojan War and the politics of cultural identity in fifteenth-century Europe," shows instead how Trojans, the mythical ancestors of choice of the Italians (not to mention the English, the Burgundians, and the Habsburgs), are identified with contemporary Ottoman Turks in fifteenth-century manuscript illuminations and paintings. Harper argues that this identification between Trojans and Ottomans responds to the military and territorial threats posed by the Ottoman Empire in the aftermath of the spectacular victories in the fifteenth century. Some commentators located a Trojan lineage for the Turks in order to accommodate them within the European community. As a result, the visual representations of Trojans as Turks in manuscript illuminations also evoked the worldly riches of ancient Rome. Yet as the Ottoman Empire continued to gain power, attempts to contain the threat that they posed produced instead a series of counter-attempts to demonize, as well as convert, the Turk. Hence, by the sixteenth century, Trojans were presented not as Turks, but as ancient Romans. While this complex process of analogy and comparison highlights anxieties about European colonization by the Turks – how can you colonize your own people? – it also charts an early history of the use of the legacy of ancient Rome for purposes of propaganda that anticipates the future of European colonialism.

Our final section, "Memory and nostalgia," examines the ways in which medieval studies and the idea of the Middle Ages functioned in a colonial framework. As historians of the Holocaust, African-American slavery, and, most recently, the Partition of India have documented, the traumas of displacement and of loss of property and territory produce a series of complex narrative responses. Highlighting the experiences of shock and conflict, and the processes of recollection and forgetting, the chapters in this section reveal how the Middle Ages and medieval studies signified in the formation of colonial as well as postcolonial subjectivities. They provide a vocabulary for, as well as a distraction from, the experiences of colonialism. Most notably, these essays show how medieval histories and cultures offered the possibility of rewriting the past, by providing a wonderful mythos and genealogy to justify, smooth over, and suppress aspects of history in response to what Allen Frantzen calls "the desire for origins."[35]

In "Analogy in translation: imperial Rome, medieval England and British India," Ananya Jahanara Kabir explains how British imperialism in India was conceptualized through a series of analogies with medieval English history, and, in particular, the conquest of England by the Romans, the Saxons, and the Normans. These analogies cast, for example, the Hindus as the Anglo-Saxons, and the Persians, seen as invaders into India, as the Normans; while the British played a variety of roles, including Romans, Normans, and Anglo-Saxons. Such analogies offered a means of assimilating the complexities of the colonialist encounter, but they problematized the concurrent analogy between the British and Roman empires. These competing, as well as conflicting, analogies reflected not only colonial struggles for linguistic and cultural as well as geographical domination of India, but also the struggle among historians in England to establish a coherent narrative of English history. By closely focusing on imperial medievalism, Kabir nuances and develops arguments advanced by both postcolonialists and medievalists for the colonies being the laboratory of Empire, especially in the context of constructing the concept and canon of English literature. As she also suggests in conclusion, however, this necessary unmasking of the consequent celebration of racial purity should also be open to recuperating moments of countermemorial nostalgia that operate within this discourse of collective colonial memory.

In the case of the British nostalgia for the Middle Ages, collective memory acts as a justification and frame for colonial activities. Michelle R. Warren's *"Au commencement était l'île*: the colonial formation of Joseph Bédier's *Chanson de Roland"* charts a different territory by explaining how the individual memory of a French colonial subject inflected his landmark edition of the *Chanson de Roland*, a cornerstone of the French national literary heritage. Warren sets out the medieval philologist's colonialist background, explaining Bédier's divided allegiances, as a Créole, to his home, the island of Bourbon (now named Réunion), and, as a patriotic French citizen, to France. Warren reveals how medieval studies served as a means of healing the split between his two homelands. Yet in the process, as Bédier's medievalism elided his own colonial past of mixture, or *métissage*, and hybridity, he also established an authoritative edition of the *Chanson* that, similarly, expunged its own foreign influences. This impulse towards racial and national purity in Bédier's medieval scholarship suggests how his obsession with origins sought to smooth out a conflicted personal and national history, in the effort to establish a continuity between past and present, centre and colony.

Whereas Kabir and Warren show how medieval history and literature provided a frame for formulating a colonial identity, Roland Greene's "The protocolonial baroque of *La Celestina*" highlights the quality of insurgency in the historical baroque that anticipates, instead, postcolonial resistance. Long identified with the colonial, the baroque aesthetic, with its artificiality and incongruousness, not only looks back to the wondrous excesses of the medieval, but also looks forward to the magical paradoxes of the postcolonial. *La Celestina*, a late medieval Spanish prose dialogue (*c.* 1499) by Fernando de Rojas, illustrates this temporal elasticity, presaging the baroque as well as its subversive reinterpretations in postcolonial Latin America. A procuress and a witch, Celestina embodies a disproportionality and eye for superfluous detail that Rojas defines with the adjective *alinde*, or "of India," and that Greene regards as a form of aesthetic disruption that reflects the shifts in perspective that proceed from, and reflect, the discoveries and cross-cultural encounters attendant upon Spanish colonialism in the West. "A baroque figure in a romance background," Celestina celebrates colonial hybridity and postcolonial resistance, even as she undermines the boundary between medieval and early modern.

As Bruce W. Holsinger's recent article "Medieval Studies, Postcolonial Studies and the Genealogies of Critique" observes, "while scholars from certain quarters of medieval studies have begun to borrow heavily from postcolonial studies, medievalists have yet to make a significant impact on the methods, historical purview, and theoretical lexicon of postcolonialism – in large part because of the seemingly intractable modernity of the postcolonial arena and its critical-theoretical apparatus."[36] We take this as our challenge, and hope that the essays in this volume will prompt our postcolonialist readers to reexamine the historical boundaries of their discipline, and challenge medievalists from all quarters to reformulate and redefine this growing field.

NOTES

1. *Très riches heures of Jean, Duke of Berry*, Musée Condé, Chantilly. Intro Jean Longnon and Raymond Cazelles, Preface Millard Meiss, trans. Victoria Benedict (New York: George Braziller, 1969), 8. On the history of the manuscript in the twentieth century, see Michael Camille, "The *Très Riches Heures*: An Illuminated Manuscript in an Age of Mechanical Reproduction," *Critical Inquiry* 17 (1990): 72–107.

2. Caroline Walker Bynum, "Wonder." Presidential Address to the American Historical Association. *American Historical Review* 102 (1997): 15.

3. Stephen Greenblatt, "Resonance and Wonder," in *Exhibiting Cultures: The Politics and Poetics of Museum Display*, ed. Ivan Karp and Steven D. Lavine (Washington and London: Smithsonian Institution Press, 1991), 42.

4. Stephen Greenblatt, *Marvelous Possessions: The Wonder of the New World* (Chicago: University of Chicago Press, 1991).

5. Erich Auerbach, "Figura," in *Scenes from the Drama of European Literature* (New York: Meridian Books, 1959), 11–71.

6. For medieval visualizations of the Magi, see James Harper, "Turks as Trojans; Trojans as Turks" in this volume, chapter 7.

7. Edward Said, *Orientalism* (New York: Random House, 1978).

8. Lisa Jardine, *Worldly Goods: A New History of the Renaissance* (New York: Doubleday, 1996).

9. We borrow this phrase, and the attendant methodological implications, from *The Social Life of Things: Commodities in Cultural Practice*, ed. Arjun Appadurai (Cambridge: Cambridge University Press, 1986).

10. On translation as a postcolonial metaphor, see Samia Mehrez, "Translation and the Postcolonial Experience," in *Rethinking Translation*, ed. Lawrence Venuti (New

York and London: Routledge 1995), 120–38; Maria Tymoczko, "Postcolonial Writing and Literary Translation," in *Post-Colonial Translation: Theory and Practice*, ed. Harish Trivedi and Susan Bassnett (London: Routledge, 1999), 19–40; on the violence of translation, see Eric Cheyfitz, *The Poetics of Imperialism: Translation and Colonization from the Tempest to Tarzan* (New York: Oxford University Press, 1991) and Tejaswini Niranjana, *Siting Translation: History, Post-Structuralism and the Colonial Context* (Berkeley and Los Angeles: University of California Press, 1992).

11. Sir William Jones, *A Discourse on the Institution of a Society for Inquiring into the History, Civil and Natural, the Antiquities, Arts, Sciences, and Literature of Asia. By the President* (15 January 1784). See also *Between Languages and Cultures: Translation and Cross-cultural Texts*, ed. A. Dingwaney and L. Maier (Philadelphia and London: University of Pennsylvania Press, 1995), 7.

12. *Post-Colonial Translation*, ed. Trivedi and Bassnett, 5.

13. Maria Tymoczko, *Early Irish Literature in English Translation* (Manchester: St Jerome, 1999), 17.

14. David Hume, "Of the Academical or Sceptical Philosophy," in *An Enquiry Concerning Human Understanding*, ed. Charles W. Eliot (The Harvard Classics 37, New York: P. F. Collier and Son Co., 1909–14), 3.2.

15. Immanuel Kant, *Observations on the Feeling of the Beautiful and the Sublime* (1764), trans. John T. Goldthwait (Berkeley: University of California Press, 2003).

16. Walter Benjamin, "The Task of the Translator," in *Illuminations*, trans. Harry Zohn (New York: Schochen, 1968), 75.

17. Benjamin, "The Task of the Translator," 82.

18. Benjamin, "The Task of the Translator," 75.

19. See *Post-Colonial Translation*, ed. Trivedi and Bassnett.

20. Benedict Anderson, *Imagined Communities* (London: Verso, 1983).

21. See, for example, Kathleen Davis, "National Writing in the Ninth Century: A Reminder for Postcolonial Thinking about the Nation," *Journal of Medieval and Early Modern Studies* 28 (1998): 611–37, and Carolyn Dinshaw, *Getting Medieval: Sexualities and Communties, Pre- and Postmodern* (Durham, NC: Duke University Press, 1999).

22. Ruth Evans, "Historicizing Postcolonial Criticism: Cultural Difference and the Vernacular," in *The Idea of the Vernacular: An Anthology of Medieval Literary Theory 1280–1520*, ed. Jocelyn Wogan-Brown, Nicholas Watson, Andrew Taylor, and Ruth Evans (University Park, PA: Penn State Press, 1999), 366.

23. See Kathleen Biddick, *The Shock of Medievalism* (Durham, NC and London: Duke University Press, 1998).

24. Jeffrey Jerome Cohen, *The Postcolonial Middle Ages* (New York: St. Martin's Press, 2000).

25. *Postcolonial Moves: Medieval to Modern*, ed. Patricia Clare Ingham and Michelle R. Warren (New York: Palgrave Macmillan, 2003).

26. The introduction to *Decolonizing the Middle Ages*, a complete volume of the *Journal of Medieval and Early Modern Studies* 30 (2000), ed. Margaret R. Greer and John

Dagenais, claims that "the Middle Ages has itself become the object of scholarly colonization." However, the contributors frequently express anxiety about this move.

27. See Bruce Holsinger, "Medieval Studies, Postcolonial Studies and the Genealogies of Critique," *Speculum* 77 (2002): 1195–227 at 1198.

28. See Michael Hardt and Antonio Negri, *Empire* (Cambridge, MA: Harvard University Press, 2000), 21.

29. See also their discussion of scholasticism as the precursor of the Renaissance:

> It all began with a revolution. In Europe, between 1200 and 1600, across distances that only merchants and armies could travel and only the invention of the printing press would later bring together, something extraordinary happened. Humans declared themselves masters of their own lives, producers of cities and history, and inventors of heavens. They inherited a dualistic consciousness, a hierarchical vision of society, and a metaphysical idea of science; but they handed down to future generations an experimental idea of science, a constituent conception of history and cities, and they posed being as an immanent terrain of knowledge and action. The thought of this initial period, born simultaneously in politics, science, art, philosophy, and theology, demonstrates the radicality of the forces at work in modernity. (*Empire*, 71)

30. The conference was organized by Alfred Hiatt, Ananya J. Kabir, and Richard Sarjeantson. For further information, see http://www.trin.cam.ac.uk/empires/.

31. See, among others, Aijaz Ahmed, *In Theory: Classes, Nations, Literature* (New York: Verso, 1992); Homi Bhabha, "The Other Question," in his *The Location of Culture* (London: Routledge, 1994), 66–84; on critiques from an Arab perspective, see Nabil Matar, "The Question of Occidentalism in Early Modern Morocco," in *Postcolonial Moves: Medieval to Modern*, ed. Ingham and Warren, 153–70.

32. Nabil Matar, *Islam in Britain 1558–1685* (Cambridge: Cambridge University Press, 1998) and *Turks, Moors and Englishmen in the Age of Discovery* (New York: Columbia University Press, 1999); *Piracy, Slavery and Redemption: Barbary Captivity Narratives from Early Modern England*, ed. Daniel Vitkus (New York: Columbia University Press, 2001); *Three Turk Plays from Early Modern England*, ed. Daniel Vitkus (New York: Columbia University Press, 2000); Andrew Hadfield, *Literature, Travel and Colonial Writing in the English Renaissance: 1545–1625* (Oxford: Clarendon Press, 1999); Jerry Brotton, *The Renaissance Bazaar: From the Silk Road to Michelangelo* (Oxford: Oxford University Press, 2002).

33. Lisa Jardine and Jerry Brotton, *Global Interests: Renaissance Art between East and West* (Ithaca: Cornell University Press, 2000), 61.

34. See Biddick, *The Shock of Medievalism*; Dinshaw, *Getting Medieval*, and Davis, "National Writing in the Ninth Century."

35. Allen J. Frantzen, *The Desire for Origins: New Language, Old English and Teaching the Tradition* (New Brunswick and London: Rutgers University Press, 1990).

36. Holsinger, "Medieval Studies, Postcolonial Studies," 1197.

PART I

The afterlife of Rome

Anglo-Saxon England and the postcolonial void

Nicholas Howe

If nature abhors a vacuum, historiography loves a void because it can be filled with any number of plausible accounts. By void, I mean somewhat metaphorically a period or culture for which evidence is scarce on the ground, perhaps because of some seemingly cataclysmic event, and thus one for which narratives can be and have been snatched from the air. When such a void falls between two better-documented periods, then it becomes all the more irresistible as a topic; for it can be made to yield a narrative of decline that extends forward to the future or a narrative of origin that works backward to the past. Either way, the narrative is likely to say less about the void than about the contiguous period because that is where the evidence can be found. In some instances, these two types of narrative are brought together: the decline of one culture becomes the origin of another, ruin gives way to creation, progress is enacted, a happy ending is celebrated. And the void is quietly elided. In other instances, the two narratives just miss each other and do not come into alignment, as happens when engineers miscalculate the route of a tunnel being cut through a mountain from both sides. And then there is a more troubling possibility: What if the era we designate a void is best taken as belonging to itself rather than as fulfilling a previous period or anticipating a subsequent one? What if its story evades narratives of continuity?

These questions are inspired by the status of Anglo-Saxon England as a postcolonial society in the most literal sense of the term: as one that existed after the Roman Empire ceased to function as a political, military, and economic entity in Britain and before *Englalond* emerged late in the Anglo-Saxon period as an incipient nation within the larger sphere of Christendom.[1] Put this way, the prospect of studying a postcolonial

Anglo-Saxon England that extends into the eighth or ninth century carries with it a great deal of terminological and historical baggage: the imperial center and the peripheral province; the empire in decline and the development of a nationalist ethos; the shifting status of paganism and Christianity; as well as the often contentious field of postcolonial studies itself.[2] At the start of a postcolonial Anglo-Saxon England lies a period of almost two centuries from 410 to 597 – defined by the convenient dates for the withdrawal of the Roman legions and the arrival of Roman missionaries – for which the evidence is very scattered, sometimes contradictory, often tantalizingly incomplete, and usually found in sources written for an explicitly partisan purpose. It is no accident that James Campbell should have called these years "the lost centuries" and cautioned: "The natural vice of historians is to claim to know about the past. Nowhere is this claim more dangerous than when staked in Britain between AD 400 and 600."[3]

The interpretative problem of the void lies in identifying the traces left behind in their texts and structures by the inhabitants of the period, as well as in the more retrospective interpretations of those who wrote or built later in the Anglo-Saxon period. Elleke Boehmer has suggested one reading by which to classify a wide variety of medieval English writing as postcolonial:

> Marlow in Conrad's *Heart of Darkness*, for example, draws atten-
> tion to the similarities between the British colonization of Africa and
> the conquering of Britain by imperial Rome many centuries before.
> According to this view, *Beowulf* and Chaucer's *Canterbury Tales* could
> be read as postcolonial texts.[4]

To set absolute limits on what might or might not be usefully termed postcolonial in the context of Old English literature would be premature, though I have been guided by Boehmer's assertion that "*postcolonial* literature is that which critically scrutinizes the colonial relationship."[5] To expect a stable or reasonably coherent understanding of a postcolonial Anglo-Saxon England would also be premature given the state of our knowledge, though certain lines of inquiry can be followed.

Most immediately, insular writers both Celtic and Saxon employ a vividly memorable trope for memorializing the imperial presence of Romans in Britain and thus for identifying their own temporal distance from these predecessors. In his *Ruin of Britain*, written *c.* 540?, Gildas offers a passionate jeremiad denouncing the corrupt state of Celtic Britain during the period of Germanic attacks. Gildas writes as a Christian, and thus in Latin; he depicts the barbarian invasion in terms that reveal both his own cultural affiliations and also his horror at the political chaos of the time:

> ita et cunctae coloniae crebris arietibus omnesque coloni cum prae-positis ecclesiae, cum sacerdotibus ac populo, mucronibus undique micantibus ac flammis crepitantibus, simul solo sternerentur, et mis-erabili visu in medio platearum ima turrium edito cardine evulsarum murorumque celsorum saxa, sacra altaria, cadaverum frusta, crustis ac si gelantibus purpurei cruoris tecta, velut in quodam horrendo torculari mixta viderentur.

> [All the major towns were laid low by the repeated battering of enemy rams; laid low, too, all the inhabitants – church leaders, priests and people alike, as the swords glinted all around and the flames crackled. It was a sad sight. In the middle of the squares the foundation-stones of high walls and towers that had been torn from their lofty base, holy altars, fragments of corpses, covered (as it were) with a purple crust of congealed blood, looked as though they had been mixed up in some dreadful wine-press.][6]

The observer here belongs within the world of *Romanitas*. He sees the events around him through its cultural forms and styles: the established order of urban life has been destroyed and its public spaces filled with the ruins of stone walls and towers; the sacred altars built to propi-tiate the gods and ensure prosperity have been shattered; the central squares of cities are littered with mutilated bodies. As Gildas knew well, these horrors were to be attributed to a migratory group of barbarians who spoke Germanic dialects rather than Latin and typically built in timber rather than stone. The destruction of masonry buildings thus becomes for Gildas the inescapable sign that his world has been van-quished. Within the cultural model known as lithicization, Gildas' scene represents a dramatic instance of cultural regression, for it reverses the exemplary model of progress by which stone replaces wood as a build-ing material because it is more permanent and fire-resistant, as well as more costly and thus more prestigious.[7] For Gildas, the Roman civ-ilization to which he held allegiance was built in stone and designed to last out the centuries. Another marker of Gildas' cultural identity, and one that he turns here to a kind of tragic pathos, is the description of the blood-soaked corpses in urban squares that look as if they had been mangled in a winepress. Gildas' simile is vivid in itself but would also have reminded his audience that wine was another attribute of *Romanitas* in Britain, as the island's extensive trade with Bordeaux and its environs demonstrates.[8]

Gildas portrays the period of the Germanic invasions as a world turned upside-down: the enduring stone structures of a Romanized society fall, the altars are desecrated, wine denotes dismemberment and bloodshed rather than the pleasures of a civilized life. Through such images, Gildas depicts this period in British history as a hellish chaos that marks an irreparable break with the past: the Roman civilization of towns has been reduced to rubble around him. This passage from *The Ruin of Britain* appears in its historical section, which stands as a kind of preface to, or warrant for, the religious jeremiad that fills the body of the work. This prefatory section registers Gildas' understanding from reading the Old Testament that history precedes polemic, that the Pentateuch and Chronicles precede the prophets Isaiah and Jeremiah.[9] That stone structures cannot survive cataclysms, that barbarians topple the enduring achievements of *Romanitas*, that blood flows in the streets like wine – these are all proof for Gildas of a historical void that seems destined to extend beyond his own lifetime, if not far into the future.

As an avid reader of Gildas, Bede followed his predecessor's lead in evoking Roman Britain as a culture of stone-built structures – and yet he did so from a very different perspective. Writing from what he thought to be the other or triumphalist side of the void, Bede could run a thread of continuity to connect the years following the withdrawal of Roman legions to the flourishing of Anglo-Saxon Christianity during his own lifetime early in the eighth century:

> Fracta est autem Roma a Gothis anno millesimo CLXIIII suae conditio-
> nis, ex quo tempore Romani in Brittania regnare cesserunt, post annos
> ferme quadringentos LXX ex quo Gaius Iulius Caesar eandem insu-
> lam adiit. Habitabant autem intra uallum, quod Seuerum trans insu-
> lam fecisse commemorauimus, ad plagam meridianam, quod ciuitates
> farus pontes et stratae ibidem factae usque hodie testantur; ceterum

ulteriores Brittaniae partes, uel eas etiam quae ultra Brittaniam sunt
insulas, iure dominandi possidebant.

[Now Rome was taken by the Goths in the eleven hundred and sixty-
fourth year after its foundation; after this the Romans ceased to rule
in Britain, almost 470 years after Gaius Julius Caesar had come to
the island. They had occupied the whole land south of the rampart
already mentioned, set up across the island by Severus, an occupation to which the cities, lighthouses, bridges, and roads which they
built there testify to this day. Moreover they possessed the suzerainty
over the further parts of Britain as well as over the islands which are
beyond it.][10]

For Bede, as for Gildas, the visible signs of Roman occupation were
made of stone and masonry: cities, lighthouses, bridges and – most
dramatically across the landscape – roads that cut from point to point
with a straight-line directness that spoke of an imperial will to power
over the earth.[11] As Robert Hardison writes, "Roman roads were laid
perfectly straight in an outlying place like Britain not because it was
easy to do it that way but to show that even this wild did not defeat the
Roman mind, which could treat it as if it were a plane."[12] Seen from
the British perspective, these Roman roads would have symbolized, as
Richard Muir observes, "the inadequacy of indigenous arrangements"
and thus would have announced the relation between the colonizing
and the colonized societies in a literally material form.[13]

Bede does not add that most of these stone constructions must have
been in a state of disrepair when he wrote more than 300 years after the
departure of the legions in 410. Eroded by the weather, overgrown with
vegetation, quarried for building materials as they were, these Roman
structures would still have denoted the presence of an imperial power
to a later people that built characteristically, though not exclusively,
in wood. Nor would the survival of these Roman constructions into
the Anglo-Saxon period have posed any great mysteries to a writer like
Bede: the textual record provided by Roman writers made clear which
colonizing power had raised those lighthouses and roads, bridges and
walls. Even if such accounts had not been available to Bede and others,
they could have learned who built these structures, and when they did so,
from the inscriptions on many of them. The Romans had mastered the
political act of using writing to assert publicly their power and celebrate

their accomplishments. What response the surviving inscriptions of Roman Britain might have evoked from Anglo-Saxons has not been much considered by scholars, but one fundamental point can be made: the language in which they were written was not a dead or lost language that required reconstruction or decipherment.[14] For a cleric with fluent Latin like Bede, these texts and inscriptions told a story of Roman occupation and then withdrawal. Their stones remained behind and could be read. These traces of Rome were not opaque or mysterious in ways that pre-Roman structures like Stonehenge or Avebury appear to have been to the Anglo-Saxons, if one may judge from their silence on the subject. Instead, the traces of empire were for Bede evidence of a void that had been filled through a new and more enduring connection with Rome, one that returned Christianity and Latin to the island.

That Roman roads survived as the visible traces of an empire that had once included the island may explain the Anglo-Saxon practice of locating churches near – but not on – them, as with the Church of the Holy Cross at Daglingworth that lies about a mile off the main Roman road between Cirencester and Gloucester and that was built with Roman stones.[15] These roads could not have been ignored in an otherwise agrarian landscape, and they may have remained useful for transport well into the Anglo-Saxon period, but they also endured as evidence for the fading transience of all that was human-made within the scope of Christian history.[16] Anglo-Saxons who knew the story of these Roman roads must have sensed about them a somewhat melancholy air not unlike that expressed in the *ubi sunt* catalogues of ruined halls and lost treasures in the Old English poetic elegies.

The poet of *The Wanderer*, for example, memorably invokes the ruination of walls and wine-halls as a measure of the decay of the earth and of the Christian desire for the heavenly home:

> Ongietan sceal gleaw hæle   hu gæstlic bið
> þonne ealre þisse worulde wela   weste stondeð,
> swa nu missenlice   geond þisne middangeard
> winde biwaune   weallas stondaþ
> hrime bihrorene,   hryðge þa ederas.
>
> [The wise man can perceive how ghostly it will be when the riches of all this world stand abandoned, as now in various places throughout

this world walls stand windblown, frost covered, buildings swept by snow.][17]

The poet completes his lamentation by stating, in a trope that resonates through Old English lyric poetry: *eald enta geweorc idlu stodon*, "the old work of giants remained empty" (line 87). For all its haunted beauty, this passage from *The Wanderer* seems by design not to be located in any specific time or place; within the poem, it occupies a spiritualized rather than historicized landscape. Yet from another perspective, that of the postcolonial period during which it was composed, the passage can be read with a more precise historical valence; for its use of ruined stonework as proof of earthly temporality and transience depends on a vision of Christian history that came with the conversion of the Anglo-Saxons.

The passages in *Maxims II* and *The Ruin* that describe old stone-built cities and then lament them as the work of giants seem more explicitly historical, though that may be because neither poem offers the Christian consolation of *The Wanderer*. The poet of *Maxims II* opens with a statement of the accepted political order in the world of human beings – that a king should rule the kingdom – and then speaks of stone-built cities that are so monumental they can be seen from a long distance:

> Cyning sceal rice healdan. Ceastra beoð feorran gesyne,
> orðanc enta geweorc, þa þe on þysse eorðan syndon,
> wrætlic weallstana geweorc.
>
> [A king should hold the kingdom. Cities may be seen from afar, those that are on the earth, the skilled work of giants, the artfully crafted work of building stones.][18]

The statement that these cities can be seen from a distance primarily refers to their prominence on the landscape but also, one suspects, opens the possibility for a more temporal vantage: these cities can be seen as having their own distant history. That the work of giants refers to baths and walls used by human beings rather than, as might possibly seem the case, stone circles like those that survive at Stonehenge or Avebury is evident from these lines. *Weallstan* specifically refers to stone that has been cut for use in building a wall.[19] Moreover, the stone walls of *Maxims II* demarcate a world ruled by a *cyning* and protect it as a human city, as the Old English word *ceaster* makes clear. The connection between *cyning* and *ceaster* here is as much political as alliterative.

Moreover, as a borrowing of the Latin *castra*, the Old English word has a larger historical resonance: to speak of a *ceaster* in a vernacular poem is to designate a walled settlement or stronghold but also to evoke, for anyone alert to the Roman inflections of the word, a more densely historicized meaning. For an Old English poet, *ceaster* would have been a necessary element in the wordstock as a synonym for the native *burg* to denote a stronghold or fortified location. Given the frequency of *castra* as an element in Old English place names, though, the Roman origin of the word could have been recognized even by those many Anglo-Saxons without Latin. Such are the ways that traces of empire linger in language, even after the colonizers have departed. This story belongs as well to the late twentieth century: place names, or at least some of them, remain on the land as testimony to a colonial past. Others are replaced in the process of decolonization by new forms with more indigenous resonances, as when Rhodesia becomes Zimbabwe. Just as *castra* became Old English *ceaster* and an element in later placenames as –*caster*, –*cester* and –*chester*, so too *burg* became Latin and then Italian as in the *Borgo San Spirito* of Rome.[20] Sometimes the provincial language leaves its own trace on the metropolitan center.

The "work of giants" as a trope for the past imperial grandeur of Roman Britain establishes a scale of material history by identifying the use of stone with a past age of superhuman accomplishment. The common historical and poetic trope of a golden age followed in an inevitable process of decline by silver, iron and even baser metals, has its equivalent in the celebration of a past era as noble because it worked in stone. *The Ruin*, as the fullest expression of this trope in an Old English text, speaks with precise and even loving attention about such features of Roman construction as the use of cut and dressed stones, roof tiles, mortar joints, and reinforcing metalwork such as clamps.[21] The reading of *The Ruin* as a poem specifically about the city of Bath is possible, but it ignores the fact that the postcolonial landscape of Anglo-Saxon England was filled with the remains of Roman baths, including some far distant from Bath at sites like Chesters near Hadrian's Wall.[22] The Roman practice of building baths at forts and other garrison sites was no doubt meant to ease the rigors of life in a military outpost, but it also had the effect – perhaps inadvertently so – of marking the spread and maintenance of imperial power and civilization. The presence of baths across the British landscape testifies to Peter Wells's claim, in *The Barbarians Speak*, that "the army was the Roman institution that had the most direct and most profound impact on the indigenous peoples of temperate Europe."[23]

The Ruin becomes a far more interesting poem if freed from any specific location and read instead as evoking sites that would not have been uncommon on the landscape. From the opening lines of the poem, as they present an envelope pattern of present tense verbs around past forms, we gain a sense that history is the flow of time between the decaying stonework in the scene and the speaker who describes it:

> Wrætlic is þes wealstan,   wyrde gebræcon;
> burgstede burston,   brosnað enta geweorc.
> Hrofas sind gehrorene,   hreorge torras,
> hrungeat berofen,   hrim on lime,
> scearde scurbeorge   scorene, gedrorene,
> ældo undereotone.

> [The building stone is wondrously crafted, broken by fate, the city places ruined, the work of giants decays. The roofs are fallen, the towers toppled, the frost-covered gate destroyed, the rime is in the mortar, built refuges from storms are damaged, torn, collapsed, eaten under by time.][24]

The terminology here of building types, as well as the emphatic rhymes to sound out the inevitability of time's passing, mark this as the most evocative use of the trope of stonework in Old English.

The single half-line *hrim on lime*– "rime on lime" or, more prosaically, "the frost on the mortar" – becomes, in context, a law of historical causation about the decline of imperial power: once its great structures are abandoned, and nature is allowed to take its course, even the work of giants decays and crumbles. The speaker of the poem has a keen eye for the literal signs of historical change: the walls, he adds a few lines later (line 10a), are *ræghar ond readfah* or "grey with lichen and stained with red." With these two colors, the poet paints the scene before him: the grey of lichen that has been allowed to grow over the abandoned structures and the red of the rusting iron clamps and reinforcing bars used in their construction. Later in the poem, the speaker will describe the collapse of the buildings' arched roofs with their tiles (lines 30–31a), another marker of Roman construction, and also will praise as *hyðelic* or "convenient" (line 41a) the ways in which the *stanhofu* or "stonehouse" enclosed the hot springs of the bath (line 38a).

If the tone of *The Ruin* is elegiac, it has about it a more plangently historicized note of loss and lament than one usually hears in Old English poetry. Its incomplete, fragmentary state in the Exeter Book makes it impossible to know if *The Ruin* moved, as do *The Wanderer* and *The Seafarer*, from describing the decay of earthly habitations to celebrating the eternal home of heaven. What remains of the poem, though, is enough to show that its poet understood the inescapable historicity of human life on earth, that the present and the past are not a single undifferentiated mass, that the remains still standing on the earth can demonstrate that those who came before were profoundly different in their ways of life. From the details of that evocation, of mortar and cut stone, of iron rebar and roof tiles, of houses and baths, the poet gives to that idea of the past its own defining architectural style and thus fixes it in a moment of its own, distant from his present.

The stones that litter the texts of Gildas, Bede, and the Old English poets can be read as the visible traces of a colonial past. The methods of Roman colonization need, especially in our own postcolonial time, to be understood on their own terms as extending full citizenship to Britons in the centuries before 410. They were not subjected to the same practices of colonial oppression that characterized European imperialism in Africa and Asia during the modern period. In this regard, 410 must be understood as marking the withdrawal of Roman troops from Britain – not the abandonment of the island by its Roman citizens. The effects of that action were certainly profound, especially for those who remained on the island and thought of themselves as belonging to *Romanitas*. Most visible from the archaeological record are the facts that money was no longer coined in Britain and that the large-scale manufacture and marketing of pottery ceased after 410 or so. As Peter Salway has said of those years, "the feature that startles anyone used to Roman sites in Britain is the almost total absence of coins or pottery."[25] Nonetheless, traces of Roman imperial power remained visible on the landscape of the Anglo-Saxons and continued to haunt their imaginations.[26] The texts I have quoted offer a line of memorial transmission and a theory of historiographical interpretation by which to understand that memory of the Roman *imperium*. In that respect, these texts bear out the claims made by Bill Ashcroft in his *Post-Colonial Transformation*:

> Place is never simply location, nor is it static, a cultural memory which colonization buries. For, like culture itself, place is in a continual and dynamic state of formation, a process intimately bound up with the culture and the identity of its inhabitants. Above all place is a *result* of habitation, a consequence of the ways in which people inhabit space, particularly that conception of space as universal and uncontestable that is constructed for them by imperial discourse.[27]

To locate the terms of Ashcroft's argument in Anglo-Saxon England, a postcolonial zone quite distant in time from the post-World War II societies he examines, one might alter his final clause to read: "constructed for them by imperial discourse and architecture." That is, the recognition of being a postcolonial zone or place of habitation that the Anglo-Saxons register in their texts is also visible through their references to the fate of Roman stone-built architecture. To be a postcolonial in Anglo-Saxon England was to live in a landscape filled with the material remains of the colonizing power: its ways of building with, most notably, dressed stone and rounded arches, as well as its practice of inscribing texts on buildings and monuments.

These Roman stones were not merely literary tropes for Gildas, Bede, and the poets of *The Wanderer*, *Maxims II*, and *The Ruin*. They were also present on the landscape, both as they survived in derelict structures and as they were visibly reused in newly built Christian churches. W. G. Hoskins has speculated that the presence of Roman ruins in townscapes may well have altered the routes taken by pedestrians: "It has been suggested, for example, in certain towns of Roman origin where the Saxon or early medieval streets do not lie exactly on the line of the Roman streets, that these must represent the irregular tracks tramped out in Saxon times by people who were forced to walk around the ruins of tumbled Roman buildings."[28] Hoskins does not identify sites where this rerouting may have occurred but his suggestion does remind us that ruins are not merely picturesque features on the landscape. They can also alter the course of daily life in seemingly trivial and yet enduring ways. The stones of Roman ruins would have been part of the familiar scene for those who lived in sites that had once been (or were near to) Roman streets, towns, camps, or forts – a condition that was common in such areas of Anglo-Saxon England as Northumbria, especially in the frontier region near Hadrian's Wall, or in the villa-rich environs around Cirencester in Gloucestershire.[29] We know nothing reliable about the circumstances of when and where Gildas or the poets of *Maxims II* and *The Ruin* lived, and thus cannot localize them within the Anglo-Saxon historical landscape. About Bede, however, we know a good deal more because he tells us the relevant facts of his life and because he spent most of it in a very circumscribed area.

From the age of seven until he died at sixty-two, Bede tells us, he lived in the monastic community of Wearmouth and Jarrow in the north of England, a region that had been very heavily built by the Romans. He also tells us that he was born in the territory of that monastery, though he does not specify the location of his birthplace. He adds that he was educated at Jarrow under the guidance of Benedict Biscop and then Ceolfrith (*HE* v.24). In his *Lives of the Abbots of Wearmouth and Jarrow*, Bede provides a lovely description of Benedict's role in building the monastic church at Jarrow:

> Nec plusquam unius anni spatio post fundatum monasterium interiecto, Benedictus oceano transmisso Gallias petens, cementarios qui lapideam sibi aecclesiam iuxta Romanorum quem semper amabat morem facerent, postulauit, accepit, adtulit.

> [Only a year after work had begun on the monastery, Benedict crossed the sea to France to look for masons to build him a stone church in the Roman style he had always loved so much. He found them, took them on and brought them back home with him.][30]

Bede goes on to relate that the church was built rapidly so that, a year after the foundation was laid, the gables had been raised and one could imagine Mass being said within it. The year was 674, Bede tells us, a year after his birth. He was thus not an eyewitness to the building of St. Peter's Church at Jarrow, though he certainly could have known monks who had been present at the time. From one of them he could easily have learned that the church was raised so quickly at least in part because it was built from reused Roman stones that had been taken from the wall that, as he notes in the *Ecclesiastical History* (i.xi–xii), was built by Hadrian to keep the Scots and Picts at bay. Or Bede might well have determined the Roman provenance of these stones from his own observations, for he was born in the region and would have grown up surrounded by them.

That Bede says nothing in the *Lives of the Abbots* about the source of the stones used at St. Peter's in Jarrow is not in itself proof that he was ignorant of their provenance. Indeed, this kind of technical matter as it relates to everyday life is rarely of interest to him. Nonetheless, it is noteworthy that he should have been familiar with a church that was built knowingly to be, among its more obvious purposes, "an impressive, monumental Roman memorial," in the words of Tim Eaton. In his illuminating study of the use of Roman *spolia* in Anglo-Saxon England, Eaton argues that the use of stones from Hadrian's Wall was a means for Benedict "to appropriate some of the authority associated with its construction."[31] Given Benedict's love for churches in the Roman style – a matter, it would seem, at least as much of material as of design – it is hardly surprising that St. Peter's at Jarrow was built from Roman stone as a matter of cultural affiliation, even if there were also considerations of economy and convenience.

The assimilation of Roman materials and thus Roman history at Jarrow extended into the interior precincts of the church. As Eaton explains, two fragments of a Roman inscription that belonged to a "war memorial or *tropaeum*" from Hadrian's Wall were used to form the horizontal arms of a cross set inside St. Peter's. The reconstructed Latin inscription speaks directly to the triumph of Roman imperial power over the barbarians:

> Son of all the deified emperors, the Emperor Caesar Trajan Hadrian Augustus, after the necessity of keeping the empire within its limits had been laid upon him by divine precept . . . thrice consul . . . after the barbarians had been dispersed, and the province of Britain had been recovered, he added a frontier-line between either shore of the Ocean for 80 miles. The army of the province built this defence-work under the charge of Aulus Platorius Nepos, emperor's propraetorian legate.[32]

If one can imagine an eighth-century monk reading this inscription, or at least making some rudimentary sense of it as a Roman military trophy, then one can also ask what he might have thought about the shifting fortunes of empire and colony and, more specifically, of the role played by Rome as the capital of Anglo-Saxon England. The highly conscious reuse of this Roman stonework with its inscription at the very center of Northumbrian Christianity would have been proof for Bede that the postcolonial void had been bridged. The island of Britannia, once a province of the *imperium*, was now a community of Christians who looked to Rome and the papacy for spiritual direction and political guidance. This process of cultural reassimilation was eased greatly by the fact that Latin was the language of the empire and army that left behind such inscriptions as well as of the clerics who turned them to their own purposes. The use of such *spolia* at a center of monastic learning such as Jarrow demonstrates that there was no religiously mandated aversion toward the imperial past of Britannia.[33] One can argue further that there was a triumphalist assertion in the Anglo-Saxon use of Roman *spolia*; it did not merely represent an act of homage to the past of imperial Rome, but also stood as a statement that the enduring empire of Rome within human history was Christian not pagan, and was ruled by a pope not an emperor. This revisionist model of historical causation allowed the imperial conquest and Romanization of the island by Claudius in 43 to be seen as a distant but necessary precondition for the later migration and then conversion of the Anglo-Saxons.

Or, in starker terms, the Anglo-Saxons entered Christendom because the island had once been a colony of Rome. Such a reading of history, by which the postcolonial void is crossed and thus explained, can be seen in the very fabric of the small church of St. John at Escomb in County Durham that dates to the late seventh or early eighth century. This church, perhaps the most beautiful example of ecclesiastical architecture to survive intact from the Anglo-Saxon period, is relatively small and simple in design. The interior of the nave is approximately 43′6″ by 14′6″, and that of the chancel is approximately 10′ by 10′.[34] Much of the exterior stone bears visible evidence of Roman origin, especially in the tooling of the outer surfaces in broached and feather-broached patterns.[35] Other stones used in the exterior walls do not bear any such signs and may perhaps have been quarried locally for the construction of the church. More directly evocative of Rome as both imperial power and papal seat is the arch that joins nave and chancel. H. M. Taylor and Joan Taylor have described this arch as possessing "outstanding dignity," a quality that is all the more evident because of the "narrow and lofty proportions of the nave." The solemnity of the interior at Escomb is heightened by the fact that the component parts of the arch are highly crafted: "the semicircular arch is itself formed of well-cut voussoirs with radial joints."[36] The arch fits beautifully into the interior space of the church, yet it was not built for use at Escomb. If anything, the church is more likely to have been built around this arch that was taken entire from a Roman building, most probably from the nearby fort at *Vinovia* or Binchester.[37] Whether the builders at Escomb planned the church around this *spolia*, or set it within their preestablished design, it is immediately visible that the arch is the defining architectural element of the building.

Indeed, for any worshiper standing in the nave, the arch directs attention toward the sacred liturgical space within the chancel; it focuses the vision of those in the nave as they look toward the altar. It also, in the act of enforcing that line of vision, distinguishes the laity from the clergy. Any arch set between nave and chancel would have something of this effect, regardless of whether it was built by Romans or Anglo-Saxons, whether it was elegant or crude in its workmanship. The fact remains, however, that the arch at Escomb was Roman-built and thus can be read as adding a historical dimension into the interior of the church: it suggests that the faith by which an Anglo-Saxon might gain salvation was introduced into the island by missionaries from Rome. Within that church building, the human progress toward the holy is demarcated by this Roman arch, and thus the interior of the church as a whole can be read as a form of historical allegory. At Escomb, as at Jarrow, the historical syncretism of the church building as being both Roman and English was made plausible, in fact could only be interpreted through the colonial past of the island.

Yet, the skeptic asks, is this reading of the arch at Escomb our postcolonial take early in the twenty-first century, a clever playing with historical materials in an act of interpretative bricolage? Would any Anglo-Saxon have thought of the church interior at Escomb in this historical way? Would he or she have done more than gaze at its beauty and register its solemnity within the church? We can never know, but certain probabilities might be registered in favor of the historical reading I have proposed. First, the artistry by which the church and the arch as a whole were brought together suggests that the builders of Escomb were alive to the beauty and significance of the arch itself. Having transported it from a ruined Roman site, they would certainly have known of its provenance. The skill and style with which the arch has been reconstructed suggest direct familiarity with its privileged status as *spolia*, and thus some awareness of its historical significance. Second, the textual evidence presented earlier in this study suggests that Anglo-Saxons, whether they used Latin or Old English, were interested in the origin of building stones and in the ways they demarcated historical periods. For them, stones found amid derelict or ruined Roman sites were not simply blocks of rock without history, inert masses with no story to tell. Third, and perhaps most telling, there is no inherent reason to assume that those who lived during the period were somehow less alert to the complications of their own history than we are some twelve hundred years later.

The material fabric of the church at Escomb is an invitation to think on the shifting patterns of history from the time of Roman imperialism to the triumph of Anglo-Saxon Christianity. Nor is that invitation reserved simply for inquiries about the distant past. It holds as well for the visitor who travels to Escomb today. Located as it is amid the old coal-mining regions of County Durham, Escomb does not have a setting of rural beauty like that of Offa's Chapel at Deerhurst. Instead, St. John's at Escomb now sits within the walls of a circular churchyard that is in turn surrounded by modern council estates. Guidebooks lament this intrusion of the modern on the Anglo-Saxon, and those who had seen Escomb told me to expect the worst, as if the church were situated in the middle of some urban wasteland straight out of Gildas. Such pastoral responses to the present are all too easy to assume and all too reductive, as one realizes at Escomb after reading that the key to the church can be found hanging on a hook at one of those very same council houses. One understands, that is, that the present and the past are set together in Escomb and in that way preserve each other's claims on our attention. In an analogous way, I suspect, an Anglo-Saxon worshiping at Escomb could not have thought about the present moment in *Englalond* without remembering that the arch inside the church was a remnant of a past that had artfully been assimilated rather than discarded as rubble on the land.

One central fact shadows all that I have written about postcolonial Anglo-Saxon England. After the withdrawal of Roman troops in 410, the population of the country declined sharply and did not return to a comparable level until sometime well after the Norman Conquest. Historians argue about the precise numbers for the island's population throughout the period – whether for pre-410, 800, or 1200, to choose regular intervals – but most agree on a general trend of sharp population loss that was not reversed for many centuries.[38] This decline in population, combined with the evident collapse of a money economy and regular trade networks, made for substantial changes in the social and economic lives of those who lived in Britain. In this less populated landscape, some land (especially any that was marginally productive) may have been left untilled as the need for agricultural goods declined along with the available human-power to produce them.[39] In certain ways, the landscape must have grown quieter as fewer people and domestic animals moved across it, as fewer fields were cultivated, and fewer trees were chopped down or otherwise harvested for fuel and building materials. The shrinking of cultivated land and the decreased need for timber products meant that woodlands "seem to have advanced during the period of instability and economic decline following the collapse of Roman rule."[40] The psychological effects that came with witnessing the reversion of arable land to woodland after 410 are perhaps beyond our ability to diagnose, but that same phenomenon carried with it a sense of historical regression that is, as I have argued, discernible in texts.

While there is no compelling reason to characterize the period after 410 in Britain as cataclysmic or apocalyptic, there is every reason to imagine that it was often difficult in terms of material circumstances and sometimes eerily melancholy.[41] This sense of melancholy is most audible in Old English poetry, even in those works that seem to have no thematic relation to the after-effects of Roman colonization, such as *Beowulf*.[42] For that reason, melancholy may be too resonant with the sentiments of a later and perhaps, in this context, anachronistic poetic tradition to be useful for describing the decades immediately after 410. Richard Muir has described the withdrawal of the legions as initiating a "prolonged phase of introspection and localism,"[43] a formulation that neatly registers both the psychological and economic consequences of that political act. That phase was brought to closure, in a move that complicates any simplistic application of postcolonial theory to Anglo-Saxon England, by the formal reconnection of the island to Rome through the agency of Christian missionaries.

What might it have meant to live in this postcolonial world, to occupy a less densely populated landscape that was dotted with buildings and other structures that had lost some or all of their original functions?[44] This question would no doubt require different kinds of answers depending on when one lived in the postcolonial years. The physical *spolia* of stonework would have taken on different uses and resonances for someone like Bede living in a reasonably peaceful and Christianized area of *Englalond* than they would have for a Briton who had fought at Mount Badon and been momentarily heartened by that short-lived victory over the barbaric Saxons. These kinds of questions are necessary as well for our own postcolonial time, and asking them may help us avoid some of the too easy binaries of a rigid postcolonial theory.

The case of Anglo-Saxon England establishes, for example, that the relations between metropole and colony, center and periphery, cannot be set in a single unchanging relation of the powerful and the dispossessed. Nor can the metropole itself be seen as fixed and unchanging. If, as I have argued elsewhere, Rome was the capital of Anglo-Saxon England, it became so in an ecclesiastical and spiritual fashion that was radically different from its role as imperial capital of the province of Britannia and yet that also depended on this previous instantiation.[45] The fact that the geography between Rome and that island known variously as Britannia/ Albion/England remained constant did not mean that the relations of political, economic, and religious power were similarly constant. In that regard, we may say that geography enabled relations between Rome and England but it alone did not determine their precise nature.

The example of postcolonial Anglo-Saxon England also suggests that politics and the relations of power are not always made visible through ideology, indigenous resistance movements, or widely circulated manifestos. Sometimes the evidence for politics and the relations of power takes very different forms, such as stones and the narrative purposes to which they can be put by writers. Meditating on the later medieval landscape of the troubadour poets, W. S. Merwin has said: "The moving of stones is the course of history, and of rubble and forgetting."[46] Sometimes the historical void is that rubble and all that lies forgotten amid its stones. At other times, that stonework seems more comprehensible as part of a familiar landscape that people traverse, farm, timber, and live upon. Landscape is, in this sense, not simply the work of nature; it is also the product of the human hands that have altered it and the eyes that have looked over it. To speak of the postcolonial landscape of Anglo-Saxon England is thus to turn to historical purposes the assertion of James Corner: "landscape is less a quantifiable object than it is an *idea*, a cultural way of seeing, and as such it remains open to interpretation, design and transformation."[47]

In a society where literacy in either Old English or Latin was an unusual skill, the historical record could not exist entirely in written form: oral accounts both reliable and fabulous survived, as we know from Bede's Preface to the *Ecclesiastical History*, as did monumental accounts in the form of earthworks, stone structures, and ruins on the landscape. The material past of Roman rule survived and provided an alternative, and perhaps more accessible, version to the written record. In doing so, the historical landscape also had a larger cultural function that transcended mere curiosity or antiquarianism. Writing of the landscape, W. G. Hoskins has said that the Anglo-Saxons had "no eye for scenery, any more than other hard-working farmers of later centuries."[48] One can wonder if farmers, Anglo-Saxon or otherwise, may have appreciated landscape in ways that were not scenic as much as they were experiential: they knew the land and its capacity to produce crops and sustain livestock; they knew what had been built on it; they knew who crossed it.[49] In that regard, the built landscape could be registered, if not appreciated, by those who might have had little interest in the picturesque. To advance this claim, one might consider an observation by D. W. Meinig in *The Interpretation of Ordinary Landscapes*: "Every nation has its symbolic landscapes. They are part of the iconography of nationhood, part of the shared set of ideas and memories and feelings which bind a people together."[50] The landscape of Anglo-Saxon England, as it held Roman ruins and also *spolia* turned to new purposes, was a way of deciphering the postcolonial void. The Romans – and they had indeed been giants – were gone, although their buildings survived to be recycled and their language turned to the purposes of Christian learning and salvation.[51]

NOTES

1. My own thinking about the relation between Roman Britain and Anglo-Saxon England has been influenced by David N. Dumville, "Sub-Roman Britain: History and Legend," *History* 62 (1977): 173–92; *The Anglo-Saxons*, ed. James Campbell (Oxford: Phaidon, 1982), especially the chapters by the volume editor; C. J. Arnold, *Roman Britain to Saxon England* (Bloomington: Indiana University Press, 1984); and J. N. L. Myres, *The English Settlements*, Oxford History of England vol. IB (Oxford: Clarendon Press, 1986).

2. For an accomplished examination of these issues, see Holsinger, "Medieval Studies, Postcolonial Studies."

3. See Campbell, "The Lost Centuries," in *The Anglo-Saxons*, ed. Campbell, 20–44 at 20.

4. Elleke Boehmer, *Colonial and Postcolonial Literature: Migrant Metaphors* (Oxford: Oxford University Press, 1995), 1. She refers here to Marlow's famous words about the Thames Estuary as also having been "one of the dark places of the earth." The contemporary London psychogeographer Iain Sinclair has described this passage, with telling irony, as "the line they all quote"; see his *London Orbital: A Walk around the M25* (London: Granta, 2002), 375.

5. Boehmer, *Colonial and Postcolonial Literature*, 3.

6. *Gildas: The Ruin of Britain and Other Works*, ed. Michael Winterbottom (London: Phillimore, 1978), 24.3; see 98 for Latin, 27 for translation.

7. For lithicization, see Richard Muir, *The New Reading the Landscape: Fieldwork in Landscape History* (Exeter: University of Exeter Press, 2000), 148; for the "reversion to timber" for building in post-Roman Britain, see Peter Salway, *A History of Roman Britain* (Oxford: Oxford University Press, 1993), 346–7.

8. See further A. C. Sutherland, "The Imagery of Gildas's *De Excidio Britanniae*," in *Gildas: New Approaches*, ed. Michael Lapidge and David Dumville (Woodbridge: Boydell, 1984), 157–68, esp. 164; for the British wine trade with the continent, see Salway, *A History of Roman Britain*, 475–7.

9. Robert W. Hanning, *The Vision of History in Early Britain from Gildas to Geoffrey of Monmouth* (New York: Columbia University Press, 1966), 52–3.

10. *Bede's Ecclesiastical History of the English People*, ed. Bertram Colgrave and R. A. B. Mynors (Oxford: Clarendon Press, 1969), 1.xi; 40–1.

11. The relation between empire and modes of transport is always revealing; as Boehmer notes: "The Romans had laid roads; the British now [in the nineteenth century] built railroads and laid telegraph cables" (*Colonial and Postcolonial Literature*, 42).

12. Robert Hardison, *Eccentric Spaces* (Cambridge, MA: MIT Press, 2000), 46; see also Richard Hingley and David Miles, "The Human Impact on the Landscape: Agriculture, Settlement, Industry, Infrastructure," in *The Roman Era: The British*

Isles, 55 BC–AD 410, ed. Peter Salway (Oxford: Oxford University Press, 2002), 141–71, esp. 156–7.

13. Muir, *The New Reading the Landscape*, 100.
14. For a very useful inventory of Roman stonework with inscriptions that was incorporated as *spolia* in Anglo-Saxon buildings, see Tim Eaton, *Plundering the Past: Roman Stonework in Medieval Britain* (Stroud: Tempus, 2000), 59–66.
15. Muir, *The New Reading the Landscape*, 165–7; and further, as he notes, *Minsters and Parish Churches: The Local Church in Transition, 950–1200*, ed. John Blair (Oxford University Committee for Archaeology, Monograph 17, Oxford: Oxbow, 1988); also Salway, *A History of Roman Britain*, 420; and Eaton, *Plundering the Past*, 17–19, 56.
16. On the survival of Roman roads in Anglo-Saxon England, see Michael Reed, *The Landscape of Britain: From the Beginnings to 1914* (London: Routledge, 1997), 265–9; and Eaton, *Plundering the Past*, 42.
17. *The Exeter Book*, ed. G. P. Krapp and E. V. K. Dobbie (Anglo-Saxon Poetic Records 3, New York: Columbia University Press, 1936), 136, lines 73–7. All translations from Old English poetry are by the author.
18. *The Anglo-Saxon Minor Poems*, ed. E. V. K. Dobbie (Anglo-Saxon Poetic Records 6, New York: Columbia University Press, 1942), 55, lines 1–3a.
19. See *An Anglo-Saxon Dictionary*, ed. Joseph Boswell, T. Northcote Toller, and Alastair Campbell (Oxford: Oxford University Press, 1998) s.v. *weallstan*. Eaton, *Plundering the Past*, 17, draws a distinction between *wercstan* "dressed freestone" and *walstan* "rubble" that does not seem to be maintained in the poetry.
20. Wilhelm Levison, *England and the Continent in the Eighth Century* (Oxford: Clarendon Press, 1946), 40–1.
21. Eaton suggests that "the work of giants" is meant at least partly to evoke the very large size of Roman stones (*Plundering the Past*, 127).
22. For such a reading of the poem, see *Three Old English Elegies*, ed. R. F. Leslie (Manchester: Manchester University Press, 1961), 22ff; and, in a more tentative statement, C. L. Wrenn, *A Study of Old English Literature* (New York: Norton, 1967), 154. Salway states that any large town in Roman Britain, as well as many smaller ones, would have had public baths (*A History of Roman Britain*, 367).
23. Peter S. Wells, *The Barbarians Speak: How the Conquered Peoples Shaped Roman Europe* (Princeton: Princeton University Press, 1999), 134.
24. *The Exeter Book*, ed. Krapp and Dobbie, 227, lines 1–6a.
25. Salway, *A History of Roman Britain*, 338.
26. See further, Reed, *The Landscape of Britain*, 60–87.
27. Bill Ashcroft, *Post-Colonial Transformation* (London: Routledge, 2001), 156.
28. W. G. Hoskins, *Local History in England*, third edn (London: Longman, 1984), 114–16.
29. H. P. R. Finberg, *Gloucestershire* (London: Hodder and Stoughton, 1955), 39.
30. *Venerabilis Baedae: Opera Historica*, ed. Charles Plummer (Oxford: Clarendon Press, 1966), 1.5; 368; J. F. Webb and D. H. Farmer, *The Age of Bede* (Harmondsworth: Penguin, 1983), 189.
31. Eaton, *Plundering the Past*, 128.

32. Eaton, *Plundering the Past*, 128.
33. In this respect, it is worth remembering Gregory the Great's injunction, in a letter to Abbot Mellitus, that Augustine of Canterbury should turn whatever pagan shrines and religious sites he found to Christian purposes (*HE* I.xxx). One might note as well the reuse of the Roman-built Church of St. Martin in Canterbury by the first missionaries (*HE* I.xxvi). Such issues are discussed in illuminating detail in Richard Morris, *Churches in the Landscape* (London: Phoenix, 1997), 6–45. For the later Anglo-Saxon practice of building churches on what had been the sites of Roman forts, see Muir, *The New Reading the Landscape*, 152.
34. For a groundplan and dimensions of Escomb, see H. M. Taylor and Joan Taylor, *Anglo-Saxon Architecture* (Cambridge: Cambridge University Press, 1965), vol. I, 235–7.
35. For photographs of such stones, see Eaton, *Plundering the Past*, 146–7.
36. Taylor and Taylor, *Anglo-Saxon Architecture*, vol. I, 235 and 236, respectively. For a photograph of the arch, see Eaton, *Plundering the Past*, 148.
37. Taylor and Taylor, *Anglo-Saxon Architecture*, 236; Eaton, *Plundering the Past*, 16.
38. Salway, *A History of Roman Britain*, 396.
39. Muir, *The New Reading the Landscape*, 11–12.
40. Muir, *The New Reading the Landscape*, 5. The standard study for later periods is Della Hooke, *The Landscape of Anglo-Saxon England* (London: Leicester University Press, 1998).
41. Salway, *A History of Roman Britain*, 332, states that by the 440s at the latest a "distinctively 'post-Roman' society had emerged in Britain" – just in time, one might add, for the arrival of the Germanic tribes. He also states, 354, that "by the middle of the fifth century Britain was materially more impoverished and institutionally more primitive than it had been when Claudius' army landed in AD 43." See also Martin Millett, *The Romanization of Britain: An Essay in Archaeological Interpretation* (Cambridge: Cambridge University Press, 1990), esp. 212–30.
42. This topic has been much discussed; see, most recently, Fred C. Robinson, "Retrospection in Old English and Other Early Germanic Literatures," *The Grove: Studies on Medieval English Language and Literature* 8 (2001): 255–76.
43. Muir, *The New Reading the Landscape*, 100.
44. For a brilliant inquiry into the psychological valences that ruins can have for those who observe or live amid them, see John Summerson, "The Past in the Future" in his *Heavenly Mansions and Other Essays on Architecture* (New York: Norton, 1998), 219–42; and the engaging survey of the subject in Christopher Woodward, *In Ruins* (New York: Pantheon, 2002).
45. Nicholas Howe, "Rome: Capital of Anglo-Saxon England," *Journal of Medieval and Early Modern Studies* 34 (2004): 147–72.
46. W. S. Merwin, *The Mays of Ventadorn* (Washington, DC: National Geographic, 2002), 77.
47. James Corner, "Preface" to *Recovering Landscape: Essays in Contemporary Landscape Architecture*, ed. Corner (Princeton: Princeton Architectural Press, 1999), x.
48. W. G. Hoskins, *The Making of the English Landscape* (London: Penguin, 1985), 55.

49. See further Nicholas Howe, "The Landscape of Anglo-Saxon England: Inherited, Invented, Imagined," in *Inventing Medieval Landscapes*, ed. M. Wolfe and J. Howe (Gainesville: University Press of Florida, 2002), 91–112.

50. D. W. Meinig, "Symbolic Landscapes: Some Idealizations of American Communities," in *The Interpretation of Ordinary Landscapes*, ed. Meinig (New York: Oxford University Press, 1979), 164.

51. For assistance of various forms, I am most grateful to Christopher A. Jones and Roxann Wheeler.

3

Mapping the ends of empire

Alfred Hiatt

It is an obvious but fundamental point that the establishment of a colony engages both colonizers and colonized in thinking beyond familiar spaces, and hence in acts of spatial representation. The notion of the colony is structured by distance – spatial distance from an imperial center or point of origin, but also temporal distance from the precolonial past. Decolonization, as a number of postcolonial critics have been quick to notice, entails understanding and rewriting history in terms of spatial configurations and meanings.[1] As a consequence, the idea of postcolonial space seems to contain within it a number of contradictory impulses. It expresses, on the one hand, a desire to unmake colonial space – to reclaim and to reconfigure – often by means of a revisionary desire to remember the space before the colony. Yet at the same time it must confront the tyranny of inheritance: the impossibility of denying the legacy of colonial space, the remarkable persistence of its borders, its buildings, its mode of spatial organization.

The premise of this chapter is that a study of maps and mapping practices has an important role to play in the elaboration of histories around the idea and the fact of colonialism. For if maps are the measure of the colony – if they both serve and enable colonial vision – they are also colonialism's detritus, what is left behind for the postcolony to work with, to redraw, and to comprehend itself. Equally importantly, maps, when understood broadly to include verbal as well as visual descriptions, can preserve spatial meanings that predate and coexist with colonization and its aftermath. In the following pages, I will advance two basic propositions: first, that certain foundational texts of medieval geographic representation can be understood as postcolonial, since they emerge from, respond to, and rework the geography of the Roman Empire; second, that the territorial expansion of Europe from the twelfth to the fifteenth centuries (and beyond) both brings about, and is made possible by, changes in mapping practices. While these arguments do imply a transition from a postcolonial Europe to a colonizing one, they are also intended to suggest the potential for coexistence of colonial and postcolonial structures.[2]

ENDS OF EMPIRE

What is a map? The word is derived from the Latin for cloth (*mappa*), an etymology that indicates something of the material basis of spatial representation, and its potential for existence outside of traditional book form. It is important to note, however, that in the medieval period maps were described also by terms such as *figura, pictura, imago, tabula,* and often *descriptio*, all of which could refer to verbal as well as visual geographical representation.[3] A *mappa mundi* could in fact consist of verbal description without any accompanying diagrammatic representation, or lists of toponyms arranged schematically. Until recently, however, scholarly focus on visual form as a means of classification has tended to obscure the verbal basis of mapping. The numerous classificatory schemes advanced over the course of the twentieth century all make a distinction between T-O maps, which show a tripartite division of the world between the continents (*partes*) of Asia, Europe, and Africa, within an encircling ocean (Fig. 2), and zonal maps, which show northern and southern hemispheres divided into frigid, temperate, and torrid zones (Fig. 3). A third category comprises navigational charts ("portolans" in Anglophone scholarship), which show detailed outlines of coastal areas, and which appear in significant numbers in the fourteenth and fifteenth centuries (though there is evidence of their existence as early as the twelfth century). These maps are particularly associated with European commerce and exploration, and have been termed "transitional" because they appear to mark a shift from medieval to modern forms and techniques of mapmaking.[4]

Recently, however, historians have suggested a change of emphasis: rather than considering the form of the map as the basis for classification, we should, it is argued, direct our attention to its function. Patrick Gautier Dalché has suggested that the function of medieval maps was

2 T-O map in a tenth-century manuscript of Isidore of Seville's *Etymologiae*: London, BL, MS Royal 6.c.i, fol. 108v. The diagram illustrates chapter 2 of Book XIV of Isidore's work, which describes the world as circular, divided into three parts, of which Asia is the size of the other two put together, and surrounded by Ocean. The function of the map here is essentially that of gloss, but its position within the main body of text should be noted.

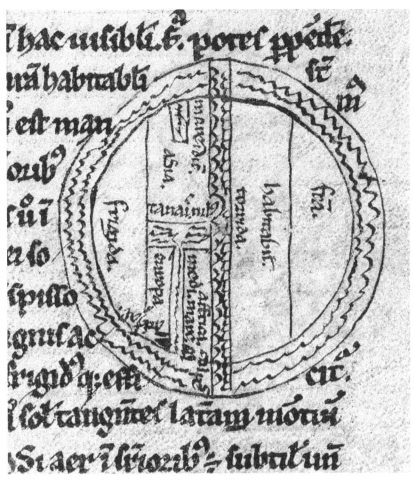

3 Zonal map in a manuscript from *c.* 1200 of William of Conches, *Dragmaticon*: London, BL, MS Arundel 377, fol. 131r. East at top; frigid zones appear at either end, while the temperate zone of the southern hemisphere is marked "habitabilis." Along with the torrid zone ("torrida"), a central band of ocean divides the two hemispheres, and flows into an encircling outer body of water. In the temperate zone of the northern hemisphere, the rivers Don ("Tanais") and Nile combine with the Mediterranean to divide the three parts of the known world. At the far east the Indian Ocean is marked ("Mare indicum"), while the westernmost extents of Europe and Africa are represented by the words "Athlas" (i.e. Mt. Atlas) and "Calpes" respectively. The location of these toponyms indicates corruption of the image in the course of its transmission, since in the *Dragmaticon* William follows the traditional location of Mt. Atlas in Africa, and "Calpes" (one of the fabled columns of Hercules) in Europe. The diagram is integral to William's text, and indeed writing overlaps the outer limits of the image.

initially that of gloss (where map is subordinate to text, often marginal and/or added by the glossator).[5] However, he argues, from the twelfth century the map itself begins to become the object of contemplation: it contains more detail and is accorded greater centrality on the page. This change of focus from form to function has had the benefit of drawing attention to the variety of contexts in which maps appear. The majority of surviving medieval world maps illustrates manuscripts that contain scientific, historical, theological, and literary texts.[6] Those that survive outside of manuscripts seem to have served a similar variety of purpose, from the spiritual to the political and military, to the commercial. Before going any further, though, it is necessary to ask what exactly is meant by a *medieval* map. Part of the problem in answering this question arises from the fact that medieval maps are in many cases amalgams of classical geographical descriptions with postclassical texts and pictorial traditions. Owing to their reliance on classical and late antique sources (at whatever remove), maps produced from the eighth and ninth centuries onwards provided not an up-to-date image of the world in the manner of a modern map, but rather a palimpsest. Accurate depictions of neither the ancient nor the medieval world, they are trans-chronological texts that incorporate features of both. It may be more profitable, then, to see "medieval" maps in terms of their *translation* of a classical geographic legacy, rather than in terms of preservation and innovation. The advantage of using the concept of translation is that, instead of examining medieval maps for the dead hand of tradition and the fresh wind of change in spatial representation, one begins to see interpretation, refashioning, and renewal – the manipulation of classical and early Christian texts, and simultaneously the utilization of their authorizing force.

A close examination of the foundational texts of medieval geography reveals their position, both spatially and temporally, at the ends of classical society and dominion. I am referring above all to two authors of profound importance for ecumenical mapping in the Middle Ages – the representation, that is, of the "known" continents of Africa, Asia, and Europe: Paulus Orosius and Isidore of Seville. Orosius' life and his best-known work, *Historiarum adversum paganos libri vii* (The Seven Books of Histories against the Pagans), evidence a complicated identification with, and critique of, the Roman Empire, at the same time as an exposure to the Greek culture of the Mediterranean region. Probably born in Braga (in present-day Portugal), Orosius fled the Iberian peninsula in 414 for North Africa as a result of Vandal invasions. In Africa he was received by the Christian community at Hippo, where his mentor St. Augustine seems to have encouraged him to reflect on the relationship between Christianity and the empire under which it emerged.

Orosius' geography is, as recent scholarship has argued, not simply a background to his historical narratives; rather, it imbues them at every level, and it is central to his expression of Christian expansionism.[7] Orosius' personal positioning in this regard is intriguing: a Christian, he explicitly identifies himself as a Roman (despite his geographical distance from Rome); his own migrations, from Iberia to North Africa (and subsequently to Palestine on an embassy to Jerome), trace the extent, yet also the decay, of Roman imperial power. What emerges from his history is an optimistic refiguration of Roman imperial space, based on the universalizing potential of Christianity:

> latitudo orientis, septentrionis copiositas, meridiana diffusio, magnarum insularum largissimae tutissimaeque sedes mei iuris et nominis sunt, quia ad Christianos et Romanos Romanus et Christianus accedo.

> [The breadth of the East, the vastness of the North, the extensiveness of the South, and the very large and secure seats of the great islands, are of my law and name because I, as a Roman and a Christian, approach Christians and Romans.][8]

This Christian geography inevitably draws on and to a large degree replicates imperial space – it takes the Empire's names, its territorial divisions, its classification and numeration of peoples.[9] But it also supplements this space: Orosius takes his description of the world, and therefore the site of universal history, well beyond the extent of empire.[10] This in itself is no departure from classical geographical texts, which had as their objective the description of the extent of the known world. What is different about Orosius' geography, however, is that it assimilates itself to the imperial dream of territorial expansion to the ends of the earth in the name of a cause that completely refashions it.

Two centuries after Orosius, Isidore of Seville – probably born in Carthagena (Byzantium) but raised in a Seville then under Visigothic rule – composed two works of lasting importance for medieval geography: *De rerum natura* and his *Etymologiae* (especially books IX and XI–XV thereof). In seventh-century Visigothic Spain, Roman institutions and law were still known and at least in part still maintained.[11] But the center had not held. Isidore's geographical description in the *Etymologiae* shares the pattern of Orosius' division into the three *partes* and islands, although Isidore also mentions a fourth, unknown, part of the world, beyond the equatorial Ocean. More than Orosius, however, the etymological foundation of the description results in an emphasis on the theme of naming, and hence a discourse of foundation. Isidore, that is, insists on a simultaneous linguistic and spatial ordering, and in so doing he consciously returns to classical models. Like Orosius (and he is clearly in numerous ways influenced by him), Isidore describes spatial contiguity: regions are described by the natural feature or neighboring region that defines their boundaries at all four compass points.[12] So, for example, his description of Assyria begins with its etymology, then positions it by reference to surrounding regions and natural features, and finally records its most famous commodities, noting (in a light-hearted but telling aside) their impact on Greek and Roman culture:

> Assyria vocata ab Assur filio Sem, qui eam regionem post diluvium primus incoluit. Haec ab ortu Indiam, a meridie Mediam tangit, ab occiduo Tigrim, a septentrione montem Caucasum, ubi portae Caspiae sunt. In hac regione primus usus inventus est purpurae inde primum crinium et corporum unguenta venerunt et odores, quibus Romanorum atque Graecorum effluxit luxuria.

> [Assyria is named after Asshur the son of Shem, who was the first to inhabit that region after the flood. This region touches India to the east, to the south Media, to the west the Tigris, to the north Mount Caucasus, where the Caspian gates are. In this region the first use was devised for purple; from that place unguents and perfumes for the hair and the body first came, with which the extravagance of the Romans and Greeks abounded.][13]

Place here is defined by a mixture of historical and geographical referents: spatial identity is established through reference to contiguous areas, while economic and cultural significance come from *inventiones* (of purple and perfumes) and crucially from the consequent relation to Greek and Roman cultures. There is a move, then, from first postdiluvian cultivation (Assur) to location within the Greco-Roman orbit.

Isidore's wish to historicize inevitably involves him in an account of the history of spatial organization, and here the colonial nature of the spaces he describes is frequently apparent. At the conclusion of his description of the three *partes* of the known world he makes the following series of statements:

> Provinciae autem ex causa vocabulum acceperunt. Principatus namque gentium, qui ad reges alios pertinebant, cum in ius suum Romani vincendo redigerent, procul positas regiones provincias appellaverunt. Patria autem vocata quod communis sit omnium, qui in ea nati sunt. Terra autem significari, ut praediximus (13, 3, 1), elementum: terras vero singulas partes, ut Africa, Italia. Eadem et loca: nam loca et terrae spatia in orbe terrarum multas in se continent provincias, sicut in corpore locus est pars una, multa in se continens membra; sicut et domus, multa in se habens cubicula: sic terrae et loca dicuntur terrarum spatia, quorum partes sunt provinciae; sicut in Asia Phrygia, in Gallia Raetia, in Hispania Baetica. Nam Asia locus est, provincia Asiae Phrygia, Troia regio Phrygiae, Ilium civitas Troiae. Item regiones partes sunt provinciarum, quas vulgus conventus vocat, sicut in Phrygia Troia; sicut in Gallicia Cantabria, Asturia. A rectoribus autem regio nuncupata est, cuius partes territoria sunt. Territorium autem vocatum quasi tauritorium, tritum bubus et aratro. Antiqui enim sulco ducto et possessionum et territoriorum limites designabant.

> [Provinces indeed are named for a particular reason. For when the Romans by conquering brought under their law the government of nations, which used to pertain to other kings, they called distant regions provinces. A fatherland (*patria*) is so called because it is common to all who are born in it. By land (*terra*) is meant, as we said earlier, the element [i.e. earth]: but "lands" signify separate entities, like Africa, Italy. Areas (*loca*) are the same: for areas and expanses of land throughout the world contain in themselves many provinces, just as in a body there exists one entity, containing within itself many limbs; just as a house has within itself many rooms: thus lands and areas are called expanses of lands (*spatia terrarum*), the parts of which are provinces; such as Phrygia within Asia, Raetia within Gaul, and Baetica within Spain. For Asia is an area (*locus*), Phrygia is a province

of Asia, Troy is a region of Phrygia, Ilium is a city of Troy. So the regions are parts of provinces, which ordinary people say together, thus "Troy in Phrygia", thus "Cantabria and Asturia in Gallicia." But by correct people the word "region" is spoken, the parts of which are territories. The word territory is almost "tauritory," oft-trodden by bull and by plough. For by the ploughed furrow the ancients used to designate the boundaries of both properties and territories.][14]

This hierarchy of forms rests on a principle of repeated metonymy from earth itself to the territory. But the explanation of the term *provincia* makes the element of colonization in this schema unavoidable, and suggests the historically constructed nature of such spaces. It draws Isidore on to an uneasy combination of classical political theory with geographical description. The space of the *patria* is set against that of the *provincia*, but that evocative notion of the native land, *communis omnium*, is quickly left behind, though not erased, by the distinction between *locus, provincia, regio*, and *civitas*. What emerges from this passage is not simply an acknowledgment of imperial naming and control of space as the result of conquest, but also a sense of the multicultural nature of empire, its encompassing of a variety of places and peoples, from Phrygia to Spain. And there is a strong emphasis on the very rootedness of provincial culture in the earth. Vulgar disorder – misnaming and garbling – is contrasted with antique order, and the latter is, crucially, connected with cultivation. The tilling of the soil establishes limits of possessions and territories: Isidore in this passage cuts to the heart of empire, to its combination of war and agriculture in order to lay claim to the earth. In so doing he aligns himself with the ancient project, with the design and repetition of limits. But he writes beyond the time of constitution and during the time of reconfiguration – after the colony, but still within its space.

Despite much speculation, there is no concrete evidence to suggest that the texts of Orosius and Isidore were originally accompanied by maps.[15] Nevertheless, the influence of their verbal descriptions on medieval mapmakers was great, and can be illustrated by two examples of medieval world maps: the Beatus maps and the Hereford *mappa mundi*. The Beatus maps accompany Beatus of Liébana's eighth-century commentary on the Apocalypse, and survive in fourteen manuscripts of the commentary that date from the tenth to the thirteenth centuries.

The purpose of these maps was to illustrate the apostolic mission of extending Christianity throughout Asia, Africa, and Europe prior to the Apocalypse. The fourteen surviving maps can be divided into two main groups, but the maps of both groups combine Orosian and Isidorean elements.[16] The organization of regions corresponds on many examples to the descriptions of Orosius and Isidore: for example, the most detailed Beatus map, drawn in the eleventh century in the Gascon abbey of Saint-Sever, depicts prominently in Asia Major, between the Tigris and Euphrates, the regions of Mesopotamia, Babilonia, Caldea, and "Eodemon," in the exact order stated by both writers (Fig. 4). This map, at the same time, also includes numerous quotations from Isidore, and a characteristic feature, not found in Orosius, but contained in Isidore's *Etymologiae*: the representation of an ambiguous "fourth part of the world, across Ocean deeper within the south, unknown to us due to the heat of the sun."[17] Equally notable is the way in which the Saint-Sever map translates the Isidorean model by interjecting elements of contemporary spatial significance. The region of Gascony is considerably enlarged, and the map's own origins displayed by means of a substantial representation of the "Ecclesia Sancti Seueri," rivaled only by the structures that denote Rome, Jerusalem, Constantinople, and Antioch.

The Hereford *mappa mundi* (Fig. 5), probably compiled in the last decade of the thirteenth century, explicitly acknowledges Orosius as one of its sources in the bottom right corner of the map's frame: "Descripcio Orosii de ornesta mundi, sicut interius ostenditur" [Orosius' account, *De Ornesta mundi*, as is shown within].[18] In the bottom left and at the top of the frame appear two scenes that seem to confirm this connection: a Last Judgment scene, with the Virgin Mary intervening on behalf of mankind at the top of the map, and at the bottom a representation of the emperor Augustus handing a charter to three surveyors, instructing them to describe the world and report back to the Senate. Amongst a number of explanations offered for these scenes, the most persuasive reading sees them in terms of a connection drawn on several occasions by Orosius between the reign of Augustus, the birth of Christ, and the eventual cessation of human miseries.[19] The map, of course, draws on many more sources than Orosius, but in explicitly acknowledging the "Descriptio Orosii" it signals its inheritance of both the imperial survey, and a post-imperial refashioning of the survey in terms of an evangelical

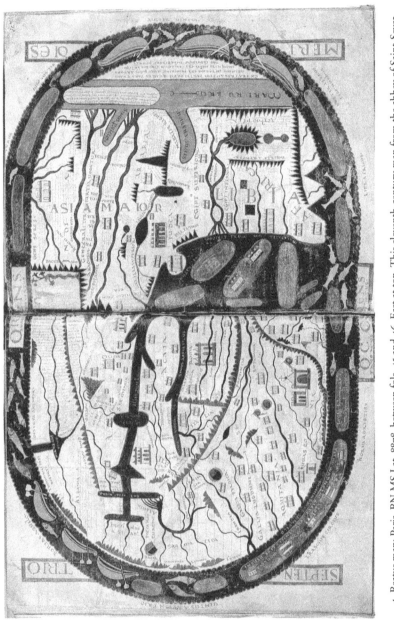

4 Beatus map: Paris, BN MS Lat. 8878, between fols. 45 and 46. East at top. This eleventh-century map from the abbey of Saint-Sever illustrates Beatus' commentary on the *Apocalypse*. Asia is divided into Major and Minor in the top half of the map; in the lower half the prominent Mediterranean separates Europe and Africa. At the far south of the map the Red Sea (Mare Rubrum) separates the known world from a strip of *terra incognita*. Prominent towns and structures on the map include the "Ecclesia Sancti Seueri" in the southwest of Europe, Rome, Jerusalem (above the toponym 'Iudea'), Constantinople, and Antioch.

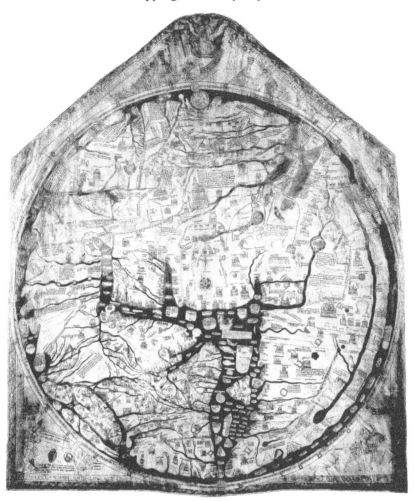

5 Hereford Map, *c.* 1290 (1.59m × 1.29–1.34m). East at top. The map contains an
extraordinary level of detail conveyed in 1091 inscriptions, and copious illustrations.
Jerusalem is located at the centre, and Paradise at the top of the map. The frame of the
map contains three scenes of structural and thematic significance: Christ in Judgment
with the Virgin Mary intervening on behalf of humanity at the top; Augustus Caesar
handing a charter to three surveyors instructing them to map the entire world (bottom
left); and an enigmatic rider gesturing back at the map accompanied by a hunter and two
greyhounds, and the words "passe auaunt" (bottom right).

Christianity.[20] With a remarkable amalgam of historical, geographic, mythographic, and ethnographic information filling the expanse of the three continents of the known world, the Hereford map is both spatial history and spatial future. It is a document that represents the earthly paradise, the birth of Christ, and the Resurrection, while gesturing at the same time, through the image of Caesar and the surveyors, to the exercise of temporal power, and the geographer's privileged perspective as viewer, and epitomizer, of the world.

In summary, then, I would argue that the works of Orosius and Isidore, texts that had a lasting impact on geographical representation, share a number of common features that allow them to be seen as post-colonial. These features include the places and dates of their composition: in North Africa and the Iberian peninsula, at times when Roman institutions and, crucially, a Roman mode of spatial organization still informed political and social life, but when it was also subject to sudden change, and in general characterized by a fluidity of boundaries. Secondly, and just as importantly, both of these texts draw on geographical descriptions that date from the high points of the Roman Empire, most notably the geography contained in Pliny's *Natural History*, but both subtly adapt and refashion these descriptions. A more detailed analysis would explore the ways in which these texts were received and interpreted in medieval Europe, how they provided models for later historians and geographers, and how they were repositioned as "European" texts. In what remains of this essay, however, I would like to concentrate on important changes in geographical representation that date from the twelfth century, and that can be linked with a revival of European colonialism. Two factors, I will suggest, were of central importance to the reemergence of a colonial cartography within Europe: the crusading impulse, and the desire for expanded commercial opportunities. Both crusade and trade depended upon travel, and not only encounters with foreign peoples, but also cohabitation with them.

CRUSADE CARTOGRAPHY

The notion of the crusade, particularly in its early formulations, appropriated and refigured the idea of the pilgrimage. Pilgrimage routes had long been the subject of itineraries, and a number of surviving medieval maps are thought to be derived from, or to have served to some degree as, guides for pilgrims.[21] This function could without a great deal of difficulty be adapted to the interests of crusaders, and there is a certain amount of evidence that the impulse not merely to travel to sites of religious significance, but to conquer, occupy, and populate them, was accompanied by a cartographic impulse. Maps associated with crusading, and particularly maps of the Holy Land, retain many points of continuity with late classical and earlier medieval geographical description. However, the emphasis has changed, from the residue of the Roman project of provincial organization and administration, or the route of the traveler and the location of specific holy sites, or the space of sacred history, to a concern with issues such as fortification, and the history of occupation.[22] This change of emphasis is not wholly discordant with the strand of Orosius' thought that approved of Christian expansionism backed by a secular polity, but whereas these elements were formerly latent in geographical representations based on Orosius and other late antique authors, they become manifest in maps that are motivated by, or respond to, crusade. At the same time new developments in cartographic technology fed into crusade-related maps. Navigational charts provided a much more detailed and more accurate image of the Mediterranean coastline, and their impact extended to maps produced to suit ideological or intellectual, rather than immediately practical, purposes.[23]

Maps that can be associated with an interest in the crusades, or that derive information from the reports of crusaders, are also noticeable for their representation of commercial information, such as the location of trading posts and the commodities to be found in each region. Two contrasting maps of the Holy Land, produced in the mid-thirteenth century by the St. Albans chronicler Matthew Paris, give a sense of the changed spatial dynamic of *Terra Sancta* at this time. The first of these is preserved in manuscripts of his *Chronica majora* and his *Historia Anglorum*, the latter containing detailed information about the crusades, the crusader kingdoms, and battles between crusaders and Saracens (Fig. 6). This map extends from Armenia to Egypt, and contains numerous captions that identify various natural and man-made features, describe the merchandise traded in the area and the religious significance of the Holy Land, and note the territory held by Saracens and Christians. At the bottom right of the map, a large block of text

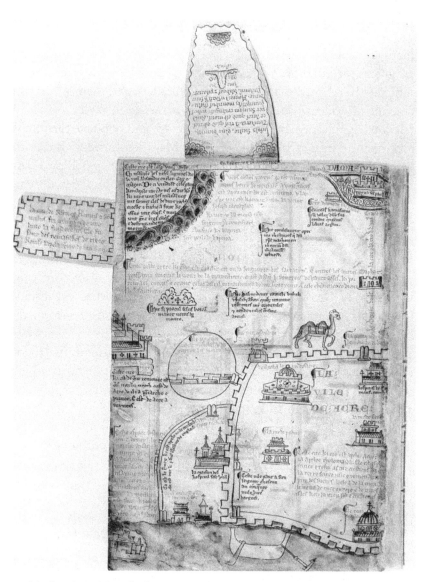

6 Matthew Paris, Map of Palestine I: London, BL, MS Royal 14.C.VII, fols. 4v–5r. East at top. In this manuscript the map of the Crusader Kingdom prefaces Matthew's *Historia Anglorum*, though similar versions of it also illustrate two manuscripts of the *Chronica majora*; in both locations it immediately follows and extends a pictorial itinerary from London to Apulia via Rome. Particularly notable features of the map are the prominence given to the city of Acre (much larger than the walled city of Jerusalem to its southeast, and Damascus at the top centre of the image), the representation of crusader ships off the coast, the enclosure of Gog and Magog and origin of the Tartars in the far northeast, and the large bloc of text to the right that describes Africa. The Bactrian camel above Acre represents the commercial as well as military significance of the city.

6 (*cont.*)

is devoted to a description of Africa, including its physical extent and its peoples. The crusading emphasis is apparent in almost every aspect of the map: crusader ships arrive on the coast; exaggerated prominence is given to the city of Acre, which includes within its crenellated walls the fortresses of the Knights Templar and the Teutonic Knights, and the headquarters of Pisan and Genovese merchants; at the top of the map Damascus is represented as a walled crusader fort, connected by road to Jerusalem.[24] Paris's second, rather more restrained, map of Palestine was preserved on a bifolium at the beginning of a St. Albans Bible (Fig. 7). The map is divided, from north to south, into a series of lands – Antioch, Armenia, the "Old Man of The Mountain," Syria, Israel, Egypt, and the land of the sultan of Babylon. While the sense of a crusade in progress is far less evident, numerous sites of significance to crusaders are noted, such as crusader castles, and in the far north of the map the dwelling of the Assassins ("habitacio assessinorum"). Here too the ethnic divisions that characterize earlier geographical representations are supplemented by religious categories: a prominent note in red ink marks the "terra a paganis et sarracenis inhabitata. cuius dominus Soldanus damasci" [Land inhabited by pagans and Saracens, ruled by the sultan of Damascus].

An even more polemical use of maps that shows the impact of crusade on spatial organization can be seen in the world map and the map of Palestine that accompanied Marino Sanudo's *Liber secretorum fidelium crucis* of 1320–21. Sanudo, a Venetian merchant, produced the book to advocate a resumption of the crusades following the loss of Christian-held territories in the preceding century. To illustrate his tract Sanudo enlisted the assistance of one of the most prominent cartographers of the time, an expert in the production of navigational charts, and the first European mapmaker to sign his works on a regular basis: Pietro Vesconte.[25] Vesconte's sources for his map of Palestine (Fig. 8) included not only navigational charts, but also a thirteenth-century pilgrim's account of the Holy Land. In addition, much of the information related on the map is explicitly derived from Arab sources, and so too, it seems likely, is its unusual use of a grid.[26] The map is often described as radical by historians of cartography because of its combination of new standards of accuracy with "traditional scholastic geography" (its inclusion, for example, of the twelve tribes, the pillar of salt formerly

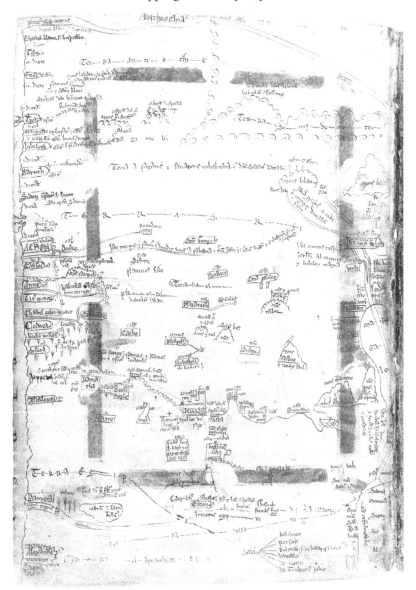

7 Matthew Paris, Map of Palestine II: Oxford, Corpus Christi College MS 2, fol. 2v.
North at top. The map extends from Antioch to Alexandria, and is divided, from north to
south, into a series of "terrae" including Armenia, Syria, Egypt, and the land of the Sultans
of Babylon and Damascus. Prominent cities and landmarks include Jerusalem, Bethlehem,
Mount Carmel, Sodom, Gomorrah, and Lot's wife.

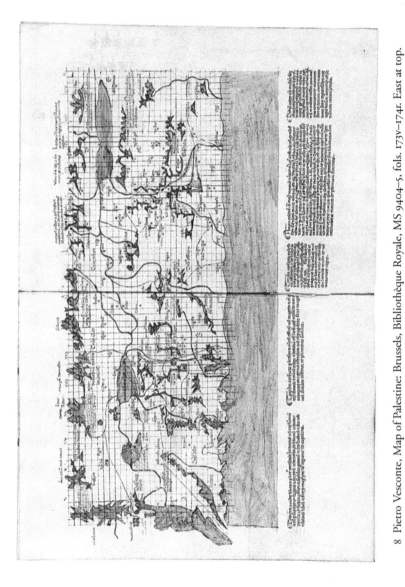

8 Pietro Vesconte, Map of Palestine: Brussels, Bibliothèque Royale, MS 9404–5, fols. 173v–174r. East at top. Vesconte's map illustrates Marino Sanudo's *Liber secretorum fidelium crucis*. The most striking feature of this map is the use of a grid, but it is a record of biblical history as well as contemporary space, which shows the locations of the twelve tribes of Israel and Lot's wife.

known as Lot's wife, and Job's tomb).[27] And its use of the grid as a
lexical aid – references in Sanudo's text could easily be located on the
map – is undoubtedly highly significant. But what is most striking
about Vesconte's map, when it is compared to the images produced
just over half a century earlier by Matthew Paris, is the altered political
configuration. There is on Vesconte's map no sense of the crusades as
an ongoing process, no sense of land as the cause and setting for violent
conflict. Instead, the map of Palestine has been redrawn – now so much
better known, it is comprehensible by means of the principle of the grid,
replete with specific locations of biblical events, but also largely devoid of
a crusader presence. It is, from the European perspective, unfortunately
postcolonial: clarity has been gained through absence. But by placing
the map, with all its carefully designed referentiality, in the context of a
call for a resumption of the crusades, Sanudo holds out the possibility
that it may be used as a blueprint for reconquest.

ETHNOGRAPHY, CARTOGRAPHY, AND COLONIZATION

Hopes of colonial expansion into Palestine gradually faded over the
course of the fourteenth and fifteenth centuries, but Europe was on
the move in other areas: in the Atlantic, in parts of northern Europe,
including some still pagan areas, and, from the fifteenth century, along
the north and west coasts of Africa. Such expansion was assisted by
maps, though it also changed them, forcing in many areas a revision of
earlier geographical description.

But if maps were central to spatial division and ordering in an era of
rapid colonization, what role did they play in the conceptualization of
ethnic identity within and without Europe, and how may this be related
to questions of colonial expansion? At a basic level, the division of the
known world between the three continents was also an ethnographic
division, between peoples descended from the three sons of Noah. This
connection between ethnography and geography was, as the descriptions
of Orosius and Isidore show, quite fundamental to classical and early
medieval mapping practices. The number and names of *gentes* (a word
that can be translated variously as peoples, tribes, or races) in certain
areas were frequently noted, alongside topographic and natural historical

features. And this kind of information about peoples just as frequently found its way into medieval maps, usually in the form of verbal notes, but occasionally as pictorial representation. In one sense, then, there is continuity between medieval representations of peoples on maps, and the many examples of sixteenth-century maps that show ethnographic scenes in the New World, and in other areas recently discovered by Europeans. But certain key differences between pre- and post-Columban representation of native peoples should be noted.

First, there is a predominantly textual basis for most pre-Columban representation: illustrations of peoples tend to be based on written descriptions, often of considerable age, rather than first-hand observation or accounts of contemporary explorers. One of the best-known features of medieval *mappae mundi* is the representation of monstrous races, usually in the southernmost part of Africa, but also in Scythia and India. Amongst the more frequently represented of these races were Anthropophagi (cannibals), Antipods (possessing feet turned in opposite direction to body), Blemmyae (with faces on chests), Cynocephali (dog-heads), Essedones (eaters of their parents' corpses), Sciopods (having one large foot, used to provide shade from the sun), and Troglodytes (cave-dwellers).[28] The majority of these peoples was ultimately derived by medieval writers from the work of Iulius Solinus, the third-century adaptor of Pliny's *Natural History*. The presence of such peoples on world maps could, at times, be linked to Christianizing motivations: the Cynocephali, for example, became associated with Saracens, and this connection was noted by inscriptions on maps such as that of the fifteenth-century "Borgia map," which depicts a dog-headed king and two subjects with the accompanying inscription: "Ebinichibel rex est sarracenus ethiopicus cum populo suo habens faciem caninam et incedunt omnes nudi propter solis calorem" [Ebinichibel is a Saracen Ethiopian king having along with his people a dog face, and they all walk around naked because of the heat of the sun].[29] One important point to make here is the level of choice that medieval mapmakers had in the representation of such peripheral regions, given the range of written sources at their disposal. Thus, two maps may show quite different images in the same area, despite otherwise being extremely similar. The southernmost region of Africa could be simply marked "Ethiopia" (as it is on the late twelfth-century Sawley world map), following Orosius' description, which studiously avoided retailing Solinus' marvels. It could also be depicted in accordance with Isidore's mention, in Book xiv of the *Etymologiae*, of huge dragons and serpents in the area; and, of course, it could be shown with an array of "monstrous species" in the Plinian tradition, as it is on the major thirteenth-century world maps such as the Hereford *mappa mundi*.[30]

Such manipulations of variant textual traditions also allowed for the introduction of information from more contemporary accounts, such as *Mandeville's Travels* or the *Travels* of Marco Polo. Texts such as Polo's *Travels* continued earlier geographers' preoccupations with political structures – regions are described in terms of the number of kingdoms, or other polities, found in them; the dimensions of such polities; and the methods by which political authority is exercised in them. Certain medieval maps, such as the remarkable Catalan Atlas, clearly give visual form to such matters. The Atlas, probably assembled by the Majorcan Jew Abraham Cresques before 1375 for Charles VI of France, consists of twelve panels that, together, form an image of the known world.[31] In Europe, there are no images of people, although, in the navigational chart tradition, flags are shown to represent separate dominions. In Asia and Africa, however, the Atlas is notable for a series of seated figures, representing rulers of various kinds, and by extension their polities (Fig. 9). These figures undoubtedly construct zones of exoticism beyond the familiar European, North African, and Near Eastern regions – beyond, one might say, the world of detailed classical geographical description. In a map designed for a European king they also have a more explicitly political purpose: the orientation of European kingdoms in relation to those of Africa and Asia – a display of their distance, their differences, the possibility of travel, but more fundamentally their configuration. This spatial organization of non-European kingdoms is not an imperial formulation as, one way or the other, most of the classical Roman descriptions were. In fact, like almost all medieval formulations of world space, it indicates the relatively small size and influence of Europe. But in its provision of a political vision, its incorporation of Polo's *Travels* (the earliest surviving map to do so), its sense of Asia and Africa as spaces that contain discrete political entities and offer clear commercial opportunities, it foreshadows the European pursuit of political influence and commercial control.

9 Catalan Atlas: Paris, BN MS ESP 30, detail showing Guinea. North at top. The Catalan Atlas is rich in ethnographic and political detail, particularly in Asia and Africa. The seated king is described in the accompanying caption as the "lord of the blacks of Guinea . . . the most wealthy and most noble lord of the whole of this region."

The representation of polities on the Catalan Atlas suggests a second key difference between early modern and medieval ethnographic representation: the absence of conquest as a structure that determines the European view. As a consequence, the drawing of "natives" – of peoples encountered, conquered, and/or colonized – is relatively rare on medieval maps. On sixteenth-century maps, by contrast, one often finds depictions of scenes (accurate or not) of indigenous peoples.[32] This is not, as I have tried to suggest, because of the absence of conquest, colonization, and encounter with foreign – both European and non-European – peoples over the course of the Middle Ages (and particularly, as Robert Bartlett has emphasized, from the tenth and eleventh centuries onwards).[33] Instead it reflects the basis of much medieval cartography in written textual sources, and the primarily navigational and mercantile orientation of traditions such as the navigational chart that had greater autonomy from verbal descriptions: maps, in other words, tended to translate text rather than experience, word rather than vision. What is clear from numerous medieval examples, however, is that certain mapmakers and their audiences reveled in the representation of non-European peoples, and that this ethnographic dimension contributed to a sense of the map as a multicultural document, a text that incorporated a variety of attested and hypothesized ethnic groups as well as places. In this sense at least, maps are imbued with the notion of cultural encounter, whether their objective was conquest, commerce, pilgrimage, or all three.

CONCLUSION

The aim of this chapter has been to contribute to a rethinking of the "post" of postcolonialism. It is clear from an examination of the legacy of Roman imperialism that the impetus that colonization gave to mapping large areas existed long before the sixteenth century. It is extremely important to consider classical colonial practices of the division, regionalization/provincialization of space not simply as some kind of precursor to modern colonial practices, but as a central aspect of the formulation of colonial discourses. Those discourses are of the *colonia*, the Roman settlement in the midst of a barbarian population – of interaction with peoples inside and outside the settlement, and with the metropolitan power in whose name it exists. But as I have tried to show, what is also crucial (and again, crucial not just for medievalists, but for all interested in the phenomenon of colonialism) is an engagement with the way in which colonial formulations live on after the colony. As medieval examples show, imperial space can be remarkably tenacious, thanks to the very extent and detail of its vision, to its provision of representational models, and to its principle of ordering information in the forms of catalogues, lists, surveys, as well as narratives. What medieval maps and geographical descriptions also show is the capacity for imperial order to be translated – to be reworked and reshaped, if not easily erased. And it may be this effort of translation, of filling in the margins, and of replacing and reformulating information, that helps to define the postcolonial.

A final point: one advantage of the study of maps from previous eras is the opportunity to see places lost, forgotten, renamed, rewritten – to see and perhaps to comprehend something of a previous spatial dynamic. Consider the medieval map of Palestine, and the modern map of the Middle East. The medieval European maps of Palestine, such as those of Matthew Paris or Pietro Vesconte, are susceptible to Christian, Jewish, and Muslim readings: all these cultures have contributed to the maps, and all can be found on them, albeit with vastly different significations – crusaders, Old Testament tribes, infidel enemy. Now, the very act of comparing medieval maps of this area to modern ones is, I am aware, polemical. Why? Because while place names are in many cases the same – Jerusalem, Gaza, Damascus, and so on – their meaning has changed, and the configuration of space around them has changed as a result of the establishment of modern-day Arab states and the state of Israel. Even – particularly – the name of the map is fraught: are we looking at a map of Palestine? Israel? The Holy Land? The Middle East? All these titles convey different, and highly charged, meanings. It is therefore not surprising to find that the provision of accurate, detailed, and mutually acceptable maps is amongst the more contentious issues of early twenty-first-century diplomacy. The possession of such maps is a crucial precondition for effective negotiation: to be mapless, as Edward Said has pointed out, is to be deprived of the means to contest decisions and advance alternative plans for territorial division.[34] It is also to be deprived of the rhetorical force that the knowledge of land carries with it when it is textualized in the form of a map.

This potential for mapping to be contentious underlines a crucial point about maps: not only do they convey spatial history, they also suggest the potential for future change. Precisely because maps leave a record of the history of places and their changing representation over time, they offer the possibility of imagining and constructing a different spatial order. If spatial configurations have changed in the past as a result of political, economic, and social factors, they can change again, and more crucially they can be changed on and by maps. It is therefore necessary to emphasize that the spatial dynamic represented on maps is not neutral, and a consequence of this point is the capacity to read images of land in terms of the histories they incorporate or erase. Such histories are very frequently ones of contestation and encounter, but it is also important not to lose sight of narratives of curiosity, accident, and imagination, because these too are forces that have made, and that will continue to make, maps.

NOTES

1. For example, Paul Carter, *The Road to Botany Bay: An Essay in Spatial History* (London: Faber and Faber, 1987); Graham Huggan, "Decolonizing the Map: Post-Colonialism, Post-Structuralism and the Cartographic Connection," *Ariel* 20 (1989): 115–31.

2. I am skeptical of the value of the concept of the "midcolonial" advanced by Jeffrey Jerome Cohen, "the time of the 'always-already,' an intermediacy that no narrative can pin to a single moment of history in its origin and end." See *The Postcolonial Middle Ages*, ed. Cohen, 3. Cohen is right to point out (along with many other medievalists) that the history of colonies begins well before "the modern world order." But that history is full of quite abrupt moments of origin and end, of significance for both colonizers and colonized, which should not be elided in a haze of intermediacy.

3. On the use of "mappa" and other terms to designate maps see David Woodward, "Medieval Mappaemundi," in *Cartography in Prehistoric, Ancient, and Medieval Europe and the Mediterranean*, ed. J. B. Harley and David Woodward, *The History of Cartography*, vol. 1 (Chicago: University of Chicago Press, 1987), 287–8; Patrick Gautier Dalché, *La "Descriptio Mappae Mundi" de Hugues de Saint-Victor: texte inédit avec introduction et commentaire* (Paris: Etudes Augustiniennes, 1988), 89–95.

4. For a summary of classification schemes see Woodward, "Medieval Mappaemundi," 294–9, 343–58, and Evelyn Edson, *Mapping Time and Space: How Medieval Map-makers Viewed Their World* (London: British Library, 1997), 2–9. On navigational

charts see Tony Campbell, "Portolan Charts from the Late Thirteenth Century to 1500," in *The History of Cartography*, vol. 1, 371–463; M. de la Roncière and M. Mollat du Jourdin, *Les Portulans: cartes marines du XIIIe au XVIIe siècle* (Fribourg: Office du Livre, 1984); and Patrick Gautier Dalché, *Carte marine et portulan au XIIe siècle: Le "Liber de existencia riveriarum et forma maris nostri Mediterranei" (Pise, circa 1200)* (Rome: Ecole Française de Rome, 1995), 24–30.

5. Patrick Gautier Dalché, "De la glose à la contemplation. Place et fonction de la carte dans les manuscrits du haut moyen âge," *Settimane di Studio del Centro Italiano di Studi sull'Alto Medioevo* 41 (1994): 749.

6. For a study of maps according to these contexts see Edson, *Mapping Time and Space*.

7. Andrew Merrills, *History and Geography in Late Antiquity* (Cambridge: Cambridge University Press, forthcoming). See also Eugenio Corsini, *Introduzione alle* Storie *di Orosio* (Turin: Giappichelli, 1968), 73–83.

8. Paulus Orosius, *Historiarum adversum paganos libri vii*, ed. C. Zangemeister (Leipzig: Teubner, 1889), 144 (v.ii.3); I have used the translation in *The Seven Books of History against the Pagans*, trans. Roy J. Deferrari (Washington, DC: Catholic University of America Press, 1964), 176.

9. See Yves Janvier, *La Géographie d'Orose* (Paris: Société d'Edition "Les Belles Lettres," 1982), 231, who points out that Orosius' information dates from different periods of the Empire. Edson notes Orosius' reliance on Pomponius Mela's first-century AD *Chorographia*, and his retention of antiquated names, even in areas with which Orosius was familiar from personal experience: *Mapping Time and Space*, 34; cf. Janvier, *La Géographie d'Orose*, 232: "l'Espagne d'Orose représente un extraordinaire retour en arriére."

10. Janvier, *La Géographie d'Orose*, 149–53, 251–2; Merrills, *History and Geography*. This practice of supplementation is extended in later rewritings of Orosian geography: see *The Old English Orosius*, ed. Janet Bately (EETS SS 6, Oxford: Oxford University Press, 1980), and Sealy Gilles, "Territorial Interpolations in the Old English Orosius," in *Text and Territory: Geographical Imagination in the European Middle Ages*, ed. Sylvia Tomasch and Sealy Gilles (Philadelphia: University of Pennsylvania Press, 1998), 79–96.

11. On this issue see further the stimulating discussion in *The Visigoths: From the Migration Period to the Seventh Century. An Ethnographic Perspective*, ed. Peter Heather (Woodbridge: Boydell, 1999), 503–11. Jacques Fontaine, *Isidore de Seville et la culture classique dans l'Espagne wisigothique*, 3 vols. (Paris: Etudes Augustiniennes, 1959–83), vol. II, 831–62, argued that the location of Visigothic Spain, combined with a period of religious and political stability, encouraged a renaissance of antique culture in the seventh century.

12. Hans Philipp, *Die historisch-geographischen Quellen in den Etymologiae des Isidorus von Sevilla*, 2 vols. (Berlin: Weidmannsche Buchhandlung, 1913), vol. II, 31–4.

13. Isidore of Seville, *Etymologiarum sive originum libri xx*, ed. W. M. Lindsay, 2 vols. (Oxford: Clarendon Press, 1911), XIV.iii.10. Translation mine.

14. Isidore of Seville, *Etymologiarum*, XIV.v.19–22. Cf. Philipp, *Quellen in den Etymologiae des Isidorus von Sevilla*, vol. II, 129–31, who notes Isidore's reliance on Servius' commentary on the *Aeneid*.

15. The eighth-century "Albi map" is one of the few examples of a map accompanying a manuscript copy of Orosius' geographical description, and it is the oldest detailed terrestrial map in existence. Its toponyms seem to show a greater reliance on Isidore's description than on Orosius': Edson, *Mapping Time and Space*, 32–3, Anna-Dorothee von den Brincken, *Fines Terrae: Die Enden der Erde und der vierte Kontinent auf mittelalterlichen Weltkarten* (MGH Schriften 36, Hanover: Hahnsche Buchhandlung, 1992), 32–3.

16. See John Williams, "Isidore, Orosius and the Beatus Map," *Imago Mundi* 49 (1997): 7–32.

17. Isidore of Seville, *Etymologiarum*, XIV.5.17: "Extra tres autem partes orbis quarta pars trans Oceanum interior est in meridie, quae solis ardore incognita nobis est." For discussion see Williams, "Beatus Map," 17–23, and Edson, *Mapping Time and Space*, 149–59.

18. *The Hereford Map: A Transcription and Translation of the Legends with Commentary*, ed. Scott D. Westrem (Turnhout: Brepols, 2001), 7. As Westrem notes, the word "ormista" or "ormesta" was used to describe Orosius' work in Europe from at least the eighth century (6).

19. See David Lawton, "The Surveying Subject: The 'Whole World' of Belief: Three Case Studies," *New Medieval Literatures* 4 (2001): 9–37, esp. 14–22. For contrasting explanations see Valerie I. J. Flint, "The Hereford Map: Its Author(s), Two Scenes and a Border," *Transactions of the Royal Historical Society*, sixth series 8 (1998): 19–44, and the discussion in Naomi Reed Kline, *Maps of Medieval Thought: The Hereford Paradigm* (Woodbridge: Boydell, 2001), 51–83. For a summary of arguments about the purpose and meaning of the outer frame of the map see *The Hereford Map*, ed. Westrem, xxiv–xxv, 4–10.

20. Patrick Gautier Dalché has recently identified a major source for the map in a twelfth-century text entitled "Expositio Mappe Mundi," which sets out the content and spatial arrangement of a world map; it appears to have been closely followed by the maker(s) of the Hereford map: *The Hereford Map*, ed. Westrem, xxxiv–xxxvii. The EMM itself incorporates a large number of classical and late antique sources: Patrick Gautier Dalché, "Décrire le monde et situer les lieux au XIIe siècle: l'*Expositio mappe mundi* et la généalogie de la mappemonde de Hereford," *Mélanges de l'Ecole Française de Rome. Moyen Age* 112 (2001): 343–409.

21. Such as the Hereford map, the mapped itineraries contained in Matthew Paris's *Chronica majora*, and possibly some of the Beatus maps, as well as fifteenth-century post-crusade maps of the Holy Land: see Edson, *Mapping Time and Space*, 14, 118, 143, 153.

22. The maps of Asia and Palestine that accompany the copy of Jerome's *Liber locorum* contained in a twelfth-century French manuscript are examples of maps concerned primarily with the representation of sacred history: Edson, *Mapping Time and Space*, 26–30.

23. On the varied function of navigational charts see Campbell, "Portolan Charts," 438–45; Gautier Dalché, *Carte marine et portulan au XIIe siècle*, 83–102.

24. For discussion of Paris's maps of Palestine see Richard Vaughan, *Matthew Paris* (Cambridge: Cambridge University Press, 1958), 244–7; Suzanne Lewis, *The Art of Matthew Paris in the* Chronica Majora (Aldershot: Scolar Press, 1987), 347–64; Konrad Miller, *Mappae Mundi: Die ältesten Weltkarten*, 6 vols. (Stuttgart: Roth, 1895–98), vol. III, 68–94.

25. On Vesconte and Sanudo see Nathalie Bouloux, *Culture et savoirs géographiques en Italie au XIVe siècle* (Turnhout: Brepols, 2002), 45–68; Bernhard Degenhart and Annegrit Schmitt, *Marino Sanudo und Paolino Veneto: Zwei Literaten des 14. Jahrhunderts in ihrer Wirkung auf Buchillustrierung und Kartographie in Venedig, Avignon und Neapel* (Tübingen: Ernst Wasmuth, 1973), 60–87.

26. See P. D. A. Harvey, *The History of Topographical Maps: Symbols, Pictures and Surveys* (London: Thames and Hudson, 1980), 144–6.

27. See e.g. Kenneth Nebenzahl, *Maps of the Holy Land: Images of Terra Sancta through Two Millennia* (New York: Abbeville Press, 1986), 43.

28. See Woodward, "Medieval *Mappaemundi*," 330–2.

29. Roberto Almagià, *Monumenta cartographica Vaticana*, 4 vols. (Vatican City: Biblioteca Apostolica Vaticana, 1944–55), vol. I, 27–9; Woodward, "Medieval *Mappaemundi*," 332.

30. E.g. Munich, Bayerische Staatsbibliothek, CLM 10058, f. 154v: cf. Gautier Dalché, *La "Descriptio Mappae Mundi" de Hugues de Saint-Victor*, 81–6. It should be noted that Isidore also mentions other animals, as well as many peoples of diverse and monstrous appearance, without going into detail.

31. *Mapamundi: The Catalan Atlas of the Year 1375*, ed. Georges Grosjean (Dietikon and Zurich: Graf, 1977).

32. Perhaps the most striking examples are to be found on the sumptuous productions of the "Dieppe School" of cartographers, whose works include Jean Rotz's *Boke of Idrography*, the Vallard Atlas, and the world map of Pierre Descaliers.

33. Robert Bartlett, *The Making of Europe: Conquest, Colonization and Cultural Change 950–1350* (Princeton: Princeton University Press, 1993).

34. Edward Said, "Palestinians under Siege," *London Review of Books*, 14 December 2000.

4

"On fagne flor": the postcolonial *Beowulf*, from Heorot to Heaney

Seth Lerer

> Someone, he added, ought to draw up a catalogue of types of buildings listed in order of size, and it would be immediately obvious that domestic buildings of *less* than normal size – the little cottage in the fields, the hermitage, the lockkeeper's lodge, the pavilion for viewing the landscape, the children's bothy in the garden – are those that offer us at least a semblance of peace, whereas no one in his right mind could truthfully say that he liked a vast edifice such as the Palace of Justice on the old Gallows Hill in Brussels. At the most we gaze at it in wonder, a kind of wonder which in itself is a form of dawning horror, for somehow we know by instinct that outsize buildings cast the shadow of their own destruction before them, and are designed from the first with an eye to their later existence as ruins.
>
> W. G. Sebald, *Austerlitz*[1]

Tearing into Heorot, soon after Beowulf arrives, Grendel breaks down the hall's door barely with a touch. He stands, maddened at the entry:

> Raþe æfter þon
> on fagne flor   feond treddode,
> eode yrre-mod.[2]

In the translation of Seamus Heaney, he is "pacing the length of the patterned floor with his loathsome tread," but that is but a part of it. Grendel stands "on fagne flor," a floor seemingly decorated or patterned in some way. The word *fag* or *fah* appears throughout the poem to connote the patterned objects of the warrior's treasury: swords, hilts, coats of mail, helms, and the like. But here, I think it means something quite specific. Grendel stands not just on a patterned floor, but a tessellated one: a mosaic relic of an older, Roman architectural past. Much like the paved road that Beowulf and his men traverse on their way to

77

Heorot – "stræt wæs stan-fah" (line 320) – this floor represents the archaeology of the Anglo-Saxon postcolonial imagination. It offers up a vision of a vernacular present set on an ancient relic. It exemplifies the status of the poem's fictive world (and, perhaps, its historical readership) as living in the afterlife of Rome.

Anglo-Saxon England was acutely conscious of its life on Roman floors. In many ways, it built itself upon the ruins of the colonizers. Churches and dwellings were built on Roman foundations (though, on occasion, old villas and roads were apparently abused, or desecrated), and there is evidence throughout Anglo-Saxon literary and historical writing for a deep, cultural consciousness of the Roman past. While much has been made of all these elements in Anglo-Saxon history, little has been made of them (especially in recent criticism) in *Beowulf*; but I want to argue here not simply for a stratum of the Roman past under the poem's archaeology. Instead, I hope to make a slightly different and more literary point, one calibrated to the poem's current reception, as well as to its possible contemporary resonances.[3]

For our modern sense of a postcolonial *Beowulf* – one voiced in Seamus Heaney's translation and the various paratexts that have surrounded it (the introduction, the reviews) – has this historical texture behind it.[4] And furthermore, the two must be approached in tandem: Heaney's translation brings out the sense of a postcoloniality to the Anglo-Saxon literary experience, where we may see the lens of a current political angst magnifying the legacy of ancient loss. As Heaney puts it in the introduction to his translation, the lament of the Geatish woman, for example, "could come straight from a late-twentieth-century news report, from Rwanda or Kosovo; her keen is a nightmare glimpse into the minds of people who have survived traumatic, even monstrous events and who are now being exposed to a comfortless future" (xx–xxi).

Such an exposure to a comfortless future is the fate of those who would survive the death of their own culture, be it the Survivor's people who had amassed the treasure he buries or, for that matter, Wiglaf's who must live on after Beowulf's death. Heaney's translation – in its local idiom and its larger, global framing – may attempt to relocate our reading of the poem in these current frames. But they are also the historical frames for the poem's narrative: a narrative of elegy and loss, one conscious of a life lived on the barely maintained artistry and artifice of Roman Britain, one fearful of just what lies hidden in the wondrous arches left by leaders who have gone.

The word "colonial" comes ultimately from the Latin *colonia*, settlement, itself derived from the verb *collo*, meaning (among other things) to till the land, to live in, or to cultivate.[5] The *colonus* was a settler, and the cultural expansion signaled by the term was not limited to imperial politics. Early in the *Aeneid*, Carthage itself appears as an outpost of another nation:

> Urbs antiqua fuit (Tyrii tenuere coloni)
> Karthago . . .
>   (1.12–13)
>
> [There was an ancient city, Carthage, held by settlers from Tyre . . .]

And what is, too, the masterplot of the *Aeneid* but the settlement of Rome itself, the making of a nation founded by the drifting warriors of Troy?

Eventually, the world *colonia* came to mean a specific administrative unit of settlement. In the early Empire, it was something like a town filled with old soldiers. Later, the term denoted the biggest or most important of the settlements (followed, in descending order, by *municipia*, *civitates*, *vici*, and then *pagus*).[6] London, Bath, Chichester, Lincoln, Gloucester – these were some of the *coloniae*: in the words of the historian Peter Salway, "one of those essential bastions of Roman stability, a Romanized community that organized and ran itself on Roman lines derived eventually from the formal structure of Rome itself."[7]

Always, the Romans left the markers of their manners: paved roads, baths and amphitheaters, villas rich with tessellated floors and muraled walls. Their massiveness and artifice must have astounded native populaces.[8] Even after they were left in ruins they could still amaze. At the beginning of the eighth century, Bede could look back on the majesty of Roman handiwork, *ciuitates farus pontes et stratae*, or in the Old English of his later, Alfredian translator:

> & ceastre & torras & stræta & brycge on heora rice geworhte wæron, þa we to dæg sceawian magon.
>
> [And cities, and towers, and paved roads and bridges had been built during their rule, which we may still see today.][9]

Bede's impressions were echoed by Æthelweard in the tenth century, with some embellishment.

> Urbes etiam atque castella nec non pontes plateasque mirabili ingenio condiderunt, quæ usque in hodiernam diem videntur.
>
> [They made cities, forts, bridges, and streets with wonderful skill, and these are to be seen to this day.][10]

It is the wonder at these public works that Æthelweard notices, a wonder that filled many of his Anglo-Saxon peers before and after him. St. Cuthbert saw the old "city wall and the well formerly built in a wonderful manner (*mire*) by the Romans" when he visited Carlisle in 685.[11] Some time in the 780s, Alcuin extolled the Roman foundations of York, with its "high walls and lofty towers," and he praised the city's location ("a healthy place of noble setting") as attractive to *multos colonos* – many different settlers.[12] In 839, a document known as the *Cartularium Saxonicum* called London itself "that celebrated place built by the skill of the ancient Romans."[13] By the early eleventh century, when *Beowulf* and the poems of the Exeter Book and the Vercelli Book were being written down, the praise of Roman industry and edifice had become something of a trope.[14] That sense of the remarkable (*mirabilis*) finds its vernacular equivalent in the Old English term *wrætlic*. Take, for example, the opening of *The Ruin*, a poem generally acknowledged to be about some ancient Roman city, such as Bath.

> Wrætlic is þes wealstan,   wyrde gebræcon;
> burgstede burston,   brosnað enta geweorc.
> Hrofas sind gehrorene,   hreorge torras . . .
>
> [Remarkable is that stone wall, broken by fate;
> the city foundations shattered, the work of giants decayed.
> The roofs have fallen in, the towers in ruins . . .][15]

This "work of giants," too, becomes an idiom of architectural marvel. Look at the opening of the Cotton *Maxims*, with its gnomic avowals of the ideals of kingship phrased in terms of an ancient empire.

> Cyning sceal rice healdan.   Ceastra beoð feorran gesyne,
> orðonc enta geweorc,   þa þe on þisse eorðan syndon,
> wrætlic weallstana geweorc.

[A king should rule a kingdom. Cities are seen from far away, the skillful work of giants, which still remain on this earth, the remarkable work of stone walls.][16]

That word *ceastra* is here, as in all Old English writing, a self-conscious loan-word from the Latin, *castra*, and cannot but refer to the settlements of Roman forts (it would eventually pass into later English as the name, and suffix, *chester*).[17] Here, too, as in *The Ruin*, the remarkable artifice of stonework still stands. Early Anglo-Saxon settlers built almost exclusively in wood, and even up until the Conquest there were no English monumental buildings in dressed stone. This architectural habit made not only the older Roman edifices noteworthy; it made the new Norman castles – from that same Latin root – equally marvelous, and terrifying. The poem on the death of William the Conqueror from the *Peterborough Chronicle* sustains this idiom, as it begins with a reflection on its subject's achievements: "Castelas he let wyrcean."[18] He had castles built, an imposition of a new political order signaled by a change in architecture.

The marvels of stonework could be seen by Anglo-Saxons not just on horizons but beneath their feet. Paved roads still criss-crossed Britain. The word *stræt* was, like *ceastra*, a loan from the Latin and referred almost exclusively to the roads of Roman legacy. "Stræt wæs stan-fah" in *Beowulf*. The street was stone paved (the phrase can mean, I think, nothing else), for this is the remnant of a road set from the sea to inland settlement and the one that Beowulf and his men follow on their way to Hrothgar's hall. It is a phrase designed to conjure in the audience's mind an image of that earlier construction, much as the similar phrasing in *Andreas* is calibrated to evoke that saint's torture in an ancient city.

Drogon deormodne   æfter dunscræfum,
ymb stanhleoðo,   stærcedferþne,
efne swa wide swa   wegas to lagon,
enta ærgeweorc,   innan burgum,
stræte stanfage.

[They dragged the one bold in spirit up to the caves,
that strong-hearted one around the stone cliffs,
even as far as the road to the sea,
the ancient work of giants, then inside the city
with its stone-paved streets.][19]

Stræt, ceastra, torre; street, city, tower. This is the canon of Roman work-manship according to Bede, and it fills these Old English poetic reflec-tions on their ruin.

But central to the quality of stonework was its ornament. Words like *orðonc* and *wrætlic* are the vernacular equivalents for the *miraculi ingenio* with which such things were constructed and adorned. And so too, in association with these words, is the Old English element *fah*, or *fag*. The word appears throughout the Anglo-Saxon literary corpus to connote a surface glimmer or a decoration, or a stain. Ælfric's eleventh-century glossary translated it as *varius, vel discolor*: varied in appearance, or of different colors.[20] It is the second element in many compounds – *ban-fah, blod-fah, gold-fah, searo-fah, wyrm-fah*, and nearly a dozen others – some of them *hapax legomena*, all calibrated to evoke a well-worked or remarkable surface.[21] The *stan-fah* streets of *Beowulf* and *Andreas* are thus roads covered with a surface of stone. What is, then, the *fagne flor* of Heorot?

Though there appears to have been something of a flurry of debate about this term a generation ago, recent critics have apparently ignored it – either because the meaning was so obvious that it required no discussion, or because the meaning was so opaque that an explanation was impossible. It has been taken, by some almost intuitively, to refer to a tessellated or mosaic floor; by others, it has been seen simply as a shining, decorated, or even blood-stained one.[22] There is that single place name, Fawler in Oxfordshire, that has been understood to be derived from *fag-flor* – a place where there must have been a Roman villa with mosaics.[23] But that is about it.

Recent archaeological work, however, provokes me to revive this image of a Roman floor and, furthermore, to take it somewhat more specifically – and also metaphorically – than others have.[24] Mosaic floors in Roman villas filled the British landscape. The last two centuries of the *coloniae* produced what must have been hundreds of such floors (around 400 actually survive, in some form), and schools of mosaic art devel-oped such that by the end of the fourth century, identifiable motifs and techniques were appearing, clustered around certain geographical loca-tions. Now, the central question for those who have speculated on the *fagne flor* and other shards of Roman life in *Beowulf* has been whether or not post-Roman settlements were built on the remains of villas. Could

Heorot be something like a Saxon hall built on the tessellated floor of an abandoned mansion? There is a fair amount of indirect archaeological evidence for such a phenomenon. Roman buildings sometimes stayed in active use after the Empire had gone. A good example is Redlands Farm, Stanwick, Northamptonshire. At this site, a second-century villa was apparently rebuilt and remodeled in the middle of the fourth century. By the fifth century, portions of the house had fallen into disuse, and were demolished. But there still remained a central core of building (substantially reduced in size and function), clearly in use in the post-Roman period. Salway's *Illustrated History of Roman Britain* nicely shows the various stages of this occupation, and it also offers reproductions of its original tessellated floor. Clearly, someone was still living on this Roman floor (even if, at a certain later point, the *tesserae* had been removed and piled up on a dump).[25]

There may have been a hearth built over the old pavement, and some other sites have revealed hearths built on tessellations. An example such as the villa in Keynsham, Somerset, has been taken as evidence either of immigrant appropriation of old sites or of a declining standard of living by either Romano-British or Germanic settlers.[26] More generally, Saxon settlers reused a great deal of the Roman architecture that they found. Masonry was carted off and used for churches. Tiles and stones show up in buildings; columns were reused; arches seem to be transported from ruins to reuse.[27] There is even evidence of villa bath-houses transformed into corn-drying kilns and stackyards.[28] Finally, Germanic-style buckles and belt-fittings have been recovered from older Roman sites. Were Anglo-Saxons living on Roman remains, or were they simply pillaging them? Were they mercenaries, engaged by remaining Britons after the Romans had left, or were they truly settlers?[29]

Whatever archaeology may recover, however, there is another philological and literary line of inquiry that has not been explored. Though much energy has been expended on *fag*, or *fah*, nothing has been said of *flor* – as if it were too obvious to worry about. *Flor* glosses Latin *pavimentum*, and the compounds *florstan* and *stanflor* gloss *tessella*.[30] If we recall the gloss for *fah* (*varius, vel discolor*), Old English *fagne flor* connotes a varicolored pavement: precisely the idiom that Pliny used in his *Natural History* to describe mosaic flooring. Paved floors (*pavimenta*), Pliny notes, were first developed by the Greeks; they were originally painted, but then decorated with mosaics. At Pergamum, he goes on, Sosus became famous for laying out the floor of his so-called unswept room, "because by means of small cubes tinted in various shades, he represented on the floor refuse from the dinner table and other sweepings, making them appear as if they had been left there" (*quoniam purgamenta cenae in pavimentis quaeque everri solent velut relicta fecerat parvis e tessellis tinctisque in varios colores*). In Roman times, Pliny continues, tessellated pavements had become common by the Cimbertian War (end of the second century BC), "as is shown by the famous verse from Lucillius: 'With paviour's skill and wavy inset stones'" (*est Lucillianus ille versus: Arte pavimenti atque emblemate vermiculato*).[31]

Pliny's description of the origins and popularity of tessellated or mosaic pavements would not only have resonated with later Roman practice. It would have provided even later viewers of that flooring with a critical vocabulary for its description. The very fact that the Old English glossaries record words like *tessera* and *pavimentum* implies, of course, that Anglo-Saxons had the visual experience of such antique floors. And what does *fah* mean but, to appropriate Pliny's terms, *tinctis in varios colores*?

I suggest that the phrase *fagne flor* is a vernacular translation of this Plinian vocabulary and, furthermore, that it connotes the very kind of flooring that would have been understood as the mark of a great house. But whatever the sources for this idiom, the fact remains that *Beowulf* is not a work of natural history or historical topography but a poem: it imaginatively re-creates or reimagines aspects of an early culture for an Anglo-Saxon audience. As in the many instances of swords, shields, and armor, of building details, of historical names and locales, of religious practices, the poem does not conform to historical exactitude. Rather, as we have come to recognize, it conforms to an imagination of the past in all its vicissitudes. The *fagne flor* of Heorot is something of a comparable imagination: a memory of magnificence, an allusion to something old, rich, artistic, and alien.

And what that memory may be is one of the most notable aspects of Roman tessellation in Britain. While social class and personal taste clearly influenced the choice of decoration, scenes from nature and mythology, from classical literature and, on occasion, Christian narrative fill these floors. Intriguingly, a large number of these mosaics have scenes of Orpheus. At least nine floor mosaics survive with an Orphic figure, harping and subduing the beasts of creation. He appears more than any other single mythological figure, and, as D. J. Smith writes in a survey of Romano-British mosaics, "in no other province have so many representations of this theme in mosaic been recorded."[32] A beautiful example of an Orphic pavement of the mid-fourth century is that of the Littlecote villa near Hungerford, which would have lain at the center of a great villa. Another example, too, is the so-called Woodchester Great Pavement, probably installed sometime between 325 and 350 – a huge bit of flooring, which originally must have lain 47 square feet.[33] Perhaps the early Christian fascination with Orpheus is responsible for their proliferation (the argument being that the allegorical associations among Orpheus and the psalmist, the soothing of the beasts and the miracle of creation, and the story of his hell descent, all resonated with an early Christian idiom). Perhaps it was just taste. Whatever the reasons, Orpheus appears on British mosaics in ways that struck the Roman and, perhaps too, the Anglo-Saxon imagination.

For what I imagine at this moment is the monster, angered by the music of the hall and moved to action. He suffered when he heard the joy loud in the hall, the sound of the harp and the song of the scop.

> Þa se ellen-gæst   earfoðlice
> þrage geþolode,   se þe in þystrum bad,
> þæt he dogora gewham   dream geyrde
> hludne in healle;   þær wæs hearpan sweg,
> swutol sang scopes.
> (lines 86–90)

In Tolkien's memorable phrasing, Grendel is "maddened by the sound of harps,"[34] an impression brought out by Heaney's translation of these lines (for all their syntactic liberties):

> It harrowed him
> to hear the din of the loud banquet
> every day in the hall, the harp being struck
> and the clear song of the skilled poet.

And so, what better image than that monster standing on the harper's floor, the shattered Orpheus beneath his feet? What better image for that hall mosaic than the very subject matter of the scop's song in the hall, the shaping of creation, the representation of "cynna gehwylcum, þara ðe cwice hwyrfaþ" (line 98, every kind of creature that moves alive)? And what better image, too, for the Old English translator of the *Consolation of Philosophy*, whose Orpheus not only can sway woods and rivers and tame the beasts but also (and this is a detail nowhere in the Latin tradition) "þa stanas hi styredon," cause the very stones to stir.[35]

The Anglo-Saxons, too, had stirred the stones of Roman ruin, and so too have the inhabitants of *Beowulf*. The *fagne flor* and *stan-fah stræt* share in a collection of such rattled Roman remnants: perhaps, as well, the dragon's barrow, with its ruined arch (*stanboga*, line 2545), another work of giants comparable to the *mirabile* ruins seen by others, and here seen by Beowulf himself:

> Seah on enta geweorc
> hu ða stan-bogan   stapulum fæste
> ece eorð-reced   innan healde
> (lines 2717–19)[36]

Heaney's translation specifically brings out (or imposes?) the Roman quality to this construction:

> He steadied his gaze
> on those gigantic stones, saw how the earthwork
> was braced with arches built over columns.

The dragon guards a treasure hoard not unfamiliar from the Roman leavings. Indeed, the *Anglo-Saxon Chronicle* records for the year 418 (an entry written, however, in the late ninth century) that "in this year the Romans collected all the treasures which were in Britain, and hid some in the ground, so that no one could find them afterwards, and took some with them into Gaul."[37] Stories abound of Saxons being buried with troves of Roman coins.[38] Sutton Hoo itself was filled with artifacts already old (and some, at least, of continental workmanship) at the time of their burial. And in a pit at Snettisham in Norfolk, archaeologists have found a pile of golden torques, probably from the first century.[39]

So: there remain throughout the poem bits and pieces not just of an ancient artistry but of specifically a Roman and colonial one. These things are remnants of an age of otherness – an age when people came to settle and then left. But that narrative of the colonial is also the poem's, for what are Hrothgar and his retinue but colonizers of some strange landscape? Look how they enter in the narrative – Hrothgar, favored in war, assembling around him friends and relatives into a retinue that grows into a powerful armed force (*mago-driht micel*, line 67a). And then, it came into his mind to build a great hall, worthy of his great host (note how the half-line *medo-ærn micel* [line 69a] echoes *mago driht micel*). This is the work not of giants, however, but of men (*men gewyrcean*, line 69b). He sends throughout the world for artisans to decorate his place. It took shape on the landscape, Hrothgar saw it, found it good, and named it Heorot (lines 74–9). In this scene, redolent with images of the creation, soon to be echoed by the scop's song of God's Creation, Hrothgar becomes something of a colonizer himself. Like the Romans, his is a true *colonia*, made up originally of soldiers. And, like anyone who would attempt to rear a civilization in the wilderness, he calls for workmen to adorn it. Some have found in his call for such artisans "geond þisne middan-geard" an implication that his *fagne flor* may well be tessellated in imitation of a continental style.[40] But all have imagined Hrothgar simply making something of a place in his own homeland.

I do not see it so. The *pagus* on which Hrothgar builds his hall is already inhabited. There Grendel lurks – indeed, he more than lurks. *Swa rixode* (line 144a), thus he ruled. Grendel has taken back the landscape, made himself now the ruler of this stead.

> Heorot eardode,
> sinc-fage sel sweartum nihtum;
> (lines 166–7)

[He dwelled in Heorot, that richly adorned hall, in the dark of night.]

And when Grendel has been killed and his mother has avenged his death, Hrothgar must direct Beowulf over a landscape that, though nearby, is a world away from anything these Danes (or anybody else) have seen. "Nis þæt feor heonon mil-gemearces" (lines 1361–2). It is not far, when measured in miles. True, but miles are not the measurement here. We are no longer in a world that can be plotted out by human strides, but rather in a forest of the imagination. And, so too, do ghosts of Romans rise up here. For what else is that measurement in miles than an allusion to the Roman milestones that still dotted the Anglo-Saxon (and, indeed, the entire Northern European) landscape?[41] No bit of stone can direct the hero how to go or measure his grim progress.

Finally when Beowulf himself dies, and the woman keens and friends lament, just what has passed? How can we not see such a moment through our own dark lenses of oppression? Surely, Seamus Heaney does so, as he freely translates the lament of the Geatish woman.

> A Geat woman too sang out in grief;
> with hair bound up, she unburdened herself
> of her worst fears, a wild litany
> of nightmare and lament: her nation invaded,
> enemies on the rampage, bodies in piles,
> slavery and abasement. Heaven swallowed the smoke.
> (lines 3150–5)

In this passage, Heaney makes a Latinate, international vocabulary out of the Old English compounds, and in the process writes a song for our own times. Here is the Old English text, from the Wrenn–Bolton edition Heaney uses:

> Geatisc meowle
> . . . bunden-heorde
> song sorg-cearig.   Sæde geneahhe,
> þæt hio hyre here-geongas hearde ondrede
> wæl-fylla worn, werudes egesan,
> hynðo ond hæft-nyd. Heofon rece swealg.

The half-line *song sorg-cearig* (line 3152a), which would literally be trans-lated as "she sang full of, or caring with, sorrow," becomes in Heaney's version "she sang out in grief." *Sæde geneahhe* (line 3152b), a simple phrase that means "she said often," becomes "she unburdened herself" (as if in lovely echo of her bound up hair). The phrase *hyre here-geongas* (line 3153), "the goings of the army into the country," becomes "her nation invaded." The words *hynðo* and *hæft-nyd*, that mean, in essence, "a bring-ing low" and something like "distress of a prisoner," become "slavery" and "abasement." There is a progress in this passage, in Heaney's ver-sion, that moves to powerfully evocative terms grounded in a Latinate or international vocabulary. But there is more than mere translation going on here. Heaney brings in phrasings corresponding to no words in the Old English. To what does "wild litany" refer? Where are the "bodies in piles" here? And there is much that may not even be in *Beowulf*'s Old English at all. These lines present one of the poem's most textually corrupt passages. The manuscript is badly damaged; words are illegible. Klaeber sought a reconstruction, markedly different from that of C. L. Wrenn and W. F. Bolton, which gives a markedly different understanding of this moment.[42] The fact remains that what we have here is no "translation" at all, but an evocative reflection on an editorial invention. Heaney's words present no version of an Old English idiom or vision of an Anglo-Saxon practice but a picture of our modern, scarred political body. Who can read the half-line "bodies in piles" and not think of the mass graves that litter the latter half of the twentieth century? Who cannot read of an "invasion" and "abasement" – that last word as pungent as the rising smoke – and not think of Heaney's own Northern Ireland? Even heaven becomes a predatory being here, swallowing the smoke much as Grendel had swallowed up his hated Danes or, as we might well say today, one nation swallows up another.

Or as Rome sought to swallow up its Britain. Talk of slavery and abasement must recall that early Heaney poem, "Freedman," ostensibly about the ancient Roman occupations but more pointedly about the modern British. Here is the poem in full, complete with the scholarly epigraph Heaney gives it.

> *Indeed, slavery comes nearest to its justification in the early Roman Empire: for a man from a 'backward' race might be brought within the pale of civilization, educated and trained in a craft or a profession, and turned into a useful member of society.* (R. H. Barrow, *The Romans*)

Subjugated yearly under arches,
Manumitted by parchments and degrees,
My murex was the purple dye of lents
On calendars all fast and abstinence.
'*Memento homo quia pulvis es.*'
I would kneel to be impressed by ashes,
A silk friction, a light stipple of dust –
I was under that thumb too like all my caste.

One of the earth-starred denizens, indelibly,
I sought the mark in vain on the groomed optimi:

Their estimating, census-taking eyes
Fastened on my mouldy brow like lampreys.

Then poetry arrived in that city –
I would abjure all cant and self-pity –
And poetry wiped my brow and sped me.
Now they say I bite the hand that fed me.

"Subjugated yearly under arches," brilliantly distills the image of *Roman-itas* as framed in architecture – a phrasing resonant with those *stan-boga* that arch over ancient edifice or dragon's barrow. It leads, too, to that impression of "slavery and abasement" deep in the keen of Heaney's Geatish woman, while the ashes and the dust remain but the mementos of a fallen world. And, much as in the world of Hrothgar's hall, poetry too comes to that city: now not a Roman *colonia* but another settlement of former military men, listening to the sweet song of the scop (*swutol sang scopes*).

"Freedman" is a poem about living after, about the imagination of a postcolonial world, and in his Introduction to the *Beowulf* translation Heaney writes as something of his own freed man in coming to Old English. His *Beowulf* – for all the fires of its funerals or the smoke of its sadness – is a poem lit by the fires of his own imagination, a poem about coming after something else. There is not just a postcolonial but almost a postliterary feel to *Beowulf* in Heaney's hands, as if the poem needs to be appreciated as the next thing after "literature" itself. "Readers coming to the poem for the first time are likely to be as delighted as they are discomfited by the strangeness of the names and the immediate lack of known reference points." He goes on:

> An English speaker new to *The Iliad* or *The Odyssey* or *The Aeneid* will probably at least have heard of Troy and Helen, or of Penelope and the Cyclops, or of Dido and the golden bough. These epics may be in Greek and Latin, yet the classical heritage has entered the cultural memory enshrined in English so thoroughly that their worlds are more familiar than that of the first native epic, even though it was composed centuries after them . . . First-time readers of *Beowulf* very quickly rediscover the meaning of the term "the dark ages," and it is in the hope of dispelling some of the puzzlement they are bound to feel that I have added the marginal glosses which appear in the following pages. (xi–xii)

Notice the vocabulary here: *enshrined; native epic; the dark ages; dispel.* There is the contrast not just between the classical and the vernacular, but between the sacred and the profane, the elevated and the native, the lucent and the dark. Part of Heaney's job is thus to *illuminate* in the root sense of that word, to bring a light unto the darkness. Such imagery will be familiar to readers of Heaney's earlier poetry: "All I know," he announces in "The Forge," "is a door into the dark."[43] To *dispel*, in his Introduction, is to demystify, to scatter whatever spells may have been cast by the poetry's dark magic. So when Grendel appears "as a kind of dog-breath in the dark" (xviii), he carries with him the smell not just of the fearful monsters of the distant past, but of the still familiar creatures who inhabit Heaney's literary barnyards: the drowned feral cats of "The Early Purges"; the rogue bull of "The Outlaw"; or the weird "turnip-man's lopped head" at Halloween, that

> Blazes at us through split bottle glass
> And fumes and swims up like a wrecker's lantern.
>
> Death mask of harvest, mocker at All Souls
> With scorching smells, red dog's eyes in the night –
> We ring and stare into unhallowed light.
> ("No Sanctuary")

Such poetry rings with an almost uncanny familiarity for anyone accustomed to the shape of Grendel's habitation – here rendered in the voice of Heaney's Hrothgar.

> A few miles from here
> a frost-stiffened wood waits and keeps watch
> above a mere; the overhanging bank
> is a maze of tree-roots mirrored in its surface.
> At night there, something uncanny happens:
> the water burns.
> (lines 1361–6)

These creatures live in an "unhallowed light." They live, to be more literal about it, in a land not far from here, measured in miles.

But Heaney's job for his own reader is to measure out the poem in miles: to make it conform, at least in part, to familiar verities of literary experience, to dispel its strangeness. And so, he stresses the poem's "mythic potency," alludes to Yeats, and calls up archetypes of phantasms, agons, and deep imagery. The poem's use of gold – "gleaming solidly in underground vaults, on the breasts of queens or the arms and regalia of warriors on the mead benches" – becomes in Heaney's vision something like the glories of that earlier Irish poet's Byzantium, "persisting underground as an affirmation of a people's glorious past and an elegy for it" (xvii). The transitoriness of earthly wealth finds its survival in the language of the poet. *Beowulf* is not so much an elegy for a past age, as it is the occasion for an elegiac reading. It reflects on the ways in which poetic language can, paradoxically, both inhume the past and bring it back imaginatively to life. Writing of the poem's monsters, Heaney observes that the poem needs them "as figures who call up and show off Beowulf's physical might and his superb gifts as a warrior" (p. xviii). But surely what he means is that the poem needs them as figures who call up and show off the *poet's* imaginative might and his superb gifts as a story-teller – for which we may read, as well, Heaney's own recognition that they pose a challenge to his own gifts as a translator.

Translating *Beowulf* is Heaney's own self-represented agon: his response to the call from the editors of Norton, his rise to the occasion of monstrous representation. It is his Herculean labor. And with each death there comes not just the keening of a person but the lament of a people. Politics – not Swedish wars or English dynastic disturbance, but modern, everyday conflict – is never far from this *Beowulf*. Episodes such as the well-known "Father's lament" rise, he avers, "like emanations from some fissure in the bedrock of the human capacity to endure."

> Such passages mark an ultimate stage in poetic attainment . . . At these moments of lyric intensity, the keel of the poetry is deeply set in the element of sensation, while the mind's lookout sways metrically and far-sightedly in the element of pure comprehension . . . And nowhere is this more obviously and memorably the case than in the account of the hero's funeral with which the poem ends. Here the inexorable and the elegiac combine in a description of the funeral pyre being got ready, the body being burnt, and the barrow being constructed – a scene at once immemorial and oddly contemporary. The Geat woman who cries out in dread as the flames consume the body of her dead lord could come straight from a late-twentieth-century news report, from

Rwanda or Kosovo; her keen is a nightmare glimpse into the minds
of people who have survived traumatic, even monstrous events and
who are now being exposed to a comfortless future. We immediately
recognize her predicament and the pitch of her grief and find ourselves
the better for having them expressed with such adequacy and dignity
and unforgiving truth. (xx–xxi)

This great extended reading offers up a vision of the postcolonial sublime. Like all sublime experiences, it trades in fragments, in the burst of
"lyric intensity" (a phrase that could come right out of an Augustan or
a Romantic reader of Longinus). The brilliant metaphor – "the keel of
the poetry" – takes us back to the stormy seas not just of *Beowulf*
but of the canon of classical and vernacular poetry that the English
Augustans and Romantics considered emblematic of the sublime. And
where that keel is set is in the "element of pure comprehension," a
phrase that recalls Tolkien's grand praise of the poem's "elements . . . all
most nearly in harmony."[44] The political resonances of these passages
in *Beowulf* come for Heaney (as all sublime experiences must come) in
immediate recognition. And if that recognition helps us "find ourselves
the better," it may be a betterment as much aesthetic or spiritual as political, a betterment akin to Longinus' own sense of *hupselon*, elevation.
The soul "takes a proud flight, and is filled with joy and vaunting, as
though it itself had produced what it had heard."[45]

And yet, it is Heaney himself who is producing what we hear. His
own translation stands as the vehicle as well as testimony to the sublime
experience. If *The Norton Anthology*'s invitation opened up a door into
the dark, then it is philology that turns on the light. Reviewing his
experience of early English language in school, in the university, in the
shards of the words that still survived in local dialect, Heaney remarks
how he discovered the true meaning of the Old English verb *þolian*. It
means "to suffer," but it survives, too, in British, Irish, and American
dialects.

What I was experiencing as I kept meeting up with *thole* on its multicultural odyssey was the feeling which Osip Mandelstam once defined
as a "nostalgia for world culture." And this was a nostalgia I didn't
even know I suffered until I experienced its fulfillment in this little

> epiphany. It was as if, on the analogy of baptism by desire, I had
> undergone something like illumination by philology. (xxvi)

Heaney undergoes illumination by philology. The study of the word
reveals not just a history of culture but a history of the self. Heaney's
obsession with *þolian* makes him now the rightful son and heir to generations of "my father's people." He realized, he writes, that he wanted
Beowulf to sound as if it were "speakable by one of those relatives"
(xxvii).

But if this is a philological move, it is also a political one. This is
a "multicultural odyssey," an encounter with the worlds of literature.
To use Osip Mandelstam to explicate an Anglo-Saxon verb (by way of
Northern Irish English) is to distill that now-tired "multicultural" into
purity. Epiphany, baptism: these are the Greek words for the religious
life. They take us back, philologically as well as politically, to an old
time: a time when it was once a crime to be a Christian, when one could
genuinely *thole* for a belief.

All I know is a door into the dark. When Grendel breaks the door
of Heorot with a touch and stands upon the *fagne flor*, he shatters any
doorways to the light. He rules his landscape in the darkness, hates the
illuminations of the celebrating Danes, is condemned by God. I have
focused on this floor, and its potential Roman resonances, in large part
because my rereading of *Beowulf* through Heaney's version makes the
poem full of doors and floors. There is a kind of grim domesticity to
Heaney's *Beowulf* that brings out that sense of a Roman public and
domestic past embedded in the Anglo-Saxon idiom. For a people who
would build hearths on mosaics; who would turn bath-houses into
granaries; who would pull out the cobble of a massive past and mortar it
into a local present – these are a people who are constantly *domesticating*
(in the root sense of that word) the ancient other. Go back to the
"Life of St. Cuthbert" for another encounter with that past and its
domestications.

> Coming from the south to the river which is called the Wear, on
> reaching a place called Chester-le-Street, he [i.e., Cuthbert] crossed it
> and turned aside on account of the rain and tempest to some dwellings
> used only in spring and summer. But it was then winter time and the
> dwellings were deserted, so that he found no man to succour him

and his horse, wearied as they were by their journey and by lack of food. So he unsaddled his horse and led it into the dwelling-place and, fastening it to the wall, he waited for the storm to cease. As he was praying to the Lord, he saw his horse raise its head up to the roof of the hut and, greedily seizing part of the thatch of the roof, draw it towards him. And immediately there fell out, along with it, a warm loaf and meat carefully wrapped up in a linen cloth. When he had finished his prayer, he felt it and found that it was food provided before-hand for him by God through sending forth of his angel who often helped him in his difficulties.[46]

Cuthbert, as Bertram Colgrave has observed in his edition of this passage, "was doubtless travelling along the Roman road."[47] He finds deserted dwellings, and in taking shelter becomes the beneficiary of a miracle. Warm food appears out of cold buildings – not just from anywhere, but from the roof. Manna from heaven, rephrased as barnyard tale. Cuthbert finds divine blessing on the Roman road – much as, in Carlisle, he would have a vision of the horrible defeat of Ecfrith by the Picts exactly at the moment when his guide is pointing out the Roman ruins.[48] At moments such as these, the street or edifice becomes a locus of illumination. Cuthbert has sought out a door, a place of refuge, a small domestic space. And in such spaces, the sublime appears.

So, too, for Heaney. His now-famous, big-voiced Scullion ancestors inspired his translation. "A simple sentence such as 'We cut the corn to-day,' took on immense dignity when one of the Scullions spoke it. They had a kind of Native American solemnity of utterance, as if they were announcing verdicts rather than making small talk" (xxvii). To associate the Scullions with the Native Americans is to transmute Heaney's Irish into Indians – to make them both the shattered people under domination, yet to recognize that in them both lies an enduring dignity that, in our modern world, survives only in language. And yet, "we cut the corn today" could come right out of one of Heaney's early poems ("Digging," or "Churning Day") where manual labor serves as stand-in for the act of writing poems.

And there, again, is Grendel at the door. Now, in Heaney's translation, we can see this horrid knock rephrased in language that recalls a local landscape, that associates domestic and grand, old and new.

Spurned and joyless, he journeyed on ahead
and arrived at the bawn. The iron-braced door
turned on its hinge when his hands touched it.
Then his rage boiled over, he ripped open
the mouth of the building, maddening for blood,
pacing the length of the patterned floor
with his loathsome tread, while a baleful light,
flame more than light, flared from his eyes.
He saw many men in the mansion, sleeping,
a ranked company of kinsmen and warriors
quartered together.
(lines 720–30)

What is a *bawn*? Heaney comments on his choice of word:

> In Elizabethan English, bawn (from the Irish *bó-dhún*, a fort for cat-
> tle) referred specifically to the fortified dwellings which the English
> planters built in Ireland to keep the dispossessed natives at bay, so it
> seemed the proper term to apply to the embattled keep where Hroth-
> gar waits and watches. (xxx)

But there is more behind it. The *OED* offers an etymology from Irish
babhun, "of unknown derivation," and defines it as "A fortified enclosure, enceinte, or circumvallation; the fortified court or outwork of a
castle." But it also notes that it means "A cattlefold," citing an 1850 note
from *Notes and Queries*: "The word bawn or bane . . . is still applied in
the south of Ireland to the . . . place for milking the cows of a farm . . .
Before the practice of housing cattle became general, every country gentleman's house had its bawn." So what is it: the castle or the barn, the
big house or the little, the mark of grandeur or the place of simplicity?
Surely both connotations are at work in such a weird word, made even
more striking later in the passage when Heaney translates the same Old
English word (*recede*) as "mansion." *Mansion*: a word from Latin by way
of Old French, certainly as far from the native Irish "bawn" as one could
get. And I think that is the point. Heorot is a shifting structure here, part
native settlement, part foreign imposition. Its status on the landscape is
an odd one, with its patterned floor and iron-braced door. This is, now,
no longer the mere "hall" of earlier in the poem but something that
must capture its profoundly alien and imposed quality to Grendel. For,
in this passage in the translation, we are meant to see Heorot through

Grendel's eyes: a castle thrown up by invaders, a mansion that has no business being in the moor-land.[49]

This double image of the hall returns us, too, to Cuthbert in the wilderness. For, in his turning from the Roman street, he too finds habitation. But if his pathway is akin to the *stan-fah stræt* that Beowulf and his men follow, it leads him not to a great hall but to little huts (in Latin, *habitacula*, *domunculi*). And yet, in that little dwelling lies great wonder, sustenance from God. In Heorot's great hall, however, lies the food for terror: Hrothgar's men, whom Grendel would cannibalize. The *fagne flor* on which he stands at this moment becomes a place of desecration – and, soon in the poem, a place of battle, as Beowulf will wrestle with the monster and eventually tear his arm off. That body part becomes a *tacen*, sign or symbol, displayed, as the poem puts it, "under geapne hrof" [under the gaping roof, line 836]. For Cuthbert, though, the little dwelling's roof conceals a symbol of a different kind, a sign of divine sustenance, a blessing and a miracle.

These houses of the postcolonial, post-Roman, and postdevastation landscapes are bawns of both kinds, then: grand fortifications or small places of the barnyard. In Heaney's world, "we cut the corn today" becomes a statement of both farmland domesticity and moral power – a maxim not unlike those of the Anglo-Saxon gnomes: "Cyning sceal rice healdan." But what happens after the king has ruled? What happens in the afterlife of any *rice*? The Cotton *Maxims* tell us, in the lines that follow, which I quote again, now to present as a temporal commentary on that opening line:

> Ceastra beoð feorran gesyne,
> orðanc enta geweorc, þa þe on þysse eorðan syndon,
> wrætlic weallstana geweorc.

After the Empire, those great *ceastra* can be seen from far away – but *feor* also means, in Old English, far back in time. This is how Hrothgar uses the word, in the opening of his so-called sermon to Beowulf, a lecture on rulership not far removed from the precepts of those *Maxims*:

> . . . se þe soð ond riht
> fremeð on folce, feor eal gemon,
> eald eðel-weard . . .
> (lines 1700–2)

An old guardian of his people does that which is true and right for his people, he bears in mind all that has gone before. Heaney translates these lines as concerned with respecting "tradition," but I think that is inaccurate. The idea here is an awareness of past things, a recognition that we live in a world that came after something else. The poet of the Cotton *Maxims* does not look out merely at a literal horizon to see buildings, but looks back into a past when such great edifices, the work of the giants, filled the landscape. They remain in this world; the phrase recalls the Old English Bede on the "ceastre & torras & stræta & brycge" of that old Roman "rice." All of which may be seen today ("þa we to dæg sceawian magon"). And all of this recalls that poignant moment in that modern novel of post-Holocaust existence, W. G. Sebald's *Austerlitz*, which I use as my epigraph. It is the little house that offers us a sense of peace (how like the little house of Cuthbert's miracle, or the barnyard bawn), but it is those great buildings that "cast the shadow of their own destruction before them, and are designed from the first with an eye to their later existence as ruins." The ruin of Heorot is already present in its building, as the poet says. And the great works of giants stand in their greatness only to be "feorran gesyne," seen far away in the past. All that is left now, in the words of *The Ruin*, are structures "wyrde gebræcon," broken by fate. Or, as Heaney's Latin line reminds us: "*Memento homo quia pulvis es*" [remember, man, that you are dust].

Is there, in the end, a postcolonial *Beowulf*? I have suggested here that the Old English poem, and its translation by Seamus Heaney, both explore the idea of the "post-": that sense of coming after something, whether it be in the cultural elegiacs of the Anglo-Saxon meditation on the Roman past or in the political idioms of current Northern Irish evocations of a family history or national aspiration. There is, too, as I have sought to expose, something of the colonial in *Beowulf* itself: a story about settlers in a hostile, ancient landscape, where monsters tread or dragons breathe. *Urbs antiqua fuit*, there was an ancient city. Or, in the words of "Freedman": "Then poetry arrived in that city." This a poetry of *pulvis*, a poetry of things left in the dust. *Gold on greote*, as the Anglo-Saxon has it. And, so too, for the poem on its own. For *Beowulf* remains a ruin, charred and fractured, barely legible at times. That passage on the Geatish woman's song is not just hard to read or badly scarred. It is the moment when the text itself becomes that ruined edifice on which we build a literary tradition.

And every now and then, something arises that reminds us of a past we cannot escape. Beowulf, old and infirm, yet still his kingly self, must fight a dragon who has held sway, the poem states, "þreo hund wintra," three hundred years (line 2278). Three centuries after the end of empire, a poem seeks to understand its legacy. Or still, perhaps, at the end of an empire three centuries old and now dissipated – save, maybe, in the poet's home – a modern translation and its reader seek to understand its dragons.

NOTES

I am grateful to Deanne Williams and Ananya Jahanara Kabir for welcoming my essay into this volume and for their supportive commentary during its writing; to Kathleen Davis for her critique of an earlier draft (and for discussion of her essay, "National Writing in the Ninth Century") and to Toni Healey for inviting me to present a shorter version of this material at the 2002 MLA Convention in New York.

1. W. G. Sebald, *Austerlitz*, trans. Anthea Bell (New York: Random House, 2001), 18–19.

2. *Beowulf*, lines 724-6. All quotations from *Beowulf* are from *Beowulf*, ed. C. L. Wrenn and W. F. Bolton, third edn (London: Harrap, 1973), the text printed with *Beowulf*, trans. Seamus Heaney (New York: Farrar, Straus, Giroux, 2000). I also reference *Beowulf*, ed. F. Klaeber, third edn (Boston: Heath, 1950). Unless otherwise noted, all translations are my own.

3. See Michael Hunter, "Germanic and Roman Antiquity and the Sense of the Past in Anglo-Saxon England," *Anglo-Saxon England* 3 (1974): 29–50; J. C. Higgitt, "The Roman Background to Medieval England," *Journal of the British Archaeological Association*, third series 36 (1973): 1–15; Peter Salway, *Roman Britain* (Oxford: Oxford University Press, 1981); Salway, *The Oxford Illustrated History of Roman Britain* (Oxford: Oxford University Press, 1993); Michael E. Jones, *The End of Roman Britain* (Ithaca: Cornell University Press, 1996); Howard Williams, "Ancient Landscapes and the Dead: The Reuse of Prehistorical and Roman Monuments as Early Anglo-Saxon Burial Sites," *Medieval Archaeology* 41 (1997): 1–32; Tyler Bell, "Churches on Roman Buildings: Christian Associations and Roman Masonry in Anglo-Saxon England," *Medieval Archaeology* 42 (1998): 1–18. The classic essay of Rosemary J. Cramp, "*Beowulf* and Archaeology," *Medieval Archaeology* 1 (1957): 57–77, still sets the lines of inquiry into relationships between the poem and the material past. See also Catherine M. Hills, "*Beowulf* and Archaeology," in *A Beowulf Handbook*, ed. Robert E. Bjork and John D. Niles (Lincoln: University of Nebraska Press, 1997), 291–310.

4. Technically speaking, Anglo-Saxon England may not be a "postcolonial" society, as it is not the survivor of colonial occupation (in the way that one can assuredly speak of India, or certain nation-states of Africa, or even Ireland as postcolonial societies). My concern, however, is with Anglo-Saxon England as a society concerned with coming after the Roman colonial *imperium* and, thus, as a culture acutely conscious of its post-Roman situation. My approach differs, therefore, from those concerned with applying postcolonial literary and cultural theory to medieval texts in order to expose their ideological concerns with national identity and Europeanness. Representative of such approaches are the contributions collected in *The Postcolonial Middle Ages*, ed. Cohen, many of which focus on issues of Orientalism in medieval literature (and thus drawing on the work of Edward Said). Finally, I need to stress that, even though *Beowulf*'s narrative takes place in continental Scandinavia, it is an Anglo-Saxon poem for an English audience, and therefore its sense of Roman history and its architectural idiom remain largely insular.

5. *Oxford Latin Dictionary*, ed. P. G. W. Glare (Oxford: Clarendon Press, 1968), s.v. *colonia, collo.* See, too, the *Oxford English Dictionary*, s.v. *colony.*

6. See the discussion in Salway, *Oxford Illustrated History*, 74–5, 385.

7. *Oxford Illustrated History*, 364–5.

8. See Hunter, "Germanic and Roman Antiquity."

9. Bede, *Ecclesiastical History* I.12, and *The Old English Version of Bede's Ecclesiastical History*, ed. Thomas Miller (EETS OS 95, London: Oxford University Press, 1890), 44.

10. *The Chronicle of Æthelweard*, ed. and trans. A. Campbell (London: Nelson, 1962), 5–6.

11. "An Anonymous Life of St. Cuthbert," in *Two Lives of Saint Cuthbert*, ed. and trans. Bertram Colgrave (Cambridge: Cambridge University Press, 1940), 122–3. See Colgrave's note: "The impression made by the Roman remains upon the Angles and the Saxons was considerable" (334).

12. *Alcuin: The Bishops, Kings, and Saints of York*, ed. and trans. Peter Godman (Oxford: Clarendon Press, 1982), 4–7, lines 19–34.

13. *Cartularium Saxonicum*, ed. W. De G. Birch (London: Phillimore and Co., 1885–93), no. 424, cited in Hunter, "Germanic and Roman Antiquity," 35.

14. The rhetoric of wonder survives into post-Conquest meditations on the relics of the Roman past. William of Malmesbury, in the early twelfth century, remarked on the "mira Romanorum artificia," and writers such as Giraldus Cambrensis, Ranulph Higden, and the author of the *Gesta Stephani* all offer comparable comments. See Higgitt, "Roman Background," 3.

15. *The Exeter Book*, ed. Krapp and Dobbie, 227, lines 1–3.

16. "Maxims II," in *Poems of Wisdom and Learning in Old English*, ed. T. A. Shippey (Cambridge: Brewer, 1976), 76, lines 1–3.

17. See *Bright's Old English Grammar and Reader*, ed. F. N. Cassidy and R. N. Ringler, third edn (New York: Holt, 1971), 374. For more detail on *chester* place names, see the commentary and bibliography in Bell, "Churches on Roman Buildings," 6

(who also remarks on *stan*-based place names as evidence of settlements on Roman foundations).

18. The poem on the death of William, known as the "Rime of King William," is edited in C. Clark, *The Peterborough Chronicle, 1070–1154*, second edn (Oxford: Clarendon, 1970) for the year 1086.

19. *Andreas: The Vercelli Book*, ed. G. P. Krapp, Anglo-Saxon Poetic Records 2 (New York: Columbia University Press, 1932), 37, lines 1232–6. For discussion of this passage and its possible relevance to *Beowulf*, see Marijane Osborn, "Laying the Roman Ghost of *Beowulf* 320 and 725," *Neuphilologische Mitteilungen* 70 (1969): 246–55; Leslie Whitbread, "*Beowulf* and Archaeology," *Neuphilologische Mitteilungen* 69 (1968): 63–72; Yasuharu Eto, "*Andreas* lines 1229–52," *Explicator* 52 (1994): 195–6.

20. "Ælfric's *Glossary*," in *Aelfric's Grammatik und Glossar*, ed. Julius Zupitza (Berlin: Weidmann, 1880). See also *An Anglo-Saxon Dictionary*, ed. Joseph Bosworth and T. Northcote Toller (Oxford: Oxford University Press, 1882–98), s.v. *fag*.

21. For an inventory, see Klaeber's glossary, s.v. *fag, fah* (327).

22. See Osborn and Whitbread; the notes to the relevant lines in the Wrenn–Bolton and Klaeber editions; and Cramp, "Beowulf and Archaeology," 76.

23. As far as I can tell, the reference to Fawler first appears in A. H. Smith, *English Place-Name Elements* (English Place Name Society 25, Cambridge: English Place Name Society, 1956), 164, 176; it is repeated in Cramp, "*Beowulf* and Archaeology," 76, and then passes into the discussions in Wrenn–Bolton, Osborn, and just about anyone else who considers this passage.

24. The following discussion is indebted to the researches presented in *The Roman Villa in Britain*, ed. A. L. F. Rivet (London: Routledge and Kegan Paul, 1969), especially D. J. Smith, "The Mosaic Pavements," 71-126, and Graham Webster, "The Future of Villa Studies," 217–50.

25. For Redlands Farm Villa, see Salway, *Illustrated History*, 253 (reconstruction), 326 (ground plans), 424 (village plans), and most strikingly the color plate following p. 426, picturing the central house foundations.

26. Webster, "Future," 232–3.

27. See Hunter, "Germanic and Roman Antiquity," 36–7, and Higgitt, "Roman Background," 4; Williams, "Ancient Landscapes" and Bell, "Churches on Roman Buildings."

28. Webster, "Future," 232, where the examples are from Lullingstone, Kent; Atworth, Wiltshire; and Barnsley Park, near Cirencester.

29. Webster, "Future," 235–6, citing Sonia Chadwick Hawkes and G. C. Dunning, "Soldiers and Settlers in Britain, Fourth to Fifth Century," *Medieval Archaeology* 5 (1965): 1–70.

30. See Ælfric's Glossary, *pavimentum, flor*. Latin *tessellae* is explained there, as well, as "*lytle ferðscite florstanas*" (little four-cornered floor stones), while *tesellis* is elsewhere glossed as "*stanflorum*." See Cramp, "*Beowulf* and Archaeology," 76, who records the glosses for *florstan* and *stanflor*, but does not pursue the argument.

31. Pliny, *Natural History*, ed. and trans. D. E. Eichholz (Loeb Classical Library 36, London: Heinemann, 1962), 144–7.

32. Smith, "Mosaic Pavements," 88.

33. For reproductions and illustrations, see Salway, *Illustrated History*, 422–3, and plate following 384, respectively.

34. J. R. R. Tolkien, "*Beowulf:* The Monsters and the Critics," in *Interpretations of Beowulf: A Critical Anthology*, ed. R. D. Fulk (Bloomington: University of Indiana Press, 1991), 14–44 at 35.

35. *King Alfred's Old English Version of Boethius De Consolatione Philosophiae*, ed. W. J. Sedgfield (Oxford: Clarendon Press, 1899), 101, corresponding to *Cons. Phil.* III.m.12. I can find no pre-Old English references to Orpheus' music causing stones to move.

36. Klaeber is doubtful: "There is certainly no need to take *stanbogan* or *stapulas* as architectural terms pointing to the specific Roman art of vault-building" (219). Wrenn–Bolton glosses *stapol* as pillar, post, column, or colonnade. For the use of older Roman arches in later Saxon buildings, see Higgitt, "Roman Background," 4–5.

37. "Her Romanae gesomnodon al þa goldhord þe on Bretene wæron & sume on eorþan ahyddon þæt hi nænig mon siþþan findan ne meahte & sume mid him on Gallia læddon." *Two of the Saxon Chronicles Parallel*, ed. Charles Plummer, 2 vols. (Oxford: Clarendon Press, 1892, 1899).

38. See Hunter, "Germanic and Roman Antiquity," 38.

39. See the picture in Salway, *Oxford Illustrated History*, plate before 129.

40. See the discussion in Cramp, "*Beowulf* and Archaeology," 76 and Osborn, "Laying the Ghost," 248–9.

41. See Ivan D. Margary, *Roman Roads in Britain* (London: John Baker, 1973), 502–3.

42. For a survey of the immense textual and paleographical problems in this passage, see Tilman Westphalen, *Beowulf 3150–55: Textkritik und Editionsgeschichte*, 2 vols. (Munich: Fink, 1967).

43. All quotations from Heaney's earlier poetry are from *Poems, 1965–1975* (New York: Farrar, Straus, Giroux, 1980).

44. Tolkien, "*Beowulf:* The Monsters and the Critics," 31.

45. Longinus, *On the Sublime*, ed. and trans. W. R. Roberts (Cambridge: Cambridge University Press, 1935) VII.2.54–5.

46. Colgrave, ed. and trans., *Two Lives*, 71.

47. Colgrave, ed. and trans., *Two Lives*, 314.

48. Colgrave, ed. and trans., *Two Lives*, 122–3.

49. Heaney goes on: "Putting a bawn into *Beowulf* seems one way for an Irish poet to come to terms with that complex history of conquest and colony, absorption and resistance, integrity and antagonism" (xxx).

PART II

Orientalism before 1600

Alexander in the Orient: bodies and boundaries in the *Roman de toute chevalerie*

Suzanne Conklin Akbari

One of the great criticisms leveled against Edward Said's groundbreaking study, *Orientalism*, was that it posed one monolithic entity, "the West," against another, variously identified as "the Orient," "the East," or "Islam." This formulation was seen as both homogenizing the "Oriental" subject, and conflating a broad spectrum of Western views, ranging from antiquity to the late twentieth century, into a single discourse, Orientalism.[1] Ironically, the most influential postcolonialist interventions made during the 1980s, including Bhabha's theory of colonial mimicry and the notion of subalternity as formulated by Spivak, were founded on Said's strategically reductive presentation of the "Oriental" subject.[2] For those studying premodern cultures, however, the more pressing concern has been Said's conflation of Western views. As I have argued elsewhere, the binary opposition of East and West, fundamental to Said's theory, cannot be projected back onto a Middle Ages which seldom conceived the world as bipartite. Medieval maps and encyclopedias almost invariably present a tripartite world, divided between the three known continents: Asia, Europe, and Africa. The opposition of a coldly rational Occident and an overheated, passionate Orient has its origins not in classical antiquity but in fourteenth-century reconceptualizations of north-western Europe and its relationship to the surrounding world.[3]

Admittedly, neither the binary opposition of East and West, nor the discourse of Orientalism, is completely absent from medieval texts. Several historical chronicles discuss the transmission of imperial might through the westward movement of *translatio imperii*; in addition, a wide range of texts, including the Alexander romances, the Prester John Letters, and travel narratives such as the *Milione* of Marco Polo and

The Book of John Mandeville, present an Orient replete with luxurious goods, wealth, and wonders. There are, however, significant differences between modern and premodern manifestations of both the East–West opposition and its attendant Orientalism. This chapter probes these differences by focusing on Thomas of Kent's *Roman de toute chevalerie*. This late twelfth-century Anglo-Norman poem depicts a world in the process of being conquered by Alexander the Great, who places ceremonial markers defining the boundaries of his empire at "treis fins del mond" (line 5945) (three ends of the earth): the extreme East, North, and South.[4] The fourth cardinal direction is absent: Alexander does not bother to venture to the West, where dwell the Irish, Spanish, and British. Despite this curious absence, the romance takes what I term a "westward turn" in its closing sections, which describe Alexander's mortal remains being returned from the East, Babylon, to the central regions of his empire. The narrative's own genealogy, from the putative Greek original of Alexander's letter to his tutor, Aristotle, to the letter's Latin translation, to the Anglo-Norman poem, traverses a similar path, moving from remote regions to the familiar space of the vernacular. This multiple westward turn in the *Roman* – geographical, corporeal, and linguistic – lays the foundation for the establishment of imperial might in a long-forgotten corner of Europe, and for the emergence of a new construction of Western identity.

LOCATING THE WEST

Thomas of Kent's account of Alexander's conquests draws heavily on a template of universal history and geography and a binary opposition of East and West furnished by a particular group of medieval texts: twelfth-century histories consciously patterned after Paulus Orosius' *Seven Books of History against the Pagans*, a historiographic counterpart to Augustine's *City of God*.[5] Orosius uses the dichotomy of East and West in order to structure his narrative in terms of *translatio imperii*, the gradual movement of imperial domination from the kingdom of Babylon to the rule of the Caesars in Rome. Orosius begins with a tripartite division of the world into Asia, Africa, and Europe.[6] However, his presentation of the chronological succession of empires soon reveals a westward movement based upon the poles of the ancient city of Babylon and the modern city of Rome: "siquidem sub una eademque conuenientia temporum illa cecedit, ista surrexit . . . tunc Orientis occidit et ortum est Occidentis imperium" [thus, at the exact same moment, the one fell and the other arose . . . thus the empire of the East fell and that of the West was born](1:87–8; II.2.10). However, closer examination reveals this opposition of East and West is rooted in a four-part historical sequence, itself ordered about the four cardinal points of the earth.

Between the might of eastern Babylon and western Rome, Orosius declares, came the short-lived empires of Macedonia in the North and Carthage in the South:

> Inter Babylonam regnum quod ab oriente fuerat, et Romanum quod ab occidente consurgens hereditati orientis enutriebatur, Macedonicum Africanumque regnum, hoc est quasi a meridie ac septentrione breuibus uicibus partes tutoris curatorisque tenuisse. Orientis et occidentis regnum Babylonium et Romanum iure uocitari, neminem umquam dubitasse scio; Macedonicum regnum sub septentrione cum ipsa caeli plaga tum Alexandri Magni arae positae usque ad nunc sub Riphaeis montibus docent; Carthaginem uero universae praecelluisse Africae et non solum in Siciliam Sardiniam ceterasque adiacentes insulas sed etiam in Hispaniam regni terminos tetendisse, historiarum simul monumenta urbiumque declarant. (III:17–18; VII.2.4–6)

> [During the time between the Babylonian Empire that existed in the East and the Roman Empire which, raising itself up in the West, was nourished by the heritage of the East, there intervened the Macedonian and African Empires . . . in the North and the South they held, for a brief time, the roles of guardian and protector. I know that no one has ever doubted that the Babylonian and Roman Empires are rightly called that of the East and that of the West. We are taught that the Macedonian Empire was in the North not only by its very geographical location (lit. "celestial zone"), but also by the altars placed by Alexander the Great at the foot of the Riphaean mountains, which still remain to this day. The testimony of books of history as well as city monuments attest that Carthage had preeminence over all of Africa, and had extended the boundaries of its rule not only as far as Sicily, Sardinia, and the other nearby islands, but even as far as Spain.]

Here, the ostensibly simple movement from Babylon to Rome, following the natural path of the sun, proves to be more complex. Although
Macedonia and Carthage are not true heirs to the Babylonian empire,
they hold its authority in custody until the true heir, Rome, reaches
maturity. The opposition of North and South, Macedonia and Carthage,
counterbalances that of East, Babylon, and West, Rome, adumbrat-
ing a pattern in world history that makes visible the hidden truth
of Christian history. As Fabrizio Fabbrini argues, this pattern follows
the perfect geometrical design of a cross, rendering visible a deeper
Christian *telos* invested in "a fifth Empire, qualitatively different from
the others."[7] This city is not ruled by an earthly emperor, but by Christ.
In this evocation of the Christian empire of the spirit, it is possible to
see the conformity of Orosius' view of history to that of his mentor,
Augustine.

Orosius undeniably describes both time and space as quadripartite,
with the four cardinal points corresponding to the four empires. While,
in its broadest terms, *translatio imperii* moves from East to West, its
actual trajectory moves from East, to North, to South, to West – from
Babylon, to Macedonia, to Carthage, to Rome. Speaking as a Roman,
however, Orosius mentions only three of the four regions in describing his place in the world: "latitudo orientis, septentrionis copiositas,
meridiana diffusio . . . sedes mei iuris et nominis sunt quia ad Chris-
tianos et Romanos Romanus et Christianus accedo" [The breadth of
the East, the vastness of the North, the extensiveness of the South . . .
are of my law and name because I approach Christians and Romans
as a Roman and a Christian](11:86; v.2.3). For Orosius, the West is,
as it were, a personal center. Although it is not the center of the
world, it is the place from which he encounters the world as a Roman
citizen.

The *Roman de toute chevalerie* also describes the far reaches of the
earth using only three of the four cardinal directions, omitting the West.
Alexander is said to have conquered "tuit le mond" [all the world] (line
5943), having placed his standard at each of the "treis fins del
mond" [three ends of the world] (line 5945), that is, at the extreme East,
North, and South. The only region left unexplored and unconquered is
the West, simply because (as Thomas says) there is nothing there worth
conquering:

Ore n'i ad [a] dire si sul occident non
Ou meinent ly Yreis, Espaniol e Breton,
Qe la terre habitable ne seit alé environ.
(lines 5948–51)

[Now there is nothing at all to be said about the West, where the
Irish, Spanish and British live, for the habitable land does not extend
around there.]

This omission is made even more striking by the detailed accounts of
Alexander's placement of commemorative markers or "mercs" at the
other extreme edges of the known world. He ventures into the East as
far as the "mercs" of Hercules, and exceeding even the latter's reach,
places his own "temples" and "auters" (line 5947) at the "fin d'orient"
and constructs "columpnes de metal" (line 6546) at the far reaches of
the North to enclose the unclean tribes of Gog and Magog. Finally,
having surrounded the East and the North, he turns southward to the
kingdom of Ethiopia (line 6639). In each of these locations, Alexander
makes ritual sacrifices and receives divine messages that prophesy his
inevitable downfall. In the East, he encounters the oracular trees of
the sun and moon; in the North, on Mount "Chelion," he hears the
voice of God; and in the South, Alexander sacrifices on the "ardant
mont" [burning mountain](lines 6883–93) where a disembodied voice
tells him that he will never see his home again. Alexander's encounters
with these liminal points, located at the extreme margins of the known
world, are significant in two respects. For humanity as a whole, they
represent man's greatest and most extreme accomplishments. For the
individual, however, they represent danger and inevitable destruction.
In these places at the "fin del mond," the divine is audible and one's
own end is in sight.

There is a deeper significance to be found in this patterning of world
geography in the *Roman de toute chevalerie* after the Orosian scheme.
Thomas of Kent's description of Alexander's sequence of conquests follows the same sequence reported in Orosius' quadripartite account of
translatio imperii from East, North and South, and finally to Rome in
the West. Alexander's path of conquest follows a similar trajectory – up
to a point. Following his encounter with Darius and the conquest of
Babylon, Alexander ventures into the furthest East, going beyond the

varied lands of India to the shores of the eastern Ocean. He then heads
North to subdue the unnatural races of Gog and Magog, and then to
the South to survey the heterogeneous nations of Ethiopia. Alexander,
however, never ventures into the West: a disjunction between the *Roman
de toute chevalerie* and Orosius' chronicle that repays closer scrutiny.
On a superficial level, Alexander never ventures into the West because,
as Thomas states, the West houses only the straggling populations of
Ireland, Britain, and Spain. On a deeper level, however, the absent voyage into the West signals Alexander's role as a harbinger of imperial
conquests to follow: the conquest of the known world by Rome, the
great city of the West, and the subsequent rise of European might in the
far western regions.

This point is supported by Alexander's special place in medieval historiography, as evidenced by the detailed comparisons of Alexander and
Augustus Caesar found in Orosius' *Seven Books against the Pagans*. As
a proud man and relentless conqueror who ultimately falls prey to the
excesses of the flesh, Alexander is no hero to the devout Christian:
Orosius accordingly emphasizes both his appeal and his limitations.
Alexander's undeniable might, however, makes him a fitting counterpart to the Roman emperor who achieved universal peace and con-
cord, preparing the way for the establishment of Christianity on the
foundations of the Empire. Once again, Orosius makes the comparison
through symbolic geography. Representatives from all over the world
assembled in homage to Alexander after his eastward return to Babylon
(1:172; III.20.3). Correspondingly, Augustus Caesar receives homage
from the far corners of the world not in his imperial seat at Rome,
but in the distant lands of the West:

> Caesarem apud Tarraconem citerioris Hispaniae urbem legati Indo-
> rum et Scytharum, toto Orbe transmisso, tandem ibi inuenerunt,
> ultra quod iam quaerere non possent, refuderuntque in Caesarem
> Alexandri Magni gloriam: quem sicut Hispanorum Gallorumque
> legatio in medio Oriente apud Babylonam contemplatione pacis adiit,
> ita hunc apud Hispaniam in Occidentis ultimo supplex cum gentilicio
> munere eous Indus et Scytha boreus orauit (II:233; VI.21.19–20).

> [After having crossed the whole world, the ambassadors of the Indians
> and Scythians finally found Caesar in Tarraco, a city of furthest Spain,
> beyond which they could not have continued to seek him, and they

transferred to Caesar the glory of Alexander the Great. In the same way that a legation of Spaniards and Gauls intending to make peace came to him (i.e., Alexander) in Babylon, in the middle of the East, just so the Indian of the Eastern Ocean and the Scythian of the Boreal River beseeched him (Caesar) on their knees in Spain, at the extremity of the West, offering tribute from their peoples.]

Alexander appears here as both counterpart and harbinger of Augustus. Just as Rome is said to be the heir to Babylonian might, as *translatio imperii* moves from East to West, so all the lands of the East come to the furthest point West to pay tribute to Augustus Caesar, just as long ago all the lands of the West came to "the middle of the East" to pay tribute to Alexander. Augustus thus perfects, not simply repeats, Alexander's triumphs. As Orosius puts it, in spite of all his great achievements, "Alexandro uero apud Babylonam . . . interiit" [Alexander died in Babylon] (1:172; III.20.4); by contrast, Augustus exercised imperial power so complete that "ab oriente in occidentem, a septentrione in meridiem ac per totum Oceani circulum cunctis gentibus una pace conpositis" [from the East to the West, from the North to the South, and over the entire circuit of the Ocean, all nations were arranged in a single peace] (II:234; VI.22.1). At that moment, the world is prepared for the crucial moment in salvation history: that is, the Incarnation.

By the twelfth century, the negative view of Alexander as tyrannical conqueror, possessed by pride and destroyed by lust, had begun to give way to a more positive image that emphasized his daring, bravery, and might.[8] Simultaneously, the symbolic geography of Orosius, in which imperial power moved from the East to the North, South, and then West, was fundamentally altered. Where Orosius had stated that the mantle of empire was handed from Babylon to Macedonia, to Carthage, to Rome, twelfth-century chroniclers such as Otto of Freising replaced these nations with Babylon, Persia, Greece, and Rome.[9] As a result, the notion of *translatio imperii* was made more emphatically and more simply a movement from East to West, with Greece as a new middle ground, belonging fully neither to the East nor to the West. This change erases the imperial history of Carthage, deleting Africa from the sequence of imperial power in European historiography.[10]

It was in this context that the *Roman de toute chevalerie* was composed. The story of Alexander reemerges as both cautionary and inspirational, with Alexander exemplifying the qualities not just of the ideal conqueror, but of the ideal knight. His "chevalerie" (that is, his possession of the qualities appropriate to a knight) is exercised both on the battlefield and in the bedroom, as he rallies his troops in wartime and gives pleasure to his lady in time of peace. In addition, for the medieval reader of the romance, Alexander is a mediator between the familiar space of home and the exotic terrain abroad, as the reader sees the curiosities of the world – from the monstrous races of Ethiopia to the marvelous luxuries of India – through his eyes.

FROM THE TOMB OF DARIUS TO THE CHAMBER
OF CANDACE

The *Roman de toute chevalerie* is both a heroic portrait of one man – Alexander – and a history of the rise and fall of the Macedonian Empire. It also has an encyclopedic character, including several long accounts of the monstrous races and natural marvels to be found at the extreme limits of the *ecumene*, drawn from a version of the legend of Alexander composed in the fourth century by Julius Valerius, the marvels of the East described in the *Letter of Alexander to Aristotle*, and a variety of works of natural philosophy, including Pliny's *Historia naturalia*, Solinus' *Collectanea rerum memorabilium*, and Aethicus Ister's *Cosmographia*.[11] This idiosyncratic compilation has been attributed to a now-lost Old French original, hypothetically titled *Alexandre en Orient*, which provided a common source of parallel passages in the two main Alexander romances of the twelfth century, the *Roman d'Alexandre* and the *Roman de toute chevalerie*.[12] However, while the author of the *Roman d'Alexandre* refers to a vernacular ("romans") antecedent, Thomas of Kent refers to a Latin source: "d'un bon livre en latin fist cest translatement" [I made this translation from a good book in Latin (line P 21)].[13] More significant than the (probably insoluble) question of whether the *Alexandre en Orient* really existed is the fact that Thomas self-consciously presents his *Roman de toute chevalerie* as a work of translation ("cest translatement"). The fictitious assertion of a Latin source appears to be an effort to claim greater authority for Thomas's narrative, giving the vernacular romance a stabilizing foundation in an ancient text.

Latinity, in the Middle Ages, does not necessarily connote Rome. Nonetheless, the absent West in Thomas's adaptation of Orosius' symbolic geography is still evident on a linguistic level, in the Latin language – the language of the Roman Empire – that, Thomas asserts, lies behind the *Roman de toute chevalerie*. The claim of a Latin original thus does more than simply ground the poem's authority on a firmer basis: it embeds Alexander's story in Latin prose as well as in Roman history. This move is central to Thomas's effort to domesticate the unpredictable and dangerous peripheries of the globe by connecting them to the stable center of imperial Rome. The monstrous races of Ethiopia, the marvelous diversity of India, and the hideous uncleanness of the races of Gog and Magog are reined in by the discipline of Alexander's military conquest, and by the order imposed by the poet's metrical line.

Thomas's comment on his sources immediately follows his account of the death and interment of the Persian king Darius. This moment is significant both on the level of *translatio imperii* and on the level of the individual, for it marks not only the transfer of imperial power (in Orosius' terms) from the East to the North, but also the transformation of Alexander into an Oriental king. Other narratives of Alexander similarly signal the interment of Darius as a crucial moment. In Walter of Châtillon's *Alexandreis*, for example, the monumental tomb of the Persian king, topped with a crystalline globe and inscribed with an elaborately rubricated map of the earth, both memorializes Darius and pays tribute to Alexander's new status as king of all the Orient, and ruler of the world.[14] Alexander's intention is to be not simply Darius' conqueror but his heir: an almost filial piety motivates not only the construction of this magnificent memorial, but also his first act following the tomb's erection, as Alexander sets out to find and punish Darius' killer. In the *Roman de toute chevalerie*, too, the tomb of Darius demarcates a turning point in the narrative. Unlike Orosius' presentation of him as a northern king ruling over rapidly expanding eastern territories, Alexander becomes, after the death of Darius, part of the Orient he now rules.

This transformation, however, seems far off during the initial stages of the conflict between Alexander and Darius, where Darius is depicted as a Saracen king, patterned after the depictions of Saracens found in the *chansons de geste* and romances. Like those "pagans," Darius is early on said to be "orgoillus" (proud, line 27); he rules over a vast and heterogeneous army of "cent mil Sarazin" [a hundred thousand Saracens] (lines 1604–8) that, in every respect, is identical to the Saracens of the *chansons de geste*, even down to their worship of "Apolin" and "Tervagant" (lines 1605, 1391–2, 2270).[15] These associations project Alexander, Darius' opponent, forward in time as a crusader king, identifiable with the contemporaneous European Christian effort to take the Holy Land.[16] And yet Alexander is also heir to Darius and his dominion, becoming the ruler over his heterogeneous group of subjects, and king not only of the whole Orient, but of the whole world: "tuit le mond est Alisandre a bandon,/De touz roys terriens ad il subjecion" [all the world has surrendered to Alexander; he has subjected all earthly kings] (lines 5943–4).

The fate of Darius, then, becomes an uncanny harbinger of Alexander's own fate. The process of Darius' interment – the ritual preparation of the body, the exacting design and construction of a fitting monument – anticipates the final disposition of Alexander himself.

> A deus ciriziens fet Alisandre overir le corps,
> Mult bien le fet laver dedenz e dehors;
> Font arder la boele qe ne la mangent pors.
> E cusent le en un paille e enbalment le cors,
> E puis [l]'envolupe[nt] en quir de deus tors,
> En bere le metent entre deus chevals sors.
> (lines 3710–15)

> [Alexander had the body opened by two surgeons, and had it very well washed, both inside and outside. He had the guts burned, so that pigs would not eat them. And they placed the body on a silken cloth and embalmed it, and then wrapped it in the hide of two bulls and placed it on a bier drawn by two sorrel horses.]

The ritual preparation of Darius' body – interred "en guise de Persien" (line 3722) [in the Persian manner], his body placed "en sarcu de fin or" (line 3725) [in a sarcophagus of pure gold] – anticipates that of Alexander's body after his death by treachery, embalmed in a "sarcu de fin or" (line 7982). Being king of the Orient, Alexander is naturally buried as an Oriental king, with one crucial difference: location. While Darius' tomb is a fixed mausoleum, a monument to the fallen glory of Persia,

Alexander's golden sarcophagus is mobile. Carried by his men back westward, it lies in Alexandria, one of the twelve cities founded by the conqueror and named after him. This bodily translation emblematizes the *translatio imperii* narrated in the *Roman de toute chevalerie* – both the transmission of imperial power from Persia to Macedonia explicitly recounted, and its transmission further west, to Europe, which is implicit in the depiction of Alexander as a model of "toute chevalerie."

Between the golden sarcophagus of Darius and the golden sarcophagus of Alexander lies a sprawling account of the marvels of the world, as Alexander ventures into the furthest regions of the East, North, and South in his passionate endeavor to explore everywhere and conquer everything. The magnificent *mappa mundi* which adorns Darius' tomb in the *Alexandreis* comes alive, as it were, in the *Roman de toute chevalerie*'s account of the abundant luxuries found in the "fin d'Orient," the hideous tribes of Gog and Magog found in the northern wastes, and the monstrous races populating the torrid regions of the South. Significantly, the trajectory of Alexander's route of exploration and conquest – East, North, and South – follows that found in Orosius' universal chronicle, as the Persian Empire gives way to Macedonia, to Carthage, and finally to Rome. Alexander thus embodies the spirit of conquest, summing up the path of *translatio imperii* in the life of a single man. The westward track of *translatio imperii*, however, in which imperial power devolves upon Rome, is mirrored not in Alexander's acts, but in the fate of his dead body.

Alexander's voyage into the East is characterized in terms of doubleness. The land itself is double, for India is divided into two parts: "En la fin d'orient, de Inde i ad deus paire,/Inde superior e Inde la maire" [In the furthest East, there are two Indias, Upper India and Greater India] (lines 4601–2).[17] This doubling has a temporal dimension as well, for there are two summers, and two harvests (lines 4619–20). The resulting plenty extends not just to the abundant crops but also to the numerous cities and great number of "diverses genz" [diverse peoples] (line 4623). The East is filled with "merveiles" (line 4626), as Thomas illustrates in his long catalogues of the various peoples and wondrous animals to be found in India. When Alexander encounters the Indian king Porus, he has only one demand: he asks Porus to take him to the "fin d'orient" (line 5359), as far as the "mercs" left by Hercules long ago (line 5377).

There, an aged native comes up to Alexander to tell him about the further marvels to be found further east, beyond the pillars of Hercules, in the land of Taprobane.[18] Predictably, Alexander insists on going "ou Hercules n'osa" [where Hercules did not dare](line 5484). In Taprobane, the doubleness of the East is reinforced, with two summers, two harvests, and, furthermore, two winters. In this easternmost region, Alexander encounters further marvels, exploring until there is no more to be found: "Par tote [Ynde] est alez cerchant la region" [He went throughout all India, exploring the region](line 5938).

Alexander's exploration of the Orient is interrupted when a messenger comes down from the North, begging the conqueror to come back with him to deal with the hideous tribes of Gog and Magog, who live "vers aquilon" [in the place of the north wind]. This horrible "nacion" is "vers humeine nature" [against human nature]: their favorite food is "char d'ome" [human flesh] but they also eat dogs instead of venison, serpents, toads, frogs, and slugs (lines 5961–70). The uncleanness of these tribes is manifested not just in their cannibalism (and in eating man's best friend), but also in their consumption of foods that are unclean because they fall outside normal categories, such as frogs and toads.[19] The tribes of Gog and Magog are, in some ways, homogeneous: Thomas describes them as a single "nacion" (line 5961), united in their unclean behaviors and in their common descent from Nimrod, "Nembroth le traitur" (line 5980).[20] Despite this apparent homogeneity, however, the northerners demonstrate a range of diversity similar to that encountered earlier during Alexander's travels throughout the East. One group lives on the sea and eats human flesh; another eats mice; still another is made up of metalworkers, and so on. Among this diverse lot, Thomas gives special emphasis to the Turks, who eat both humans and dogs, "char vive" [living flesh] and "ordure" [filth](line 6021). They are "cruel e dure" [cruel and hard], given to "lecherie e chescune luxure" [lechery and every wanton behavior](lines 6019–20). Thomas goes beyond his source, the *Cosmographia* of Aethicus Ister, in his emphasis on the Turks and in his description of the climatic qualities associated with the northern region they inhabit. In this chilly, arid land, "Il n'i put nul blé crestre, ne nul fruit n['i] m[e]ure;/En esté, en yver ont toz jors la froidure" [no wheat can grow there, nor any fruit or berry; in summer and in winter, they have constant cold](lines 6048–9).[21]

The catalogue of the tribes of Gog and Magog goes on to include those who swim in the sea, those who build "estranges nefs" [strange boats](line 6057) that travel underwater, unnamed dwarves, and "Rifaires" who constantly fight "vers autres Sarazins" [against other Saracens](line 6090).[22] Alexander's role as conqueror demands his cleansing the world of the tribes of Gog and Magog: "De cest[e] ordure est trestuit le mond soillez" [the entire world is made dirty by this filth](line 6338). Having established the borders of the known world through conquest, Alexander also must bear the burden of maintaining the order of his territory within. Accordingly, he withdraws to Mount Chelion to make sacrifices, where the voice of God instructs him on how to enclose Gog and Magog. Forging columns of metal, reinforced with bitumen, Alexander seals up the unclean tribes in an enclosure from which they will emerge only in the time of Antichrist (lines 6574–8).[23] It is this accomplishment, for Thomas, that makes Alexander "the Great," himself as marvelous as the marvels he discovers.

Having swept through the regions of the East and North, Alexander turns his glance southward:

> Les deus parties del mond ad pres environé . . .
> Al regné de Ethiopie ad il ost mené,
> E veu tel[es] choses qe point nen ay conté
> (lines 6637–40)

> [He surrounded two parts of the world . . . and turned his host toward the kingdom of Ethiopia, and saw such things as I have not yet begun to tell.]

Ethiopia – used here, as usual in twelfth-century maps and geographies, to represent the southernmost habitable region – is replete with marvels, and marvelous diversity. Its many kingdoms are filled with

> Gent de meintes maneres e de diverse colur:
> Aquanz i sunt noir, autres blanc cum flur,
> Aquanz sunt coloré, aquant ont palur.
> (lines 6681–4)

> [People of many different characters and of different colors: some there are black, others white as a flower; some are ruddy, others pale.][24]

Unlike medieval encyclopedists, who attribute the racial diversity of the southern regions to the effects of climate, Thomas describes it as the consequence of their unusual behavior:

> En Ethiope ad gent de diverse nature,
> De diverse lignee, de diverse parleure,
> Car trestoz en sunt de diverse engendrure.
> (lines 6702–4)

> [In Ethiopia are people of diverse natures, of diverse lineages, of diverse languages, because everyone there is diversely engendered.]

Thomas explains that Ethiopians' great diversity is due to their sexual promiscuity, such that no man knows his father, nor any father his sons: "Tuit sunt commun entr'els cum bestes en pasture" [All is common among them, like beasts in the field] (line 6708). As in the regions of the East and North, the southern expanse contains a numerous, heterogeneous collection of peoples: some who have a dog for their king, others who have four eyes and worship Mercury; those who eat lions and have one eye, those who bark like dogs, those who ride elephants, those who have no mouths and communicate by sign language, and so on.

As Alexander moves through Ethiopia, its resemblance to the Indian regions where he began becomes more evident. The marvelous races, the wondrous animals, and even the land itself recall the India he left behind, for there are said to be two Ethiopias (line 6776) just as there were two Indias (line 4601). In a reenactment of his behavior in the northern wastes, Alexander withdraws to a mountain to make a sacrifice. A voice speaks to him once again, but this time it tells him that he will never return, that his insatiable thirst to see the world will end not in the safe haven of home, but abroad. At last, Alexander has received tribute from every nation, and seen everything there is to see: "Ne remeint a veer nule merveille seue,/De mostre ne d'engin ne de beste mue" [No more marvels remained to be seen, neither monsters nor quaint inventions nor crouching beasts] (lines 6923–4). Therefore, Alexander returns; but he returns not back to Macedonia, but back to "Inde major" (line 6929). In a curious sense, the Orient has itself become home to this king of the Orient. Accordingly, the following episodes are focused on Alexander's identity and his ultimate fate, as he encounters the oracular trees at the very farthest limits of the East, and is entertained by the Oriental queen

Candace in her private chamber. Both the grounds surrounding the trees and the chamber of Candace are said to be enclosures; these enclosures, however, represent not the secure, domestic spaces of home but instead unsettling locations where identity is revealed to be contingent, and danger is close at hand.

Initially, Alexander's encounter with Candace seems as though it could have taken place in the courts of France or England. This Oriental queen is "bele e blanche" (line 6943; cf. line 7751), fair-skinned and blonde as any European. As Alexander approaches the queen's palace, disguised as a messenger called Antigone, she listens to her minst-rels play "un nouvel son/Coment danz Eneas ama dame Didon" [a new song of how Lord Aeneas loved Lady Dido](lines 7650–51).[25] Perhaps remembering the fate of Dido, "Pensive en est Candace del torn de l[a] chançon" [Candace is made thoughtful by the turn of the song] (line 7655). She approaches Alexander first, sending messengers bearing luxurious gifts ranging from camels loaded with baskets of emeralds to a thousand armed Ethiopians (lines 6971). Candace's purpose here is not merely to propitiate Alexander: she also sends an artist along with her delegation, commissioned to make a portrait of the Macedonian. On his return, the portrait is used as a model for the construction of a life-size statue that will greet the conqueror during his encounter with Candace, which immediately follows his visit to the oracular trees of the sun and moon.[26]

After displaying all her rich treasures, Candace confronts Alexan-der with the truth of his identity: "Vous estes Alisandre; le non por quei changez?" [You are Alexander; why have you changed your name?] (line 7685). Alexander insists that he really is just "Antigone," the king's messenger, whereupon Candace takes Alexander off to a "privé man-age" or private room (line 7698): "Alisandre," says Candace, "veez cy vostre ymage"[Alexander, see here your image] (line 7699). By not only tricking Alexander, but actually trapping him alone in her private room, deep within the palace walls, Candace gains ascendancy over Alexander. Generously, however, Candace tells him not to be ashamed, because "tuit temps est usage/Qe femme deceit homme" [it always happens that woman deceives man](lines 7710–11). Now that you're under my "discipline," says Candace, "Aloms ore juer suz cele cortine" [Let's go play now behind those bed-curtains](lines 7748–49). They go "desur le lit parler d'amur fine;/Recordent la lesçon qu'afiert a tel doctrine" [onto the bed to speak of "fine amour," to rehearse the lesson that goes along with that doctrine] (lines 7755–6). Alexander has entered a kind of carnal paradise, where the deceptive nature of woman renders man powerless, and where no secrets can be held back.

Several scenes of enclosure punctuate Alexander's journeys throughout the world, ranging from the walling up of the tribes of Gog and Magog in the North, to the oracular cave in the deepest South, to the grove containing the trees of the sun and moon in the land furthest East, which is said to be "enclos . . . tot entur" [entirely enclosed] (line 7134). Like the grove of trees, where "flairent . . . les espices cum ceo fust Paradis" [the spices smelled as fragrant as if it were Paradise] (line 7101), Candace's bedchamber is a location which is at once paradise-like and threatening, offering both sensuous pleasure and imminent danger. The series of enclosures near the end of the narrative, including the grove of trees and the bedchamber of Candace, will end with a final enclosure: the "sarcu de fin or" (line 7982) which encloses Alexander's dead body, like the one in which he enclosed the body of his predecessor, Darius. The private room in which Alexander and Candace meet is a place at once strange and familiar: strange, because it is located in an eastern locale, decorated with curious and rare treasures, but familiar because it is a place where the knight Alexander can play at "fine amour" with a lady who is both "beautiful and white." The distant center of oriental luxury proves to epitomize the courtly ideal found (for the European reader) at home. In spite of its reassuring familiarity, this locale proves to be dangerous, for here Alexander's own identity becomes peculiarly fluid. In Candace's realm, he is known as Antigone, the messenger of Alexander, in order to protect himself from enemies in this alien land. Only in the queen's bedroom is he known by his right name, for she alone knows his true identity. He wavers between being Antigone and Alexander, messenger and king, depending upon his location.

THE TRANSLATION OF ALEXANDER

The destabilization of identity experienced by Alexander in the distant Orient signals the incipient end of the narrative. Having reached the "treis fins del mond" [three ends of the earth] (line 5945) and placed monumental markers at the extreme East, North, and South, the great conqueror's own end is in sight. His dead body, lavishly anointed with oriental unguents and spices, is returned to Egyptian Alexandria, a formerly foreign land recently absorbed into the Macedonian Empire, and soon to become a province of greater Rome. Exploration to the very periphery of the world is necessarily followed by a return to the central regions of the realm. However, that exploration included only three of the four cardinal directions: Thomas declares that Alexander does not journey to the West, where the Irish, Spanish, and British are found, because of the lack of habitable territory there. How, then, to understand the significance of the westward turn which concludes the *Roman de toute chevalerie*, in the form of Alexander's bodily translation to Alexandria and the text's literal translation from Greek to Latin, from Latin to Anglo-Norman? The movement westward represents domestication and stabilization, an assimilation through translation of the dangerous Orient – at the price, however, of the traveler's own identity.

Translation, in the *Roman de toute chevalerie*, is a process carried out both in the macrocosm and in the microcosm, in the passage of empires and in the passage of the single man. Alexander's bodily translation proceeds from Babylon to Alexandria, as his golden sarcophagus makes its way westward. This movement is reflected in the *Roman de toute chevalerie*'s account of its own textual transmission: Thomas declares that he translated his text from a "good book in Latin" (that is, the *Letter from Alexander to Aristotle*), which itself was thought to be a Latin translation of a Greek original. In it, Alexander tells of the great marvels of the East, none of them more amazing than the oracular trees of the sun and moon located at the very tip of the Orient. Those trees speak not only Greek but "indiene parole" (line 7178), words translated from the Indian language into Greek, into Latin, into Anglo-Norman. Thomas himself reflects on the nature of such translation in the passage where he names himself and describes the genesis of his book:

> E tut içoe ai dist, quei i fu et coment.
> La verité ai estrait, si l'estorie [ne] ment.
> N'ai sez faiz acreu, çoe vus di verreiement,
> Mes beles paroles i ai mis nequedent.
> N'ai acreu l'estoire ne jo n'i ost nient;
> Pur plaisir as oianz un atiffement;

Home ne deit lange translater autrement;
Qui d[ir]eit mot por mot, trop irreit leidement.
(lines P 10–17)

[I have told all of it, what happened there and how.
I have extracted the truth, if the story doesn't lie.
I have not exaggerated his deeds, that I tell you truly,
although I did add some pretty words here and there, nevertheless.
I have not embellished the story, nor have I omitted anything.
For the pleasure of the hearers there is some decoration;
One may not translate any other way;
He who does it word for word does very badly.]

Translation necessarily entails transformation; not alteration of the substance of the story, the "verité," but the incorporation of new words that both convey truth and give pleasure. The beauty of the language, like the beauty of Alexander's golden sarcophagus, lies in the act of movement, in the translation across tongues, and across cultures.

The Alexander romances, and the *Roman de toute chevalerie* in particular, offer crucial insights into the dynamism of medieval conceptualizations of the shape of the world. The modern dichotomy of East and West can be fitted to medieval texts only awkwardly, owing to the much more common conceptualization of a tripartite world, made up of the known continents of Asia, Europe, and Africa. Even Orosius' chronicle, which posits a movement of empires from the East into the West, begins with the tripartite division of the world, a formula repeated in the opening of the *Roman de toute chevalerie*:

En trois la departirent . . .
L'une est Aufrike, Asye est la seconde,
Europe est la tierce.
(lines 34–6)

[They divide (the world) in three . . . One is Africa, Asia is the second, Europe is the third.]

The opposition of East and West in the work of Orosius is strikingly different from the modern dichotomy in that the westward flow of imperial might is interrupted by what Orosius calls the "guardianship" of the northern kingdom of Macedonia and the southern empire of Carthage. This quadripartite structure, as Fabbrini argues, is intended to represent the cross, a symbol of how Christian history is embedded within the development of the secular world. The opposition of East and West in the later medieval chroniclers who base their work on Orosius, such as Otto of Freising and Ordericus Vitalis, differs even more greatly, for these chroniclers had to adapt their symbolic geography to accommodate the special role of Jerusalem in the context of the crusades. In the *Roman de toute chevalerie*, the quadripartite structure of the world found in the Orosian account is even more elaborately developed, as the variable effects of climate are illustrated in the course of Alexander's voyages to the ends of the earth.

He travels, however, into only "treis fins del mond": conspicuously, Alexander does not venture into the West. For Orosius, the West is Rome, the fourth and greatest of the world empires that paves the way for the advent of the spiritual empire of Jesus Christ. In the history of Alexander, however, the West represents the future, both the proximate future of Alexander's body, translated westward in its golden sarcophagus, and the more distant future of the European nations to come. Alexander's world, in the *Roman de toute chevalerie*, is the prehistory of the European nations; accordingly, its symbolic geography anticipates the fulfillment of imperial ambitions in the West, as the uninhabitable wasteland of the "Irish, Spanish, and British" gives rise to the modern nations familiar to the twelfth-century reader. The richly elaborated vision of the Orient found in texts like this Anglo-Norman poem made it possible to conceive of an idea of the West that was founded upon humble origins, but imbued with the infinite potential for growth and expansion.

NOTES

1. Assessments of Said's binary opposition of East and West are many: see especially Robert Young, *Colonial Desire: Hybridity in Theory, Culture, and Race* (London and New York: Routledge, 1995) and Aijaz Ahmed, *In Theory: Classes, Nations, Literature* (New York: Verso, 1992).
2. See the cogent assessment of the relationship of Bhabha's work, especially *The Location of Culture*, to Said's *Orientalism*, in Ato Quayson, *Postcolonialism: Theory, Practice or Process?* (Cambridge: Polity, 2000), 39–47. Spivak has mediated the European and North American reception of the work of the Subaltern Studies collective by translating its radical historiography into poststructuralist terms; see Gayatri Chakravorty Spivak, "Subaltern Studies: Deconstructing Historiography," *Subaltern Studies* 4 (1985): 330–63, and "Can the Subaltern Speak?" in *Marxism and the Interpretation of*

Culture, ed. Cary Nelson and Lawrence Grossberg (Urbana: University of Illinois Press, 1988), 271–313. For the interrelation of Spivak and Said's work, see *Selected Subaltern Studies*, ed. Ranajit Guha and Gayatri Chakravorty Spivak, Foreword by Edward W. Said (Oxford and New York: Oxford University Press, 1988), v–x, and Spivak, *A Critique of Postcolonial Reason: Toward a History of the Vanishing Present* (Cambridge, MA: Harvard University Press, 1999), 264–72 and *Death of a Discipline* (New York: Columbia University Press, 2003), 105 n6. Thanks to Ritu Birla for help with these references.

3. Suzanne Conklin Akbari, "From Due East to True North: Orientalism and Orientation," in *The Postcolonial Middle Ages*, ed. Cohen, 19–34.

4. *The Anglo-Norman Alexander (Le Roman de toute chevalerie) by Thomas of Kent*, ed. Brian Foster and Ian Short, 2 vols. (Anglo-Norman Text Society 29-33, London: Anglo-Norman Text Society, 1976–77). References to the *Roman de toute chevalerie* are cited in the body of the text by line number; translations are my own.

5. One of the most famous examples is Fulcher of Chartres, where the historian reflects on the paradoxically backward flow of *translatio imperii* to be found in the European-ruled Holy Land: "Consider, I pray, and reflect how in our time God has transferred the West into the East. For we who were Occidentals now have been made Orientals." See *Historia Hierosolymitana, (1095–1127)*, ed. Heinrich Hagenmeyer (Heidelberg: Carl Winter, 1913), 748 (III.27.2–3); translated in *The First Crusade: The Chronicle of Fulcher of Chartres and Other Source Materials*, ed. Edward Peters, trans. A. C. Krey, second edn (Philadelphia: University of Pennsylvania Press, 1998), 281.

6. Paulus Orosius, *Historiarum adversum paganos libri vii*, in *Orose: Histoires (Contre les Païens)*, ed. and trans. Marie-Pierre Arnaud-Lindet, 3 vols. (Paris: Les Belles Lettres, 1990), 1:15–16; 1.2.1–12. Citations refer to the volume and page number of the edition, followed by book and chapter numbers. Translations are adapted from Arnaud-Lindet's very literal modern French translation; a more idiomatic English translation can be found in *The Seven Books of History Against the Pagans*, trans. Deferrari.

7. Fabrizio Fabbrini, *Paulo Orosio: uno storico* (Rome: Edizioni di Storia e Letteratura, 1979), 364–5; translation mine.

8. On views of Alexander in the twelfth century, see George Cary and D. J. A. Ross, *The Medieval Alexander* (Cambridge: Cambridge University Press, 1956), 208–9 and *passim*; Martin Gosman, *La Légende d'Alexandre le Grand dans la littérature française du 12e siècle une réécriture permanente* (Faux titre 133, Amsterdam and Atlanta: Rodopi, 1997), 143–67.

9. On the significance of this change, see Fabbrini, *Paulo Orosio*, 14 n57.

10. Compare the often minimalist depiction of Africa on medieval world maps described in Scott D. Westrem, "Africa Unbounded on an Unstudied European *Mappamundi* (ca. 1450) and in Related Cartography," in *Making Contact: Maps, Identity, and Travel*, ed. Glenn Burger, Lesley B. Cormack, and Natalia Pylypiuk (Edmonton: University of Alberta Press, 2003), 3–21, esp. 4 and 12–14.

11. A full study of the sources of the *Roman de toute chevalerie* can be found in Johanna Weynand, *Der Roman de toute chevalerie des Thomas von Kent in seinem Verhältnis zu seinen Quellen* (Bonn: Carl Georgi, 1911).

12. On the conjectural *Alexandre en Orient*, see Armstrong's comments in *The Medieval French Roman d'Alexandre*, vol. VI: *The Version of Alexandre de Paris*, ed. Edward C. Armstrong (Princeton: Princeton University Press, 1976), vii and 22ff.

13. *Roman d'Alexandre*, ed. Armstrong, 88–9 (line 15 in the version of Alexandre de Paris). Note that Foster and Short's edition of the *Roman de toute chevalerie* numbers the lines of the poem according to manuscript D; where D lacks an episode, they restart the numbering, adding the letter of the supplementary manuscript. Hence lines P1–178 follow line 3921 in D. On the limitations of Foster and Short's edition, see Gosman, 290–2.

14. Walter of Châtillon, *Alexandreis* VII.42–77, ed. Marvin Colker, *Galteri de castellione Alexandreis* (Padua: Antenore, 1978); *The Alexandreis of Walter of Châtillon: A Twelfth-Century Epic*, trans. David Townsend (Philadelphia: University of Pennsylvania Press, 1996), 126–7. On this passage, see Christine Ratkowitsch, *Descriptio picturae: Die literarische Funktion der Beschreibung von Kunstwerken in der lateinischen Grossdichtung des 12. Jahrhunderts* (Vienna: Verlag des Österreichischen Academie der Wissenschaften, 1991), 167–8, and Maura K. Lafferty, "Mapping Human Limitations: The Tomb Ecphrases in Walter of Châtillon's *Alexandreis*," *Journal of Medieval Latin* 4 (1994): 64–81.

15. On the pagan "anti-Trinity" of Apolin, Mahum, and Tervagant in the *chansons de geste*, see Suzanne Conklin Akbari, "Imagining Islam: The Role of Images in Medieval Depictions of Muslims," *Scripta Mediterranea* 19–20 (1998–99): 9–27; on the names of the gods, see C. and Y. Pellat, "L'idée de Dieu chez les Sarrasins des chansons de geste," *Studia Islamica* 22 (1965): 5–42.

16. Noting a similar case of the interchangeability of ancient heroes with contemporary knights, Christine Chism argues that the figure of Alexander in the Middle English *Wars of Alexander* served as a vehicle for the concerns and the "ideology of the fourteenth-century British chivalry" (136) in "Too Close for Comfort: Dis-Orienting Chivalry in the *Wars of Alexander*," in *Text and Territory*, ed. Tomasch and Gilles, 116–39.

17. On maps and in prose geographies, India is divided into two, three, or even more parts. See von den Brincken, *Fines Terrae*, 162.

18. In connection with the figure of the local informant, a native who offers direction and information in an unfamiliar territory, compare Ora Limor's description of the "knowing Jew" in "Christian Sacred Space and the Jew," in *From Witness to Witchcraft: Jews and Judaism in Medieval Christian Thought*, ed. Jeremy Cohen (Wolfenbütteler Mittelalter-Studien 11, Wiesbaden: Harrassowitz, 1996), 55–77.

19. See Mary Douglas, "The Forbidden Animals in Leviticus," *Journal for the Study of the Old Testament* 59 (1993): 3–23.

20. This unusual detail comes not from the *Cosmographia* of Aethicus Ister, the source for much of Thomas's account of Gog and Magog, but from the *Apocalypse* of

pseudo-Methodius; noted in Smithers' edition of *Kyng Alisaunder* 2: 135–36 (note to line 5954).

21. Compare the source passage in the *Cosmographia* of Aethicus Ister, where the chill of the northern climate is not emphasized, and the natives even celebrate a late-summer religious festival: *Die Kosmographie des Aethicus*, ed. Otto Prinz (MGH, Quellen zur Geistesgeschichte des Mittelalters 14, Munich: Monumenta Germaniae Historica, 1993), 120–1, cap. 4.

22. Thomas of Kent uses the term "Sarazin" to refer to pagans in general, not just those found in the Orient, and also applies it to the pre-Christian period. Diane Speed suggests that such generic usage of the term was standard in twelfth- and thirteenth-century England; see "The Saracens of *King Horn*," *Speculum* 65 (1990): 564–95, esp. 566–7.

23. The standard source on the tradition of the encounter of Alexander with the tribes of Gog and Magog is Andrew Runni Anderson, *Alexander's Gate, Gog and Magog and the Inclosed Nations* (Cambridge, MA: Medieval Academy of America, 1932). See also Andrew Gow, *The Red Jews: Antisemitism in an Apocalyptic Age, 1200–1600* (Leiden: E. J. Brill, 1995) and "Gog and Magog on *Mappaemundi* and Early Printed World Maps: Orientalizing Ethnography in the Apocalyptic Tradition," *Journal of Early Modern History* 2 (1998): 61–88; Scott D. Westrem, "Against Gog and Magog," in *Text and Territory*, ed. Tomasch and Gilles, 54–75.

24. Compare the climatic maps which illustrate Isidore, *Etymologiae* XIII.6, in which the northern habitable extreme is labeled with the Riphaean Mountains and the southern extreme with Ethiopia; examples in von den Brincken, *Fines Terrae*, plates 13–15.

25. This may refer to the twelfth-century romance of *Eneas*; see *The Anglo-Norman Alexander*, ed. Foster and Short, vol. II, 73.

26. On the oracular trees in the *Liber floridus*, *Roman de toute chevalerie*, and *Kyng Alisaundre*, see my *Idols in the East*, chapter 2 ("From Jerusalem to India") (forthcoming, University of Pennsylvania Press).

6

Gower's monster

Deanne Williams

I cannot strecche up to the hevene
Min hand, ne setten al in evene
This world.

(John Gower, Confessio Amantis i.1–3)

John Gower starts his *Confessio Amantis* by throwing up his hands in frustration. Although it may not be possible to stretch his hands to heaven and confer order on creation like God, Gower seeks to confer order on his own literary universe. Consequently, Gower's *Confessio Amantis* is a classic example of medieval textual culture, with its encyclopedic, almost architectural structure, complete with Latin summaries and verse headings, redactions of classical and vernacular source material, and systematic moralizations. Its compendious nature and sheer size bring together the idea of literary authority, *auctoritas*, with its Latin root, *augere* (to expand; to increase).[1]

Yet this combination of order and authority has made Gower unsympathetic to some contemporary readers, who regard him as a kind of pernicious dinosaur, one whose lamentations that the world is going to the dogs are not only woefully nostalgic, but also deeply conservative. For these readers, Gower embodies the repressions, prejudices, and unwavering hierarchalism associated with the "alterity" of the Middle Ages: a period that has been conceived of in opposition to the humanist sensibilities of the Renaissance.[2] This Gower celebrates social structure and the status quo: he presents the 1381 rebels as animals, endorses the legitimacy of committing murder while on crusade, and manifests a masculinist acceptance of rape.[3] However, this is only one side of the story. Gower has his supporters as well as his detractors, and more

positive appraisals of Gower call attention to his ethical and philosoph-
ical preoccupations, and find his work to offer an urbane psychological
sensitivity that is indebted to the vernacular *dits amoreux* of Machaut
and Froissart; a sophisticated and coherent exposition of the relationship between ethics in the political sphere and the morality of human
love; and a learned and nuanced negotiation, "in the ironic traditions
of Ovid, Jean de Meun, and Chaucer," of the competing discourses of
ethics and politics, cosmology and theology, and eros.[4]

Whether he is regarded, on the one hand, as a representative of the
old guard or, on the other, as a paragon of humanist individualism,
the reception of Gower offers an ongoing commentary on the figure
of "moral Gower," Chaucer's famous epithet from *Troilus and Criseyde*,
weighing and reweighing the reputation for "virtu" and "moralitee"
that once earned him a place as one of the "primier poetes of this
nacion."[5] The range in critical responses to Gower also reflects the
prevailing views of the Middle Ages that motivate medieval studies.
As unruly peasants, heterodox dissenters, and Others of various stripes
have begun to populate our vision of the medieval, Gower recalls a no-
longer-fashionable vision of the Middle Ages as a time of authority and
piety. At the same time, however, his humanist and reformist sensibilities
provide an occasion for scholars such as James Simpson to critique the
structures of periodicity that define the "medieval" in opposition to the
Renaissance, a precursor to modernity.[6]

This range reflects the profound division that is fundamental to
Gower's *Confessio Amantis*. Indeed, Gower takes "divisioun" as the major
theme of his Prologue: the "moder of confusion" (Prol. 852), it is the
major cause of the world's problems, infecting empires, kings, popes,
and the people. This thematic division expresses itself formally, as well.
The orderly structures of medieval scholasticism are evinced by Gower's
deployment of organizational techniques, from *ordinatio* and *compilatio*
to rubrication and gloss, and by the highly controlled environment in
which he produced his manuscripts. These structures work against a
fascination with narratives of chaos, metamorphosis and monstrosity
that make this ostensible orderliness spin out of control, and mock its
very pretensions.[7] It expresses itself in the perversity of Genius's moralizations (as, for example, when Pyramus and Thisbe becomes a story
about not being late), as well as in the overarching erotic narrative which

works both in tandem and in tension with the text's framing treatment of empire formation.[8]

It has been difficult, therefore, for us to reach a consensus on Gower because his work itself is so divided. With *Confessio Amantis* in English, *Vox Clamantis* in Latin, and *Mirour de l'omme* in Anglo-Norman, Gower's works reflect the polylinguistic vitality and sharp social divisions of late medieval England, with French associated with royalty and the aristocracy; Latin, the language of the church and of higher education; and English, a less prestigious language of the people that was, in Gower's generation, just beginning to come into its own as a literary language.[9] Gower's dividedness is thus a product of England's cultural and linguistic divisions, and of the dynamics of *translatio imperii et studii* – the translation of empire and of learning – that produced them, as England was subject to Roman as well as Norman rule. The multiple acts of translation from Latin and French that are required to produce a text such as the *Confessio*, which Gower dubs "a bok for Engelondes sake" (Prol. 24) are a testament to England's history of conquest. The *Confessio Amantis* is a product of the challenges he faced when he began to compose poetry for king and court in the English vernacular, "in oure englissh" (Prol* 23) as he calls it: a challenge that he took up, as he recalls in his revised version of the Prologue, during a rowing expedition on the Thames.[10]

In *Confessio Amantis*, Gower uses the biblical figure of Nebuchadnezzar, king of Babylon, as a figure for England's condition of cultural hybridity. Whereas the confessor, Genius, and the besotted lover, Amans, invoke the traditions of French love poetry and Latin learning, by narrating Nebuchadnezzar's transformation into a monster, along with his apocalyptic dreams and exile into the wilderness, Gower highlights the diverse cultural influences and the important role of translation in medieval English literary culture. As visions of the nightmarish Other and versions of the most private aspects of the self, monsters make a regular appearance in medieval English texts that seek to define cultural or national identities: from *Beowulf* to Mandeville's *Travels*, from Geoffrey of Monmouth's *Historia* to the corpus of Arthurian romance. As Jeffrey Jerome Cohen argues, the medieval monster embodies the Lacanian concept of *extimité*: an "intimate alterity" in which terrifying – and terrifyingly proximate – Otherness is made central to the integrity of individual or collective identity.[11] Neither a terrifying antagonist that needs to be vanquished, nor an uncanny creature in an unsettling encounter, Gower's Nebuchadnezzar is, instead, a figure for the act of translation itself, bringing together the familiar and the strange, and revealing the continuities and conflicts that exist between the civilized human and the barbarian exile.[12] Nebuchadnezzar's metamorphosis provides Gower with a paradigm for addressing his relationship to the literary process of translation: the frightening yet potentially revelatory metamorphic process in which one thing becomes something else, while retaining a vestige of what it once was. In this way, Nebuchadnezzar allows Gower to reveal, and to revel in, the dignity of his own hybridity.

Nebuchadnezzar is well known to contemporary audiences because he gives his name to the rogue ship in the recent film, *The Matrix*, in which the unwilling hero, Neo, is transported by Morpheus (in Ovid, the god of sleep). *The Matrix* presents a futuristic image of the computer age in order to mount a critique of postmodern complacency, and the "Nebuchadnezzar" is the vessel from which a small rebel community confronts corporate dystopia. The Wachowski brothers chose the name Nebuchadnezzar because of its associations with apocalyptic change, the conflict between dreams and waking life, and the loss of what is safe and known. Morpheus (played by Lawrence Fishburne) welcomes Neo (played by Keanu Reeves) "to the desert of the real" – a computer-generated simulacrum that has masked the extent to which humans have become slaves to machines.[13] The "Nebuchadnezzar" is the place where Neo learns, through a series of dreams-within-dreams, how technology (along with some excellent martial arts moves) can be used to facilitate community and ethical responsibility, to expand human potential, and, most importantly, to resist an exploitative, technocratic new world order. *The Matrix* implies that the ultimate source for this is not some kind of demonic outsider, but instead the self. In other words, the contrast between endless skyscrapers and countless clones, and the post-nuclear/medieval asceticism of the rebel band on the "Nebuchadnezzar," represents an internalized psychological conflict between our love of technology and passive acceptance of technocracy, and the keen desire for a more authentic, alternative, form of community: something new, something Neo.

As *The Matrix* reveals, Nebuchadnezzar is a creature of contradictions. The historical Nebuchadnezzar made a string of conquests
through the Middle East. As Gower puts it, "al the world in thoryent,/
was hoole at his commaundement" (*Confessio Amantis* 1.2789–90).[14]
Nebuchadnezzar's conquests, and in particular his siege of Jerusalem,
made him a popular figure for worldly pride: Judith, Isaiah, Ezekiel and
Jeremiah, as well as Daniel, mention his tremendous military successes
and his triumphs as a conqueror. The Prologue to *Confessio Amantis*
holds Nebuchadnezzar up as the source for the chaos, division and, most
importantly, mutability that wrack the contemporary world: "Hou that
this world schal torne and wende" (Prol. 591). Gower proceeds to relate
the biblical story of Nebuchadnezzar's prophetic, apocalyptic dream, in
which a statue with a golden head, silver chest, bronze belly, iron thighs,
and feet made of iron and clay appears, is smashed by a stone which is
rolling down a mountain, and dissolves. A powerful visual metaphor for
the tales of imperial decline that follow (from the Babylonians to the
Persians, to the Greeks, to the Romans, etc.), Nebuchadnezzar's statue is
interpreted by Daniel as a prophecy of the eventual downfall of Babylon.

Gower goes on to describe how the world has been weakened, not only
by Babylon's imperial power, which Gower describes using words such as
"subjeccion" (line 683) and "possessioun" (line 6840), but also, and more
importantly, by its subjection to the principle that Babylon represents:
conquest and empire-building, followed by inexorable decline:

> . . . All the world in that partie
> To Babiloyne was soubgit
> And hield him stille in such a plit,
> Til that the world began diverse.
> (Prol. 674–5)

As king of Babylon, Nebuchadnezzar is defined through military
achievements that, for Gower, constitute an anticipation of, and ana-
logue to, the impressive successes of Islamic expansion in the Middle
Ages.[15] The idea of Nebuchadnezzar as a heathen tyrant and of Babylon
as fearsome eastern Other illustrates a kind of biblical proto-Orientalism
that defines civilized Christianity against the dangerous Babylon: a discourse that resonates powerfully with current international affairs. However, it is important to recognize the extent to which Gower interprets

Nebuchadnezzar's story as a prophecy of the instability of empire itself, adding to Daniel's interpretation a discussion of recent church history and contemporary English politics. Gower uses the story of Nebuchadnezzar to make a universally applicable point, to address issues that are close to home, thus establishing a common ground instead of demonizing the Other.

Hence, Nebuchadnezzar is a figure for sympathy as well as repudiation: he is not only a heinous unredeemable tyrant but also a flawed, yet educable, man. His prophetic dreams set him apart from other biblical bad guys, placing him in the company of Daniel, Moses and other prophets.[16] In this way, Gower uses Nebuchadnezzar to introduce both the apocalyptic account of macrocosmic decline and division that frames *Confessio Amantis*, and the collection of individual transformations that Genius narrates to Amans throughout. In Book I, which is devoted to the sin of Pride, Gower relates the story of Nebuchadnezzar's physical metamorphosis into a monster, with eagle's feathers and bird's claws, and his exile to the wilderness, where he eats grass on all fours like an ox. Eventually, Nebuchadnezzar regains his human shape, and emerges from the wilderness a new, humbled man: full of praise and thanks to God for restoring his form.

The story of Nebuchadnezzar's metamorphosis is of a piece with Gower's own fascination with beast transformation: he bestializes the participants of the 1381 Rising in *Vox Clamantis*; gives human sin an animal face in *Mirour de l'omme*; and, of course, narrates a series of Ovidian metamorphoses throughout *Confessio Amantis*. As Caroline Walker Bynum points out, popular tales of physical transformation such as Marie de France's werewolf tale, *Bisclavret*, offered a means of expressing and accounting for widespread experiences of social, political, and individual change.[17] Moreover, the monstrous form into which Nebuchadnezzar is shaped is not only a figure of visual shock and awe – but, like his apocalyptic dream, a figure that demands a reading, an explication, a translation. The word "monster," from the Latin *monstrum*, comes from the root *monere*, to warn (as well as the cognate verb *demonstrare*, to reveal). To show and to warn: *monstrum* was used to translate the Greek word *teras*, which gives us the word *teratology*, or the interpretation of prodigies. As Cohen sums up, "The monster exists only to be read."[18]

Medieval English authors use Nebuchadnezzar in order to reflect upon the challenges of interpretation and identity-formation raised by England's history of overlapping cultural and linguistic influences. In *Cleanness*, the intensely physical details of Nebuchadnezzar's transformation provide a powerful, visual illustration of his status as outsider, as exile, forming part of a larger, unfolding narrative that highlights the exemplary and regenerative purpose of correct behavior. Nebuchadnezzar's transformation is one in a series of traumatic paradigm shifts: from the old, antediluvian world, to Noah's ark, to the new, dry land and covenant; from the sexual hotbed of Sodom and Gomorrah, to the hills where Lot's daughters do their business, to the new generations that they spawn; from the destruction of the Temple in Jerusalem to Babylon and, ultimately, salvation. Nebuchadnezzar earns the wrath of God because of his personal attachment to his empire ("Moȝt never myȝt bot myn make such anoþer," line 1668):[19]

> Þus he countes hym a cow þat watz a kyng ryche,
> Quyle seuen syþez were ouerseyed, someres I trawe.
> By þat mony þik fytherez þryȝt vmbe his lyre,
> Þat alle watz dubbed and dyȝt in þe dew of heuen;
> Faxe, fyltered and felt, floȝed hym vmbe,
> Þat schad fro his schuldres to his schere-wykes,
> And twenty-folde twynande hit to his tos raȝt,
> Þer mony clyuy as clyde hit clyȝt togeder.
> His berde ibrad alle his brest to þe bare vrþe,
> His browes bresed as breres aboute his brode chekes;
> Holȝe were his yȝen and vnder campe hores,
> And al watz gray as þe glede, with ful grymme clawres
> Þat were croked and kene as þe kyte paune.
> (lines 1685–97)

[Thus he who was a rich king now finds himself a cow. While seven years were passed in summers, I believe, thick feathers grew over his limbs in that time, and all was daubed and drenched in the dew of heaven. Hair, tangled and shaggy, covered him, spreading from his shoulders to his groin. Twenty times around his toes it wrapped, where many burrs like plaster knit it together. His beard covered everything from his breast to the bare earth, his brows bristled like briars about his broad cheeks, hollow were his eyes beneath his shaggy hairs, and he was as gray as a kite with horrible claws that were as crooked and sharp as a kite's talons.] (translation my own)

Nebuchadnezzar has become the classic medieval wild man: it is as if he has taken on all of the qualities of the wilderness he inhabits. With his feathers and fur, briar and burrs, Nebuchadnezzar's appearance plays into the preoccupation with the tension between wilderness and court, province and town, margin and center that defines the poems of the so-called *Pearl*-poet in British Library MS Cotton Nero a.x. (a manuscript that also contains another great monster-story, *Sir Gawain and the Green Knight*). In the case of Nebuchadnezzar, it seems, the medium is the message. While he experiences the prophecy of his downfall, translated to him by Daniel, as a physical transformation, the detailed anatomy of his distress renders, in striking detail, Gregory the Great's argument that humans are, essentially, God's monsters, incorporating the nature of the divine, the bestial, the horticultural, and even the lapidary.[20] On the one hand, Nebuchadnezzar's transformation is a form of self-realization, as he has essentially become as beastly and as monstrous as he always was: the poem's intense account of the sacking of Jerusalem underscores his brutality in that regard.[21] This illustrates Daniel's larger argument about the decline of empire. On the other hand, however, his transformation offers a poignant vision of human imperfection. As Allen Frantzen puts it, "the abjected and exalted worlds come together."[22] As this passage highlights the conflict between external form and internal condition, it preserves the intimation of human consciousness: "countes he hym" [he counts himself, he considers himself] a cow, a beast. Paradoxically, despite Nebuchadnezzar's monstrous form, he retains the distinctly human power to name the animals.

For Chaucer, Nebuchadnezzar provides a focus for anxieties concerning the potential failures of language and translation. In the *House of Fame*, Nebuchadnezzar appears in the context of Chaucer's request to Venus to give him access to Helicon's well, so that he might have sufficient words to communicate his dream: to translate it, therefore, from visual images into English:

> Now herkeneth, every maner man
> That Englissh understonde kan,
> And listeneth of my dreme to lere,

For now at erste shul ye here
So sely an avisyoun
That Isaye, ne Scipioun
Ne Kynge Nabugodonosor,
Pharoo, Turnus, ne Elcanor,
Ne mette such a dream as this.
Now faire blisfull, O Cipris,
So be my favour at this tyme!
And ye, me to endite and ryme,
Helpeth, that on Parnaso duelle,
Be Elicon, the clere welle.
(lines 509–22)

Calling for the attention of an English audience, Chaucer uses Nebuchadnezzar to address the experience of cultural inbetweenness raised by the genre of the *House of Fame*: the medieval dream vision. Chaucer operates within a genre that emerged out of the medieval tradition of the vernacularized and moralized Ovid, and was popularized by French poets such as Machaut and Froissart: making an act of multiple linguistic as well as cultural translation, a fusion of classical and vernacular, high and low. Chaucer's uncertainty here expresses the sense of being an outsider. Nestled somewhere in the middle of a list of dreamers that ranges from prophets such as Isaiah, to tyrants such as the Pharaoh and the mysterious, Arabic-sounding Elcanor in the *Monk's Tale*, Nebuchadnezzar is part of a tradition of dreamers whose visions already have been glossed and understood, unlike Chaucer's dream, which remains subject to the ambiguities of mediation, translation, and interpretation. In this passage, Chaucer's uncertainty concerning the possibility of genuine communication focuses upon the "sely" or blessed quality of his dream: he brashly suggests that it trumps all others. Yet just a few lines before, he expresses anxiety that his dream is a mere "fantome and illusion" (line 493).[23]

Chaucer associates Nebuchadnezzar with a similar kind of ambiguity in the *Monk's Tale*. Just as Nebuchadnezzar appears in the middle of a list of prophets and tyrants in the *House of Fame*, Chaucer's monk places him in between Hercules and Belshazzar, the hero and the tyrant. He develops this sense of uncertainty with the inexpressibility *topos*. First, the Monk complains that Nebuchadnezzar's "myghty trone, the precious tresor, /The glorious ceptre, and roial magestee . . . with tongue unnethe may discryved be" (*Canterbury Tales* VII.2143–6). He then goes on to explain how, in Babylon, "clerk ne was ther noon,/That wiste to what fyn his dremes sowned" [that could find the meaning of his dreams] (lines 2157–8). For the Monk, Babylon is a land of misunderstandings: Nebuchadnezzar is visited by dreams that he cannot understand, and, on the subject of God, he just does not get it at all: "he wende that God, that sit in magestee/Ne myghte hym nat bireve of his estaat" (lines 2167–8). Ultimately, Nebuchadnezzar's transformation, which turns him into a kind of absurd bird-man ("And lik an egles fetheres wax his heres, / His nayles lyk a briddes clawes were," lines 2175–6), is reversed when God "yaf hym wit." This wit allows the king finally to understand his place in the world and live in fear: "and evere his lyf in feere, / Was he to doon amys or moore trespace" (lines 2178–80).[24]

Nebuchadnezzar's status as a figure for the complex dynamics of cultural translation, and the ambivalence and uncertainties attendant upon the collision between two worlds, is confirmed by the passion with which he is, ultimately, rejected. Following the climactic tearing of the pardon in Langland's *Piers Plowman*, Will the dreamer compares his visions to those of Nebuchadnezzar. He concludes that he has given up on dream interpretation altogether:

Ac I have no sauour in **songewarie** for I se it ofte faille.	**dream interpretation**
Caton and Canonistres coundseillen vs to leue	
To sette sadnesse in Songewarie for *sompnia ne cures*.	**don't pay attention to dreams**
Ac for þe book bible bereþ witnesse	
How Daniel diuined þe dremes of a kyng	
That Nabugodonosor nempneþ þise clerkes –	
Daniel seide, 'sire kyng, þi **sweuene** is to mene	**dream**
That vnkouþe knyȝtes shul come þi kyngdom to cleyne;	
Amonges lower lordes þi lond shal be departed.'	
As Daniel diuined in dede it fel after:	
The kyng lees his lorshipe and lasse men it hadde.	
(VII.154–64)	

With the first "Ac" [but], Will renounces the idea that his crazy dreams can be accorded any meaningful kind of interpretation at all. His frustration emerges out of a dispute concerning translation and interpretation: after the priest has translated the pardon from Latin into English ("For I shal construe ech clause and kenne it thee on English," VII.106), he declares that it is no pardon at all. This declaration prompts Piers to tear up the pardon, rejecting altogether its message that good works produce salvation. Yet with the second "Ac," Will's reference to Nebuchadnezzar retains his biblical association with "songewarie," or the translation and interpretation of dreams, as well as his identification with paradox and irresolution. First Will gives up on dreaming altogether. He is finished with it. And immediately afterward, Will comes up with a crucial counter-example, supplied by Nebuchadnezzar and Daniel, which is that dreams can come true.

Will's rejection of "songewarie" and his subsequent acceptance of Daniel's interpretation of Nebuchadnezzar's dream illustrate the divided, ambivalent nature of the story of Nebuchadnezzar: he is evil yet educable, occupying a place somewhere on the continuum between Isaiah and the Pharaoh (though we do not know quite where). Biblical commentators were not even clear on whether his transformation is meant to be taken as a miracle or a metaphor.[25] Nebuchadnezzar's apocalyptic dream and his movement between registers – linguistic, eschatological, and otherwise – produce a series of acts of interpretation: by Daniel, by himself, and by readers. These acts are echoed and illustrated by his physical transformation, just as, in turn, Nebuchadnezzar's transformation into a beast requires him to make the connection between his physical and his spiritual conditions. His cry is the commentary.

Of course, the word "translation" has both a physical and a linguistic meaning. For example, in response to an ongoing exegetical debate concerning whether Nebuchadnezzar's was a literal or a figurative transformation, Robert Burton's *Anatomy of Melancholy* insists, "Nabuchadnezzar was really translated into a beast."[26] Gower highlights this crossover in meaning in his discussion of alchemy, when an account of the physical translation of metals into gold by famous alchemists segues into an account of famous literary translators such as Jerome: "Out of Caldee, Arabe and Grek / With gret labour the bokes wise / Translateden" (IV.2657–60). As a word for physical transformation, "translation" is often tied to the idea of improvement. John Lydgate uses it to talk about the transmigration of souls: "The sacred forsaide of Crist ascensioune / Was sometyme prefigurid in Helyes [Elijah's]

translacioune." And Chaucer uses it to describe Griselda's radical transformation from ragged pauper to chic madame in *The Clerk's Tale*:
"Unnethe peple hire knew for hire fairness / when she translated was in
swich richesse" (*The Canterbury Tales* IV.384–5).

While the idea of saints and other religious figures being conveyed
rapturously into another sphere gives "translation" an upbeat, revelatory
aspect, it also contains negative, downwardly mobile associations that
place it within the doom-ridden context of an apocalyptic vision. Gower
uses it in his account of the fraudulent election of Pope Boniface:
"And that thei loke wel algate,/That non his oghne astat translate /Of
holi cherche in no degree/Be fraude ne soubtilite" (II.3043–6). Indeed,
medieval literary translations are, more often than not, a movement
down the ladder of prestige: from Latin into French, from French into
English. The ascendant language is transformed into, absorbed by, its
inferior, just as Nebuchadnezzar's human shape and kingly figure shift
down to that of a monster. Hence, Gavin Douglas uses it to describe
his process of translating the *Aeneid*: "ay word by word to reduce ony
thing" (Prol. 410), and Caxton explains the process of translation as: "to
reduce it into Englysshe."[27]

Shakespeare's "Bless thee, Bottom, bless thee. Thou art translated"
(III. i. 113–4) from *A Midsummer Night's Dream*, brings together both the
positive and the negative associations of translation.[28] It creates an ironic
juxtaposition between Bottom's ass's head, which recalls Ovid's tale of
King Midas, who receives ass's ears in punishment for his bad musical
taste, and Bottom's pride of place in Titania's fairy land: a supernatural
space where he is treated like a god, or, at the very least, a gentleman. The
ambivalent value attached to translation has its root in the biblical story
of Babylon, Nebuchadnezzar's hometown. According to the Bible, translation first becomes necessary with the collapse of the Tower of Babel,
the *fons et origo* of linguistic confusion. The Prologue to the *Confessio
Amantis* explains how this tower was built by the proud Nembrot
to memorialize his "emprise," specifically, his territorial conquests:

> And over that thurgh Senne it come
> That Nembrot such emprise nom,
> Whan he the Tour Babel on heihte
> Let make as he that wolde feihte
> Ayein the hihe goddes myht

Wherof divided anon ryht
Was the langage in such entente
Ther wist non what other mente,
So that they myhten noght procede.
(Prol. 1017–24)

The collapse of the Tower of Babel, a kind of linguistic analog to the story of the Fall, gives rise to the division of tongues, creating the necessity to interpret between them. The story brings together a narrative of imperialist expansion (and, specifically, of eastern expansion) and anxieties concerning a more general apocalyptic decline, with the individual dynamic of pride and fall. For Gower, the Towel of Babel, like Nebuchadnezzar's dream of the disintegrating statue, illustrates this argument of inevitable deterioration: the world "appeireth" (1.1198), it is always deteriorating, and "men sayn it is now lassed/An wers plyght than it was tho" (Prol. 56–7). But it is in the context of a world that "appeireth" that Gower finds his *métier* as translator and compiler. Daniel's acts of interpretation take place with a sense of desperation: in captivity, under threat of death, and following the destruction of his city. Similarly, Gower, in the face of what he regards as imminent destruction, translates words and texts as desperately as Nebuchadnezzar brays in the wilderness. Thus, if Babylon brings with it the idea of inevitable change and decline, which is the inexorable movement of *translatio imperii*, it also brings with it the need to interpret between the tongues, making communication, and linguistic translation, impossible yet absolutely essential.

Nebuchadnezzar's apocalyptic dream speaks to conquest and cultural domination, as well as to the importance of interpretation. Gower places heavy emphasis upon the role of Daniel, Nebuchadnezzar's captive, who is forced to learn the Chaldean language and adopt their practices. Having experienced personally the translation of empire and culture, Daniel is the only one who can expound the meaning of the dream, "when that the wiseste of Caldee, / Ne cowthen wite what it mente" (1.666–7). Nebuchadnezzar's metamorphosis resonates with the experience of exile, the wilderness, and hybridity: each reflects, for Gower, England's status as a site of multiple conquests and cultural influences. While the ambivalent value of translation suits the conflicted status of Nebuchadnezzar as, on the one hand, an image of the beginning of the end, and, on the other, of human perfectability, as a linguistic process it raises the question of cultural integrity being dismantled, as well as of the possibility of cultural integrity at all. It speaks to a world of flux and change: as Ovid puts it, "nec perit in tot quicquam, mihi credite, mundo / sed variat faciemque novat" [nothing perishes in the whole universe; it does but vary and renew its form].[29] The paradox of translation is the paradox of transformation – of metamorphosis itself – where identity is not a question of rigid distinctions, binaries, and either/or, but instead exists on a continuum where things are never totally lost, but also never fully themselves.

Thus, when Gower enumerates the minutiae of Nebuchadnezzar's transformation – its effect on preferences for food and drink and taste in clothing, and its uncanny replacement of hands with claws, of skin with fur, etc. – he highlights the metamorphic point of divergence between beast and human. By placing contradictory attributes on the same line, Gower anatomizes the relationship between Nebuchadnezzar's present and past conditions and creates his own, syntactic monster:

> Tho thoghte him colde grases goode
> That whilhome eet the hote spices,
> Thus was he torned fro delices:
> The wyn which he was wont to drinke,
> He tok thanne of the welles brinke
> Or of the pet, or of the slowh,
> It thoughte him thanne good ynowh:
> In stede of chambres well arraied,
> He was thanne of a busshe well paied,
> The harde ground he lay upon,
> For othre pilwes hath he non . . .
> In stede of mete, gras and stres
> In stede of handes longe cles,
> In stede of man a bestes lyke
> He syh; and thanne he gan to syke
> For cloth of golde and for perrie
> Which him was wonte to magnefie.
> When he behield his Cote of heres,
> He wepte, and with fulwoful teres
> Up to the hevene he caste his chiere
> Wepende, and thoghte in this manere;
> Thogh be no wordes myghte winne,

Thus seide his herte, and spake withinne
(1.2976–3003)

The repetition of "in stede" highlights the tension between his external shape and his internal condition: instead of meat, grass; instead of hands, claws. The word "Cote," which applies to the king's fur, but also recalls his golden garments, enacts this collision of human and bestial form at a lexical level. Gower also suggests that Nebuchadnezzar's monstrous hybridity, half-human, half-beast, brings a concomitant decline in taste: the hard ground suits him fine for a bed, the bushes for his home, grass for food. Yet, at the same time, Nebuchadnezzar is horrified not only by how he has changed physically, but also by how low his tastes have fallen. He has become his worst nightmare: a barbarian. And he shapes his beastly form into a human gesture to express his misery:

And thogh hym lacke vois and speche,
He gan up with his feet areche,
And wailende in his bestly stevene
He made his pleignte unto the hevene.
He kneleth in his wise and braieth . . .
(1.3023–27)

This is Christopher Ricks's favorite part of the *Confessio*. He writes: "'braieth is everything that is still unredeemably animal . . . and yet it is within an air's-breath of being human. (No animal can pray.) You must prick up your ears to make quite sure what word you have heard: prayeth? brayeth?"[30] For Ricks, the poetic texture of this passage justifies the high praise that he gives Gower's "verbal felicities."

But it is more than simply a poetic *tour-de-force*. This slippage between human and beast illustrates the conundrum of *translatio imperii et studii* itself. Nebuchadnezzar's bray recalls the old story of the Greek construction of Persian barbarism: according to the Greeks, the Persians were without language because they spoke no Greek; their utterances, which sounded to the Greeks like meaningless babble, *barbarbarbar*, produced the idea of the *barbarian*.[31] The bray also contributes to an ongoing discussion concerning the English vernacular. Thomas Warton recalls this discussion when he writes, in 1774, "If Chaucer had not existed, the compositions of John Gower, the next poet in succession, would alone have been sufficient to rescue the reigns of Edward III and Richard II from the imputation of barbarism."³² As Warton suggests, medieval English culture struggled under the specter of the barbarous: an anxiety which dates from the Roman occupation, when the island was judged an uncivilized wasteland.³³ Britain's mythical Trojan ancestor, Brutus, supplied the island with its name, Britain, as well as with an irresistible pun on "brute" that can be found in texts ranging from Laȝamon's *Brut* to Caxton's description of his native tongue as "brode and rude."³⁴ As Gower himself concedes, "This once used to be called the island of Brut . . . the people of this land are wild."³⁵ Yet Nebuchadnezzar's barbarous babble speaks directly to God, who rewards him for his honesty by returning him to human form: "in a twinklinge of a lok / His mannes forme ayein he tok, / And was reformed to the regne" (lines 3033–5). Indeed, as John of Trevisa contends: "rude words and boystous percen the herte of the herer to the inrest poynte, and planten ther the sentence of thynges" [rude and crude words pierce the heart of the listener to the inmost point, and plant there the true meaning of things].³⁶ The rude barbarian is uniquely capable of getting to the heart of the matter.

We find, therefore, an allegory for Gower's own poetic enterprise in the story of Nebuchadnezzar. When Gower segues from the apocalyptic discourse and political analyses of the Prologue into the personal, amatory woes of Amans in the *Confessio Amantis*, he makes a generic move from prophecy, political treatise, and estates satire to dream vision and *ars amatoria*. With this shift in gears, however, the *Confessio Amantis* reveals itself to be as hybrid, generically, as Nebuchadnezzar is physically. Whereas each of Chaucer's *Canterbury Tales* represents a different generic form (saint's life, romance, fabliau, etc.), Gower defines his literary form as a whole through the interpenetration of genres. The parade of hybrids that begins with Nebuchadnezzar includes the Sirens, like women above the navel, and fishes beneath (1.484ff); and the Gorgons, with their gruesome snake-hair (1.402ff), illustrating the extent to which Gower is creating a kind of literary monster. These hybrid forms also provide an image of Gower's labors as author, translator, and encyclopedist, as he brings together texts from a variety of different worlds – the classical and the vernacular, the ancient and the contemporary – and chooses the English language, which is, itself, a hybrid, as the appropriate medium. They allow Gower to trace the roots of larger political problems that preoccupy him in the Prologue back to the individual:

> If a man were
> Mad altogether of o matiere
> Withouten interrupcioun
> There scholde no corrupcioun
> Engender upon that unite.
> (Prol. 983–7)

His wistful fantasy of bodily integrity is countered with tales of Gorgons, Sirens, and Midas with his ass's ears (v.153ff).

Nebuchadnezzar's metamorphosis thus speaks to the process of literary and cultural translation. A text or a culture is made into something different, yet it retains an aspect of its former self, just as the monstrous Nebuchadnezzar retains a sufficient amount of his human consciousness to be made miserable by his monstrous shape. This dynamic extends into the realm of erotic love, when the Petrarchan tropes of love-longing that describe Amans' pain bleed into the biblical topography of spiritual exile:

> For I was forther fro my love,
> That erthe is frome the heven above,
> And for to speke of any spede,
> So wyste I me none other rede,
> But as it were a man forsake,
> Unto the wood my way gan take.
> (Prol. 105–10)

The lovesick Amans is in both the wood of the dream vision and the wasteland of Nebuchadnezzar's exile: Gower puns on "wood" as a topographical signifier, and as a psychological state of madness (which, in Middle English, is "wod"). As Genius explains, Amans' passion has the potential of transforming him into a beast. The melancholy endemic to lovesickness, for example, transforms the plaintive cries of a lover into the lowing of a bull:

> The ferst of hem Malencolie
> Is cleped, which in compaignie
> An hundred times in an houre
> Wol as an angri beste loure,
> And noman wot the cause why.
> (III.27–31)

Amans admits that his erotic frustrations have this effect: like those who sin seven times daily, "So bere I forth an angri snoute/Ful manye times in a yer" (III.125–9). Even worse, little costumes and capers designed to display himself to his lover make Amans "lich unto the Camelion" (I.2696–8). This motif of physical translation is extended in the series of Ovidian metamorphoses that Genius relates as he anatomizes the sins of love. These include Acteon, turned into a stag (I.136ff); Ceyx and Alcyone, who turn into kingfishers (IV.2928ff); and Calistona, transformed into a bear (VI.6228ff). Ultimately, like Nebuchadnezzar, Amans finds himself on the ground, casting up his eyes piteously to the heavens:

> So hard me was that ilke throwe
> That ofte sythes overthrowe,
> To grounde I was withoute brethe.
> And ever I wisshed after dethe,
> Whan I out of my peyne awoke
> And caste up many a pitous loke,
> Unto the hevene, and sayde thus.
> (I.117–23)

Gower brings home the parallel between Nebuchadnezzar and Amans when Genius interrupts Amans' weeping and wailing: Amans is startled, or, in Middle English, "abrayde" (line 154).

As a spiteful despot cum humble penitent, as a prophetic dreamer, gifted with foreknowledge of the apocalypse, and as a lamenting beast in the wilderness, Nebuchadnezzar is a figure for juxtaposition and the swift shifting of gears. He represents collisions between empires as well as between modes of existence: animal, human, and divine. As he moves between three conditions – the bestial, the human, and the prophetic – he brings a number of different worlds into contact: Babylon and Jerusalem; the city and the wasteland; the lap of luxury and a life of abjection. He also personally experiences the jarring confrontation between the dream life and the waking life; the state of the villain and that of the penitent; the experience of ignorance and of spiritual bliss. The story of Nebuchadnezzar suggests how we can be, simultaneously, one thing *and* the other: a paradigm that defeats the kind of binaries that distinguish East from West, civilized from barbarian, self from Other. Nebuchadnezzar is both/and as opposed to either/or: a tasteless barbarian and an expansionist conqueror; an ignoramus and a visionary; a king and a monster; a human and a beast. He at once embodies the binaries, and transcends the conflict between them.

Gower's handling of Nebuchadnezzar moves between the heinous Other of apocalyptic discourse, and the endlessly mutable, interpretative (and interpreting) self of the medieval dream vision. In this way, it addresses the questions posed by *translatio imperii et studii*: whereas a view of the world through the lens of empire produces a divided vision of the world in which Nebuchadnezzar is a heathen tyrant, the cultural translations that emerge in his story undermine difference, as they proceed in the hope of mutual understanding. This binary speaks to the paradoxes of postcoloniality, which negotiates and renegotiates the dialectics of purity and hybridity. This dichotomy between the self / Other binary and the hybrid continues to motivate postcolonial theory: the true choice, it seems, is not between East and West, colonizer and colonized, and self and Other, but instead between a mentality of unassimilable cultural difference and multicultural diversity and cosmopolitanism. Gower's alienated, ambivalent, yet compelling Nebuchadnezzar offers an alternative to these dichotomies that is monstrously resistant to classification: both. It speaks, as well, to medieval studies, where the jury remains out on whether the "medieval" is fundamentally Other, in which case it is the task of medieval studies to recover its various alterities, or if it is, instead, a source of continuity, however mediated (or mutated), and therefore a vision, and a version, of ourselves. And it speaks to the reception of Gower, as medievalists have failed to reach a consensus on whether he is a dead white male or a tolerant humanist. Gower's ambiguity as translator and author, moreover, confirms Homi Bhabha's thoughts on cultural translation: "that it is the 'inter' – the cutting edge of translation and negotiation, the inbetween – that carries the burden of the meaning of culture."[37] In this respect, then, it is the unassimilable Gower who conveys a most accurate vision of the Middle Ages. At the same time that translation functions as an act of negotiation between languages and cultures, it highlights foreignness, difference, and slippage. However, as F. Scott Fitzgerald famously observed, "the true test of a first-rate mind is to hold two contradictory ideas at the same time."[38] As the *Matrix Reloaded* depicts the destruction of the "Nebuchadnezzar," revealing its futility as a vehicle for redemption, we are reminded that Nebuchadnezzar was also the name of a US army division in Iraq, and that the story of Nebuchadnezzar, king of Babylon, continues to offer a powerful pretext.

NOTES

Douglas Gray, Helen Cooper, and Malcolm Parkes encouraged my interest in Gower long ago: this chapter is dedicated to them, with thanks. Comments and suggestions from Terry Goldie, Seth Lerer, and Simon Palfrey contributed to this project in important ways, as did valuable feedback from James Simpson and the Cambridge Medieval Seminar. A Huntington Library fellowship made completing this chapter a pleasure.

1. See Malcolm Parkes, "The Influence of the Concepts of *Ordinatio* and *Compilatio* on the Development of the Book," in *Scribes, Scripts and Readers: Studies in the Communication, Presentation and Dissemination of Medieval Texts* (London: Hambledon Press, 1991), 25–70.
2. See Hans Robert Jauss, "The Alterity and Modernity of Medieval Literature," *New Literary History* 10 (1979): 181–227. See also the words of the scholar H. A. Taine on Gower: "et quel style! Si long, si plat, si interminable traîné dans les redites." Quoted in John Hurt Fisher, *John Gower: Moral Philosopher and Friend of Chaucer* (New York: New York University Press, 1964), 2.
3. See Paul Strohm, "Form and Social Statement in *Confessio Amantis* and *The Canterbury Tales*," *Studies in the Age of Chaucer* 1 (1979): 17–41; Winthrop Wetherbee, "John Gower," in *The Cambridge History of Medieval English Literature*, ed. David Wallace (Cambridge: Cambridge University Press, 1999), 590; Steven Justice, *Writing and Rebellion: England in 1381* (Berkeley: University of California Press, 1994) and, in particular, his chapter on Gower entitled "Insurgency Remembered," 193–254; Carolyn Dinshaw, "Rivalry, Rape and Manhood: Gower and Chaucer," in *Chaucer and Gower: Difference, Mutuality, Exchange*, ed. R. F. Yeager (Victoria, BC: University of Victoria, 1991), 130–52.
   On Gower's response to the Rising, see David Aers, "'Vox Populi' and the Literature of 1381," in *The Cambridge History of Medieval English Literature*, and Janet Coleman, *English Literature in History, 1350–1400* (New York: Columbia University Press, 1981), 126–56.
4. See John Burrow, "The Portrayal of Amans in *Confessio Amantis*," in *Gower's Confessio Amantis: Responses and Reassessments*, ed. A. J. Minnis (Cambridge: D. S. Brewer, 1983), 5–24 at 9; Alastair Minnis, "Moral Gower and Medieval Literary Theory," in *Gower's Confessio Amantis*, 50–78 at 57; James Simpson, *Sciences and the Self in Medieval Poetry: Alan of Lille's Anticlaudianus and John Gower's Confessio Amantis* (Cambridge: Cambridge University Press, 1995), 134–6.
   Minnis places Gower within a medieval conception of authorship as commentary, critique, and ethical prod, and sees him as assimilating "Ovidian ethics to the

Christian scheme of the Seven Deadly Sins with the concomitant emphasis on the universal nature of moral standards" (57). By contrast, for Simpson, Gower is not so much a coherent assimilator as a poet of "deeply planted structural incongruities" that mean that there is "no reliable authority figure from within the text" (138).

On Gower's debt to the *dits amoreux* see also Nicolette Zeeman, "The Verse of Courtly Love in the Framing Narrative of the *Confessio Amantis*," *Medium Aevum* 60 (1991): 222–40.

5. See *Troilus and Criseyde* v.1856, in *The Riverside Chaucer*, ed. Larry D. Benson (Boston: Houghton Mifflin, 1987), all references to Chaucer are to this edition; Thomas Hoccleve, *Regement of Princes, and Fourteen Poems*, ed. F. J. Furnivall (EETS ES 72, London: Oxford University Press, 1887), 72; James I of Scotland, *The Kingis Quair*, ed. A. Lawson (London: Oxford University Press, 1910), 100; George Ashby, *Active Policy of a Prince*, ed. M. Bateson (EETS ES 76, London: Oxford University Press, 1899), 13.

On Gower's literary reputation, see N. W. Gilroy-Scott, "John Gower's Reputation: Literary Allusions from the Early Fifteenth Century to the Time of *Pericles*," *Yearbook of English Studies* 1 (1971): 30–47, and Derek Pearsall, "The Gower Tradition," in *Gower's Confessio Amantis*, ed. Minnis, 179–98. On Shakespeare's use of Gower as a figure for authority see my "Papa Don't Preach: The Power of Prolixity in *Pericles*," *University of Toronto Quarterly* 71 (2002): 595–622.

6. See James Simpson's discussions of Gower, in *The Oxford English Literary History*, vol. II: *Reform and Cultural Revolution, 1350–1547* (Oxford: Oxford University Press, 2002), and *Sciences and the Self.*

7. On the production of Gower's manuscripts see Malcolm Parkes, "Patterns of Scribal Activity and Revisions of the Text in Early Copies of Works by John Gower," in *New Science Out of Old Books: Studies in Manuscripts and Early Printed Books in Honour of A. I. Doyle*, ed. Richard Beadle and A. J. Piper (Aldershot: Scolar Press, 1995), 81–121.

8. For Simpson, the text is "driven by the iterative force of desire, which seeks refuge from the relentlessness of history by fragmenting it" (*Reform and Cultural Revolution*, 140).

9. On the post-Conquest linguistic situation, see Richard Foster Jones, *The Triumph of the English Language: A Survey of Opinions concerning the Vernacular from the Introduction of Printing to the Restoration* (London: Oxford University Press, 1953); see also Deanne Williams, *The French Fetish from Chaucer to Shakespeare* (Cambridge: Cambridge University Press, 2004).

10. This is at a time when aristocratic and royal readers tended to have only French and Latin works in their collections; see Janet Coleman, *Medieval Readers and Writers* (New York: Columbia University Press, 1981), 18 ff.

11. See Jeffrey Jerome Cohen, "Monster Culture, (Seven Theses)," in *Monster Theory: Reading Culture*, ed. Jeffrey Jerome Cohen (Minneapolis: University of Minnesota Press, 1996), 3–25 at 4, and, for further elaboration, his *Of Giants: Sex, Monsters and the Middle Ages* (Minneapolis: University of Minnesota Press, 1999).

12. The classic study of medieval translation is Rita Copland's *Rhetoric, Hermeneutics, and Translation in the Middle Ages* (Cambridge: Cambridge University Press, 1991). See especially her discussion of Gower's *Confessio Amantis* (202–20) in which she demonstrates the distance of the translations from their original sources.

13. As Slavoj Zizek contends, this simulacrum supplies a metaphor for the insular dream world of the contemporary West, which, decadent, prosperous, and technologically prodigious, aches for, at the same time that it is terrified by, a calamitous interruption. See Slavoj Zizek, *Welcome to the Desert of the Real: 5 Essays on September 11 and Related Dates* (London: Verso, 2002).

14. See *The English Works of John Gower*, ed. G. C. Macaulay (EETS ES 81, 82, London: Oxford University Press, 1900, reprinted 1969). All references to this text will be to this edition.

15. On Islam and Christian apocalypticism, see R. W. Southern, *Western Views of Islam in the Middle Ages* (Cambridge, MA: Harvard University Press, 1962): "It was not difficult for them to find in Islam and its founder the signs of a sinister conspiracy against Christianity. They thought they saw in all its details – and they knew very few – that total negation of Christianity which would mark the contrivances of Antichrist" (24).

16. Emile Mâle provides an image of Nebuchadnezzar with Daniel, Jeremiah, Isaiah, and Moses – from Nôtre Dame la Grande in Poitiers – see *L'Art religieux du XIIe siècle en France* (Paris: Librairie Armand Colin, 1928), 143–4. Penelope Reed Doob suggests that it comes from the iconography of the Ordo Prophetarum. See *Nebuchadnezzar's Children: Conventions of Madness in Middle English Literature* (New Haven: Yale University Press, 1973), 75.

17. See Caroline Walker Bynum, *Metamorphosis and Identity* (New York: Zone Books, 2001).

18. See Cohen, "Monster Culture," 4. Other useful treatments of the monstrous in medieval art and culture include John Block Friedman, *The Monstrous Races in Medieval Art and Thought* (Cambridge, MA: Harvard University Press, 1981) and Jean Céard, *La Nature et les prodiges* (Traveaux d'Humanisme et Renaissance 158, Geneva: Librarie Droz, 1977).

19. *The Poems of the Pearl Manuscript* ed. Malcolm Andrew and Ronald Waldron (London: Edward Arnold, 1978).

20. "Together with the angelic hosts, man possesses the wisdom whereby he knows that God is the supreme creator in the world. Man feels, hears, tastes, sees and walks; hence man possesses a kind of animal nature. Man also grows in height together with the trees; and by virtue of his special quality he possesses existence in the manner of stones." See Gregory the Great, *Moralia in Job*, ed. Marci Adraien (Turnhout: Brepols, 1979).

This is one of Gower's favorite concepts. He uses it in the Prologue of the *Confessio Amantis*:

> For men of Soule resonable
> Is to an Angel resemblable,
> And lich to beste he hath fielinge.

And lich to trees he hath growinge;
The stones ben and so is he:
(Prol. 949–53)

He makes this point also in *Mirour de l'omme* (26,869) and in *Vox Clamantis* (vii.viii.639).

21. See Bynum's discussion of Lycaeon in *Metamorphosis and Identity*, 169.
22. Allen Frantzen, "The Disclosure of Sodomy in *Cleanness*," *PMLA* iii (1996): 451–64 at 461.
23. Note also the ambiguity of the word "sely" that Chaucer uses to describe the dream. It means "blessed" and "good" as well as "happy," and its more modern significance, "hapless" or "silly."
24. This idea of Nebuchadnezzar's educability is picked up in *The Parson's Tale*, as well: "This tree saugh the prophete Daniel in spirit upon the avysioun of the king Nabugodonosor, whan he conseiled hym to do penitence. /Penaunce is the tree of lyf to hem that it receyven, and he that holdeth hym in verray penitence is blessed, after the sentence of Saloman" (x. 126–7).
25. One of the questions that dominates exegetical discussion of Nebuchadnezzar is, of course, whether his is a literal or a figurative metamorphosis. See Bynum's discussion of Gervais of Tilbury, in *Metamorphosis and Identity*, 85.
26. Robert Burton, *Anatomy of Melancholy* (Oxford: Henry Cripps, 1632), i.ii.
27. See *Virgil's Aeneid Translated into Scottish Verse by Gavin Douglas, Bishop of Dunkeld*, ed. David F. C. Coldwell, vol. ii (Edinburgh and London: William Blackwood and Sons, 1957), 14, and Caxton, Prologue to the *Eneydos*, in *Caxton's Own Prose*, ed. N. F. Blake (London: André Deutsch, 1973), 79.
28. William Shakespeare, *A Midsummer Night's Dream*, ed. Peter Holland (Oxford: Oxford University Press, 1994).
29. Ovid, *Metamorphoses*, trans. Frank Justus Miller (The Loeb Classical Library, London: William Heinemann and New York: G. P. Putnam's Sons, 1916), xv.254–5.
30. See Christopher Ricks, "Metamorphosis in Other Words," in *Gower's Confessio Amantis*, ed. Minnis, 24–49 at 31–2.
31. On classical ideas of barbarism see V. Y. Mudimbe, "The Power of the Greek Paradigm," *South Atlantic Quarterly* 92 (1993): 361–85.
32. See Thomas Warton, *The History of English Poetry*, 2 vols. (London: Thomas Tegg, 1824), vol. ii, 305. Leland writes: "Let us then bear with whatever is infelicitous in Gower, and set him forth as the first 'polisher' of the native tongue. For before his time, the English language lay uncultivated and almost entirely unformed. There was no one who could write any work elegantly in the vernacular worthy of a reader" (*Script. Brit.* 1.414, cited in Simpson, *Oxford Literary History*, 25).
33. On the discourse of English barbarism from the Roman perspective, see Mary Floyd-Wilson, *English Ethnicity and Early Modern Drama* (Cambridge: Cambridge University Press, 2003).

34. Cf. "this simple and rude English"; "this rude English"; "this rude and symple English" (among many others) in *Caxton's Own Prose*, ed. Blake, 99, 134.

Gower participates in this tradition in the Latin verse that opens the *Confessio Amantis*:

> Torpor, ebes sensus, scola parva labor minimusque
> Causant quo minimus ipse minora canam:
> Qua tamen Engisti lingua canit Insula Bruti
> Anglica Carmente metra iuvante loquar.
> Ossibus ergo carens que conterit ossa loquelis
> Absit, et interpres stet procul oro malus.

> [Dull wit, slight schooling, labor less
> Make slight the themes I, least of poets, sing,
> Let me, in Hengist's tongue, in Brut's isle sung,
> With Carmen's help tell forth my English verse.
> Far hence the boneless one whose speech grinds bones
> Far hence be he who reads my verses ill.]

trans. Siân Echard and Clare Fanger, *The Latin Verses in Gower's Confessio Amantis: An Annotated Translation* (East Lansing: Colleagues Press, 1991).

35. *Vox Clamantis* in *The Major Latin Works of John Gower* (Seattle: University of Washington Press, 1962), Book I, ch. 20. Gower goes on to observe: "They are fair of form but see, by nature, they have more cruel fierceness than wolves . . . Yet I do not think there is a worthier people under the sun if there were mutual love among them."

36. See *The Idea of the Vernacular: An Anthology of Medieval Literary Theory, 1280–1520*, ed. Jocelyn Wogan-Browne, Nicholas Watson, Andrew Taylor, and Ruth Evans (University Park, PA: Penn State Press, 1999), 327.

37. Homi Bhabha, "The Commitment to Theory," in *The Location of Culture*, 30.

38. F. Scott Fitzgerald, *The Crack-Up* (New York: New Directions, 1945).

7

Turks as Trojans; Trojans as Turks: visual imagery of the Trojan War and the politics of cultural identity in fifteenth-century Europe

James G. Harper

In Italo Calvino's 1972 *Le città invisibili*, Marco Polo describes the imaginary city of Zora to Kublai Khan:

> Questa città che non si cancella dalla mente è come un armatura o reticolo nelle cui caselle ognuno può disporre le cose che vuole ricordare: nomi di uomini illustri, virtú, numeri, classificazioni vegetali e minerali, date di battaglie, costellazioni, parti del discorso . . . per essere meglio ricordata, Zora languí, si disfece e scomparve. La terra l'ha dimenticata.[1]

> [This city which cannot be expunged from the mind is like an armature, a honeycomb into whose cells each of us can place the things he wants to remember: the names of famous men, virtues, numbers, vegetable and mineral classifications, dates of battles, constellations, parts of speech . . . in order to be more easily remembered, Zora has languished, disintegrated, disappeared. The earth has forgotten her.]

Calvino's words might equally apply to Troy, an obliterated city that remains a perennial motif in Western literature and visual arts. Like placing things in a honeycomb, the imagining of Troy is an action that inevitably reflects the identity politics of the cultural moment that remembers and re-creates it. This chapter argues that a collective anxiety in Europe, which developed in the face of the military and the cultural threat of the Ottoman Empire, influenced the way in which Europeans imagined Troy and the Trojans. It concentrates on the visual imagery of the fifteenth century, a period that saw the apex and subsequently the partial suppression of a trend among European artists to dress the ancient Trojans in the costume of contemporary Ottoman Turks, and demonstrates that the trope of *translatio imperii* underpins both the adoption and the rejection of the representation of "Trojan as Turk."

In the late medieval period, as awareness of the Ottoman Empire was just beginning to register in the Western imagination, conventional imagery of the Trojan War showed the Trojans caparisoned as medieval knights. The fifteenth-century trend toward the depiction of Trojans as Turks grew up alongside the persistence of this older chivalric mode. The conventions of High Renaissance art, by contrast, displaced both of these, preferring the use of *all'antica* Roman costume for the Trojans. The shift towards the classical is generally explained as a reflection (and inevitable result) of the reverence for antiquity that is a hallmark of the Renaissance. While this essay does not propose to reject this interpretation entirely, it intends to challenge its hegemony, and enrich it with a second, concurrent reading. Explored within a colonial discourse, the evidence of the visual imagery suggests that the reoccupation of the symbolic territory of the Trojan legend compensated – at least in part – for the ongoing loss of real territory to the expanding Ottoman Empire.

Visual treatments of peoples are inherently less schematic than verbal descriptions.[2] Writers from Homer to Benoît de Sainte-Maure distinguished Greek and Trojan by naming them, rather than by relying on ethnic descriptors or costume details. Homeric references to the specific appearance of the Achaeans and Trojans are, with a few notable exceptions, vague: helmets are "dazzling," shields "glittering," and heroes "broad-shouldered" or "fair to see."[3] Such descriptors require the active compensation of the reader's imagination to produce a visual image.[4] Some of the later accounts give the artist more to work with, but still are hardly prescriptive. In the late antique *De excidio Troiae historia*, which falsely claims the truth-status of an eyewitness account, Dares the Phrygian gives brief descriptions of physique and character:[5]

> Priamum Troianorum regem vultu pulchro magnum voce suavi aquilino corpore . . . Alexandrum candidum longum fortem oculis pulcherrimis capillo molli et flavo ore venusto voce suavi velocem cupidum imperii . . . Aeneam rufum quadratum facundum affabilem fortem cum consilio pium venustum oculis hilaribus et nigris.
>
> [Priam, the king of the Trojans, had a handsome face and a pleasant voice. He was large and swarthy . . . Alexander [i.e. Paris] was fair,

tall, and brave. His eyes were very beautiful, his hair soft and blond, his mouth charming, and his voice pleasant. He was swift, and eager to take command . . . Aeneas was auburn-haired, stocky, eloquent, courteous, prudent, pious, and charming. His eyes were black and twinkling.][6]

Dares gives similar descriptions for the Greeks, without suggesting any patterns of discernible ethnic difference between Greek and Trojan. Each side has its swarthy, its fair, its blond, and its bearded. Medieval versions of the legend were content to follow the patterns of non-differentiated physical description established in the late antique texts. Benoît de Sainte Maure's *Roman de Troie* (*c.* 1160) follows Dares, embellishing somewhat, though in a formulaic fashion. The same may be said for the less poetic *Historia destructionis Troiae* (1287) of Guido delle Colonne. Significantly, these texts do not even assign ethnic or racial alterity to King Memnon, even though this Trojan ally hails from far-off Ethiopia, and the geographic distance of his origins is acknowledged in the epithet Ημαθιωυα [son of the day].[7]

Yet one must assume that the Greeks and their Trojan enemies at the very least dress differently. In Book II of the *Aeneid*, as their city falls around them, Coroebus suggests to a band of his fellow Trojans: "mutemus clipeos Danaumque insignia nobis/aptemus. dolus an virtus, quis in hoste requirat? . . . spoliis se quisque recentibus armat./vadimus immixti Danais haud numine nostro" [let us exchange shields (with some slain Greeks) and don Danaan emblems; whether this is deceit or valor, who would ask in warfare? . . . (and so) each man arms himself in the new-won spoils. We move on, mingling with the Greeks, under (the protection of) gods not our own].[8] Here, the difference in costume is significant enough to make Coroebus' ruse plausible, yet the reader is given no indication of the distinguishing characteristics of that difference. The precise visual appearance of the Trojans remains elusive and thus mutable, a fact borne out in the wide variety of depictions of Trojans in art over the centuries. Filling in the blanks, as it were, visual artists interpreted the differences suggested in the textual narratives and, inevitably, did so in manners that reflected the interests and discourses of their own eras.

For the ancient Romans, easternness was a defining factor in the depiction of the Trojans, and Roman artists often showed them wearing the Phrygian cap, a generic signifier of "the Orient."[9] Though this distinctive, forward-curling headgear originated in ancient Phrygia and not in Troy, the Romans deployed it as an identifying attribute in a range of contexts, giving it to the noble Trojan, to enslaved Dacian captives, and to the god Mithras, whose cult was of Indo-Iranian origin. Early Christian artists within the Roman Empire also gave the Phrygian cap to the Three Magi, whom the Bible identifies simply as "wise men from the East."[10]

The most notable exception to the ancient Roman trend of depicting the Trojans as "Orientals" is the figure of Aeneas. According to the *Aeneid*, this Trojan prince escaped the destruction of his native city and founded a new line in Italy. Though Virgil maintained the tradition that Romulus founded the city of Rome (probably because it was too well-rooted to displace) he embellished a complementary foundation myth by which Aeneas was the progenitor of the Julio-Claudian house and the Roman "race."[11] The *translatio imperii* laid out in the *Aeneid* was a key component of imperial and dynastic legitimization as well as a source of pride for Roman citizens. Anachronistically, ancient Roman artists often depict Aeneas wearing Roman garb, an iconographic choice that signals his privileged status as ancestor and emphasizes continuity between Troy and Rome. As contradictory as Orientalized and Romanized interpretations of the Trojan may seem, however, they were not mutually exclusive, and could even coexist in the same image. For example, a second-century AD marble sarcophagus in the Museo Nazionale in Rome (Fig. 10) shows Aeneas departing for the hunt. A cuirassed (and hence Roman) Aeneas is accompanied by Phrygian-capped (and hence "Oriental") comrades.[12] This mixed band of Trojans simultaneously signifies the closeness and the distance of Troy.

With its dissonant commingling of signs, the Aeneas sarcophagus embodies the tension that faced every Western artist who took on the theme of Troy. In a chronological and geographical sense the Trojans are Other, yet at the same time, as putative ancestors, they are somehow familiar. Every Trojan image exists somewhere on a triangular field that is defined by three considerations: geographical distance, chronological distance, and cultural distance. In the Aeneas sarcophagus, the

10 Anonymous sculptor, marble sarcophagus with Aeneas departing for the hunt, second century AD, Museo Nazionale Romano, Rome.

Phrygian caps serve to express the distance of place, a factual component of the story expressed by way of an ahistorical detail. Yet making Aeneas resemble a contemporary Roman (he bears a striking resemblance to the Antonine emperors) effectively minimizes the cultural distance between the Romans and their legendary ancestors, obviously a matter of importance to the patron. The designers of the sarcophagus gave minimal value to the third consideration, time, sacrificing reference to the chronological distance of the narrative in favor of emphasis on other aspects of the story.

Medieval artists, on the other hand, tended to deprioritize both the chronological distance and the easternness of Troy. Instead, their images, most often illustrations of manuscript chronicles or romances, emphasize cultural closeness by depicting both the Greeks and the Trojans as medieval knights.[13] This parallels the literary treatment of the same themes in contemporary chivalric epics like Benoît de Sainte-Maure's twelfth-century *Roman de Troie*. The reliance of medieval writers on the formulae and *topoi* of the chivalric genre conditioned artists' responses to Trojan subjects, and both literary and artistic products of the period reveal the desire on the part of their consumers to recognize their own ideals in the exploits of Hector and Achilles. Moreover, like the ancient Romans, the late medieval European courtly elites for whom the manuscripts were produced regarded themselves as Trojan descendents. Though its roots were Roman, the idea of constructing mythical Trojan genealogies saw its fullest flowering in the Middle Ages. While the Holy Roman Emperor held the firmest claim to the line of Aeneas, countless other dynasts made parallel claims to Trojan descent and *Trojanitas*.[14] Invoking the legitimacy, nobility, and destiny associated with the *translatio imperii*, propagandists deployed creative etymology to connect the Franks to the Trojan Franco, the Britons to the Trojan Brute, and so forth.[15] Even the Republic of Venice participated in the trend, claiming foundation not by a dynasty but by a band of "Free Trojans."[16]

The appearance of the Ottoman Turks on the European scene during the late Middle Ages must be seen against this efflorescence of "pan-Trojanism." Seeking to explain the rise of a new empire, European thinkers elaborated on an old theory that associated the Turkic peoples of central Asia with the Trojans. The connection goes back to at least the seventh century, when the pseudo-Jerome explained that the Turks were descended from an eponymous Trojan named Torquatus.[17] Having fled their destroyed city, they took refuge in the Asian interior, where they lived in obscurity for millennia, finally reemerging to take back what was rightfully theirs. Although many authors repeated this story, so long as Turkish expansionism remained a distant, Asian phenomenon European interest in the topic was limited to a small and pedantic specialist audience. Interest in the Turks increased exponentially, however, in the fourteenth century. A series of spectacular Ottoman military victories over the Byzantine Empire led to the establishment of the first Ottoman base on European soil in 1354.[18] A century later, in 1453, the Byzantine capital of Constantinople fell to Sultan Mehmet II, and in 1480 the Ottomans briefly occupied Otranto, an important port city in southern Italy.[19] As these events unfolded, medieval indifference to the Ottoman Turks gave way to an increasing curiosity. Fifteenth- and sixteenth-century Europeans gathered ethnographic material, costumes, and images of Turks, and eagerly consumed travel literature that recounted (with varying degrees of accuracy) their origins, habits, and appearance.[20] Turbaned figures appear with increasing frequency in Western art from the fourteenth century, sometimes directly indicating

Turkish identity, and other times signifying a generic easternness, much as the Phrygian cap had for the ancient Roman viewers. The interest in the Islamic world, which has specific roots in the confrontation of the Ottoman Empire and the European polities, coincides with what some scholars identify as "an awareness of race . . . dawning in the European consciousness," and what others term the "invention of race."[21]

Inevitably, as the Ottoman Empire developed into an increasingly direct threat to the western European states, European interest in the Turks became complicated and eventually dominated by anxiety. Attempting to name the Other, and to fit it into an established and familiar order, is a standard way of exercising control in the face of alterity. The explanation that the Turks were descendants of the Trojan prince Torquatus (or, in an alternate version, Turcus) was, therefore, comforting to some European thinkers. The theory had the authority of destiny, and fitted events into a preestablished order. It dignified the new Ottoman victors with an ancient heritage, so that their conquests became less offensive to an age that valued nobility. Finally, it suggested that with the retaking of their historic territory, the descendants of Turcus might settle down and stay put. The legend of the Trojan origins of the Turks drew further support from the critics of the Byzantine Empire, some of whom found the Fall of Constantinople a fitting end for the "decadent Greeks." In contrast to the Byzantines, the Ottoman Turks were seen by many as austere and disciplined.[22] The model of the admirable Turk, distinguished by his military valor, obedience to authority, and perseverance, was later overshadowed by the more negative stereotypes that are a familiar part of the Orientalist discourse. But for a time, a focus on Trojan virtue, destiny, and the prerogatives of Trojan descent rendered the early Ottoman successes less transgressive in the European imagination.

The theory of the Trojan origins of the Turks influenced artists, who began depicting Trojans in Turkish garb in the fourteenth century. The earliest examples appear in Spain, where artists were able to draw on a more direct experience of the Islamic world than was available anywhere else in Western Europe. Operating on the dual assumption that the Turks should share appearance, costume, and architectural style with both their putative ancestors and their Iberian co-religionists, an illuminated manuscript of the *Roman de Troie*, executed in 1350 for King Alfonso XI of Castile, gave colorful *morisco* costumes to the Trojans and Umayyad architectural motifs to Troy.[23] Initially less well equipped to imagine Islam, the rest of Europe caught up as knowledge of the Turks and their appearance spread. Typical of the Italian manifestations of this trend is the appearance of Aeneas in an *Aeneid* manuscript illuminated by the Florentine painter Apollonio di Giovanni around 1460, in a turban, tarboosh, and richly brocaded kaftan.[24] Though it never displaced all other iconographic possibilities, the "Turkified Trojan" was one of the primary iconographic strains in Western European imagery of the Trojan War by the fifteenth century.

The appeal of an Oriental Troy, eclectic but with distinct Turkish attributes, can be seen in Jean de Courcy's illumination of a manuscript of the *Chronique universelle*, dated 1431 (Fig. 11). On one page, the artist dresses a quartet of city founders and select members of their entourages in eclectically exotic eastern costume. For Dido, the founder of Carthage (lower left), the fantastic garb suits the erotically tinged otherness often associated with the African/Phoenician queen.[25] Likewise, the turbans, tarbooshes, and kaftans visible among the entourages of Priam the Younger at the upper right of the image, and Antenor at the upper left, reflect the theory of the Trojan origin of the Turks. Astonishingly, though, de Courcy shows Romulus, the founder of Rome, at the bottom right in a version of the same Turkish-inspired ensemble. Romulus' costume is the most exotic and the richest of all the city founders, signaling that his foundation was the most important and lasting of the four.

Showing Romulus as a Turk requires a four-step exercise in anachronism, free association, and fallacious logic. Step One: Romulus is the descendant of Aeneas, so they should dress alike. Step Two: Aeneas is a cousin of Turcus, so *they* should dress alike. Step Three: Turcus is the ancestor of the Ottoman Turks, so *they* should dress alike. Finally, the conclusion: Romulus should dress in the Turkish manner. For de Courcy, the connection of Trojan and Turk was so strong that it could even be projected onto the imagining of ancient Rome. Turkish dress had become an attribute of *Trojanitas*, and hence, by extension, of *Romanitas*. The wealth, luxury, and sophistication that the costume evoked for contemporary viewers, moreover, would certainly have underscored the message of the power and magnificence of ancient Rome.[26] De Courcy's

11 Jean de Courcy, *Antenor, Priam the Younger, Dido and Romulus as City Founders*, illuminated manuscript page from the *Chronique universelle* (inv. 20124, fol. 154), 1431, Bibliothèque Nationale de France, Paris.

illumination demonstrates that, for the fifteenth-century mind, Turkish associations could have neutral even forcefully positive meaning.

One of the most notable examples of the imagery of an "Orientalized Troy" is a tapestry series designed around 1465 by the Coëtivy Master and produced at Tournai (Figs. 12–14).[27] The series enjoyed great popularity, with sets entering the collections of Charles VIII, king of France, Charles the Bold, duke of Burgundy, Matthias Corvinus, king of Hungary, Henry VII, king of England, James IV, king of Scotland,

Ludovico Sforza, duke of Milan, and Federico da Montefeltro, duke of
Urbino. The Coëtivy Master commingles the familiar with the exotic:
while continuing the medieval mode of showing both Trojan and Greek
in contemporary European dress, he also uses the turban, tarboosh, and
other elements of Turkish garb as signs of Trojanness. Considering the
wide dissemination of the series at the highest levels of court culture,
and its ownership by sovereigns who claimed descent from the House
of Priam, we can assume that the imagery of the cycle was not regarded
by its initial viewers as transgressive.

   The tapestry illustrated here is the eighth of eleven large-scale panels
in the series (Fig. 12). It divides into three distinct narrative scenes, all
based on the *Roman de Troie*.[28] In the battle scene to the left (Fig. 12),
inscriptions identify the chief protagonists: on the Greek side are
Achilles, Telamon, Agamemnon, Antilochus, and Menelaus; while on
the Trojan side are Paris, Troilus, Brunnus, and Philimenis, as well as
the Trojan ally King Memnon of Ethiopia. At the center of the panel
(Fig. 13), set off from the battle scene by the architectural frame of the
Temple of Apollo, is the non-Homeric scene in which Paris, accompanied by an armed band of Trojans, ambushes and kills Achilles. Finally,
the third section of the tapestry bears a battle scene (Fig. 14) in which Ajax
avenges Achilles' death, slaying Paris on a crowded battlefield. Among
the faces in the around are certain figures whom the artist intended us
to recognize as Asian and African.

   In the visual arts of late medieval Western Europe, it was conventional
to use rich, bejeweled costumes and fanciful headdresses, including the
turban, to signify Asia, Asiatic peoples, and "Easternness." Likewise it
was conventional to use black skin to represent Africa and African peoples. The best index of this is the iconography of the Adoration of the
Magi, one of the most commonly depicted Christological scenes in the
late medieval and early Renaissance periods.[29] Although the Bible gives
neither the names, the origins, nor even the number of the Magi, stating
merely that they came "from the east," medieval legends and exegetical texts developed the Three Kings as distinct personalities, assign-
ing each a name and eventually also associating each with one of the
three known continents. To quote the Pseudo-Bede: "Mystice autem
tres Magi, tres partes mundi significant, Asiam, Africam, Europem, sive
humanum genus, quod a tribus filiis Noe seminarium sumpsis" [the

12 The Coëtivy Master, detail of the left section of *The Death of Troilus, Achilles and Paris*, eighth tapestry from an eleven-piece set of the *History of the Trojan War*, designed *c.* 1465; woven in the Netherlands, probably at Tournai, between *c.* 1475 and *c.* 1495, Museo Catedralico, Zamora.

mystery of the three Magi is also that they signify the three parts of the world, Asia, Africa, Europe, which is to say the [entire] human race, which takes its seed from the three sons of Noah].[30] The diversity of the Magi was an invention that emphasized the universal claims of Christianity. By the late medieval period, many artists were choosing to

13 The Coëtivy Master, detail of the central section of *The Death of Troilus, Achilles and Paris*, eighth tapestry from an eleven-piece set of the *History of the Trojan War*, designed *c.* 1465; woven in the Netherlands, probably at Tournai, between *c.* 1475 and *c.* 1495, Museo Catedralico, Zamora.

14 The Coëtivy Master, detail of the right section of *The Death of Troilus, Achilles and Paris*, eighth tapestry from an eleven piece set of the *History of the Trojan War*, designed *c.* 1465; woven in the Netherlands, probably at Tournai, between *c.* 1475 and *c.* 1495, Museo Catedralico, Zamora.

render the message explicit by dressing Gaspar as a European king, giving a turban or "Asiatic" headdress to Melchior, and coloring Balthazar with the dark pigmentation of a sub-Saharan African. Though these conventions do not apply to every single image of the Adoration, they were certainly recognized as standard attributes of the Magi (and of their continents of origin) by the time the Coëtivy Master designed the Tournai tapestries.[31] The iconography of the Three Magi provides a key to understanding fifteenth-century perceptions of "Africanness" and "Asianness," and we can assume that for the audience of these tapestries, costume and pigmentation carried the same specific geographic and ethnic associations that they did in the imagery of the Adoration.

Throughout the panel, the Coëtivy Master distinguishes between heroes and supernumeraries. The heroes are labeled with their names. They receive richer, more elaborate costumes than the anonymous soldiers. While most of the Greek foot soldiers wear round helmets and armor that has a distinctly fifteenth-century look, their champions have fancier, jeweled armor and crested helmets. The Trojan protagonists are dressed much like their Greek counterparts: though they have somewhat more fantastic helmet shapes, it is mainly their names that allow the viewer to distinguish them from the Greeks. Most striking, however, are the Trojan supernumeraries, some of whom actually have more colorful costumes than their commanders. At the lower right of the first battle scene (Fig. 12), a Greek engages in *mano a mano* combat with an enemy who wears a turban and an earring. Though some of the heroes in both armies wear full moustaches and beards, this man's whiskers are shaved between his lip and nose, the resulting half-moustache an attempt to convey Turkish Otherness. In the central scene (Fig. 13), while Paris wears the same armor he wore on the battlefield and the unwitting, unarmed Achilles wears contemporary northern European courtly dress, the nameless artist counts on the supernumeraries to convey the sense of eastern alterity. Of the dozen visible henchmen of Paris, half of them wear distinctly Turkish costume items.[32] The fallen Trojans in the foreground include one in a yellow turban and another wearing a fanciful helmet with a turban wrapped around it. Behind Paris another yellow-turbaned figure looks on. Finally, behind Achilles, a bearded Trojan swordsman wears a bulbous "turban helmet," of a type that historians of armor have identified as distinctly Ottoman.[33] In the third scene of the panel, the heroes again look like contemporary Europeans, while the Trojan supernumeraries receive consciously ethnicizing costume treatments. The crowd of heads gathered beneath the banner that reads "ILLION" is peppered with turbans, turban helmets, and even a high-crowned, brimless red helmet that looks like an armored fez. In the foreground of this battle scene, a bearded, turbaned man ferociously attacks a Greek, grabbing him by the shoulder as if to pull him from his mount.

Most notable of all, though, are the black-faced figures near the right margin of the panel.[34] Each wears a turban, and the one closer to the foreground has a golden earring as well. These figures must represent the Ethiopian allies of Troy, as specified in most versions of the legend.[35] The "eyewitness" account of Dictys of Crete states: "At sequenti die Memnon, Tithoni atque Aurorae filius, ingentibus Indorum atque Aethiopum copiis supervenit, magna fama, quippe in unum multis milibus armatis vario genere spes etiam votaque de se Priami superaverat" [Memnon, the son of Tithonus and Aurora, arrived with a large army of Indians and Ethiopians, a truly remarkable army which consisted of thousands upon thousands of men with various kinds of arms, and surpassed the hopes and prayers even of Priam].[36] Dares the Phrygian also tells us that King Memnon came from Ethiopia, and that he was the only non-Trojan on Hector's five-man command team.[37] Literary sources show a recognition that the Ethiopians were black-skinned: Quintus Smyrnaeus, for example, designates them as "melambroton Aithiopeian", literally "the Ethiopians, those from the land of the dark-skinned men" (11.31–2). Yet in the battle scene to the left of the panel, the Coëtivy Master depicted Memnon as white, following the lead of Benoît and Guido delle Colonne, who say nothing of the Ethiopian king's skin color, but describe him as having "un chief cresp e aubornaz" [curly auburn hair] (Benoît), or "crinibus autem crispatis et flavis" (Guido), neither option suggesting Africanness.[38] As with the Greek and Trojan heroes, the artist has treated the African champion in a way that encourages contemporary Europeans to identify with him. Meanwhile, the job of signaling the otherness of the Ethiopians is given to the nameless soldiers, the military subalterns of this allied commander.

Some scholars try to connect the Tournai tapestries to contemporary crusade rhetoric, using the opposition of East and West to read the Greeks as representative of Europe and the Trojans as surrogates for the Ottoman Empire.[39] Yet through foundation myths and the *topos* of *translatio imperii*, late medieval Europeans were more inclined to identify themselves as Trojans than as Greeks.[40] The operative identity politics are more complex, moreover, than exclusive use of either the East–West model or the ancestor–descendant model allows. By depicting Europeanized protagonists and Orientalized or Africanized supernumeraries, the artist created hybrid national groups that simultaneously convey geographical distance and cultural closeness. In this sense, the Coëtivy Master's treatment of Troy shares much with that of the Aeneas sarcophagus (Fig. 10) which also features a hybrid band of Trojans. This is a different sort of hybridity from that which Homi Bhabha has theorized: in this case, the culture of Troy constructed by the artist is that of the distant past, while the desires that shape it are those of a relatively uniform culture, that of a late medieval courtly elite. The hybrid here is the artistic solution that, however iconographically dissonant, reconciles variant and even opposite currents of meaning. In both the Tournai tapestries and the Aeneas sarcophagus, an artist risks identity confusion to attain multivalence, simultaneously suggesting closeness and distance.

The iconographic license that allowed the depiction of the Trojans (and even the Roman Romulus) as Turks is, however, increasingly restricted during the second half of the fifteenth century. As the Ottomans began to colonize parts of Eastern Europe, a sense of emergency mounted in the Catholic West. Some writers, including the canon regular Timothy of Verona, used the legend of the Trojan origins of the Turks to fan the flames of fear. In an alarmist treatise written in the wake of the Fall of Constantinople, entitled *Ad excitandum omnes principes contra Theucram*, Timothy invokes European foundation myths to suggest that Mehmet the Conqueror has designs on the entire Trojan diaspora, and, having retaken Troy, is on his way to Italy to claim the land where his great-great-uncles Aeneas and Antenor lie buried.[41] On the other hand, orthodox crusade polemicists such as Pope Pius II (r.1458–64) rejected outright any connections between the Turks and the Trojans. Aside from his own statements on the matter, Pius commissioned Niccolo Sagundino to research and write an account of the origins of the Turks, the *De Turcarum origine*.[42] Their refutation of the legend was absolute, and in its place they proposed a Scythian descent for the Turks. Pius II writes in his *La Discritione de l'Asia e Europa*:[43]

> Ut eorum confutetur error qui gentem Troianam Turcas esse affirmant, ac Teucros vocant. Turcae (ut Ethicus philosophus tradit) in Asiatica Scythia ultra Pericheos montes, & Taracuntas insulas, contra Aquilonis uberas sedes patrias habuere.

> [In order to put to silence the error of those who assert that the Turks are the descendants of the Trojans, [I say that] the Turks (as the philosopher of the Ethics lays out) have their place of origin in Asian Scythia, beyond the Pericheos mountains and the Tarcuntine Islands, opposite Aquilonia.]

Countering contemporary accounts of the Turks as admirable, disciplined, and valorous, he continues:

> Gens truculenta & ignominiosa, in cunctis stupris ac lupanaribus fornicaria, comedit quae caeteri abominantur. Iumentorum, luporum, ac vulturum carnes, & quod magis horreas, hominum abortivum.

> [A savage and ignominious people, entirely given over to rape and fornication in brothels, they eat those things that others would abhor: the meat of beasts of burden, of wolves, and of vultures, and, even more horrifyingly, aborted human fetuses.]

Pius goes beyond merely disproving an implausible theory and proposing an alternate one: his visceral description locates the Turks as the revoltingly impious opposites of Virgil's "Pius Aeneas."

On a personal level, Pius must have felt a strong sense of identification with *Trojanitas*. His baptismal name was Aeneas, and as a Renaissance humanist he had steeped himself in the culture of classical antiquity. As ruler of Rome and bearer of the ancient priestly title *pontifex maximus* he was, moreover, the direct heir of Augustus and hence also of Aeneas. But the violence of his invective can hardly be attributed to personal reasons. In fact, an important point of propaganda hung on the matter: Pius was convinced of the necessity of a crusade against the Ottoman Empire, and throughout his pontificate promoted this cause among the European princes. From his point of view, it was urgent that the rise of the Ottoman Empire be framed as a transgression of the proper order of things. The less that the Turks shared with the Europeans, the better: Pius' crusade was not to be a chivalric joust between "Trojan cousins" but rather a clash of order against chaos, good against evil, and civilization against barbarity. The legends of the Trojan War, which accord a noble dignity to both Greeks and Trojans, were ill-suited to the struggle at hand.

Meanwhile, Pius II deployed the mythical Trojan origins of European dynasties to help rally the Christian princes. Publicly praising the duke of Burgundy for his willingness to commit to the crusade, the pope added: "Dicendum esset de nobilissimo familie genere, cuius originem ab Ilio repetunt" [mention should be made of the exalted rank of his family, which traces its origin back to Ilium].[44] However, the unity of purpose that Pius was striving to kindle in the hearts of the Christian rulers never materialized, and the pope's crusade fizzled with his death in 1464. In the century that followed, the seemingly invincible Ottomans enjoyed a steady stream of military victories, taking island after island from the Venetian Empire, colonizing Greece and the Balkans, and even laying siege to the imperial capital of Vienna in 1529. In the increasingly militant, crisis-aware atmosphere of Europe during this period of Ottoman expansionism, there was less and less room for the ambiguity of images that conflated Trojans, the ancestors of Christian Europe, with Turks, the enemies of Christian Europe. Instead, the image of the Turk acquired an increasingly negative load of meaning in a variety of artistic and iconographic contexts. At the turn of the sixteenth century, for instance, Albrecht Dürer linked the figure of the Ottoman Turk with the Antichrist in his *Apocalypse* series, while numerous decorative cycles of the sixteenth century fantasized victory and degraded the enemy by showing chained Turkish prisoners.[45] At the same time, Western polemicists aggressively reclaimed exclusive ownership of *Trojanitas*, and the dignity and destiny associated with it. In such a climate, the trend of representing Trojans in Turkish garb withered. While some artists, such as Lucas Cranach, continued the medieval mode of representing them as contemporary knights, many others responded to events in a more up-to-date, Renaissance way, by depicting the Trojans as ancient Romans.[46]

While the Turkish or "Oriental" references had largely disappeared from Trojan War imagery by 1500, the turbaned Magus, who made his

15 Federico Barocci, *The Flight of Aeneas from Troy*, oil on canvas, 1598 (autograph copy of the 1586–89 original), Villa Borghese, Rome. *Instituto Centrale per il Catologo e la Documentazione, Ministero Beni e Attivita Culturali, Rome.*

appearance in Western art at about the same time as the turbaned Trojan, remained a consistent presence in Renaissance and even baroque images of the Adoration. The difference between the Magi and the Trojans, however, is their relationship to European identity. There was no need to emphasize the cultural closeness of the Magi, but rather the opposite. Corresponding to the three known continents, the distant provenance of the trio and their diverse racial and costume types symbolized the ideal unity of the world's people under the spiritual leadership of Rome. Even as the Ottoman Empire threatened to colonize Europe, the presence of a turbaned Magus kneeling at the manger represented the hope that the Turks could be converted to Christianity.[47]

There was no redeeming propaganda value to the turbaned Trojan, however, and Federico Barocci's *Flight of Aeneas from Troy* exemplifies the new and increasingly dominant trend of depicting Romanized Trojans (Fig. 15). Among the countless examples from the late fifteenth and early sixteenth centuries, Barocci's Aeneas is a climactic example of the type.[48] He appears in the painting as an ancient Roman, clad in armor that reflects the artist's detailed and deliberate study of the archaeological evidence at hand in Rome. Instead of turban and kaftan, he wears a crested helmet, buskins, and a cuirass that are identical to those seen on ancient statues of Roman emperors. The monumental column that stands out against the burning city behind the figures is a clear reference to the commemorative columns of imperial Rome. Both the Column of Marcus Aurelius and the Column of Trajan remained standing in Barocci's time, as they do in our own, as visible connectors of *Roma antica* to *Roma moderna*.[49] The round building next to the column, meanwhile, is a reference to a more recent Roman building, Bramante's 1504 Tempietto.[50] Inasmuch as Bramante intended his design to evoke classical Roman style, the Tempietto may be considered a dual reference, condensing *Roma antica* and *Roma moderna*.

The connections of Troy to Rome, established through costume and setting, emphasize the Trojan heritage of the Romans and the message of *translatio imperii*. The depiction of Trojans in Roman costume is, of course, no less anachronistic than the depiction of Trojans as Turks. Yet Barocci's calculation is the reverse of that made by Jean de Courcy in his manuscript illumination of Romulus founding Rome (compare Figs. 11 and 15). While the early fifteenth-century painter projected his version of *Trojanitas* forward onto a Roman, the late sixteenth-century painter projects *Romanitas* backward, onto a Trojan. Returning to the triangular field imagined in an earlier section of this chapter, Romanizing images such as Barocci's eliminate suggestions of geographic distance, while emphasizing the antiquity of the narrative event. At the same time, since self-identification with Roman antiquity was a hallmark of Renaissance thought, the Romanized Trojan also emphasized a cultural closeness (imagined or real) of Troy to Barocci's audience, the courtly elites of the late sixteenth century. The shift in emphasis from easternness to antiquity parallels the writings of Pius II: both the visual imagery and the polemical treatises represent an aggressive and possessive retaking of Troy for the West.

To summarize, the depiction of Trojans in Turkish garb begins in the fourteenth century, with the dawning European awareness of the Ottoman people, and draws strong impetus from the theories of the Trojan origins of the Turks. Under the vigorous counterattack of anti-Turkish propagandists, the origins theory withered: simultaneously, depictions of the Trojans began to take on a doctrinaire classicism. While this coincided with the increasing authority of antiquity in all areas of Renaissance thought, it is also true that the same period saw a general increase in the realization of the propagandistic potential of art. The result of these combined forces is that by the sixteenth century there were very few depictions of the Trojans as Turks, and images of Trojans as ancient Romans predominated. From its origins in Italy, the new, classicizing iconography spread throughout Europe, so that even such a profoundly unclassical artist as Pieter Schoubroeck (*c.* 1570–1607), a Flemish painter of phantasmagoric fire scenes, dresses his fleeing Trojans in Roman garb.[51]

There are, of course, exceptions to the trends. Giulio Romano's frescoed "Hall of Troy" at the Palazzo Ducale in Mantua, finished in 1538, appears at first to be an orthodox, High Renaissance treatment of the Trojan War narratives, with combatants on both sides dressed in the manner of ancient Romans. However, a close look reveals that Giulio's Trojans are another anachronistically hybrid band, for the artist gives the turban and tarboosh to some of the less conspicuous supernumeraries. Yet the reasons for these inclusions (and, it follows, their meaning) differ from those operative in the Tournai tapestries. The Duke of Mantua, who commissioned the "Hall of Troy," was married to the Byzantine Greek princess Margherita Paleologa, a member of the ruling family that Mehmet the Conqueror had driven from Constantinople. This dynastic connection determined the pro-Greek position that Giulio Romano takes in his frescoes, which are an exception to the general Trojanophile tendencies of the European courts.[52] Blatantly anti-Trojan, the cycle focuses on Paris, the least creditable son of Ilium. When Aeneas appears, he is neither performing heroic deeds nor founding new races, but escaping under Venus' cloak of invisibility: a narrative moment that Bette Talvacchia labels "a vignette of dishonor."[53]

Giulio Romano, fully aware of the theory of the Trojan origin of the Turks, deploys the connection in reverse to cast the Trojans as enemies and to flatter the Grecophile ducal family. By his time the figure of the Turk, demonized by the Renaissance polemicists, had acquired a strongly negative symbolic load, and could no longer stand as a neutral or even positive sign, as it had in the time of de Courcy. Recognizing this, Giulio activates the discredited tradition of the Turks as Trojans to define the Trojans with the negative attributes of the Turks. He thus not only underscores the idea that the Trojans are the enemy, but suggests that they share some of the "depraved" tendencies that were, by then, popularly associated with the Turks. The Greeks in the fresco who fight against and defeat this hybrid force stand, by implication, as its moral opposite.

What are the ramifications of this study for a volume that deals with postcolonial approaches to the Middle Ages? First of all, the cases and trends examined here demonstrate that Europe, which scholars are often inclined to regard exclusively as conqueror and colonizer, actually occupies a much more ambiguous position in the premodern period. While it is true that some aspects of the European curiosity about the Turks fit the traditional models of exoticism or Orientalism, fifteenth- and sixteenth-century Europeans were by no means assured of their dominance of the world. On the contrary, this period was defined by the anxiety of being colonized by a powerful enemy Other.[54] While none could deny Ottoman military prowess, it was imperative that it be given a morally reprehensible frame, and European writers and artists responded to the crisis by depicting the enemy as barbaric, despotic, dangerous, and luxurious. Conversely, and just as defensively, they crafted a morale-boosting myth of Europe's own superiority, informed in part by the virtues of Pius Aeneas and the grand destiny of the *translatio imperii*. Trends in visual imagery allow us to track this process, while an understanding of it allows us to reconstruct the context that shaped the images.

Significantly, the patterns that this chapter tracks are strongest in Italy, the part of Europe that expressed the firmest claims to Trojan descent, that felt most directly threatened by Ottoman expansionism, and that, through the papacy, gave voice to the most unambiguous crusading rhetoric. The trends were present but less universal in France, for instance, where enmity toward the Habsburgs led to frequent French alliances with the Ottoman sultan. Likewise in England and Holland, distance from the battlefronts and eventually the rise of Protestantism softened the sense of common cause with pope and emperor.[55] Rombout van Troyen's 1652 *Siege of Troy*, a relatively rare late example of the depiction of turbaned Trojans, reflects a distance from emergency as much as it does the baroque exoticism of the Rembrandt school.[56] Nevertheless the iconic image of the Fall of Troy, repeated by countless

Western artists from the early sixteenth century forward, from Rome to London, is that of a heroic Aeneas, with his father on his back and his son at his side, dressed in the cuirass armor of classical Roman antiquity. Reviewing the evidence of hundreds of prints, sculptures, canvases, and ceramics from all parts of Western Europe, one could say that Pius II had won: though the Christian armies would never regain control of Constantinople, the Roman propagandists had at least managed to maintain control of an imaginary Troy.

NOTES

1. Italo Calvino, *Le città invisibili*, third edn (Turin: Einaudi, 1972), 13. The translation is from *Invisible Cities*, trans. William Weaver (New York: Harcourt Brace Jovanovich, 1974), 15–16.
2. The formulation of this statement follows the felicitous phrasing of Paul Kaplan, *The Rise of the Black Magus* (Ann Arbor: UMI Research Press, 1985).
3. In *The Iliad*, Hector is described as "κορυθαίολος" (11.816); Homer describes the blinding "αὐγὴ χαλκείη κορύθων ἄπο λαμπομενάων θωρήκων τε νεοσμήκτων σακέων τε φαεινῶν" (XIII.341–2); Menelaeus' "μετάφρενον εὐρύ" (X.29); and Paris as "ἐῖδος ἄριστε" (III.39). See *The Iliad*, trans. A. T. Murray, rev. edn William F. Wyatt (Loeb Classical Library 170–1, Cambridge, MA and London: Harvard University Press, 1999).
4. Exceptions include Homer's celebrated *ekphrasis* on the shield of Achilles, in Book XVIII of *The Iliad*. See Andrew Sprague Becker, *The Shield of Achilles and the Poetics of Ekphrasis* (Lanham, MD: Rowman and Littlefield, 1995).
5. There is some debate about the dating of the *De excidio Troiae historia*. In referring to it and to Dictys Cretensis' *Ephemerii belli Troiani* as "late antique," I follow Marie Tanner, *The Last Descendent of Aeneas: The Hapsburgs and the Mythical Image of the Emperor* (New Haven: Yale University Press, 1993), 53.
6. See Dares Phrygius, *De excidio Troiae historia*, ed. Ferdinand Meister (Stuttgart and Leipzig: B. G. Teubner Verlagsgesellschaft, 1991), XII.10–11; 18–22. For translation see *The Trojan War: The Chronicles of Dictys of Crete and Dares the Phrygian*, trans. R. M. Frazer (Bloomington: Indiana University Press, 1966), 143.
7. Hesiod assigns the epithet *Ημαθίωυα* to Memnon (*Theogonia*, 984–5). By suggesting that Memnon comes from the same direction as the rising sun, he exaggerates the position of Ethiopia, which lies more to the southeast than the east. See Frederick Paley, *The Epics of Hesiod*, second edn (London: Whittaker and Co., 1883), 273.
8. Virgil, *Aeneid* II.389–90. The fuller version of the passage reads: "atque hic successu exsultans animisque Coroebus, / 'o socii, qua prima' inquit 'fortuna salutis / monstrat iter, quaque ostendit se dextra, sequamur:/ mutemus clipeos Danaumque insignia nobis / aptemus. dolus an virtus, quis in hoste requirat? / arma dabunt ipsi.' sic fatus deinde comantem /Androgei galeam clipeique insigne decorum / induitur laterique Argivum accommodat ensem. / hoc Rhipeus, hoc ipse Dymas omnisque

173

iuventus / laeta facit; spoliis se quisque recentibus armat. / vadimus immixti Danais haud numine nostro." [And here, flushed with success and courage, Coroebus cries, 'Comrades, where fortune first points out the road to safety, and where she shows herself auspicious, let us follow. Let us change the shields and don Danaan emblems; whether this is deceit or valor, who would ask in warfare? Our foes themselves shall give us weapons.' So saying, he then puts on the plumed helmet of Androgeos, and the shield with its comely devise, and fits to his side the Argive sword. So does Rhipeus, so Dymas too, and all the youth in delight; each man arms himself in the new-won spoils. We move on, mingling with the Greeks, under gods not our own.] See Virgil, *Aeneid*, trans. H. Rushton Fairclough, rev. edn G. P. Goold (The Loeb Classical Library revised edition, Cambridge, MA and London: Harvard University Press, 1999).

9. Although they were from Asia Minor, the Trojans were not Phrygian. Nevertheless, some ancient authors refer to them as such: see Andrew Erskine, *Troy between Greece and Rome: Local Tradition and Imperial Power* (Oxford: Oxford University Press, 2001), 3.

10. Matthew (2:1–12) is the only one of the four evangelists to mention the Three Magi.

11. The notion of the Trojan origins of certain Roman families existed prior to Augustus' time, and may have had currency as early as the sixth century BC. However, the emperor's vigorous promotion of it as a state myth ensured that it would be most closely associated with his rule. The Julii, the family of Julius Caesar and his adoptive son Augustus, had chosen Aeneas as an ancestor long before the dictator and first emperor were born, basing their claim on the similarity of their family name to that of Iulus, a figure who appears in the legend as, alternately, the son or grandson of Aeneas. The political success of the house of Caesar, therefore, accounts for much of the success of the myth of the Trojan origins of Rome, as they parlayed their family legend into an institutionalized state myth. Moreover, the promotion of the myth, which brought with it the claims to ancient nobility and descent from the Gods, assisted Roman imperialism in the Greek world, where the name of Romulus had little resonance. See Erskine, *Troy between Greece and Rome*, 15–46.

12. The sarcophagus, housed at the Museo Nazionale in Rome (inv. # 168 186) depicts Aeneas departing for the Hunt. See Guntram Koch and Hellmut Sichtermann, *Römische Sarkophage* (Munich: C. H. Beck, 1982), 134 and fig. 139.

13. See Benoît de Sainte-Maure, *Le Roman de Troie en prose, version du Cod. Bodmer 147*, ed. Françoise Vielliard (Series Bibliotheca Bodmeriana, Textes 4, Cologny and Geneva: Fondation Martin Bodmer, 1979).

14. See Tanner, *The Last Descendant of Aeneas*, 11–118.

15. In a particularly ambitious passage of mythmaking, the early fourteenth-century Milanese Dominican Galvaneus Flamma posed the following Trojan founders: Pisius (Pisa), Janus (Genova), Palerius (Palermo), Missinus (Messina), Brundius (Brindisi), Tatentus (Taranto), Capus (Capua), Salernus (Salerno), and a female founder, the eponymous Verona. For a concise summary of foundation myths,

see *Troia: Traum und Wirklichkeit*, ed. Barbara Theune-Grosskopf (Stuttgart: Verlagbüro Wais und Partner, 2001), 190–203.

16. On *translatio imperii*, see, among other sources, the proceedings of the October 2002 conference *The Fall of Troy in the Renaissance Imagination*, ed. Alan Shepherd (Toronto: Center for Renaissance and Reformation Studies, forthcoming). See also Elizabeth A. R. Brown, "The Trojan Origins of the French: The Commencement of a Myth's Demise 1450–1520" in *Studies in Ethnic Identity and National Perspectives in Medieval Europe*, ed. Alfred P. Smyth (New York: St. Martin's Press, 1998), 135–79.

17. See Alexandre Eckhardt, "La légende de l'origine troyenne des Turcs," *Kőrösi Csoma-Archivum* 2 (1967): 422–33, and Robert Schwoebel, *The Shadow of the Crescent: The Renaissance Image of the Turk, 1453–1517* (New York: St. Martin's Press, 1967), 188–9.

18. In 1354, the Ottoman Prince Suleyman established a European base at Gallipoli, from which the Turks led raids and expeditions against southeastern Europe.

19. On the brief Ottoman occupation of Otranto, see Charles Verlinden, "Le présence turque à Otrante (1480–1481) et l'esclavage," *Bulletin de l'Institut Historique Belge de Rome* 53–4 (1983–84): 165–76, and more recently, Kurt W. Treptow, "Albania and the Ottoman Invasion of Italy, 1480–1481," *Studia Albanica* 27 (1990): 81–106. For contemporary Italian responses to it see *Gli umanisti e la guerra otrantina: testi dei secoli XV e XVI*, ed. Lucia Gualdo Rosa, Isabella Nuovo, and Domenico de Filippis (Bari: Edizioni Dedalo, 1982).

20. See Mustafa Soykut, *The Image of the "Turk" in Italy: A History of the "Other" in Early Modern Europe: 1453–1683* (Berlin: K. Schwarz, 2001), 2ff, and Bronwen Wilson, "Reflecting on the Turk in Late Sixteenth-Century Venetian Portrait Books," *Word and Image* 19 (2003): 38–58.

21. See Thomas Hahn, "The Difference the Middle Ages Makes: Color and Race before the Modern World," *Journal of Medieval and Early Modern Studies* 31 (Winter 2001): 1–37.

22. On the European admiration of the Ottomans see Soykut, *The Image of the "Turk" in Italy*, 8.

23. Hugo Buchthal, *Historia Troiana: Studies in the History of Mediaeval Secular Illustration* (London: Warburg Institute, 1971), 15. Among other things, Buchthal points to the use of Islamic-style sitting poses in his discussion of the manuscript Escorial h.i.g, commissioned by King Alfonso XI of Castile and completed in 1350.

24. On Apollonio di Giovanni's *Aeneid* manuscript, Biblioteca Riccardiana, no. 492, see Margaret R. Scherer, *The Legends of Troy in Art and Literature* (New York and London: Phaidon, 1964), 187–8.

25. On the eroticism of Dido, see Marilynn Desmond, *Reading Dido: Gender, Textuality, and the Medieval Aeneid* (Minneapolis: University of Minnesota Press, 1994), 30–3, and *A Woman Scorn'd: Responses to the Dido Myth*, ed. Michael Burden (London: Faber and Faber, 1998).

26. On the European association of Islamic luxury goods with wealth, luxury, and sophistication, see Jardine and Brotton, *Renaissance Art between East and West*,

and Rosamond E. Mack, *Bazaar to Piazza: Islamic Trade and Italian Art 1300–1600* (Berkeley: University of California Press, 2002).

27. See Jean-Paul Asselberghs, "Les tapisseries tournaisiennes de la Guerre de Troie," *Revue Belge d'Archéologie et d'Histoire de l'Art* 39 (1970): 93–183 esp. 115–18. See also Thomas Campbell, *Tapestry in the Renaissance: Art and Magnificence* (New York: Metropolitan Museum of Art, 2002), 55–64.

28. The battle scene itself is actually a conflation of two separate battles (numbered the eighteenth and nineteenth in the medieval romances). See Asselberghs, "Les tapisseries tournaisiennes."

29. The classic study on the racial and geographical associations of the Magi in art is Paul Kaplan, *The Rise of the Black Magus in Western Art*. Kaplan writes: "there are several reasons why an art historical approach to the problem of white attitudes towards blackness is perhaps superior to other methods. The distinctive color and physiognomy of black Africans make them much easier to identify in pictures than in written records. Furthermore, in the period before 1500, visual descriptions of blacks are generally less schematic than verbal ones, and they were accessible to a larger audience. When confronted with the task of delineating physiognomies, painting and sculpture were unquestionably more supple and more adventurous than prose and poetry in this era" (1). This statement suggests why the study of visual arts is less riddled with the ambiguities that vex the study of blackness in literature (a famous example of which is the confusion surrounding Shakespeare's *Othello*). For the "Oriental" treatment of the Magi in late medieval and early Renaissance art, see Franco Cardini, *La Cavalcata d'Oriente: I Magi di Benozzo a Palazzo Medici* (Rome: Tomo Edizioni, 1991), 51ff.

30. See the Pseudo-Bede, *In Matthaei Evangelium exposito*, ed. J. P. Migne, *Patrologia Latina* (Paris, 1844–64), vol. 92, col. 13, as cited in Kaplan, *The Rise of the Black Magus*, 33.

31. For the ubiquity of the black Magus during the later fifteenth century, see Kaplan, *The Rise of the Black Magus*, 2–3.

32. That the henchmen are all Trojans is supported by the narrative sources: for the ambush in the Temple of Apollo, Dares specifies that Hecuba "chose the bravest of the Trojans and stationed them in the temple." See Frazer, *The Trojan War*, 160–1.

33. On the "turban helmet" see David Alexander, "Two Aspects of Islamic Arms and Armor: Part I. Turban Helmets," *Metropolitan Museum of Art Journal* 18 (1984): 97–104. The earliest surviving helmet of this type was made at Bursa during the reign of Sultan Orhan (1326–60).

34. Interestingly, the *petits patrons* (preparatory sketches) for the Tournai panels reveal that the black-skinned figures were added at a late point in the design process.

35. On European perceptions of the blackness of the Ethiopians, see Kaplan, *The Rise of the Black Magus*, 4; 22–34; 48–58. One of the black-skinned figures in the Tournai tapestry holds a golden banner featuring a sword-bearing lion rampant. The same banner appears in the battle scene to the left of the same panel, where it is juxtaposed with the figure of King Memnon. It is tempting, though hardly necessary to the interpretation presented in this chapter, to read the lion as the militant "Lion of the

Tribe of Judah," a symbol deriving from the Book of Revelation that the Ethiopian kings were using at the time of the European Renaissance. For the history of this motif, see Sven Rubenson, *The Lion of the Tribe of Judah: Christian Symbol and/or Imperial Title* (Addis Ababa: Haile Sellassie I University, 1965), 3. Rubenson claims that the association of Ethiopian royalty with the lion "might have been already [operative] in ancient times, but it was in any case a fully developed concept by AD 1520." At different moments, the Ethiopian Lion of Judah has been shown passant and rampant, brandishing alternately a cross and a sword.

36. Dictys Cretensis, *Ephemeridos belli Troiani libri*, ed. Werner Eisenhut (Leipzig: B. G. Teubner, 1958), IV.4. For the English translation see Frazer, *The Trojan War*, 89.

37. See Dares, *De excidio* XVIII, 23, and Frazer, *The Trojan War*, 148. Campbell confuses King Memnon of Ethiopia (who fought on the side of the Trojans) with King Merion, son of Idomeneus (who fought on the side of the Greeks). The source of the confusion is the tapestry workshop's mistranscription of the king's name in the Latin and French verses in the upper and lower margins of the panel. These narrate how "Merion" attacks Achilles to recover the body of the fallen Trojan prince Troilus, a deed which the textual sources actually give to Memnon (the idea that Merion should attack his own allies is, of course, nonsensical). The workshop did get the inscription right on Memnon's sword, however, which clearly reads "le Roy Menon."

38. See Benoît de Sainte-Maure, *Le Roman de Troie*, trans. Constans, 287. Guido delle Colonne's description of Memnon specifies: "crinibus autem crispatis et flavis" (VIII.259). See *Historia destructionis Troiae*, ed. Nathaniel Griffin (Cambridge: The Medieval Academy of America, 1936); for the English translation see Guido delle Colonne, *Historia Destructionis Troiae*, trans. Mary Elizabeth Meek (Bloomington: Indiana University Press, 1974), 85.
It is worth noting that Dares the Phrygian, the source for many of the later accounts of Memnon's role in the Trojan War, causes some confusion by introducing Memnon into the narrative as an Ethiopian, and referring to him later as the "Persarum ductor" [leader of the Persians] in his account of Memnon's death. See *De excidio Troiae historia*, 40, and Frazer, *The Trojan War*, who translates the same phrase as "King of the Persians" (160).

39. Scott McKendrick argues convincingly against this line of interpretation, asserting that "there is nothing in them [the tapestries] which is either strictly programmatic in intention or potentially programmatic in one direction." See "The Great History of Troy: A Reassessment of the Development of a Secular Theme in Late Medieval Art," *Journal of the Warburg and Courtauld Institutes* 54 (1991): 43–82 at 80.

40. The fifteenth-century reader received information on the Trojan War from pro-Trojan texts such as Benoît and Guido. On the general neglect of the original Homeric texts in favor of these later works, see McKendrick, "The Great History of Troy," 43. On the general trend of pro-Trojan imagery (to which Giulio Romano's Hall of Troy is a notable exception), see Bette Talvacchia, "Homer, Greek Heroes, and Hellenism in Giulio Romano's Hall of Troy," *Journal of the Warburg and Courtauld Institutes* 51 (1988), 235–42 at 235. The grecophilia in the nineteenth- and

twentieth-century West is a later construction, related to the nineteenth-century liberal desire for identification with the Greeks as inventors of democracy, as well as to Orientalist issues. The modern Orientalist view of a Troy that is Eastern and thus deserving of censure may be summed up by the words of the Victorian author William Mure, who wrote in 1854 of the "oriental licentiousness of Priam's court." See Erskine, *Troy between Greece and Rome*, 8.

41. Schwoebel, *The Shadow of the Crescent*, 30–1.

42. Niccolo Sagundino, *De Turcarum Origine* (Viterbo, 1531).

43. Pius II (Aeneas Silvius Piccolomini), *Aeneae Sylvii Piccolominei Senensis, qui post adeptum pontificatum Pius eius nominis secundus appellatus est, opera quae extant omnia, nunc demum post corruptissimas aeditiones summa diligentia castigata & in unum corpus redacta, quorum elenchum versa pagella indicabit* (Basel: Henric Petrina, 1551; reprinted Frankfurt: Minerva G.M.B.H., 1967), 383. There is an alternate version of the text in the 1544 Vinegia edition. Translation my own.

44. Pius II, *Commentarii* XII.26–7. The Latin transcription used here is taken from *Pii Secundi Pontificis Maximi Commentarii*, ed. Ibolya Bellus and Iván Boronkai (Budapest: Balassi Kiadó, 1993), 592; the English translation used in the text above is taken from Florence Gragg, *Memoirs of a Renaissance Pope: The Commentaries of Pius II* (New York: Capricorn Books, 1962), 348.

45. For the connection between Dürer's Apocalypse and the Ottomans, see the work of Heather Madar, including "The Mark of the Beast: Ottoman Turks in Dürer's Apocalypse" (MA thesis, University of California, Berkeley, 1999), and her essay on Dürer's depictions of the Ottoman Turks, in *The Turk and Islam in the Western Eye (1453–1750)*, ed. James Harper, forthcoming.

46. Cranach's 1508 print of the *Judgment of Paris* is an example of the extension of medieval trends into the High Renaissance period.

47. This notion, which R. Schwoebel (*The Shadow of the Crescent*, 221) describes as "optimism, born of anxiety," finds expression in Pius II's letter proposing conversion to Sultan Mehmet II, for which see M. C. S. Tekindag, "Thought on the Letter sent by Pope Pius II to Sultan Mehmet the Conqueror," in *Lectures Delivered on the 511th Anniversary of the Conquest of Istanbul* (Istanbul: Fen Fakültesi Döner Sermaye Basimevi, 1967), and, more recently, and comprehensively, Luca d' Ascia, *Il Corano e la Tiara: L'Epistolo a Maometto II di Enea Silvio Piccolomini (Papa Pio II)* (Bologna: Edizioni Pendragon, 2001). The idea that one might hope for the conversion of the sultan, and hence for the conversion of the Ottoman people, continued to lodge in the imagination of Europeans long after the time of Pius II. In an episode from the seventeenth century, three English Quakers travel to Istanbul, where they hope to perform, personally, the conversion of the sultan. For this frankly bizarre story, see James Harper, "The Barberini Tapestries of the Life of Urban VIII: Program, Politics and Perfect History for the Post-Exile Era," PhD dissertation, Philadelphia: University of Pennsylvania, 1998, ii–iv.

48. For the two versions of this subject, both autograph works, see Nicholas Turner, *Federico Barocci* (Paris; Vilo, 2000).

49. The connection that the columns establish between *Roma antica* and *Roma moderna* became even stronger after the renovations of Pope Sixtus V (r. 1585–90). He rededicated both monuments, applied new inscriptions and erected statues of St. Peter and St. Paul atop them, in the positions originally occupied by statues of Marcus Aurelius and Trajan.

50. Ronald E. Malmstrom was the first to note these connections in his "Note on the Architectural Setting of Federico Barocci's *Aeneas' Flight from Troy*," *Marsyas* 14 (1968/69): 43–7.

51. For Pieter Schoubroeck's *Burning of Troy*, see Theune-Grosskopf, *Troia: Traum und Wirklichkeit*, 266 (fig. 276). For a somewhat later but parallel example of the mix of a Boschian phantasmagoric landscape and a Romanizing Aeneas group, see *Aeneas Fleeing the Destruction of Troy*, by Daniel van Heil (1604–62), illustrated in *The Burlington Magazine* 122 (1980): xii.

52. Talvacchia, "Homer, Greek Heroes, and Hellenism," 235.

53. Talvacchia, "Homer, Greek Heroes, and Hellenism," 236.

54. Daniel J. Vitkus writes: "what has often been forgotten is that while the Spanish, Portuguese, English and Dutch ships sailed to the New World and beyond . . . the Ottoman Turks were rapidly colonizing European territory. Thus in the sixteenth and seventeenth centuries, the Europeans were both colonizers and colonized." See "Turning Turk in *Othello*: The Conversion and Damnation of the Moor," *Shakespeare Quarterly* 48:2 (1997): 145–76 at 146. For an assessment of the "colonial discourse" of European fear of colonization in the face of the expanding Ottoman Empire, see also Matar, *Turks, Moors and Englishmen*, 8–11 and 19–42.

55. For an account of the relatively friendly relations between England and the Islamic peoples of the Ottoman Empire, the northern African regencies and Morocco, see Matar, *Turks, Moors and Englishmen*, 3–6, 20.

56. The painting is reproduced in *The Burlington Magazine* 131 (June 1989): xxi. By 1652, the Dutch artist's distance from emergency was due to reasons not only geographical and political, but also chronological: collective fear of annihilation at the hands of the Ottomans was already beginning to wane by the mid-seventeenth century, even in the Mediterranean world.

PART III

Memory and nostalgia

8

Analogy in translation: imperial Rome, medieval England, and British India

Ananya Jahanara Kabir

> Caractacus, Cassibelauneas and Boadicea represent the old state of native feeling in India. The "groans of the Britons," entreating the Romans to continue their protection to them, represent the new era which is dawning upon India.
>
> Sir Charles Trevelyan as recorded in Parliamentary Papers, 1843–44

At first glance, this suggestive analogy between sub-Roman Britain and British India, articulated by colonial administrator, writer, and politician Charles Trevelyan during a parliamentary discussion of the benefits of teaching English to Indians, reiterates unhesitatingly one of the most durable tropes of the British Empire: its self-fashioning in the image of imperial Rome.[1] Certainly, the material traces of this trope remain conspicuous in both postimperial and postcolonial spaces. The statue of pioneer Orientalist William Jones in London's St Paul's Cathedral, toga-clad, leaning on two volumes of the "Codes of Menu," finds visible echo in Calcutta's Victoria Memorial gardens, where Jones's contemporary, the pro-Orientalist governor general Warren Hastings still stands, dressed as a Roman senator, flanked by a Brahmin Pandit and a Muslim Maulvi poring over a Sanskrit and a Persian manuscript, respectively.[2] Juxtaposed against these metonymic reminders of their linguistic conquest of India, the Romanized figures of Jones and Hastings powerfully condense and communicate the ideological links between "the command of language and the language of command," between *pax Romana* and *pax Britannica*, and between Roman and British forms of *translatio studii et imperii*.

These links offer an obvious context for Trevelyan's analogy, itself a form of cultural translation. Yet underlying the confident emulation of linguistic and cultural imperialism are deeper anxieties about genealogy and origins that symptomatically interrupt the process of analogy as translation, as suggested by the rather unsettling reference to "the groans of the Britons." Translating the phrase "gemitus Britannorum" which, according to the fifth-century insular historian Gildas, constituted the Britons' self-description in a pleading but disregarded letter to Roman consul Aetius, Trevelyan's "groans of the Britons" interrupts and disrupts the well-known equation of British India and imperial Rome.[3] In inviting us to read against the grain of that equation, it exposes what Homi Bhabha has termed "the forgetting – the signification of a minus in the origin – that constitutes the beginning of the nation's narrative."[4] Medievalists have increasingly demonstrated that, *pace* Bhabha and others, the European nation's master narrative depended not only on othering its colonies but also on "forgetting" its medieval past to bracket off its modernity.[5] I suggest that this "forgetting" constituted maneuvers far more complex than the mere separation of medieval from modern, not least because of the concurrent analogy between Britain and Rome and the perceived relationship between Rome and medieval Europe.

The Middle Ages offered the British in India a way out of the ontological shock generated by the colonial encounter.[6] Constructing the unfamiliar present in terms of a willfully "forgotten" past rendered, in fact, both past and present mutually manageable, creating in the process a spatiotemporal grid for the post-Enlightenment, imperial self. How did imperial Britain as Rome fit into this grid? Did it compete or collaborate with imperial medievalism? In this chapter, I demonstrate that the analogy between the Roman and British empires met the analogy between medieval Britain and colonial India at precisely the moment figured in the "groans of the Britons": the gap between the departure of the Romans from Britain in the early fifth century AD and the arrival of the Angles and Saxons in the sixth. With the help of the trope of *translatio studii et imperii*, this gap sutures two trajectories of conquest into the "beginning of the nation's narrative" even while calling attention to the "minus in the origins": the erasure of Britain's Celtic past from this developing teleology.

NORMAN AND SAXON IN EIGHTEENTH-CENTURY BENGAL

> On 18 June 1822, the Sixteenth, the Queen's Light Dragoons set sail for Calcutta on board the *Marchioness of Ely*. The officers of the regiment discovered a favoured book during the voyage, the recently published *Ivanhoe*, for sometime either in December 1822 or January 1823 an Ivanhoe party was held in their honour at Calcutta. One of the party, a Captain Luard, with all the attainments expected of a young officer of the day, not only played his part in the arrangements, but also completed a sketch of the assembled dignitaries and their ladies, dressed as the leading figures in the novel.[7]

Translated from metropolis to colony, these officers of the Sixteenth can think of no better diversion than dressing up as what Macaulay termed "our Saxon and Norman progenitors."[8] This anecdote dramatically captures the *zeitgeist* of early nineteenth-century Calcutta as well as the subliminal preoccupations of those who arduously crossed the oceans to exert power in the protoimperial domain. It is not surprising that the "desire for origins," undoubtedly sharpened by the voyage out to India, would have found compelling articulation in the idealized intertwining of Saxon and Norman played out in *Ivanhoe*. Less obvious, perhaps, but implicit in the iteration of *Ivanhoe* at Calcutta, are the resonances that Walter Scott's larger theme – the alignment of race and language with questions of power – would have borne for the officers *after* they disembarked in Bengal.

During the years 1770 and 1790, British scholars began producing a series of grammars, dictionaries, classbooks, and translations of various Indian languages. The impetus for this flurry of linguistic activity was access to the revenues of Bengal, which had been opened up by the British victory, under Robert Clive, at the Battle of Plassey in 1757. Plassey had left the British *de facto* rulers of Bengal, from which vantage point they would soon extend their hold over the rest of India. A tactical maneuver adopted by the victors was mastery of the languages they encountered, from the high-status Sanskrit, Arabic, and Persian to the quotidian Bengali and Urdu/Hindustani. A veritable army of linguists emerged to realize this ambition and the Orientalist was born, epitomized by Sir William Jones, founder of the Asiatic Society and the first person to discern structural similarities between Sanskrit,

Persian, Latin, and Greek, but equally embodied in figures like Nathaniel Halhed, author of the first Bengali grammar.[9] The production and consolidation of this linguistic apparatus "began the establishment of discursive formation, defined an epistemological space, created a discourse (Orientalism) and had the effect of converting Indian forms of knowledge into European objects."[10]

It is in this context that we should view the publication, in 1787, of John Borthwick Gilchrist's *Dictionary English and Hindostanee*, one of the spoken languages of Upper India. Seeking to acquaint his readers with the linguistic history of India, Gilchrist, a British army surgeon, offers the following comments on Hindustani in the *Dictionary*'s preface:

> Before the irruptions, and subsequent settlement of the Moosulmans, the Hinduwee, or *Hindooee*, was to India, what the Hindostanee is now to Hindoostan . . . This ancient tongue, under various modifications, is to Hindoostan, exactly what the Saxon was to England, before the Norman Conquest, while the Hindoostanee is, in fact, nothing more than the Hinduwee deluged, after repeated successful invasions by the Moosulmans, with Arabic and Persian, bearing the very same relations almost in every respect to its original basis, that the England which sprang from the parent Saxon, obscured by an influx of French and other continental tongues, now does to its own source also.[11]

This convoluted passage represents one of the earliest British uses of the Middle Ages to illuminate, through analogy, the Indian present. "Exactly," "nothing more than," "the very same," "almost in every respect" – through these qualifiers, Gilchrist collapses differences between medieval England and contemporary India, forcing his evidence into the contours of analogical reasoning. It is a moot point how exact or historically valid these comparisons are; what is important is the use of analogy as a rhetorical tool in order to clear new epistemological space; as well as the marshalling of the medieval past of Britain into this service.

Analogy implies more than the limited and static scope of the metaphor or simile. A metaphoric comparison between the European Middle Ages and India could, for instance, produce a statement such as, "Indian languages are still in the Middle Ages"; its equivalent in simile would be "Indian languages are still like languages in the Middle Ages." Analogical comparisons, in contrast, are comparisons of systems and movements, enabling the user to perform a kind of semiotic calculus. Through his analogy, Gilchrist compares not merely Saxon to Hindu and Norman to Muslim; rather, he captures into the same discursive arena the relationship between Saxon and Norman on the one hand, and that between Hindu and Muslim on the other. By mapping the development of English from "the parent Saxon" on to the development of Hindustani, he offers for both languages and the cultures that nourish them a particular interpretative lens, focused through the common idea of conquest as the dynamo of cultural change.

Hindoostan, the land of the Hindus, or those dwelling beyond the River Indus, is the Persianized form of the Arabic *Al-Hind*. *Hinduwee* and *Hindustani* refer to versions of the language spoken in a swathe across the north of India, grammatically identical but with differing lexical components. *Hinduwee* (or Hindi) derived its vocabulary largely from late reflexes of Sanskrit. Hindustani contained a high proportion of words derived from Persian, Arabic, and also Turkish languages introduced by the waves of Central Asian Muslims who entered India through the Khyber Pass from the twelfth century onwards for a variety of reasons, including plunder, conquest, trade, and peaceful propagation of Islam. Gilchrist chooses to foreground these military and expansionist dimensions of the development of Hindustani by understanding and explicating it through analogy with the Norman Conquest. In a manner uncannily prescient of *Ivanhoe*, Gilchrist's analogy between the "Moosulman invasions" and the Norman Conquest reads the latter in terms of the cultural rupture produced by conquest before linguistic rapprochement can take place.

This emphasis is evident in the backward look towards Anglo-Norman England that Gilchrist asks us to cast:[12]

> Let us make here an awful pause, and look back to England herself in the time of, and long after, William the Conqueror. Have we totally forgotten, that the Persian is to Hindostanee now, what Norman French was to the miserable oppressed English of the dark days, and can we nevertheless continue to encourage, cultivate, and extend among ourselves along with the benevolent British laws and regulations, the acquisition of a foreign, perfectly odious badge of slavery, and subjugation to the utter exclusion almost of both local dialects of the intermediate general Hindostanee language, in which the

unofficial Hindoo himself has gone ages ago, more than halfway to meet the haughty Mussulman, and with him form the bond of union at least, between the conquered and conquerors of India? (xxvii)

Thanks to the analogical structure, the "haughty Mussulman" shades into the Norman, the "miserable oppressed English" into the Hindu, and the foreign language, the "odious badge of slavery and subjugation," becomes equally descriptive of French and Persian. Gilchrist next conjures up an Anglo-Norman court, with magistrates and tribunals who speak only French, native officers and undertrappers bilingual in French and English, and "plain common [ie. English-speaking] people" (xxvii). Even as the Anglo-Gallican French judges are misled by the translation of verbal vernacular detail by the bilingual undertrappers, argues Gilchrist, so might a British judge in India well versed in Persian but ignorant in Hindustani misrepresent an innocent British subject on trial.

This lavishly imagined scene of elite monolingualism is meant to convince Gilchrist's English readers and potential users of his *Dictionary* of the importance of knowing the local vernacular. Nevertheless, it draws its inspiration not so much from the now-familiar "wily Brahmins," bilingual go-betweens who led early Orientalists up the garden path, but rather, from a particular vision of post-Conquest England and its political implications. The adjectives for Norman and Saxon point toward more radical versions of the Norman Yoke theory, that, dormant since the times of the Levellers and the Diggers, had seen a comeback in the last quarter of the eighteenth century: a revival catalyzed by the American and French Revolutions.[13]

NORMANS, MUGHALS, AND ORIENTAL DESPOTS

In 1771, the anonymous *Historical Essay on the English Constitution*, arguing for "reconciliation between Great Britain and her distant provinces," credited Alfred with the institution of the bicameral parliament, trial by jury, and democratic government. "Whatever is of Saxon establishment is truly constitutional, but whatever is Norman is heterogeneous to it, and partakes of a tyrannical spirit."[14] Widely disseminated, the *History* portrayed the formation of the English constitution through a scheme similar to that envisaged by Gilchrist and others for the formation of the English language. Just as the latter was formed from a mixture of Saxon and French, so the English Constitution:

> Consists of a mixture of the old, or first establishment, and the new, or that which took place at (and since) what is commonly called the Conquest, by William the first. These two forms of Government, the first founded upon the principle of liberty and the latter upon the principles of slavery, being so diametrically opposite, it is no wonder that they are continually at war, one with the other. For the first is grounded upon the natural rights of mankind, in the constant and annual exercise of elective power, and the latter, upon the despotick rule of one man. (8)

The phrase "natural rights" would recur a few years later in the extreme radicalism of Thomas Paine, who in his *Common Sense*, sneered at a monarchy that grounded its claims on the illegitimate acts of "a French bastard landing with an armed banditti."[15] Paine's views of pre-Conquest England were no more flattering, but in slightly less extreme positions than his, emphasis on the Norman Yoke would bring with it a default option of sympathy and admiration for the "free Anglo-Saxons."

In the same year as the *Historical Essay* was published, the French historian Augustin Thierry used literary production to argue for the oppression of the Saxons by the Normans and the recovery of the former. The inequality of the Saxons is clear in the relegation of the Saxon tongue to the "poorest and rudest" classes of the nation, which fell "as much beneath the new Anglo-Norman idiom as this was beneath the French, the language of the court."[16] The fifteenth-century resurgence of the English language saw the disappearance of linguistic inequality which "in combination with the inequality of social condition had marked the separation of the families descended from one or the other race" (390). Thierry offers further analogies between the

> state of the Greeks under the Turks and that of the English of Saxon race under the Normans, not only in the material features of the subjugation, but in the peculiar form assumed by the national spirit amidst the sufferings of its oppression, in the moral instincts and superstitious opinions arising out of it, in the manner of hating those whom it would fain, but could not conquer, and of loving those who still struggled on while the mass of their countrymen had bent the neck.[17]

Thierry's reference to the Ottoman Empire reveals how the parallel between the Muslim invaders of India and the Norman invaders of Anglo-Saxon England was constructed. The keystone here is the Oriental despot, who had already emerged as the antithesis of what would ultimately become revolutionary ideals of liberty and equality.[18] While the Islamic faith common to the Mughals and the Ottomans helped to extend the thesis of oriental despotism eastwards to India, a broadly radical championing of the underdog facilitated its westward move to post-Conquest England. The language used of William's rule in late eighteenth-century radical writings – slavery, tyranny, and despotism – is reminiscent of the parallels Gilchrist draws between Norman and Muslim rule. Thus, analogies between medieval England and India, while facilitated by the Enlightenment's disjunction of the medieval past from modernity, were further calibrated by the formula of oppressed indigenous inhabitant and oppressive invader, also derived from a variety of Enlightenment sources.

Gilchrist's analogy illustrates that, by the turn of the century, a two-tier system of comparing India to the Middle Ages had arisen: some aspects of Indian political and cultural economy were compared to the pre-Conquest period of the "free Anglo-Saxons," while others were compared to the post-Conquest period of the feudal and despotic Anglo-Normans. A great many of those writing about India in these terms were Orientalists, emergent comparative linguists before the advent of Indo-European scholarship proper. Others, such as Colonel James Tod, British Resident of Rajasthan, were fired by an analogical imagination even in the writing of travelogues and historical discourse. Tod's enormously popular *Annals and Antiquities of Rajast'han*, published between 1829 and 1832 (and, from its title, obviously written in the wake of Percy, Ossian, and Walter Scott) constructs a veritable Highlands out of Rajasthan, replete with bards, cairns, and minstrelsy.[19] Woven into this tapestry are frequent comparisons of Rajput states to the Saxon Heptarchy, Brahmins to Anglo-Saxon monks, and the Mughal adversaries of the Rajputs to despots and tyrants in the mould of the Normans.

Although lacking the rigor of their one-to-one analogical mapping, Tod shared with Orientalists such as Gilchrist, Halhed, Colebrooke, and even Jones an appreciative view of the stratum of Indian language and culture broadly corresponding to Hindu India. Another shared view was that some languages of India such as Persian, Arabic, and Sanskrit were "classical," on a par with Latin and Greek, while the languages spoken for quotidian purposes in the different regions of India were "vernacular." For the Orientalists and their ilk, Norman and Saxon, like classical and vernacular, served as epistemological categories that could reorder through analogy the thicket of new data that was India. The specific relationship between race, language, and conquest that developed thereby colored equally England's past and India's present, and, in Orientalist writings, served more of a descriptive than a normative purpose.[20]

ROMANITAS AND THE BENGAL RENAISSANCE

By the early nineteenth century, and following East India Company *causes célèbres* such as the trial of Warren Hastings, the linguistic terrain in Bengal was no longer so benign.[21] Questions of moral responsibility of the British toward the Indians, and of the Company's accountability, were at the forefront of debate and praxis. The entwining of liberalism, utilitarianism, and empire meant that such questions merged with those of educating the native populace.[22] However, the appropriate language of instruction became a bone of contention.[23] For the Orientalists, with their quarter-century of linguistic experience, the choice lay between the "classical" Indian languages and the regional "vernaculars." Their opponents, the so-called Anglicists, regarded all Indian languages as transmitters and repositories of superstition, idolatry, and arrested civilization. Fired by a combination of utilitarian conviction and evangelical zeal, they advocated English as the favored medium of instruction, successfully turning Orientalist scholarship and arguments against the Orientalists themselves.

The most (in)famous manifesto of the Anglicist position is Thomas Babington, Lord Macaulay's *Minute on Indian Education* (1835). Addressed to the General Committee on Public Education in India, it demonstrates how the Orientalist analogy between medieval England and contemporary India was thus redeployed:

> Had our ancestors . . . neglected the language of Cicero and Tacitus;
> had they confined their attention to the old dialects of our own island;
> had they printed nothing and taught nothing at the universities but

Chronicles in Anglo-Saxon and Romances in Norman French, would English have been what she now is? What the Greek and Latin were to the contemporaries of More and Ascham, our tongue is to the people of India. The literature of England is now more valuable than that of classical antiquity. I doubt whether the Sanscrit literature be as valuable as that of our Saxon and Norman progenitors.[24]

Like Gilchrist, Macaulay distinguishes between Anglo-Saxon and Norman French, associating each period, furthermore, with a specific genre of literary production: chronicle and romance, respectively. However, he diverges in offering a third phase of linguistic and cultural development to which both Saxon and Norman are contrasted: the Renaissance/Reformation and the revival of the "language of Cicero and Tacitus." Just as England was lifted out of her medieval "Dark Ages" by the light of the classics during the Renaissance, so would English perform the role of the classics in bringing Bengal, and indeed the rest of India, to its own Renaissance. This assumption is enshrined in the very phrase, "Bengal Renaissance," that is still used to describe the period of literary activity following the implementation of the Anglicist position by Governor General of Bengal, William Bentinck.

To the Orientalist analogy between Norman and Muslim, Saxon and Hindu, Macaulay adds a new twist: what the classics were to medieval English, modern English is to (contemporary-yet-medieval) India. The Evangelists had their own version of this argument: in the words of Alexander Duff, Scottish missionary, "the English in India holds the same place now which the Latin and Greek held in Europe at the period of the Reformation."[25] Both versions devolved around the trope of *translatio imperii*, inverting, in fact, its earlier use by Orientalists themselves. As Cohn points out, Nathaniel Halhed had also compared the eighteenth-century English in India to the Romans, but in a diametrically opposite way: "The English Masters of Bengal," wrote Halhed in 1778, needed to add its language to their acquisitions like the Romans, "people of little learning and less taste who applied themselves to the study of Greek once they had conquered them."[26] Discarding this rather inconvenient idea of "uncivilized Rome," the Anglicists foregrounded the transfer of Latin and Greek manuscripts to Europe after the Fall of Constantinople and the consequent Revival of Learning, in the shadow of which hovered Rome's own Hellenizing, centuries before.

Whether Utilitarian or Evangelist, therefore, in Anglicist hands, analogy becomes teleology. Through analogy, the Middle Ages, comprising Anglo-Saxon and post-Conquest England, came to represent a period for the English language comparable to Indian languages. When pressed into the service of teleology, the Middle Ages became but one stage in the overall development of English toward an ideal stage that was both classical and modern. A crucial role in this development is played by the belief that all vernacular languages must possess a "literature of one's own" to move forward in the narrative of civilization. This argument is spelled out by Macaulay's fellow Anglicist, Sir Charles Trevelyan, whose treatise *On the Education of the People of India* (1838), like Macaulay's *Minute*, was addressed to the General Committee on Public Instruction. Envisaging the "formation of a vernacular literature to be the ultimate object to which all our efforts must be directed," Trevelyan opines that "the study of English, and with it the knowledge of the learning of the West, is . . . the first stage whereby India is to be enlightened."[27] This close connection between language, literature, and liberal education engages with the value-laden distinction made between vernacular languages which possess literatures, such as the modern European languages, and vernacular languages which, in Anglicist opinion, do not: namely, those of India.

In order to improve Indian languages, and hence Indians, Trevelyan's treatise advocates a gradual process of cultural change:

> Such refinement is the last stage in the progress of improvement. It is the very luxury of language; and to speak of the delicate sensibility of a Bengalee or Hindusthanee being offended by the introduction of new ideas is to transfer to a poor and unformed tongue the feelings which are connected only with a rich and cultivated one. It will be true enough after their scientific vocabulary is settled, and they have masterpieces of their own; to think of keeping their language pure. When they have a native Milton or Shakespeare, they will not require us to guide them in that respect. (122–3)

From this passage, we may extract the following five stages whereby languages progress from being merely vernacular, to possessing vernacular literatures:

1 a poor and unformed tongue which lacks a scientific vocabulary,
2 a scientifically infused vocabulary leading to progress and improvement,
3 native Milton and Shakespeare providing the first masterpieces,
4 a rich and cultivated language, and finally,
5 the very luxury of language – refinement, purity, and stylistic concerns.

This program of improvement for native vernaculars is essentially a paradigm abstracted from a particular imbrication of the linguistic and political histories of England. Thus, we can read stage 1 as Anglo-Saxon, stage 2 as medieval, and stage 3, marked by Miltons and Shakespeares, as the Renaissance. During the European Renaissance, new exposure to the classics led to an improvement of all the "modern European languages [which] were in a state exceedingly barbarous, devoid of elegance, of vigour, and even of perspicuity . . . Hence rose a demand which the classical languages could not satisfy, and from them sprang the vernacular literature of Europe" (40–1). Trevelyan then quotes verbatim from Macaulay's *Minute* to reinforce the basic argument that "the actual state of Hindu and Mussulman literature, *mutatis mutandis*, very nearly resembles what the literature of Europe was before the time of Galileo, Copernicus and Bacon" (57).

Within this five-stage scheme, the distinctions between Norman and Saxon lost the valency born out of oppositions between "free" Anglo-Saxon and "despotic" post-Conquest England. Radical attitudes toward the Norman Yoke did remain, but they crept out of the post-Conquest box to color the presentation of the entire Middle Ages as feudal and premodern. In Evangelist versions, the feudal Norman Yoke became also the "scholastic Yoke"; as Duff comments, "arguing with the Brahmins, you find yourself transported back to the days of European darkness . . . the fine-spun distinctions and airy subtleties of the schools are vividly brought to your recollection."[28] At the same time, the positive presentation of the Anglo-Saxon period in radical thinking lost its impetus. Norman and Saxon were not altogether collapsed, and continued to be mapped, as had been done by the Orientalists, on to distinctions between Hindu and Muslim periods of Indian history. Nevertheless, the thrust of the analogy had changed, as the following quotation from Trevelyan clarifies:

> The Hindu system of learning contains so much truth as to have raised the nation to its present point of civilization, and to have kept it there for ages without retrograding, and so much error as to have prevented it from making any sensible advance during the same long period . . . The Mohammedan system of learning is many degrees better, and resembles the nations of Europe before the invention of printing, so far does even this fall short of the knowledge with which now Europe is blessed. (83–5)

Gilchrist's analogy between Norman and Muslim, Saxon and Hindu, that sharply contrasts Norman to Saxon, reappears here as two stages of "bad" and "slightly better" corresponding to the pre-Renaissance state of Europe.

However, the medieval European past remains different from the Indian vernacular present in one fundamental respect: that of what Trevelyan terms "sensible advance." In contrast to his vision of the stalled movement of Hindu society and a barely improved Muslim one (similar to John Stuart Mill's reading of India), European, specifically English, culture is presented in terms of evolutions and progressions:

> When Latin was . . . the cradle of science, the English language had not attained that fullness and correctness of which it can now legitimately boast. The style of vernacular writers was not formed; being quaint, pedantic and vitiated; composition was but in its infancy, and there were but few writers . . . Ever since the Reformation, English has been advancing to its present magnificent state of universality, copiousness and beauty. (216)

The trope of *translatio imperii* obviously influenced Trevelyan's concept of "sensible advance," but the relationship worked in both directions. Anglicist emphasis on the classics dovetailed with already established visions of the English as Roman conquerors, and encouraged the conflation of the English-led Bengal Renaissance and the political parallel between imperial Rome and protoimperial Britain. In 1845, an article in *The Calcutta Review* declared, "we are called . . . to imitate the Roman conquerors, who civilized and conquered the nations they subdued . . . to extend a superior light, further than the Roman eagle ever flew."[29] In Parliament, Trevelyan could likewise claim that "we will do more than the Romans," because of the two advantages the British had over the latter: "constitutional freedom" and "Christianity."[30]

It was during the same parliamentary discussion that Trevelyan referred to "the groans of the Britons," the phrase that forms my epigraph. Building on the comparison between imperial Rome and Britain, Trevelyan hypothesizes how the Indians would react were the British to renege on their self-styled responsibility of leading the former into "modernity" through the English language. Yet the Britons who were left groaning in the wake of the Romans, and whose groans prefigured too the arrival of the Angles, Saxons, and Jutes at the invitation of the beleaguered Vortigern, were also precursors and ancestors of the British: an equivalence especially relevant in light of the Act of Union of 1800.[31] In other words, the "groaning Britons" are ciphers for both colonized and colonizer. At this point in Trevelyan's rhetoric, analogy appears stretched almost too tightly over a complex genealogical and territorial map.

When pressed into the service of origins, the parallel between Roman and British empires inevitably though reluctantly returned to the moment when, simultaneously, Roman and Saxon met to create an idealized pair of political and genealogical forebears, and the Celtic past of Britain intruded to expose to scrutiny the "minus in the origins." In 1851, some thirty years after sketching the *Ivanhoe* party in Calcutta, Captain Luard privately published an illustrated history of British military dress.[32] Its first three sketches reconstruct the military dress of Roman, Saxon, and Norman Britain, while the final one accessorizes contemporary British soldiers with an Indian in subservient pose. The linear sequence of the illustrations demands interpretation as the teleological progress of Britain from ex-Roman colony to imperial power, even as the Roman British soldier who precedes the Saxon embodies the protocolonial layers that calque on to the Anglo-Saxon past, putative genealogies of blood with those of power. Most telling are Luard's comments on the Celtic inhabitants of the British Isles: "there is much obscurity about their dress, therefore a drawing is not attempted" (1). The non-image that haunts Luard's visual teleology represents the same aporia inscribed within Charles Trevelyan's reference to "the groans of the Britons."

A similar moment is Isaac Disraeli's insistence that the "Aborigines of this island vanished, but their name is still attached to us."[33] The gap between Briton and Britain that opens up through the "vanishing act" of the so-called aborigines is elided by Disraeli's subsequent declaration that "the Anglo-Saxons became our progenitors, and the Saxon is our mother-tongue." Disraeli's Jewish extraction foregrounds the constructedness of this maneuver, another instance of which is revealed within Alexander Duff's earlier speech urging English on to the Indians. In an extraordinarily poignant moment, the stiff-upper-lip missionary and exemplary colonial Scot suddenly laments his own loss of Gaelic through Anglicization: "On this subject I speak from painful experience, for the Gaelic is my mother tongue."[34] After the Anglicist victory in the battle over language, it became less pressing to emphasise thus Englishness through the English language and at the cost of other affiliations. In its place reappeared the "free Anglo-Saxons" as the rude yet vigorous ancestors of a seafaring power that was living up to the promise of eighteenth-century analogies with the Roman Empire. This reinstatement of the Anglo-Saxons within a motivated genealogy becomes the watermark of Victorian imperialism, but at the cost, perhaps, of the delicate balance of analogies already established between imperial Rome and imperial Britain.

Such discursive short-circuiting characterizes the work of the magisterial Oxford historian of the Constitution and of the Norman Conquest, Edward Freeman. Writing in the latter half of the nineteenth century, Freeman ostensibly exemplifies how a revival of interest in Anglo-Saxon origins sat well with the confidence of full-blown Victorian imperialism. His analysis of English political institutions presents their "most unbroken descent from the primitive Teutonic stock," "grown within the same body" as "the rude traditions and customs of the followers of Hengest and Cerdric"; with "absolutely no gap" between them and "the meeting of the Witan of Wessex which confirmed the laws of Alfred, nor that far earlier meeting which changed Cerdric from an Ealdorman into a king."[35] As for the Norman Conquest, far from "crush[ing] or extinguish[ing] the Old English spirit," it "call[ed] it out in a more definite and antagonistic form," turning the "conquering Normans" into a "band of worthy proselytes" once they had "drunk" the democratic "air of the free island."[36] An ascendant and all-absorbing Anglo-Saxon ancestry becomes the basis of the robust and ever-proliferating Englishness that, for Freeman, most emphatically encompasses also the notion of an imperial Britishness.[37]

Freeman views the Anglo-Saxon past through the lens of the imperial present, in a manner akin to the Anglo-Saxonist John Mitchell Kemble, whose work he knew and cited. For Kemble, even the imperial present is no match for the Saxon Advent:

> Familiar as we are with daring deeds of nautical enterprise, who have seen our flag float over every sea, and flutter in every breeze that sweeps over the surface of the earth, we cannot contemplate without astonishment and admiration, these hardy sailors, swarming on every point, traversing every ocean, sweeping every estuary and bay, and landing on every shore which promised plunder.[38]

Echoing Kemble's sentiment, Freeman describes the Saxon Advent as "a colony sent forth while our race was still in a state of healthy barbarism."[39] As the word "colony" implies, for Freeman more than Kemble, past and present become typologically interwoven as figures of a manifest destiny.[40] In Freeman's account, the takeover of Celtic Britain by the Angles, Saxons, and Jutes mimes English colonial adventures in India, Africa, and the Antipodes: "we won a country for ourselves and grew up, a new people in a new land." An emphasis on racial purity seamlessly dissolves the centuries between old and new fears of miscegenation and contagion: "severed from the old stock, and kept aloof from intermixture with any other, we ceased to be German and we did not become Britons or Romans."

This assertion of a pure Anglo-Saxonism had further implications and motivations. Freeman reads the transformation of Britain into England during the Anglo-Saxon period not as a Teutonicization (as did the Germanophile Kemble), but in keeping with his own predilections, as an overall Englishing.[41] This embryonic "Englishness" erases also the racial affiliations between the Anglo-Saxons and the continental Saxons, the miscellaneous barbarians who were earlier grouped together as "Gothic." Freeman's attitudes toward the "Gothic connection" oscillate between forgetting and remembering. His insistence that "we ceased to be German" is matched elsewhere by his acknowledgment of the "Teuton family" while discussing Rome's unique position of having civilized those barbarian hordes who, in Trevelyan's words, having "triumphed over the arms, yielded to the arts of Rome."[42] By civilizing those "whom she had conquered" as well as "those who conquered her" (i.e. the Goth, who restored Rome's "material fabrics," and the Frank, who restored "her political dominion"), Rome exonerates these "barbaric" cousins of the English, while adding to its own glory.[43]

The emergent discourse of Indo-Europeanism, and the new kinship structures it predicated, also enables (or perhaps forces) Freeman to bring together "the Greek, the Roman and the Teuton, [who] each in his own turn, stands out above the other nations of the Aryan family."[44] Freeman's use of Indo-European kinship structures is wedded to a redeployment of the trope of *translatio imperii*. The Teutons, Greeks, and Romans, "each in his own turn, has reached the highest stage alike of power and civilization that was to be had in his own age, and each has handed on his own store to be further enriched by successors who were at once conquerors and disciples." *Translatio imperii* separates the sheep from the goats in the Aryan brotherhood, in which imperialist and subject are otherwise comfortably juxtaposed. Even Christianity is read in terms of thus passing on the baton of civilization: "if the Aryan world of Europe has learned its arts and its laws from an elder brethren, it is from the Semitic stranger that it has learned its faith . . . but this Semitic faith, banished from its Semitic home, became the badge of Rome's dominion: the sway of Christ and Caesar became words of the same meaning."[45]

Freeman's recurrent theme thus emerges as the competition of different groups, both anterior and posterior to Rome, for Rome's heart and mind. Yet his conception of the pure Anglo-Saxon genealogy of the English has a problematic impact on the political genealogy supported by this theme: if "Britain is a land which had ceased to be Roman before its Teutonic conquerors set foot in it," it follows that the English have in them "no true Roman element."[46] *Translatio imperii* exacerbates rather than smoothes over this awkwardness:

Whatever Roman element we have in us we owe, not to direct transmission from the Elder Empire but to our conversion by Roman missionaries, to our conquest at once by Romance-speaking warriors and
Romance-speaking lawyers, to the spirit of imitation which decked
the lords of the island world with titles borrowed from the Caesars of
the mainland.[47]

The intellectual and political lineage that Freeman so stridently claims
betrays his intense awareness of the genealogical disjuncture between the
British as Anglo-Saxon, and the Roman Empire on which the British
Empire has been modeled. Quickly recovering his poise, he asserts:

> In the three homes of our folk, in the oldest England by the Eider and
> the Slei, in the newer England which we made for ourselves in the
> island world of Britain, in the newest England of all which is spread
> over the islands and continents of the Ocean, we have of a truth had
> a mission, but it has been a mission apart from the mission of our
> kinsfolk in the general course of European history.[48]

The space of analogical disjuncture thus necessitates, indeed nourishes,
the belief in the manifest destiny of Englishness and the imperial mission as both inheritor of and competitor to a transcendent *Romanitas*:
"Wherever men speak of her tongue, wherever men revere her law, wherever men profess the faith which Europe and European colonies have
learned of her, there Rome is still."[49] Yet this belief is striated by the
stubborn trace of the Celt, who "in his own person, speaking his own
tongue, lingers only in corners here and there,"[50] but lingers emphatically enough for Freeman not to be able to ignore.

In this ultimate inability to erase the "mote in the eye," Freeman,
the historian of the high imperial noon, appears not so far from an
Englishman of an earlier stage of the Raj, Reginald Heber, first Anglican
bishop of Calcutta. Better known for his *Narratives of a Journey through
Upper India* (1828) than for his poetry, Heber's fragmentary "Morte
D'Arthur" (1810–20) captures in amber, as it were, a fleeting moment
when a nostalgia for lost pasts overshadows visions of sturdy Saxons
mutating into toga-clad imperators:

> When I rehearse each gorgeous festival,
> And knightly pomp of Arthur's elder day,
> And muse upon these Celtic glories all,

Which, save some remnant of the minstrel's lay,
Are melted in oblivious stream away
(So deadly bit the Saxon's blade and sore)
Perforce I rue such perilous decay,
And, reckless of my race, almost deplore
That ever northern keel deflower'd the Logrian shore.[51]

This glimpse of the colonizer almost deploring the perilous decay exacted by the deadly blade opens up a rare moment when structures of power are undercut by a sudden awareness of cultural loss as a loss to humanity. It is simultaneously a moment when the critique of imperial medievalism lifts out of the very debris of deracination a resilient humanism that paradoxically survives *and* attests not to a clash of civilisations, but to the transformative, redemptive possibilities of translating cultures.

NOTES

1. See Norman Vance, *The Victorians and Ancient Rome* (Oxford: Blackwell, 1997). For the parliamentary discussion in question, see Reports from Committees, *Parliamentary Papers*, Nov. 1852–Aug. 1853, vol. 32, Appendix N (General Report on Public Instruction in the Lower Provinces of the Bengal Presidency for 1843–44), 177.
2. The "Codes of Menu" are the Sanskrit *Manusmriti*, a Vedic treatise on Hindu custom that became the basis for British codification of Hindu law.
3. "Agitio ter consuli gemitus Britannorum. Et post pauca querentes: 'repellunt barbari ad mare, repellit mare ad barbaros; inter haec duo genera funerum aut iugulamur aut mergimur.' Nec pro eis quicquam adiutorii habent." [To Aetius, thrice consul: the groans of the British; further on came this complaint: 'the barbarians push us back to the sea; the sea pushes us back to the barbarians; between these two kinds of death, we are either drowned or slaughtered.' But they got no help in return]. *Gildas: The Ruin of Britain and other Works*, ed. and trans. Michael Winterbottom (London: Phillimore, 1978), 95. On Gildas, see also Howe, "Anglo-Saxon England and the postcolonial void," chapter 2 in this volume.
4. Homi Bhabha, "Dissemi/Nation: Time, Narrative, and the Margins of the Modern Nation," in *Nation and Narration*, ed. Homi Bhabha (New York: Routledge, 1990), 291–322.
5. See Kathleen Biddick, *The Shock of Medievalism* (Durham, NC and London: Duke University Press); *The Postcolonial Middle Ages*, ed. Cohen; Dinshaw, *Getting Medieval*; Davis, "National Writing in the Ninth Century"; and *Postcolonial Moves*, ed. Ingham and Warren.
6. Thomas Metcalf, *The New Cambridge History of India*, vol. III.4: *Ideologies of the Raj* (Cambridge: Cambridge University Press, 1995), 68–80. I am developing this argument in detail in my monograph in progress, *Imperial Medievalism*.

7. Brian Young, "'The Lust of Empire and Religious Hate': Christianity, History and India, 1790–1820," in *History, Religion and Culture: British Intellectual History 1750–1950*, ed. Stefan Collini, Richard Whatmore, and Brian Young (Cambridge: Cambridge University Press, 2000), 91–111 at 91. On the life of Captain Luard, see James D. Lunt, *Scarlet Lancer* (London: R. Hart-Davis, 1964).

8. Thomas Babington Macaulay, *Selected Writings*, ed. John Clive and Thomas Pinney (Chicago and London: University of Chicago Press, 1972), 243. For further discussion of this point, see 191–2 below.

9. See, for Halhed, Rosane Rocher, *Orientalism, Poetry, and the Millennium: The Checkered Life of Nathaniel Brassey Halhed, 1751–1830* (Delhi: Motilal Banarsidass, 1983); for Gilchrist, Bernard Cohn, "The Command of Language and the Language of Command," in *Subaltern Studies IV: Writings on South Asian History and Society*, ed. Ranajit Guha (Delhi: Oxford University Press, 1985): 276–339 at 300–4; for Colebrooke, see Katherine Prior, Lance Brennan, and Robin Haines, "Bad Language: English, Persian and Other Esoteric Tongues in the Dismissal of Sir Edward Colebrooke as Resident of Delhi in 1829," *Modern Asian Studies* 35 (2001): 75–112; and for Jones, *Objects of Enquiry: The Life, Contributions and Influence of Sir William Jones, 1746–1794*, ed. Garland Cannon and Kevin R. Brine (New York and London: New York University Press, 1995).

10. Cohn, "Command," 282. A useful work in this context is *Orientalism and the Postcolonial Predicament: Perspectives on South Asia*, ed. Carol A. Breckenridge and Peter Van der Veer (Philadelphia: University of Pennsylvania Press, 1993).

11. J. B. Gilchrist, *Dictionary English and Hindostanee* (Calcutta: Stuart and Cooper, 1787), xx.

12. On the legacy of the Norman Conquest, see Deanne Williams, *The French Fetish from Chaucer to Shakespeare*.

13. See Christopher Hill, "The Norman Yoke" in *Puritanism and Revolution: Studies in Interpretation of the English Revolution of the Seventeenth Century* (London: Secker and Hudson, 1958), 50–122; Samuel Kliger, *The Goths in England: A Study in Seventeenth and Eighteenth Century Thought* (New York: Octagon Books, 1972); Bernard Bailyn, *The Ideological Origins of the American Revolution* (Cambridge, MA: Harvard University Press, 1971).

14. Anonymous, *An Historical Essay on the English Constitution* (London: Edward and Charles Dilly, 1771), 9–10.

15. Thomas Paine, *Political and Miscellaneous Works*, ed. R. Carlile (London: J. Ridgeway, 1819), 16.

16. Augustin Thierry, *The History of the Conquest of England by the Normans*, trans. William Hazlitt, 2 vols. (London: David Bogue, 1771), vol. II, 366. See also Lionel Gossman, "Augustin Thierry and Liberal Historiography," in his *Between History and Literature* (Cambridge, MA and London: Harvard University Press, 1990), 83–151.

17. Thierry, *History*, vol. I, xxiv–xxv.

18. Franco Venturi, "Oriental Despotism," *Journal of the History of Ideas* 24 (1963): 133–42, and Sylvia Tomaselli, "The Enlightenment Debate on Women," *History Workshop* 20 (1985): 101–24.
19. See Norbert Peabody, "Tod's *Rajast'han* and the Boundaries of Imperial Rule in Eighteenth-Century India," *Modern Asian Studies* 30 (1986): 185–220.
20. Though see Metcalf's somewhat different view: "Yet the Orientalist project as it emerged was clearly fitted to the needs of Europe. Classification always carries with it a presumption of hierarchy" (*Ideologies*, 14).
21. For the trial of Hastings, see Sara Suleri, *The Rhetoric of English India* (Chicago: Chicago University Press, 1992), 49–74. The historical moment is charmingly captured by William Dalrymple, *White Mughals: Love and Betrayal in Eighteenth-Century India* (London: Flamingo, 2003).
22. See Eric Stokes, *The English Utilitarians and India* (Oxford: Oxford University Press, 1959) and Uday Singh Mehta, *Liberalism and Empire: A Study in Nineteenth-Century British Liberal Thought* (Chicago and London: University of Chicago Press, 1999).
23. As most recently analysed by Gauri Vishwanathan, *Masks of Conquest: Literary Study and British Rule in India* (Oxford: Oxford University Press, 1989).
24. See Macaulay, *Selected Writings*, 243.
25. Alexander Duff, *Missionary Addresses, 1835–1839* (Edinburgh: Johnstone and Hunt, 1850), 43.
26. Cohn, "Command," 296.
27. C. E. Trevelyan, *Treatise on the Education of the People of India* (London: Longman et al., 1838), 23.
28. Duff, *Missionary Addresses*, 15.
29. Anonymous, "Of Government Education in Bengal," *Calcutta Review* 5 (1845): 211–63 at 221.
30. *Parliamentary Papers*, Nov. 1852–Aug. 1853, vol. 32, Appendix N, 177.
31. Linda Colley, *Britons: Forging the Nation, 1707–1837* (New Haven, CT and London: Yale University Press, 1992) and Leigh Davis, *Acts of Union: Scotland and the Literary Negotiation of the British Nation, 1707–1803* (Stanford: Stanford University Press, 1999).
32. John Luard, *A History of the Dress of the British Soldier: From the Earliest Period to the Present Time* (London: William Clowes and Sons, 1852, reprinted London: Muller, 1971).
33. Isaac Disraeli, *Amenities of Literature*, 3 vols. (London: Edward Moxson, 1841), vol. I, 27.
34. Duff, *Missionary Addresses*, 78–9.
35. E. A. Freeman, *Comparative Politics: Six Lectures* (London: Macmillan, 1873), 45–7.
36. E. A. Freeman, *Historical Essays* (London: Macmillan, 1871), 51.
37. E. A. Freeman, *The History of the Norman Conquest and Its Results*, 6 vols. (Oxford: Clarendon, 1867–79), vol. I, 604.

38. John Mitchell Kemble, *The Saxons in England*, 2 vols. (London: Longman, 1849), vol. 1, 6.
39. Freeman, *Norman Conquest*, vol. 1, 20–1.
40. See Reginald Horsman, *Race and Manifest Destiny* (Cambridge, MA: Harvard University Press, 1981).
41. For which see Hans Aarsleff, *The Study of Language in England, 1780–1860* (Minneapolis: University of Minnesota Press and London: Athlone, 1983), 193–4 and 201–2, and *John Mitchell Kemble and Jakob Grimm: A Correspondence 1832–1852*, ed. and trans. Raymond A. Wiley (Leiden: Brill, 1971).
42. Trevelyan, *Treatise*, 39.
43. Freeman, *Comparative Politics*, 44.
44. Freeman, *Comparative Politics*, 38. For Indo-Europeanism, Aryanism and Empire, see Sheldon Pollock, "Deep Orientalism: Notes on Sanskrit and Power beyond the Raj," in *Orientalism*, ed. Breckenridge and Van der Veer, 45–75; Thomas R. Trautmann, *Aryans and British India* (Berkeley: University of California Press, 1997); and Tony Ballantyne, *Orientalism and Race: Aryanism in the British Empire* (Basingstoke: Palgrave, 2001).
45. Freeman, *Comparative Politics*, 43.
46. Freeman, *Comparative Politics*, 47–8.
47. Freeman, *Comparative Politics*, 48.
48. Freeman, *Comparative Politics*, 48.
49. Freeman, *Comparative Politics*, 44.
50. Freeman, *Comparative Politics*, 50.
51. Reginald Heber, "Morte D'Arthur," Canto 3.1 in *The Poetical Works of Reginald Heber* (London: John Murray, 1841), 249. For Arthur in the imperial context, see Stephanie Barczewski, *Myth and National Identity in Nineteenth Century Britain: The Legends of King Arthur and Robin Hood* (Oxford: Oxford University Press, 2000), 201–30.

9

"Au commencement était l'île": the colonial
formation of Joseph Bédier's *Chanson de Roland*

Michelle R. Warren

In 1878, in the town of Saint-Denis, an adolescent boy read the *Chanson de Roland*. "Sous un beau manguier" [under a fine mango tree], he learned of Roland's heroic death and Charlemagne's vengeful, divine victory over their Saracen adversaries. This scene calls to mind the several encounters "suz une olive" [under an olive tree] in the *Roland* itself and in its avowed counter-text, *Le Voyage de Charlemagne*, which moves the tree from Saracen Spain to Saint-Denis "desuz un oliuer."[1] Like this olive tree of Saint-Denis, the Saint-Denis of the mango tree is "out of place," for the boy reads the *Roland* far from the Saint-Denis near Paris – on France's colony of La Réunion in the southern Indian Ocean.[2] Joseph Bédier's encounter with France's national epic on this colonial site named after the medieval center of royal and religious authority inaugurates a life-long obsession with the *Roland*, punctuated by his own edition dedicated to his island home. This edition, first published in 1922, is a product and expression of Bédier's most influential theories: it is a single-manuscript edition (the kind Bédier championed against composite editions) and it exemplifies the epic genre (which Bédier argued originated in pilgrimage routes). It also serves as a reply to Léon Gautier's *Roland*, which Bédier first read on the island and which had become a standard reference in French schools since 1880. Just as Saint-Denis doubles Saint-Denis, Bédier's *Roland* purveys continuity across geographical and temporal distances. Indeed, his nearly continuous work on this text is part of a life-long effort to heal the social and psychological ruptures of a colonial identity split between two homelands. His influential reevaluations of French literary history ultimately reveal a double effort of cultural translation – between the eleventh and twentieth centuries, and between France's south-eastern colonial edge and its metropolitan center.

QUANT I SA VA L'AUT' COTÉ LA MER . . .

Bédier's fractured relation to France is sealed in his childhood: born in Paris in 1864, he arrived on La Réunion at age six with his widowed mother.[3] It is easy to imagine the young Joseph conscious of leaving behind his home, and not yet aware that he was also coming home. And this new "home" looked nothing like the one left behind, not least of all because the population was about 40 percent non-white and spoke Creole (a strange sound to Parisian ears).[4] Bédier's arrival in the colony thus marked the beginning of a racial and linguistic consciousness that he brought back to Paris eleven years later as a university student. He thus lost his home once again, while simultaneously returning to a place he would have remembered to some degree. This second rupture shapes a double exile that will condition many of Bédier's ideas about memory, history, and national belonging.

Bédier retraces this double departure (a movement of exile that takes place entirely within France itself) in 1887, having decided to make a final trip "home" before sacrificing himself to the "life of the mind."[5] Anticipating this return to Bourbon (Réunion's first French name and the one preferred by most islanders), Bédier's letters to his friend Joseph Texte express unbridled joy.[6] After the two-month visit, however, his letters manifest a brutal psychological rupture:

> Je regrette ce voyage à Bourbon; je regrette plutôt d'en être revenu; en tout cas, ce sont des épreuves qu'on ne renouvelle pas; pour le moment, je voudrais pouvoir chasser tous ces souvenirs. Heureux encore ceux qui peuvent remonter parmi leurs souvenirs douleureux sans y retrouver quelque humiliation ou quelque honte – J'ai tant laissé à Bourbon! et pour toujours – et pour quoi faire? – Pour quoi faire romaniser, apprendre l'allemand, etc? Qui me délivrera de ce sentiment de l'*à quoi bon*?[7]

> [I regret this trip to Bourbon; I regret rather having come back from there. In any case, these are trials that one doesn't renew. For the moment, I would like to be able to chase away all these memories. Happy are those who can return among their painful memories

without finding some humiliation or some shame – I have left so much on Bourbon! And forever – and to do what? – study Romance (languages), learn German, etc.? Who will deliver me from this feeling of "what's the use?"]

Regretting both going and returning, Bédier decides never to return again and to forget, since the memories make his present life seem useless. In this moment, Bédier's homesickness seems almost to have derailed his career at its inception. And what are the unnamed humiliation and shame? The sense of being an outsider in his own home? Of being betrayed or of having betrayed? In any case, "romaniser" will become the life-long activity that takes the place of forgetting: "Oublier! voilà le désir" [To forget! That is the desire]. He says that he wants to work after four months of idleness, but he is not sure what motivates this desire. Tiring of analyzing himself, he concludes: "Seulement, que de choses, que de choses j'ai laissées à Bourbon! Je suis un sot d'être revenu. Enfin, me voilà. Je travaillerai donc." [It's just that, so many things, so many things I've left on Bourbon! I'm an idiot to have returned. Well, here I am. I will work then]. "Revenu" has now become ambiguous, expressing Bédier's split sense of place: should he have never returned to the island, or to Europe? "Work" takes the place that "forgetting" never can – the painful rupture of migration. Since the only solutions could never have been taken (never to have left Paris, never to have left Bourbon), "work" will be a labor of mourning, a constant activity that betrays a permanent homesickness. Study of the Middle Ages takes the place of the colonial past as Bédier seeks a literally postcolonial life. His nearly continuous work on the topic of origins, and especially on the *Roland*, repeatedly performs the impossibility of forgetting the ruptures of his double migration.

Although Bédier makes no further mention of the past or of Bourbon in his next letter to Texte, he cannot forget his origins; the decision not to return will not cure his homesick desire, or his sense of shame and humiliation: a number of years later, he still refers to his regrets.[8] His desires for belonging will instead find repeated and even obsessive expression in philological sublimation. There is nothing unique about Bédier's split subjectivity in relation to home: indeed, Bédier's compatriot Raphaël Barquissau considered it the general affliction of all Creoles (that is, island-born Europeans).[9] Multiple divided affiliations, moreover, are a commonplace of migration. That a failed effort to leave the colony behind, to become postcolonial in the temporal sense, subtends Bédier's critical efforts, however, prompts some rethinking about the Middle Ages he shaped for twentieth-century medieval studies.

Bédier's sense of belonging to the colony ("j'appartiens . . . à une de ces Frances d'outre mer"[10]) never leaves him. Accepting his election to the Académie Française in 1921, for example, Bédier did not fail to evoke Bourbon:

> Et j'entends aussi de chères voix lointaines: elles me viennent de mon pays, noble entre les nobles terres de douce France, ma petite île Bourbon, sans cesse tendue vers la mère-patrie, et si éprise d'amour d'elle qu'elle enivre tous ses enfants de cet amour.[11]

> [And I hear also cherished distant voices: they come to me from my country, noble among all the noble lands of sweet France, my little island Bourbon, incessantly stretched toward the motherland, and so taken with love for her that she (the island) intoxicates all of her children with this love.]

The voices of Bourbon, reaching Bédier's ears as if by magic, speak the transcendent nature of the colonial community. Claiming the island's superiority in the language of the *Roland* he was about to publish ("douce France"), Bédier turns Bourbon into the source of a patriotic nationalism whose origins he finds in the *Roland* itself.

Bédier affirmed his colonial memory once again in 1937, at the Parisian meeting of the Association Amicale des Réunionnais celebrating the election of his compatriot Admiral Lacaze to the Académie Française. Praising Lacaze's career, Bédier sympathizes with the necessity of traveling far from the island:

> Ainsi firent beaucoup d'autres créoles, car c'est notre destin d'essaimer et de courrir au loin des fortunes diverses; mais des ondes magnétiques traversent les terres et les mers et nous relient les uns aux autres par les liens d'une mystérieuse télépathie.[12]

> [Thus have done many other Creoles, for it is our destiny to swarm and to run afar after various fortunes; but magnetic waves traverse lands and seas and bind us each to the others with the bonds of a mysterious telepathy.]

Bédier describes here an expansionist Creole community that transcends geographical limits. *Essaimer* [to swarm] in particular aligns Bédier's concept of Creolity with what his compatriot Raphaël Barquissau called the "colonie colonisatrice," for young bees swarm specifically to establish new colonies.[13] Whatever their location, these new diasporic communities remain in continuous contact with the mother colony through "magnetic waves." Operating as an occult phenomenon, Creole bonds do not in fact depend on the colonial territory. Thus while Bédier may never return to Bourbon, he is also always already there, carried on the magical waves of Creole telepathy. Bédier's denials of historical and geographic rupture in relation to the colony echo through his historical theories of French ethnic and national continuity in relation to the Middle Ages.

Beyond these and other formal declarations – all occasioned by moments when he was publicly representing "France" – Bédier reportedly met regularly with other colonial migrants to the metropole:

> Joseph Bédier, qui était né à la Réunion, comme tant d'autres écrivains, recevait souvent chez lui des personages au teint plus ou moins foncé, originaires de l'ancienne île de Bourbon. Sa concierge . . . était si bien habituée à ces visites qu'elle indiquait l'étage du maître avant même qu'on le lui demandât.[14]

> [Joseph Bédier, who was born on Réunion, like so many other writers, received often at his home persons of more or less dark color, natives of the former island of Bourbon. His doorkeeper . . . was so well accustomed to these visits that she indicated the floor of the professor before she was even asked.]

Bédier's Creolity is prominent enough that this columnist assumes that he was born on the island. Most important, though, is the glimpse afforded of Bédier's relation to colonial *métissage*. As Françoise Vergès argues, the particular histories of racial mixing on Réunion condition the identity of all of the island's inhabitants.[15] The anecdote suggests an experience of racial complexities lived continuously from the colony to the metropole.

Bédier's sense of colonial identity politics was apparently acute, as his student Gustave Cohen reports:

Il était fier . . . d'être créole, né à la Réunion comme Leconte de Lisle. "Vous ne savez pas . . . ce que c'est d'être un colonial aux cheveux blonds et aux yeux bleus. Cela suppose des centaines d'années de fidélité à des origines normandes ou bretonnes, sans mélange d'aucune sorte."

"Bretonne," disait-il, mais d'après le type physique, je dirais plutôt normande.[16]

[He was proud to be Creole, born on Réunion like Leconte de Lisle. "You don't know . . . what it is to be a colonial with blond hair and blue eyes. It implies hundreds of years of fidelity to Norman or Breton origins, without mixing of any kind."

"Breton," he said, but according to the physical type, I would say rather Norman.]

Like the columnist, Cohen believes Bédier was born on the island – perhaps Bédier even said so himself. In any case, while he can convincingly impart the fact of his Creolity, he maintains that its meaning cannot be fathomed in the metropole. The remark suggests that if Bédier discovered his whiteness when he arrived on Bourbon as a boy, he experienced its loss when he arrived in Paris as a young man. In the colony, the visible traits of Bédier's face told a specific cultural history (of race, status, and politics); in the metropole, they say very little (so little, in fact, that Cohen can easily deny Bédier's actual ethnic claims). Bédier's double migration thus both amplifies the place of race in Creolity, and shows its fragility.

Racial consciousness on Bourbon rested on two rival mythologies: that all whites descend on their mother's side from Africans or Indians, and that whites descend only from Europeans.[17] The former myth is not unfounded: reportedly only six "pure" European white families inhabited the island in 1717; with the continuous arrival of new Europeans (among them a Bédier), successive generations of *métis* grew whiter. One traveler describes a veritable "rainbow family," five generations from an African matriarch to a blond great-great-grandchild.[18] "What it is," then, to be a blond Creole is to refute the myth of universal *métissage*. The principal architects of refutation in Bédier's lifetime were Marius and Ary Leblond – pseudonyms that express an entire ideological program based on Celtic superiority.[19] Bédier has reason to think that in his case, white racial purity is genealogical fact not fiction, since his father wrote down the family history back to 1680. Bédier notes, however, that the maternal line is silent before 1830 – in other words, before Bédier's own grandmother and over one hundred years after the first Bédier arrived.[20] Bédier's racial consciousness is thus formed by experience and textual historiography, and by a selective reading that assumes the continuity of white ancestry.[21] Bédier's homesickness is thus partly a longing to return to a colonial place where continuity was meaningful in ways that can never be known in the metropole: "you don't know," he insists.

Affirming his Creolity on numerous public and private occasions, Bédier reflects on the enduring meaning of personal history. The meaning he finds, however, is in some sense "meaningless," since he considers the past almost exclusively in its relation of continuity with the present. This historiographic principle is concisely illustrated in the citation of Horace that he invokes throughout his life: "Caelum non animum mutant, qui trans mare currunt." [They change their sky, not their soul, those who range across the sea].[22] In several cases, Bédier accompanied the citation with a Creole translation: "Quant i sa va l'aut' coté la mer, l'ciel i çanze, le coer i çanz' pas" [When one goes to the other side of the sea, the sky changes, the heart changes not].[23] Semantically, this citation affirms continuity by identifying the exile's faithful attachment to home – in this case, both France and Bourbon (both are "the other side of the sea"). Philologically, the doubling of Latin with Creole affirms continuity between past and present, Rome and the French colony.

Bédier's letters, speeches, and anecdotal legacy reveal an adult life shaped by homesickness – a desire for national belonging. In this respect, Bédier's psychological and intellectual profile resembles that of more recent intellectual migrants who have theorized the psychic status of "home" in postcolonial contexts (e.g. Edward Said, Salman Rushdie, Homi Bhabha). The structures of identity at work in Bédier's writings differ, however, in that he always lived within France (Bourbon was administered as a colony until 1946, when it became a *département*). In legal terms, Bédier's move to Paris is neither emigration nor immigration; in experiential terms, it is both. Bédier's efforts to suppress these dualities constitute a multiply split relationship to French identity.

Michelle R. Warren

That Bédier would periodically write and speak about Bourbon in personal contexts is not necessarily surprising. That he would do so in the middle of his scholarly work is another matter. Bourbon in fact serves a key explanatory function in three of his most influential publications – *Les Fabliaux* (1893), *Les Légendes épiques* (1908–11), and the *Chanson de Roland* (six distinct editions between 1922 and 1937). Each of these publications contributes substantially to Bédier's elaboration of a "purified" history of a France devoid of foreign influences and virtually unchanged since its origins. While this theory of literary history rests overtly on philological argumentation, it also originates in colonial experiences – experiences that preceded Bédier's philological formation. Bédier's notion of racial purity, in other words, complements his intellectual investments in other kinds of pure forms (textual, poetic, ethnic, national).

Les Fabliaux, Bédier's university thesis and first book-length publication, attacks the idea that the French tales originated in India. In the midst of arguing his conclusion that tales in fact have multiple origins, he finds his most concrete proof literally between France and Bourbon – on board the ship that brought him back from the island in 1887. Off Cap Gardafui (present-day Somalia) – the geographic nexus between east and west, south and north – Bédier reports hearing a *fabliau* told by an aged Mauritian.[24] Although the man had never left his island, he tells the story exactly as Bédier had read it in the scholarly edition of the medieval text. When the man cannot say where he first heard the tale, Bédier concludes that he represents an authentic witness of oral tradition. The tale's shipboard audience, moreover, includes an English businessman from Sydney and a seaman from the Martigues (near Marseilles). Bédier later hears the seaman telling the tale to a group that includes Basques, Corsicans, and an Arab ship-worker. Bédier concludes with ridicule for the collectors of tales who will later puzzle over the propagation of the Arabic, Provençal, Basque, etc. versions of this tale. Bédier's narrative of the scene, however, rests on equally spurious assumptions about transmission. While he identifies its genre and date with precision (thirteenth-century *fabliau*, number 122), its linguistic form is entirely unclear: the Mauritian planter could have spoken

French, Creole, or English. The description of the audience does little to clarify, since Bédier mentions both English and French speakers. The lines of transmission are even less clear when the Provençal seaman repeats the tale to Basques, Corsicans, and an Arab – and Bédier goes on to imagine possible Chinese and Italian listeners. This supposed transmission functions very much like communication in the *Roland*, where Iberian Muslims, Franks, Africans, Saxons, etc. speak to each other without mediators. What's more, Bédier keeps himself conspicuously out of the lineage of transmission by not actually retelling the tale. Invoking the published edition, he refuses to enter a stream of narrative that does in fact flow from the east and from the colony. This anecdote demonstrates the casualness of cross-cultural transmission, which occurs without writing and without major population movements, as well as the remarkable continuity of French culture (stretching from the thirteenth century to the late nineteenth, from the metropole to the distant former colony of Mauritius). Bédier concludes that it suffices for two people knowing the same language to meet for stories to take root in new contexts.[25] He leaves out, however, the colonial background that conditions this particular meeting, comprised of a motley crew of colonial migrants.

The *Fabliaux* is continued by Bédier's four-volume *Légendes épiques*, which also attacks a popular theory of origins – in this case, that epics derive from oral songs composed at the time of distant historical events and preserved through generations until collected in the texts that remain. Instead, they are purely French literary creations.[26] Bédier thus offers a national epic without *métissage* that deeply resonates with his valorization of a family history "without mixing." Bédier's overall thesis depends on a particular conception of memory, or rather, on a disbelief in memory, illustrated by family history. Bédier begins by noting how easy it is to forget the identity of relatives portrayed in household photos.[27] For Bédier, the loss of this kind of personal genealogical memory works the same as the national memory of colonialism:

> Que reste-t-il aujourd'hui dans la tradition orale d'événements bien plus considérables (que la bataille de Roncevaux en 778) de nos guerres d'Algérie, du Mexique ou du Tonkin? Ça et là, un couplet patriotique

que l'on répétera aussi longtemps que l'air n'en sera pas trop démodé, un nom propre, une historiette.[28]

[What remains today in oral tradition of events much more considerable (than the battle of Roncevaux in 778 that inspires the *Roland*), of our wars in Algeria, Mexico, or Tonkin? Here and there a patriotic couplet that will be repeated as long as the tune isn't too out of fashion, a proper name, a vignette.]

Here, Bédier conceives of the events of Charlemagne's lifetime in continuity with the modern nation, and their role in popular memory is similarly brief. Since Bédier cannot imagine continuous lineal or national memory in his present, he concludes that the epics cannot represent oral traditions deriving from distant events: this is less of a philological proof about the genesis of epics than an expression of colonial regret for how "the people" forget the glories of French history.

Whereas with the *fabliau* anecdote Bédier fantasizes the transmission of tales, here he fantasizes its failure. In both cases, the scene of fantasy is Bourbon. There, Bédier received a written document to restore the names to his family portraits:

Parfois, dans nos maisons, une vieille épée, un hausse-col, une croix d'honneur retiennent de tels souvenirs (de nos guerres), et c'est là notre folk-lore domestique: mais chacun sait combien il est pauvre et qu'il s'appauvrit encore chaque fois que la mort enlève les vieilles gens de la maison. Mon père m'a légué un livre où il a raconté (d'après de vieilles lettres, des pièces notariées, etc.) tout ce qu'il savait de sa famille, et je suis ainsi renseigné sur mes ascendants paternels jusqu'en 1680; mais de ma lignée maternelle je ne sais rien, pas même des noms propres, au delà de 1830; et mes enfants ne sauront plus remonter jusqu'à cette date de 1830; j'ai beau leur raconté les vieilles choses que je sais: ils les brouillent ou les oublient. Garder ainsi quelques temps un dépôt d'anecdotes, bientôt réduites à l'insignifiance, voilà tout ce que peut faire, abandonnée à elle seule, la tradition orale.[29]

[Sometimes in our houses an old sword, a gorget, a cross of honor retain such memories (of our wars), and that's our domestic folklore: but everyone knows how poor it is, and it becomes more impoverished each time death carries away the elders of the house. My father bequeathed to me a book where he recounted (according to old letters, legal documents, etc.) everything he knew about his family, and

I am thus informed about my paternal ancestors back to 1680. But of the maternal line I don't know anything, not even proper names, before 1830, and my children won't even know how to reach 1830. In vain have I told them the old things I know: they confuse them or forget them. Preserve thus a little while a repository of anecdotes, soon reduced to insignificance, that's all that oral tradition, left on its own, can do.]

The objects of Bédier's "domestic folklore" are all military and implicitly colonizing, the memories they (temporarily) evoke bellicose. These memories are to the nation what genealogy is to the family – its source of identity. Even in writing, however, memory remains only partial: it only goes so far (1680, 1830), it only holds so many names (more fathers than mothers). Indeed, the portraits of Bédier's great-grandmothers probably did remain anonymous. He seems to imagine, moreover, that his children will forget despite the family book. Even the written document, then, turns out to furnish only a fragile barrier to collective amnesia, as the colonial diaspora blends ever more thoroughly into metropolitan culture. Bédier's recollection of this book serves the same function here as the anecdote in the *Fabliaux*: it supports the fundamental concept on which his thesis rests – a concept formed in experiences that precede the thesis's supposedly philological motivation.[30] These are both moments in which, despite his efforts to forget Bourbon, Bédier's repressed history haunts philology. These moments betray a fundamental process of sublimation, of efforts to expiate the subject of home and cope with permanent homesickness.

Bédier's edition and translation of the *Roland* is the third example of the colonial formation of his philology. Dedicated "A L'ILE BOURBON. DIIS PATRIIS. J.B.," Bédier's *Roland* both arises from and expresses a compulsion to heal homesick desire. Indeed, Alain Corbellari refers to Bédier's relationship with the *Roland* as a "vieille histoire d'amour" (an old love story).[31] The dedication's first ambiguous letter captures Bédier's split relationship to colonial geography: the book is addressed *to* the island, yet the exact same phrase would locate the text *on* the island. The dedication thus deftly places J.B. both at a distance from the colony and within it, permitting a double gesture that reproduces Bédier's own migration: *Roland* is sent back to the island, from the island itself. This geographical tension is doubled by an etymological one: the island's official name then, as now, is *Réunion*. Inaugurated with the Revolution and revived with the Second Republic (1848), *Réunion* displaces the *Bourbon* of the *ancien régime* – and with it a dynastic memory that reaches all the way to the Middle Ages. By contrast, the dedication of the national epic to *Bourbon* perpetuates this memory, while consigning to history France's discontinuous geographic and political history. *Bourbon*, moreover, resists metropolitan innovations in favor of insular autonomy, denying the ruptures that might necessitate a "ré-union." Ultimately, "A l'île Bourbon" phrases a desire for unity while also containing personal and political ruptures.

The Latin phrase that completes the dedication is equally doubled, for "diis patriis" (blessed fatherland) names a geographical site with a genealogical principle. Bourbon and France are both in effect "ancestral lands" ("la grande et la petite patrie"), Bédier a colonial migrant with two homes. The ambiguities of dedication thus turn the little island far away into an outsized concept always close at hand. This spatial and temporal conflation shapes Bédier's sense of national belonging as a struggle to reconcile the traumatic difference between here and there, now and then. At the same time, the dedication inserts the *Roland* into a colonial context where certain differences – specifically, racial differences – defined the terms of national belonging.

Bédier's compatriot Hippolyte Foucque recounts that Bédier decided to dedicate the book to Bourbon while talking with none other than Marius and Ary Leblond.[32] Foucque's anecdote places Bédier in close relations with the "blond" architects of a Creole theory of white (and specifically Celtic) racial supremacy. When colonial racism and philology meet to send the sanctified bodies of the warriors who died for "douce France" back to Bourbon, all the strains of Bédier's intellectual project harmonize. For this book echoes the very one he read there as an adolescent. Whether Bédier received a copy of Gautier's hefty luxury edition of 1872, or one of the later editions destined for use in schools (4th and 5th edns 1875, 6th edn 1876), his own *Roland* serves as literal double: all are based on the unique Oxford manuscript (Bodleian, Digby 23), and present the medieval text and its modern translation on facing pages (a format initiated by Gautier and that underscores the equivalency of the two versions). Gautier does include some passages from other manuscripts, but both editors recognize the primacy of the

Oxford text. Gautier, however, would change his methods radically with his 7th edition, published in 1880 (the same year the *Roland* was officially adopted in the secondary schools).[33] And this composite text, based on three textual families each given equal authority, became the dominant form of the text for generations of students. Bédier identifies the singularity of Gautier's 1872 edition in his 1927 commentaries, but in his later study of the *Roland*'s editorial history he barely recognizes the existence of the 1872 edition.[34] Bédier of course famously theorized the superiority of single-manuscript editions in general, and the "éminente dignité" of the Oxford manuscript in particular.[35] He characterized critical editions based on multiple manuscripts, such as Gautier's from 1880 on, as "monstrueux" and "hybride."[36] Bédier's denigration of hybrid texts reflects his resistance to mixed forms of all kinds, a distrust of mixing (*mélange, métissage*) that derives partly from his colonial racial consciousness. His *Roland* thus serves both to revive his colonial reading experience, and to displace Gautier's "mixed" text with a purified one.

In these examples of some of Bédier's most influential work, the role of Bourbon appears determining on several levels. It is the source of a double sense of belonging and exile, of an idea of racial and cultural continuity across time and distance, and of a persistent valuation of pure forms. Bédier consistently finds his colonial ideas about memory, history, and identity confirmed in his philological and literary studies of the Middle Ages. The *Roland* is the most "popular" version of these ideas, in that it was designed to be read by a general educated public. Moreover, it is the version specifically destined to be read on Bourbon, to return to the "origins" of Bédier's encounter with the medieval French past.

POR ÇO QUE PLUS BEL SEIT

Many aspects of the *Roland* "itself" resonate with Bédier's Creole subjectivity. The epic opens with reference to the seven long years Charlemagne has already spent fighting the Saracens. Partly in response to the army's longing for home, Charlemagne accepts a peace proposal and sets off for France leaving Roland to defend the rearguard; the narrative ends with Charlemagne in tears as he is called once again to protect Christian interests far away. This commitment to two homelands (France and

Christianity) parallels the Creole's double attachments to insular and continental France. Roland himself embodies the tension between individual genius and collective identification that underlies Bédier's conception of literary production. Perhaps most famously, the *Roland* projects a surface ideology of absolute differences ("Paien unt tort e chrestiens unt dreit" [line 1015], "Pagans are wrong and Christians are right") fully compatible with Creole ideals of racial purity. At the same time, the poem recognizes, if obliquely, a background of shared histories.[37] This ideological combination replicates the processes of historical sublimation that subtend colonial society.

Through translation, Bédier acts as both reader and writer of these and other conflicts over belonging to France. By rewriting the *Roland* in his own image, Bédier brings French colonialism to bear on the medieval epic. In the process, he bolsters the purity of the epic's French identity by resisting some of its portrayals of cross-cultural communication. Various translation choices, for example, introduce a judging perspective that aligns the reader with a pro-French, anti-Arab stance. As Corbellari has shown, Bédier's treatment of *ber* and *gent* is particularly revealing. Bédier generally renders *ber* as "preux" or "prouesse" – but when it first applies to Marsile (line 680), he chooses "vaillant." While his use of "vaillant" in relation to Roland as well (line 1155) indicates that he does not distinguish consistently between mere Saracen "valor" and true Frankish "prowess," Corbellari suggests that Bédier nonetheless reacts instinctively against attributing a positive epithet to the "enemy." Indeed, elsewhere, *ber* disappears entirely from the translation when applied to Marsile (line 2617) and once is translated as "païens" (line 3472).[38] The neutral term *gent* ("people"), meanwhile, is translated fairly consistently as *engeance* ("detestable mob") when designating the Saracens. Characterizing this strategy as more of a "gloss" than a translation, Corbellari draws a direct connection to Bédier's republican colonialism. Numerous less dramatic cases further reinforce distinctions between the opposing sides: Roland's observation of the great "loss" of his fellows becomes a "massacre"; "France l'asolue" ("blessed" or "sovereign") becomes "France la sainte";[39] the "conquering" Roland becomes the "victor" (shifting the focus from process to accomplishment); a general description of battlefield deaths ("Asez i moerent e des uns e des altres") gains oppositional force with the naming of the two sides ("Des Français, des païens, beaucoup meurent").[40] These translations all amplify the poem's tendency to encourage the reader, as Stephen Nichols puts it, "to take sides with and against the characters and their positions."[41] Blocking readers' access to certain perceptions of resemblance, they translate historical complexities into ideological simplicities.

Bédier's most influential and controversial translation may be "la Terre des Aïeux" (Land of the Ancestors) for "tere majur," one of the terms used to designate Charles's land.[42] Bédier explains in his commentaries that the phrase is ambiguous, deriving from either a Latin adjective ("great land") or genitive plural ("land of the fathers"). Bédier concludes with the utmost of mystification: "Forcé de choisir dans ma traduction entre 'Grande Terre' et 'Terre des Aïeux,' j'ai mis 'Terres des Aïeux,' *por ço que plus bel seit*" (Forced to choose in my translation between "Great Land" and "Land of the Ancestors," I put "Land of the Ancestors," *por ço que plus bel seit* [*because it's more beautiful*]).[43] There is no philological basis for the translation choice, but rather an aesthetic appreciation of both form and sentiment. A key point of philology thus returns once again to the personal, and in a context of obvious patriotic importance. Bédier expresses this aesthetic judgment, moreover, in Old French, as if it were a natural part of the past – as if his own understanding were history itself, Old French his native language.[44] Lurking within the mystification of the "indigenous" aesthetic preference ("it's more beautiful," written in Old French) is a logic of deterritorialization: belonging to this land transcends space, deriving instead from a genealogical relation to ancestors. This is precisely *why* "Land of the Ancestors" is more beautiful: it can join disparate spaces under a unifying genealogical concept – such spaces, say, as Bourbon and France.

Bédier is also willing to conflate "tere majur" (a kind of Old French "greater France") with France itself:

Et ce que le poète célèbre sous le nom de "douce France," ou de "*Terre majur*" (v. 600, etc.), qui est *terra majorum*, qui est "patrie," ce n'est ni le vague empire des Carolingiens, ni l'étroit domaine des premiers Capétiens, ce n'est pas un territoire délimité; c'est une personne morale.[45]

[And what the poet celebrates in the name of "sweet France" or "Terre majur" (line 600), which is *terra majorum*, which is "homeland," is not the vague empire of the Carolingians, nor the narrow domain of the Capetians, it's not a delimited territory; it's a legal entity.]

This deft deterritorialization makes "Frenchness" an identity independent of geography . . . makes the Creole as French as the Parisian since both are answerable to the laws of the Republic, "une personne morale." In this vision, there is no east or west, north or south, only a transcendent "French" that knows no bounds. Colonial and historical differences alike are recuperated into a collectivity capable of endless, "meaningless" substitutions. The fact that Bédier's translation of "tere majur" has frequently been adopted, and without comment, keeps this tendentious memory circulating.

Bédier's patriotic musings on the transcendent French homeland exclude a third etymological possibility, first proposed by Bédier's student Prosper Boissonade – that "tere majur" translates the Arabic term *al-'arḍ al-kabīra* used to refer to the European continent.[46] Arabic etymologies remain a controversial subject, but the fact that Bédier affirms that none of the poem's linguistic forms have anything to do with Arabic (deriving from either French or fantasy)[47] suggests a conclusion motivated by something other than philology. Bédier of course knew of Boissonade's idea and had ample opportunity to consider, or at least mention, the Arabic thesis since he had read Boissonade's text before it was published (and thus well before completing *La Chanson de Roland commentée*)[48] and continued to revise his *Roland* over the next decade. While Bédier esteemed Boissonade's work very little (and in this he was not alone), his Latinization – and aestheticization – of "tere majur" participates in a broader effort to preserve pure origins. Whatever the inherent weaknesses of Boissonade's theory, which attributed the genesis of the *Roland* to the Spanish expeditions of Rotrou du Perche, it also represents a form of Arabic and Spanish "contamination" in the epic lineage that Bédier saw as so purely French.

The Arabic etymology found early acceptance in T. Atkinson Jenkins 1924 edition of the poem, and has most recently been affirmed as obvious fact by André de Mandach.[49] Roger M. Walker has given the question the most thorough treatment, demonstrating that only Ganelon and the Saracens use the expression "tere majur." Walker concludes that it is logical that all of the "traitors" adopt an oppositional, Arabic usage. Walker points out that the one instance where the narrator refers to "tere majur" is also the one instance where it is used with a definite article (as are the other examples of terms derived from Latin genitive plurals): here it probably does mean "Land of the Ancestors." This is, perhaps not coincidentally, the moment of homecoming (line 818): with the end of homesickness in sight, "The overtones of 'the land of their ancestors' fit the context perfectly at this point."[50] To imagine that both the Latin and Arabic explanations of "tere majur" are correct, as Walker does,[51] is to imagine a poet manipulating contexts and etymologies, a poet conscious of cross-cultural knowledge, of Arabic and Frankish exchange – precisely the kind of knowledge whose existence Bédier (and others) finds unimaginable.

Bédier's explicit discussions of translation itself articulate a conception of language as a desirable barrier to historical and cultural change. First, he presents his text not as a translation but as a "transcription" or "'traduction.'"[52] Placing translation under erasure in quotation marks, Bédier casts the modern French text as identical to the Old French text, itself a transcription from the manuscript. In this model of equivalences, Bédier also avoids the telling separation of "medieval" and "modern" by referring more vaguely to an "old text" and "today's language." Furthermore, he calls this language a "langage" rather than a "langue," suggesting that it does not differ fundamentally from Modern French. In contrast to his predecessors, Bédier claims to feel a particular affinity for the style of the author of the older version:

> J'admire . . . les allures aristocratiques de son art, les ressources et la fière tenue, très raffinée, d'une langue ingénieuse, nuancée, volontaire, et qui révèle un souci constant de distinguer l'usage vulgaire du bon usage.[53]
>
> [I admire the aristocratic bearing of his art, the resources and the proud carriage, very refined, of an ingenious, nuanced, determined language, and which reveals a constant care to distinguish common usage from proper usage.]

Bédier admires, in other words, the absence of any stylistic or social "mixing." The translation aims precisely to safeguard this aristocratic style: "J'ai voulu sauver dans ma traduction cette qualité souveraine du vieux maître, la noblesse." [I wanted to save in my translation this sovereign quality of the old master, nobility]. This is difficult, however, because so many structures and words are no longer in use, "ou, ce qui est pire, survivent, mais détournés de leur sens premier, affaiblis ou avilis!" [or, which is worse, survive, but diverted from their original meaning, weakened or demeaned!]. Change, then, is worse than death. Although Bédier admits that he cannot go back in time ("you can't bring back the dead," as Charlemagne's barons say about Roland), he does aspire to resemble the past by using only words with "titles older than the Renaissance."[54] Bédier's language thus seeks to perform continuity between the past and the present; continuity itself is an aristocratic quality, a sign of cultural superiority. Bédier designs the translation, like the *Roland* itself as Bédier understands it, to resist the ravages of time.[55] These linguistic theories resonate loudly with his racial consciousness and resistance to colonial *métissage*.

Through philological arguments about the *Roland*'s textual history, literary arguments about its origins, and his own modern French translation, Bédier projects a continuous and pure French identity all the way back to the eleventh century and all the way across the globe to Bourbon. In fact, in Bédier's first edition of the epic colonial memory usurps the place of medieval memory, as the dedication appears even before the title page. The result is a double cultural translation that turns the epic into a representation of the "other" congenial to Bédier's own notion of "greater France" – a unified entity undisturbed by geographic, ethnic, and temporal ruptures.

The *Roland* is merely the most dramatic product of an intellectual project devoted to questions of origin. A child of two homes, Bédier developed theories of medieval textual and mental processes that obsessed over origins. In his defenses of multiple origins for the *fabliaux*, of individual literate origins for the epic, and of "best manuscript" editions Bédier excludes origins *per se* from literary and cultural history. The result is a curiously anti-historicist historicism, one that insists upon both distance from and identity with the present.[56] Bédier's notion of history incorporates ruptures, especially colonial ones, into a continuous line of national history: there is no way to trace memory across ruptures, and so origins are lost from history; only signs of continuities remain as if perennial. Indeed, Bédier himself declares in one of his late publications: "je n'ai pas le sens du discontinu" [I have no sense of the discontinuous].[57] Thus Bédier resolves his fractured relationship with "greater France" into a permanent belonging, undisturbed by colonial migrations and the sense of "foreignness at home." In this process, the periphery is recuperated as an echo of the center, as its very foundation. Yet the obsessive nature of the recuperative effort repeatedly betrays the failure of integration.

All of Bédier's efforts grapple with conflicts between continuity and rupture, individuality and collectivity, home and elsewhere. From these postcolonial perspectives, his famous summary of the conclusion of the four-volume *Les Légendes épiques* takes on new resonance: "Au commencement était la route" [In the beginning was the road].[58] Bédier's own journey to epic origins begins *en route* from Paris to the island – and also from the island and to Paris. The beginning, then, is that state of colonial suspension between two homes – the *route* a movement both away and toward that defines the static poles of home. This journey with two beginnings shapes the *Roland* – which itself makes a double journey to the colony. Both the *Roland*'s olive tree and Bédier's mango tree are destinations that turn into relatively brief pauses *en route* to other places. In these passages, origins and destinations are both doubled by previous journeys that unsettle the traveler while conditioning a desirable if precarious sense of belonging.

NOTES

Portions of this chapter were presented at the conference "Orientalisms before 1600," Trinity College, Cambridge, July 2001. For archival assistance, I am grateful to the Bibliothèque Départementale de la Réunion (Dir. Alain-Marcel Vauthier), Bibliothèque de l'Institut de France, Bibliothèque Nationale de France, Collège de France (Fonds Bédier), ARTFL project (URL: humanities. uchicago.edu/orgs/ARTFL), Adrien Bédier, and my research assistants Khaleem Mohammed-Ali and Oona O'Connell. Conversations with Rebecca Biron, Alain Corbellari, Andrew Cowell, and Sharon Kinoshita shaped my thoughts at various points along the way. Research travel for this chapter was supported by faculty grants from the University of Miami; much of it was written under "Charlemagne's Crown" in Cassis, France, where I enjoyed the capacious hospitality of the Camargo Foundation.
1. *La Chanson de Roland*, ed. Joseph Bédier (Paris: Piazza, 1922), lines 366 (Ganelon, bearing Charlemagne's message, meets the Saracen leader Marsile), 2571 (Marsile

returns home after his army is routed by Charlemagne), 2705 (messengers arrive from Marsile's overlord Baligant, promising help against Charlemagne); *Le Voyage de Charlemagne à Jerusalem et à Constantinople*, ed. Paul Aebischer (Geneva: Droz, 1965), line 7.

2. As reported by Hippolyte Foucque, "Joseph Bédier: l'homme; le médiéviste," *Académie de l'Ile de la Réunion: Bulletin* 21 (1963–64): 119–31 at 121, and Joseph Bédier, "Discours," *Punch d'honneur offert le dimanche 5 février 1922 à Joseph Bédier à l'occasion de son élection comme membre de l'Académie française, Association amicale des Réunionnais de Paris* (1922), 13–16, cited in Alain Corbellari, *Joseph Bédier: écrivain et philologue* (Geneva: Droz, 1997), 12.

3. Foucque, "Joseph Bédier," 118–19.

4. C. B. Norman, *Colonial France* (London: W. H. Allen, 1886), 53–4.

5. *Une Amitié de jeunesse: 148 lettres inédites (1886–1900). Joseph Bédier, Emile Mâle, Joseph Texte*, ed. Christian Garaud and Janine Irigoin (New York: Peter Lang, 1999), 37.

6. *Une Amitié*, 64, 57–61.

7. *Une Amitié*, 73.

8. Speech given in San Francisco (Collège de France, C-VIII, liasse 106, 2).

9. Raphaël Barquissau, "Joseph Bédier," in *Une Colonie colonisatrice* (Saint-Denis: E. Drouhet, 1922), 67–86 at 75.

10. Speech given in San Francisco (Collège de France, C-VIII, liasse 106, 2)

11. Bédier, *Discours de réception à l'Académie française, prononcé le 3 novembre 1921* (Paris: Champion, 1921), 7.

12. Bédier, "Discours," *Bulletin de l'Association Amicale des Réunionnais* 2 (1937).

13. Barquisseau, "Joseph Bédier."

14. Anonymous, "Les amis de Joseph Bédier," *Aux écoutes*, September 3, 1938.

15. Françoise Vergès, *Monsters and Revolutionaries: Colonial Family Romance and Métissage* (Durham, NC: Duke University Press, 1999), 25–40, 64–71.

16. Gustave Cohen, *Ceux que j'ai connus* (Montreal: Editions de l'Arbre, 1946), 155.

17. Vergès, *Monsters and Revolutionaries*, 32.

18. Auguste Billiard, *Voyage aux colonies orientales* (Paris: Librairie Française de L'Advocat, 1822), 456–7.

19. Vergès, *Monsters and Revolutionaries*, 109–12.

20. Bédier, *Légendes épiques: recherches sur la formation des chansons de geste* (Paris: Champion, 1908–11), vol. III, 269–70.

21. Indeed the surviving Bédiers of La Réunion readily recognize a mixed heritage, noting that not every generation has blue eyes (Adrien Bédier, 23 June 2003).

22. In a letter to his brother (cited in Barquissau, "Joseph Bédier," 73); on a photo sent to his *lycée* (Foucque, "Joseph Bédier," 130; *Le Mémorial de la Réunion*, ed. Henri Maurin and Jacques Lentge [Saint-Denis: Australe, 1979–81], vol. V, 308n1, currently in Adrien Bédier's private collection); in a speech to the "colonie française" of San Francisco (Collège de France, C-VIII, liasse 106).

23. Barquissau, "Joseph Bédier," 73; also in Foucque ("Joseph Bédier," 130) and *Le Mémorial* (vol. V, 308).

24. Bédier, *Les Fabliaux*, third edn (Paris: Champion, 1911), 239–40. Corbellari likewise notes the imaginative (even imaginary) nature of this "proof" (*Joseph Bédier*, 114; on the *Fabliaux* in general, 71–126).

25. Bédier, *Fabliaux*, 241.

26. Bédier, *Légendes épiques*, vol. I, x, 435; vol. IV, 475; Corbellari, *Joseph Bédier*, 344–419.

27. Bédier, *Légendes épiques*, vol. III, 268.

28. Bédier, *Légendes épiques*, vol. III, 269.

29. Bédier, *Légendes épiques*, vol. III, 269–70.

30. Corbellari likewise notes the spurious nature of this proof (*Joseph Bédier*, 7).

31. Corbellari, *Joseph Bédier*, 364.

32. Foucque, "Joseph Bédier," 129.

33. Charles Ridoux, *Evolution des études médiévales en France de 1860 à 1914* (Paris: Champion, 2001), 614–15, citing reviews in *Romania* from 1875 and 1879.

34. *Commentée* 84–91; "De l'édition," 148.

35. *La chanson de Roland*, vi; *Chanson de Roland, commentée* (Paris: Piazza, 1927), 84–91, 94–177; "De l'édition princeps de la *Chanson de Roland* aux éditions les plus récentes," *Romania* 63 (1937): 433–69; 64 (1938): 145–244, 489–521, at 148. On the tradition of editing Bédier argued against, Ridoux 389–425.

36. Bédier, *Le lai de l'ombre* (Paris: Champion, 1913), xxxviii; *Commentée*, 264. On Bédier's place in the history of philological methods, see my "Post-Philology," *Postcolonial Moves: Medieval through Modern*, ed. Patricia C. Ingham and Michelle R. Warren (New York: Palgrave Macmillan, 2003), 19–45.

37. Sharon Kinoshita likewise suggests some of the ways in which the tendentious claim of difference betrays a "crisis of nondifferentiation": "'Pagans Are Wrong and Christians Are Right': Alterity, Gender, and Nation in the *Chanson de Roland*," *Journal of Medieval and Early Modern Studies* 31.1 (2001): 79–111 at 91. On the place of the oliphant in these histories, see my "The Noise of Roland," *Exemplaria* 16.2 (2004): 277–304. Corbellari, "Traduire," 75.

38. Alain Corbellari, "Traduire ou ne pas traduire: le dilemme de Bédier. A propos de la traduction de la *Chanson de Roland*," *Vox Romanica* 56 (1997): 63–82 at 69.

39. In a 1913 article, Bédier still followed Gaston Paris in translating "France la libre" ("L'art et le métier dans la *Chanson de Roland*," *Revue des Deux Mondes* 13 [1913]: 292–321 at 320; Gaston Paris, "La *Chanson de Roland* et la nationalité française," in *La Poésie du moyen âge* [1885] [Paris: Hachette, 1922], vol. I, 87–118 at 118). Bédier also reinforces Christian identity when Bramimonde's conversion by "veire conoisance" becomes "par vraie connaissance de la sainte loi" (line 3987, p. 331).

40. *Roland*, lines 1691, 2311, 2363, 2867, 3477; pp. 143, 195, 199, 239, 289.

41. Stephen Nichols, *Romanesque Signs: Early Medieval Narrative and Iconography* (New Haven: Yale University Press, 1983), 149.

42. *Roland*, lines 600, 818, 952, 1532, 1659, 1784.

43. Bédier, *Commentée*, 303.

44. Similarly, in the last line of the translation, he makes Old French his own by not translating, and instead printing "Ci falt la geste que Turoldus declinet" slightly

below the end of the translation. Adopting Old French as his own language, Bédier seals his identification with Turold as poet (Corbellari, "Traduire," 76). His identifications are in fact multiple, and include both Roland and Charles: he writes, for example, that he has spent *"set anz tuz pleins"* working on the *Légendes épiques* ("De l'édition," 152).

45. Bédier, *Commentée*, 39. In the *Légendes épiques*, Bédier considered "dulce France" as "précisément la nôtre" (precisely ours) (vol. III, 452).
46. Prosper Boissonade, *Du Nouveau sur la Chanson de Roland* (Paris: Champion, 1923), 72.
47. Bédier, *Commentée*, 49, 299–301.
48. Bédier offers comments on the manuscript (Collège de France, C-VIII, liasse 102bis; C-XII, no. 164); an advertisement for Bédier's own book includes a notice for Boissonade (Collège de France, C-VIII, liasse 8).
49. T. Atkinson Jenkins, ed., *La Chanson de Roland: Oxford Version* (Boston: Heath, 1924), 52; André de Mandach, *Chanson de Roland: transferts de mythe dans le monde occidental et oriental* (Geneva: Droz, 1993), 43–4.
50. Roger M. Walker, "'Tere major' in the *Chanson de Roland*," *Olifant* 7 (1979): 123–30 at 128–9.
51. De Mandach likewise notes the likelihood of a double understanding of the term (*Chanson de Roland*, 44).
52. *Roland*, x.
53. *Roland*, xii.
54. *Roland*, xii–xiii.
55. Corbellari, "Traduire," 65.
56. Hans Aarsleff, "Scholarship and Ideology: Joseph Bédier's Critique of Romantic Medievalism," in *Historical Studies and Literary Criticism*, ed. Jerome J. McGann (Madison: University of Wisconsin Press, 1985), 93–113.
57. Bédier, "Le moyen âge," in *L'Encyclopédie française* (Paris: Comité de l'Encyclopédie, 1935), v. 16, pp. 16'10, 3–9 at 9.
58. Bédier, *Légendes épiques*, vol. III, 367.

10

The protocolonial baroque of *La Celestina*

Roland Greene

The notion that the early modern baroque is contiguous with the seventeenth-century Hispanophone colonial world – that the colonial and the baroque are alike the outcomes of a self-awareness by the Romance cultures of the Renaissance – goes back at least to Irving Leonard's *Baroque Times in Old Mexico* (1959). That strange and suggestive book argues that with the Counter-Reformation, the rise of experimental science, and the emergence of a distinctly colonial aesthetic in the Spanish New World, the baroque becomes the mode of thought that characterizes the heart of the colonial period especially in Mexico:

> Through medieval religiosity chaotic feelings vented themselves in a fierce fanaticism which spawned an arid dogmatism, an uncompromising intolerance, an implacable persecution, and a degrading superstition. Through a degenerate chivalry, a tawdry relic of the Middle Ages, an explosive fervor fathered a morbid punctilio in personal relations and a specious code of honor which prolifically begot vengeful feuds and murderous duels. Baroque passion stimulated an urge to action, an obsession to wield power, and, from the deep recesses of the unconscious, it conjured up an extraordinary vitality and a forward thrust of energy which found no adequate outlet or satisfying release. Unlike the Promethean spark of the Renaissance, it was a vitality which denied life and expended itself in trivia. Having briefly experienced the emancipation of a fecund humanism, the distraught spirit now fell prey to a deep despondency on finding its medieval chains restored.[1]

As the colonial period enters its second century, in other words, its outlook folds back on itself to recover several prehumanist ideologies and attitudes – the mid-colonial becoming the precolonial in a feat of preposterousness.[2] Oddly, Leonard argues that even the Mexican people are baroque:

> If profusion of detail and hierarchy are among the typical charac-
> teristics of the Baroque, they were increasingly present in the ethnic
> composition of the neomedieval communities of the New World. As
> the seventeenth century advanced Hispanic civilization sank its roots
> so deeply in the Spanish American soil that its patterns are discernible
> three centuries later. Ever more intricate did the constellation of class
> and caste grow as a prolific miscegenation progressed. And the very
> fluidity of this ethnic process, which was creating entirely new human
> species, helped to insure the stability of a neomedieval order. The mul-
> tiplicity of racial types emerging from a sort of Baroque melting pot
> gave a sociological expression of the political maxim "divide and rule"
> to which Spanish policy was securely wedded.[3]

This influential view of the colonial as baroque was superseded but not entirely displaced by another conceit, of the postcolonial as baroque. The voice of this view is Roberto González Echevarría, who observes that

> modern Latin American literary tradition has been reluctant to con-
> sider itself a continuation of Spanish letters since the eighteenth cen-
> tury. This is due to several factors. First and foremost, the wars of
> independence, and the period leading to them, constituted a rejec-
> tion of Spain, a metropolis that was out of step with the mod-
> ern world the new nations wished to join. Desirous to establish an
> autochthonous literary tradition, spurred on by the romantic spirit
> of the early nineteenth century, when most Latin American republics
> became independent, Latin Americans looked elsewhere for literary
> models. In addition, particularly since the 1920s, a radical search for
> origins, which in other western literatures could easily be traced to
> Romanticism, led to the Baroque, as the only common origin with
> Spain worth recuperating.[4]

For Leonard the baroque is anything but autochthonous to the Americas – instead it gestures back to a medieval legacy that binds mid-colonial culture to the continent – while for González Echevarría it forms the basis of a new American identity, a taking-off point for modernity.

Near the center of both of these alternative accounts of the baroque as colonial or postcolonial is Fernando de Rojas's prose dialogue *La Celestina*, which inaugurates early modern Spanish literature and raises prospectively many of the social and cultural problems that would become exigent in Spanish and Spanish American societies in the sixteenth century and after. Leonard, who was renowned for his studies of the traffic in books across the Atlantic, finds *La Celestina* in several maritime inventories and colonial libraries of baroque Mexico.[5] More speculatively, González Echevarría locates *La Celestina* – "not baroque, to be sure" – at the beginning of modernity in Spanish letters, and therefore as one of the groundplans for the baroque as well as for what comes after.[6] More than perhaps any other work of its time, *La Celestina* has an ambiguous status that follows from its several prolepses: it anticipates, and speaks in a contemporary voice to, the sixteenth century, the transatlantic empire, the colonial period and the rise of creole and mestizo identities, the baroque, the advent of political and cultural independence, and postcolonial Latin America. None of this is to remove *La Celestina* from its late medieval moment. The influential historian of baroque culture José Antonio Maravall has argued, in his study of *La Celestina*, that Rojas's fiction offers us "the image of a pragmatic, secularized society whose individuals, morally distanced from one another, act in egoistic fashion. This distancing, which originates in the technical possibilities of a money economy, would signify freedom in the circumstances of a new era. But from the vantage of tradition, it can be appreciated as nothing more than a radical disordering of human existence."[7] *La Celestina* occupies its own distinctive envelope of social crisis. Still we might say, with González Echevarría, that the work can be not baroque and yet foundational to that outlook. It ought to be possible to agree with Maravall that in one sense the baroque is "a historical concept" that

> runs approximately from 1600 (without discarding the possibility that certain advanced phenomena of baroque significance appeared some years previously, in the later times of Michelangelesque Mannerism and, in Spain, with the construction of the Escorial) to 1670–80 (a time of economic change and the first echoes of modern science in Spain; cultural, political, and economic Colbertism in France; the unimpeded emergence of the industrial Revolution in England).[8]

But we should also be able to say that, in another sense, there is always a baroque, or the possibility of an eruption of artifice – in the service of incongruity, disproportion, and anachronism – against a background of orthodoxy.[9] *La Celestina*, positioned in a society whose questions antic- ipate but do not fully reach those of the later sixteenth and seventeenth centuries, nonetheless rehearses a baroque disposition in the person of Celestina – and of course, kills her off at the end of the fiction. As the succeeding century develops, she becomes increasingly legible as pro- leptically baroque, and her relevance to later Renaissance culture gets established. She stands as evidence that there are protobaroques before the explicit phenomenon of 1600 and after.

Where it first explicitly appears in early modern art and literature, the baroque represents disorienting artifice at the expense of ortho- doxy. As we have seen in the conversation between Leonard and González Echevarría, this artifice can seem forward- or backward- looking – "neomedieval" or "postcolonial" – but the precise historical evocation matters less than the sheer difference from humanist ortho- doxy. The baroque is artifice's revenge against the humanist habits of mind that domesticated incongruity, disproportion, and anachronism, and its specimens tend to enable readers and viewers to step out of their historical circumstances and participate in "a marvelous theater of sensations."[10] The outsize utterances, curved forms, and unsubor- dinated detail of the baroque represent a liberation of the senses that imagines alternative pasts, presents, and even futures in answer to the gathering regimentation of the real present. To the reader or spectator, the baroque exchanges social and intellectual uncertainty for fictional and sensory liberation, an uneven bargain that nonetheless found con- siderable appeal in the transition from the sixteenth to the seventeenth century. The enormous body of scholarship on the early modern baroque explores the working-out of that bargain.

In artistic terms, the baroque wields incommensurability as an aes- thetic principle. Against a social background of increasingly ordered knowledge, articulated state power, and stratified class relations, the sensation of the incommensurable is that the elements in a structure might escape from their structuring, might resist resolution into a logic, might prove impossible to measure one against another by a single scale. The principal works of European humanism typically allow hints

of incommensurability to disturb their surfaces, such as the existence
of slaves in Thomas More's *Utopia* and the attendant potential for
their experience to fashion an alternative narrative; or the conjoining
of religion and science in Luís de Camões' *Lusíadas*, where Vasco de
Gama describes to the Sultan of Malindi the fragile tissue of Portuguese
national destiny as compounded out of providence and technology, and
implicitly raises the question of whether a single outlook can hold these
standpoints together for much longer. Such intuitions of the incommensurable are what the baroque starts from. The energies released in its process, which might be said to mark out Calderón, Margaret Cavendish,
and Sor Juana Inés de la Cruz as different from Erasmus, More, and
Camões, often seem to foresee the breakdown of humanist order and
all its associated events, such as linear perspective, a system of value
for all things human, and comparison itself. In both debt and contrast
to humanism, the qualities of art often associated with the baroque –
logics that turn back on themselves, dynamic movement, overdevel-
oped figuration, and a cultivation of grotesqueness or monstrosity – are
among the forms of the incommensurable, a property that takes on a
new urgency in the crease between the Renaissance and the Enlightenment. Where intellectual and social life is being ever more emphatically
parceled out, the sensation of incommensurability among parcels – the
conviction that one integer overweighs another, and might overwhelm
that other in a dynamic motion – becomes a vehicle for thought, an idea
in the making. Moreover, it undoes more than humanism. As Natalie
Melas has observed,

> the version of incommensurability which posits a radical separation
> between autonomous systems seems problematic in a colonial context
> simply because colonialism is a complex of social, economic, and cul-
> tural practices predicated precisely on the eradication of autonomous
> realms. Subsuming the globe under its law, it sets all differences into
> relation with European metropolitan powers as the economic center
> and the cultural standard.[11]

In this sense, incommensurability seems a condition for the rendering of
the colonial into the postcolonial. The baroque seems always to describe
the present in terms of other times and places: in the Renaissance it seems
medieval, in the colonial era it seems postcolonial, and in the later
seventeenth century it seems these things and more – mad, diseased,

upside down.[12] In *La Celestina*, as in other precisely liminal works, we see colonial and postcolonial concerns prepared for, and a baroque under articulation. It might be insisted that the continuing power of this work owes something to these anticipations of later discourses.

There are several points of entry to the protobaroque and its relation to the colonial in *La Celestina*; among these, as I argue elsewhere, is the cultural semantics of the fiction, in which the term *resistencia* (resistance) appears for perhaps the first time in a recognizably modern fashion as the inevitable name for struggle against oppression.[13] For the present purpose, I will confine my discussion to the figure of Celestina herself, drawing out some of the ways that she anticipates and conditions the colonial baroque.[14] Her luminosity against the rest of the fiction might be said to represent the possibilities of the baroque counterposed to the world-views of Rojas's other characters. Open rather than closed, prolix and not measured, and irreconcilable to the prevalent orders, Celestina presages what the baroque will mean in the age of its ascendance a hundred years or more after the appearance of Rojas's fiction.

The beginning of *La Celestina* sees the transformation of a conventional romance into something considerably more momentous, and most readers attribute this change of climate to the arrival of the character named Celestina. The nominal protagonist of the work – which in its first edition (1499) was entitled the *Comedia de Calisto e Melibea*, and in its third (1502) the *Tragicomedia de Calisto a Melibea* – is the young aristocrat Calisto, who loves the beautiful Melibea, the daughter of the noble Pleberio.[15] The early episodes of the first act consist of dialogues between Calisto and Melibea, in which they adopt the stock attitudes of suffering lover and resistant lady, and between Calisto and his worldly servant Sempronio. The tenor of this latter exchange is established by Calisto's lovesickness and Sempronio's cynical commentary:

> CALISTO. Los ojos, verdes, rasgados; las pestañas, luengas; las cejas, delgadas y alçadas; la nariz, mediana; la boca, pequeña; los dientes, menudos y blancos; los labrios, colorados y gros[s]ezuelos; el torno del rostro, poco más luengo que redondo; el pecho, alto; la redondeza y forma de las pequeñas tetas, ¿quién te las podrá figurar? ¡que se despereza el hombre quando las mira!; la tez, lisa, lustrosa; el cuero suyo escurece la nieve; la color, mezclada, qual ella la escogió para sí.

SEMPRONIO (*Aparte*). ¡En sus trece está el necio!

CALISTO. Las manos pequeñas en mediana manera, de dulce carne acompañadas los dedos luengos, las uñas en ellas largas y coloradas, que parescen rubíes entre perlas. Aquella proporción que veer yo no pude, sin duda, por el bulto de fuera, juzgo incomparablemente ser mejor que la que París juzgó entre las tres deesas.

SEMPRONIO. ¿Has dicho?

CALISTO. Quan brevemente pude.

SEMPRONIO. Puesto que sea todo esso verdad, por ser tú hombre eres más digno.

CALISTO. ¿En qué?

SEMPRONIO. En que ella es imperfeta, por el qual defeto desea y apetece a ti y a otro menor que tú. ¿No has leýdo el filósofo do dize: "Assí como la materia apetece a la forma, así la muger al varón"?

CALISTO. ¡O triste!; y ¿quandó veré yo esso entre mí y Melibea?

SEMPRONIO. Posible es. Y aun que la aborrezcas quanto agora la amas podrá ser, alcançándola y viéndola con otros ojos, libres del engaño en que agora estás.

CALISTO. ¿Con qué ojos?

SEMPRONIO. Con ojos claros.

CALISTO. Y agora, ¿con qué la veo?

SEMPRONIO. Con ojos de alinde con que lo poco parece mucho y lo pequeño grande. Y por que no te desesperes, yo quiero tomar esta empresa de complir tu desseo.[16]

[CALISTO. Her eyes, green and wide; her lashes, long; her brows, dainty and high; her nose, neither too large nor too small; her mouth, little; her teeth, small and white; her lips, red and plump; her face, somewhat longer than it is round; her bosom, high; her breasts, so full and firm, who can describe them? How a man will stretch himself when he sees them! Her skin, smooth and lustrous, and so white it darkens the snow; her color, varied, as she would have chosen it for herself . . .

SEMPRONIO (*Aside*). This fool has got the bit in his teeth!

CALISTO. Her hands, small, but not too small, and sweetly fleshed; her fingers, long; her nails likewise, and so pink they seem like rubies among pearls. And from what I could see of her hidden parts, she's incomparably fairer than the most beautiful of the goddesses whom Paris judged!

SEMPRONIO. Have you done?

CALISTO. As briefly as I could.

SEMPRONIO. Well, even if everything you say of her is true, you, being a man, are still more worthy.

CALISTO. How's that?

SEMPRONIO. Because she is imperfect and in her imperfection she desires and lusts after you. Haven't you read what the philosophers say, that as matter desires form, so woman desires man?

CALISTO. Wretch that I am! When will Melibea desire me?

SEMPRONIO. It could happen, even though you hated her as much as you love her now, and when you possessed her you'd see her with eyes cured of their present squint.

CALISTO. With what kind of eyes?

SEMPRONIO. With clear eyes.

CALISTO. And how do I see her now?

SEMPRONIO. With magnifying eyes, which make the little seem much and the small, large. And so that you will not despair, I will bring this enterprise to the fulfillment of your desire.][17]

With the last speech quoted here, Sempronio prepares for the first appearance of Celestina, who at first will be the instrument of Calisto's gratification but shortly will become master of this "enterprise." Sempronio's account of Calisto's subjection to love – that his eyes render small things out of their true proportion – is marked with a striking choice of word: "Con ojos de alinde con que lo poco parece mucho y lo pequeño grande" [with eyes of *alinde*, which make the little seem much and the small, large]. *Alinde* is a term out of metallurgy for polished steel that serves as a mirror: as Peter Russell notes in his edition of *La Celestina*, *alinde* and its alternative *alfinde* are borrowings from the Arabic *al-hind*, or "of India." "Eyes of *alinde*" are eyes that see not clearly but through the deformations of love. With the injection of this noun, which appears only rarely in the period, Sempronio promises to arrange a fulfillment that will confirm the disproportion in Calisto's sight, and Rojas begins to render *La Celestina* into the counter-idealist work that marks the factitious boundary between medieval and early modern in European fiction. Celestina herself, we might say, enters the fiction through the opening created by this word, and with her the prospect of a baroque that sees with "eyes of *alinde*." If the eventual baroque is in large measure an effect of the new science and economics and, consequently, a disruption of scale – in which artists participate in the change of cultural outlook by depicting a new protocol between humanity and nature – then *La Celestina* is among the artifacts that first raise the possibility, and Celestina herself the figure who carries the work from one era to the next.

Even if we allow with González Echevarría that *La Celestina* is "not baroque," we might want to stipulate that Celestina is the first baroque character in literature: before Euphues, before Góngora's and Marino's personae, there is the procuress who can render a fresh world of desire as disproportion and errant detail. Here is Sempronio's introduction of her:

> Días ha grandes que conozco, en fin desta vezindad, una vieja barbuda que se dize Celestina, hechizera, astuta, sagaz en quantas maldades ay. Entiendo que passan de cinco mill virgos los que se han hecho y desecho por su auctoridad en esta cibdad. A las duras peñas promoverá y provocará a luxuria si quiere.[18]

> [Many days ago I met, out toward the edge of this quarter, a bewhiskered old woman who calls herself Celestina, a witch, astute and wise in all evil things. They say the number of maidenheads broken and repaired under her authority in this city passes five thousand. She can move the very stones to lechery if she sets her mind to it!][19]

The incongruity here is that Calisto needs a cure, not an incitement to further passion. But it matters more for cultural outlook that Celestina then intervenes in the relations of human beings and nature by undoing the results of her own work of incitement, which is another incitement: fashioning sexually experienced women into virgins, she renews the original lust of men beyond what nature and custom would allow – her two roles, procuress and witch, exchanging places again and again:

> Como aquéllos (cirujanos) dañan en los principios las llagas y encarecen el prometimiento de la salud, assí entiendo yo fazer a Calisto. Alargarle he la certenidad del remedio porque, como dizen, el esperança luenga aflige el coraçón, y quanto él la perdiere, tanto gela promete(ré). Bien me entiendes.[20]

> [Just as a surgeon will inflame a wound in order to prolong the treatment, so shall I do with Calisto and keep him uncertain of his cure. As the saying goes, hope deferred makes the heart sick, so the more hopeless he gets, the more we'll promise him. You understand me well.][21]

As Cervantes might have said, everyone who is human understands. This is the logic of a bottomless desire that figures in the ethics and aesthetics of several eras beginning with Petrarchan humanism, already a formative influence on *La Celestina*.[22] But a character who stands for such incitement in dramatic and narrative terms – who acts this way upon others, and obliges them to speak her actions into the fiction as descriptions of desire made rampant – is more than a Petrarchist, whose subjection to desire is invariably first-person and self-reflexive. Celestina is a baroque figure against a romance background. As such, she is not so much a character even in the limited early modern understanding of that term as a principle that makes *La Celestina* profuse in certain features: startling remappings of the human as against the natural and the divine; extravagant inventories of what makes human beings themselves, how their desires work; and the pervasive sense that as familiar contexts change – little becoming large and vice versa – we are not where we were when the fiction began, but have been moved by the representational crisis of the baroque. Celestina brings such an atmosphere into the fiction and gives it personhood, whereas after 1600 the baroque will become embodied not so much in one figure versus others but in entire works, styles, and eras.

Hence *La Celestina* models a protobaroque outlook in the person of Celestina; the fact that she is not the nominal protagonist but a figure who looms large through "eyes of *alinde*" stands for an aspect of baroque, in which one part – perhaps a pictorial detail in painting or a simile in poetry – can expand to force a new representational space for itself, the periphery exerting a pull on the center. (Even the dramatic asides or *apartes* – in which one character remarks to the audience on the speech of another – might, in their profusion, be considered such a baroque feature, the dialogue coming undone and a counter-perspective forcing a hearing. María Rosa Lida de Malkiel observes that with one exception, the aside "is exclusively in the mouths of the lower classes.")[23] González Echevarría has written astutely that

> the Baroque incorporates the Other; it plays at being Other . . . The Baroque assumes the strangeness of the Other as an awareness of the strangeness of Being. Being is being as monster, at once one and the other, the same and different . . . It is a sense of one's own rarity, of oddity, of distortion. Hence the plurality of New World culture, its

being-in-the-making as something not quite achieved, of something heterogeneous and incomplete, is expressed in the Baroque.[24]

One might wish to make a claim somewhat less grandiose: that as the outwork of early modern humanism, the baroque depicts the distortions and grotesqueries of human nature, and in the consolidating phase of the European colonial enterprise, it seems well adapted to newly outspoken classes such as mestizos, creoles, and other groups that stand away from the center of that enterprise. Hence there is a sort of contorted truth to observations like the one made by Leonard, that a mestizo population is itself baroque: assertions like this one represent the leading edge of a postcolonial outlook in literary and historical study of the mid-twentieth century, when what is struggling to be said – and in some quarters, such as the distinguished essay "El barroco de Indias" by the Venezuelan critic Mariano Picón-Salas, what actually is asserted – is that the baroque had an unusual force in Latin America because of "the hybrid influences that were inevitable in the collision of races and the violence of transplantation."[25] Going as far back as its precursors such as Celestina, the historical baroque is a mode of thought looking for a scene of hybridity in which to take hold. *La Celestina* is one such scene; the late colonial Americas are another.

Celestina is to the fiction of Rojas's *Celestina* approximately what the baroque is to early modern humanist and colonial culture: the principle that selects and extracts those strands of thought that might unravel the entire fabric, but in doing so fashions something more openly contradictory and complex. Mestizo and creole consciousnesses, when they emerge in the Americas during the seventeenth century, do not oppose a Europe-centered colonial outlook but render it closer to the complexity of the reality to which it ostensibly refers; likewise Celestina is both spokeswoman and critic of the social order into which she inserts herself from the edges, and she understands it better than the characters who have had no such vantage. She anticipates the outlook of a seventeenth-century colonial writer such as the Inca Garcilaso de la Vega, who describes Peruvian society before and after the Spanish conquest of 1532 from within and without; he often interprets contrasting sides and eras to each other in amphisbaenic terms, for example where he describes an especially barbaric pre-Incaic society as having run "a seminary to prepare youths – to be eaten."[26] This diagnostic function modeled in Celestina becomes only more indispensable as the sixteenth century turns into the seventeenth and such go-betweens – native and alien at once – are needed across the spheres of European societies at home and overseas. "Monster" is one of the things this kind of figure may be called, but there are more prosaic things too – spectator, anomaly, outlier, limit-case; and of course, as the seventeenth century goes along, author. Perhaps one of the principal attractions of the baroque as a vessel for colonial thought is that it gives all these standpoints a coherence they might have lacked otherwise. I think it goes without saying – I will return to this point later – that the absorption of such vantages into a colonial outlook anticipates a postcolonial outlook.

The venture into the baroque has two principal outcomes in *La Celestina*, both of which are influential in later mannerist and colonial discourses. First is the descriptive procedure by which Celestina herself enters the fiction. In the passages that characterize her and narrate her dubious activities, a certain descriptive mode, which will provide a model for much writing in the seventeenth century and later, becomes available. This mode includes the accounts of Celestina's interventions in nature, which can be described only through a seeing behind the superficial qualities and effects of a socially agreed reality. Here, for instance, is Pármeno's inventory of the materials used by Celestina in her ministrations to female clients:

> En su casa fazía perfumes; falsava estoraques, menjuý, animes, ámbar, algalia, polvillos, almizcles, mosquetes. Tenía una cámara llena de alambiques, de redomillas, de barrilejos de barro, de vidrio, de arambre, de estaño, hechos de mill faziones. Hazía solimán, afeyte cozido, argentadas, bujelladas, cerillas, llanillas, unturillas, lustres, luzentores, clarimientes, alvalinos y otras aguas de rostro, de rasuras de gamones, de cortezas de [e]spantalobos, de taraguntía, de hieles, de agraz, de mosto, destiladas y açucaradas. Adelgazava los cueros con çumos de limones, con turvino, con tuétano de corço y de garça y otras confaciones. Sacava aguas para oler, de rosas, de azahar, de jasmín, de trébol, de madreselva, [de] clavellinas, [*mosquetadas*] y almizcladas, polvorizadas con vino . . . Y los untos y mantecas que tenía, es hastío de dezir: de vaca, de osso, de cavallos y de camellos, de culebra y de conejo, de vallena, de garça y de alcaraván y de gamo y de gato montés y de texón, de harda, de herizo, de nutria. Aparejos para baños, esto

es una maravilla de las yervas y raýzes que tenía en el techo de su casa colgadas: mançanilla y romero, malvaviscos, culantrillo, coronillas, flor de saúco y de mostaza, espliego y laurel blanco, tortarosa y gramonilla, flor salvaje y higueruela, pico de oro y hoja tinta . . . Esto de los virgos, unos fazía de bexiga y otros curava de punto. Tenía en un tabladillo, en una caxuela pintada, agujas delgadas de pelligeros y hilos de seda encerados, y colgadas allí rayzes de hoja plasma y fuste sanguino, cebolla albarrana y cepacaballo. Hazía con esto maravillas, que quando vino por aquí el embaxador francés, tres vezes vendió por virgen una criada que tenía.[27]

[In her house she manufactured perfumes and counterfeited storax, benjamin, anime, amber, civet, powders, and musk. She had a room full of retorts and flasks, with vessels of earthenware, glass, tin, and brass, of a thousand different shapes. There she made mercury sublimate, skin lotions, jars of ointment, and eyebrow pencils; skin-fillers, salves, cleansers, fresheners, clarifiers, bleaches, and other waters for the face; grated asphodel, senna pods, tarragon, gall, new wine, and must, all distilled and sweetened with sugar. For softening the skin she used lemon juice, turpeth, deer and heron marrow, and other confections. She made perfume from roses, orange flowers, jasmine, clover, honeysuckle, and carnations, all powdered and mixed with musk and wine . . . It would be tiresome to recite all the oils and fats she extracted: from cows, bears, horses camels, snakes, rabbits, whales, herons, bitterns, chamois, wild cats, badgers, squirrels, porcupines, and otters. It would astonish you to learn of all the things she used for her medicinal baths, with herbs and roots which she had hanging from her roof, to wit: camomile, rosemary, marshmallow, maiden's hair, melilot, alder, mustard, lavender, white laurel, *tortarosa*, *gramonilla*, *flor salvaje*, psoralea, *pico de oro*, and *hoja tinta* . . . For the repair of maidenheads she used bladders, or she stitched them up. In a small painted box on a platform she kept a supply of furrier's needles and waxed silk, and hanging under it she had roots of *hoja plasma* and *fuste sanguino*, squill, and horsetail. She did such wonders with this, that when the French ambassador was here, she sold him one of her girls for a virgin three times running!][28]

From the vantage of a descriptive model that lives on, the decisive feature here is the enjambment of a medieval catalogue of nature with the narration of Celestina's technological prowess and its result: moreover, the assertion at the climax of the passage, "hazía con esto maravillas" [she did marvels with this], suggests that the plurality of the catalogue has become the singularity ("this") of a compounded and confected nature, a new object such as virginity or love that Celestina has made out of a vast store of raw materials. The logic here – many elements, acted on by knowledge, to become a single product invested with social meaning – becomes indispensable to many colonial-era descriptions of how an unfamiliar reality of the East or West Indies might have been made, or might be unmade in turn, by conquest; it is also precisely baroque, in that a slew of major seventeenth-century works concerned with the mastery of nature, what Francis Bacon called "Human Empire," could not do without it.

> About Mexico more than in any other part groweth that excellent tree called *metl*, which they plant and dress as they do their vines in Europe. It hath near forty kinds of leaves, which serve for many uses, for when they be tender, they make of them conserves, paper, flax, mantles, mats, shoes, girdles, and cordage. On these leaves grow certain prickles so strong and sharp that they use them instead of saws: from the root of this tree cometh a juice like unto syrup, which being sodden will become sugar. You may also make of it wine and vinegar. The Indians often become drunk with it. The rind roasted healeth hurts and sores, and from the top boughs issueth a gum, which is an excellent antidote against poison. There is nothing in Mexico and about it wanting which may make a city happy. Certainly had those who have so much extolled with their pens the parts of Granada in Spain, Lombardy and Florence in Italy, making them the earthly Paradise, been acquainted with the New World and with Mexico, they would have recanted their untruths.[29]

> We have also large and various orchards and gardens, wherein we do not so much respect beauty, as variety of ground and soil, proper for divers trees and herbs: and some very spacious, where trees and berries are set whereof we make divers kinds of drinks, besides the vineyards. In these we practise likewise all conclusions of grafting and inoculating, as well of wild-trees as fruit-trees, which produceth many effects. And we make (by art) in the same orchards and gardens, trees and flowers to come earlier or later than their seasons; and to come up and bear more speedily than by their natural course they do. We make them also by art greater much than their nature; and their fruit greater and sweeter and of differing taste, smell, colour, and figure, from their nature.[30]

"Hazía con esto maravillas" [he/she/I made marvels of this] might be the label for this motif, which is central to both *La Celestina* and the baroque of a century later. The emergence of Celestina out of the shadows of a conventional romance marks a turn toward "Human Empire": though she scarcely travels, is not an artist or a scientist, and belongs at the bottom of the social order, Celestina embodies a will to power over nature and human beings that will be taken up, in the discursive terms associated with her, by later figures in the concurrent colonial and baroque eras. She clears ground for them, which gives one important answer to the continual riddle of her longevity as a touchstone and model.

The second outcome of *La Celestina*'s baroque outlook, concomitant with the first, is the manner of representing speech it assigns to the principal figures.[31] The early twentieth-century scholar Morris W. Croll wrote that the baroque style in prose, including a battery of conventions and a complicated set of attitudes toward classical models, is a way of representing "not a thought, but a mind thinking."[32] Unusual for its date, *La Celestina* represents the speech of figures who anticipate the technical devices but also the larger fictional purposes of much seventeenth-century writing. There are many examples, not limited to the speech of Celestina herself but at her instigation erupting often across the fiction:

> CELESTINA. El propósito muda el sabio; el nescio persevera. A nuevo negocio, nuevo consejo se requiere. No pensé yo, hijo Sempronio, que assí me respondiera mi buena fortuna. De los discretos mensajeros es fazer lo que el tiempo quiere.[33]

> [CELESTINA. Opportunity moves the wise man; the fool persists. For new business, new plans. I didn't know, my son Sempronio, that such good fortune would come to me. A discreet messenger adapts to what the times require.]

> PÁRMENO. Con Sempronio me paresce que es impossible sostenerse mi amistad. Él es desvariado, yo mal sofrido: conciértame essos amigos.

> CELESTINA. Pues no era essa tu condición.

> PÁRMENO. A la mi fe, mientra más fui creciendo, más la primera paciencia me olvidava. No soy el que solía y assí mismo Sempronio no [ha] ni tiene en que me aproveche.[34]

[PÁRMENO. I think it's impossible for me and Sempronio to be friends. He talks too much and I can't suffer him. See if these two can be harmonized!

CELESTINA. But you used to have a different condition.

PÁRMENO. By my faith, as I grew, I lost the patience I had. I am not who I used to be, and this Sempronio is not who I want to be.]

PLEBERIO. ¡O vida de congoxas llena, de miserias acompañada! ¡O mundo, mundo! Muchos mucho de ti dixeron, muchos en tus qualidades metieron la mano; a diversas cosas por oýdas te compararon; yo por triste esperiencia lo contaré, como a quien las ventas y compras de tu engañosa feria no prósperamente suciedieron . . .

Yo pensava en mi más tierna edad que eras y eran tus hechos regidos por alguna orden; agora, visto el pro y la contra de tus bienandanças, me pareces un labarinto de errores, un desierto espantable, una morada de fieras, juego de hombres que andan en corro, laguna llena de cieno, región llena de espinas, monte alto, campo pedregoso, prado lleno de serpientes, huerto florido y sin fruto, fuente de cuydados, río de lágrimas, mar de miserias, trabajo sin provecho, dulce ponçoña, vana esperança, falsa alegría, verdadero dolor.[35]

[PLEBERIO. Oh life, full of troubles and misery! Oh world, world! Many have written of its practices and compared it with many things, but they spoke from hearsay. I will describe the world as one who has been cheated in its false marketplaces . . .

When I was young I thought the world was ruled by order. I know better now! It is a labyrinth of errors, a frightful desert, a den of wild beasts, a game in which men run in circles, a lake of mud, a thorny thicket, a dense forest, a stony field, a meadow full of serpents, a river of tears, a sea of miseries, effort without profit, a flowering but barren orchard, a running spring of cares, a sweet poison, a vain hope, a false joy, and a true pain.][36]

Fifty years ago, the baroque dimension of such passages would have been seen largely as a feat of style, due for inspection in the fashion of such mid-century literary historians as Croll, Lowry Nelson Jr., Frank Warnke, and René Wellek. Rightly or wrongly, I think it is now more convincing to say that the baroque here is a stance, an attitude that can appear in many literary and artistic situations from the Middle Ages on – and only its zenith is the seventeenth century. The baroque indeed displays a set of stylistic markers, but these tend to be the effects of its stance. For instance, a baroque speaker will often address the incommensurability between his past and his present, reflecting on his quondam self as though a different person, and will devise vivid figures of speech to carry the implications of that difference.[37] The famous soliloquies of Segismundo in Calderón's *La vida es sueño* (*Life Is a Dream*), exemplary of baroque as attitude, demonstrate this tendency and join it to other preoccupations of the period (such as reality versus deception, and the inherent monstrosity of humankind):

> SEGISMUNDO. ¡Válgame el cielo, qué veo!
> ¡Válgame el cielo, qué miro!
> ¡Con poco espanto lo admiro!
> ¡Con mucha duda lo creo!
> ¿Yo en palacios suntuosos?
> ¿Yo entre telas y brocados?
> ¿Yo cercado de crïados
> tan lucidos y briosos?
> ¿Yo despertar de dormir
> en lecho tan excelente?
> ¿Yo en medio de tanta gente
> que me sirva de vestir?
> Decir que sueño es engaño;
> bien sé que despierto estoy.
> ¿Yo Segismundo no soy?
> Dadme, cielos, desengaño.
> Decidme: ¿qué pudo ser
> esto que a mi fantasía
> sucedió mientras dormía,
> que aquí me he llegado a ver?
> . . .
> SEGISMUNDO. ¿Qué quizá soñando estoy,
> aunque despierto me veo?
> No sueño, pues toco y creo
> lo que he sido y lo que soy.
> Y aunque agora te arrepientas,
> poco remedio tendrás:
> sé quién soy y no podrás,
> aunque suspires y sientas,
> quitarme el haber nacido
> desta corona heredero.

Y, si me viste primero
a las prisiones rendido,
fue porque ignoré quién era;
pero ya informado estoy
de quién soy y sé que soy
un compuesto de hombre y fiera.[38]

[SEGISMUNDO. Great Heaven! What am I seeing?
What is all this?
I would be more willing to admire
If I were able to believe my eyes!
I, in the splendor of a palace? Dressed in brocade and satin?
I, attended by courtiers, so handsome, so deferential!
I, waking in a bed such as this?
I, with all these people helping me to dress?
No–no. That would be mere self-deception,
For I am awake and I know it!
I am Segismundo, am I not?
Heaven enlighten me!
Some change must have come over me while I slept!
Some inexplicable trick of fantasy
Which is the reason why I find myself here!
. . .
SEGISMUNDO. Dreaming, although I imagine myself awake?
No, I am not dreaming! I touch, and feel
What I am, and what I was! It is too late,
For you to repent it now! I know who I am,
And you can never, for all your prayers and sighs,
Rob me of my birth-right! I am heir to the crown,
And if in the past I accepted my imprisonment,
You must understand that I did not know what I was,
But now I know myself! I am nature's monster,
Part man, part beast!][39]

While the mere observation of incommensurability is a convention of humanism, the more complex effects it produces in the texture of a fiction – a self-description like Celestina's "messenger" that is no off-hand metaphor but a conceit that concretizes a new way of living in an unpredictable milieu, or Pleberio's barrage of epithets about the world, or Segismundo's passionate avowals – bear the imprint of the baroque. (Peter N. Dunn writes that, with Pleberio's concluding speech, "Rojas has put at the end of his play a little tag: if you pull it, the whole illusion can be turned inside out. A very type and model for Spain's Golden Age of wit."[40]) Part of the effect in these cases comes out of the labyrinthine rhetoric that turns one way and then another, considering alternatives in a living act of mind; another cause is the assumption that truth and fantasy are not remote from each other but adjacent, and easily confused one for the other. In other cases baroque speakers such as Sancho Panza turn aphorisms, commonplaces, and other forms of consensus inside out, set them against one another, or pile them up to establish an effect of vertiginous comparison. Details come to stand out from the larger setting, parts replace wholes, and the composition of the passage or the work is thrown into motion. Later figures such as Gracián and Pascal rethink these aphoristic inventories and produce yet another kind of baroque writing, with different points of reference for the values of economy and profusion. In observing styles we see the effects of baroque, but in decoding stances we get at the social purposes that make different styles meaningful. The dominant stance of *La Celestina* uncovers, through the social forensics of Celestina herself, the incongruities between different positions in Spanish society, and confronts them with their own language turned askew, hypertrophied, and exposed in its implications. Celestina herself is the instrument of this project who in carrying it out rehearses the emergent baroque.

I have mentioned that the protobaroque of *La Celestina* promises an openness – of language, of art, of social horizons – as against the comparatively closed outlooks and aesthetics of Rojas's other characters, and of the humanist Renaissance then underway. Such openness is never intrinsic or absolute, but emerges as a function of the osmotic pressure exerted by history and culture – what Charles S. Singleton calls "the balance of forces which the artist had created between the inside of his work and the outside" – on the properties of a given work.[41] There is, however, a long-term alliance between this property of openness and the postcolonial position especially in Latin America. The Brazilian avant-garde poet and critic Haroldo de Campos wrote some years ago of his own aesthetic as "neo-baroque," including in this designation his advances on the postcolonial initiatives begun in the 1920s by the modernists Mário de Andrade, Oswald de Andrade, and their contemporaries who saw Brazilian literature as writing its way aggressively out of its colonial condition. In the sense recalled by González Echevarría, Campos saw his baroqueness as an affirmative answer to the colonial past which is itself conditioned by the baroque:

> For the major writers of Latin America, the "nightmare of history," with all it implies for the most militant spirits . . . has been a Baroque and obsessive nightmare of writing (taken to an oxymoron-like paroxysm when it becomes aware that it is in forced and painful cohabitation with the writing-less world of the large segments of the population which are illiterate). "The masses will still taste the ritzy crackers I bake," prophesized Oswald de Andrade, in a pun enlivened by the "Prinzip Hoffnung" like that which prepares the nutritious marrow, the amniotic meal for the Anthropophagic future.[42]

For Campos as for Severo Sarduy, Octavio Paz, and other major Latin American writers of the 1960s and after, the baroque – confronted in their studies of Gregório de Matos, Góngora, and Sor Juana, respectively – is the marrow of Latin American culture that will be transmuted into tomorrow's feast.[43]

> To speak the Baroque code, in the literature of Colonial Brazil, was to try to extract the difference of the morphosis of the same. As the allegorical style of the Baroque was an alternative speech – a style in which, in extreme cases, anything could symbolize anything else . . . the "alternating current" of the Baroque brasilica was a double speech of the other as difference: to speak a code of otherness and to speak it in a state of otherness . . .

> Speaking the difference in the gaps of a universal code, the Latin American writers of the Baroque evolved among themselves a dialogue which has only now begun to be re-established . . . Gregório, the Bahian, Sor Juana the Mexican, the Peruvian Caviedes – all participated in a discourse that moved back and forth tropologically, even though there was neither exact contemporary [*sic*] nor direct allusion. This discourse was extended also as a symposium that went back in time: to it came Góngora, Quevedo, Lope, Garcilaso, Camões, Sá de Miranda, Petrarch . . . Literature, in the Colonies as in the Metropolis, was made from literature. Except that in the Colonies, it had the chance to articulate itself as a double difference. The difference of the different.[44]

To this symposium that rushes backward in history gathering in the formative models of the Hispanophone colonial world, Celestina, of course, is the missing penultimate term – so "different" in her anachronism, her sex, and her frank espousal of sensual freedom that she comes to be elided even in the chronicle of Campos, her descendant in baroque prolixity. After Petrarch but before Sá de Miranda and Garcilaso, and contemporaneous with the discovery of Brazil, Celestina enacts what counts as postcolonial for Campos, "the difference of the different." She is part of her society – participates in defining it – but is determinably different, occupying the vantage of her own baroqueness. From "her initial conversation with Pármeno," Stephen Gilman observes, "she provides – in addition to the sheer delight of her mastery of the mother tongue – the sophistry necessary to their lives. Sinfulness aside, sensual freedom exists here in function of exaggeration, prevarication, rationalization, lamentation, trivialization, and every other sort of communicative misbehavior."[45] When that sensual freedom is joined with a will to "Human Empire," the expressive result is a discourse that, while it can never be the voice of orthodoxy, at the same time will not go out of fashion for at least three hundred years. We might adjust Gilman's account and say that Celestina's is the voice not of misbehavior but of insurgency, baroque and postcolonial *avant la lettre*.

NOTES

1. Irving A. Leonard, *Baroque Times in Old Mexico: Seventeenth-Century Persons, Places, and Practices* (Ann Arbor: University of Michigan Press, 1959), 29–30.
2. The best account of preposterousness in early modern literature is that of Patricia Parker, *Shakespeare from the Margins: Language, Culture, Context* (Chicago: University of Chicago Press, 1996), 20–55.
3. Leonard, *Baroque Times in Old Mexico*, 37–8.
4. Roberto González Echevarría, Celestina's *Brood: Continuities of the Baroque in Spanish and Latin American Literature* (Durham, NC: Duke University Press, 1993), 32.
5. Irving A. Leonard, *Books of the Brave: Being an Account of Books and of Men in the Spanish Conquest and Settlement of the Sixteenth-Century New World*, second edn (Berkeley and Los Angeles: University of California Press, 1992), 116–17, 348, 401.
6. González Echevarría, Celestina's *Brood*, 4. The more informative accounts of traditional usages of *baroque* include René Wellek, "The Concept of Baroque in Literary Scholarship," *Journal of Aesthetics and Art Criticism* 5 (1946): 70–109; Lowry Nelson, Jr., *Baroque Lyric Poetry* (New Haven: Yale University Press, 1961), 3–17; James V. Mirollo, *The Poet of the Marvelous: Giambattista Marino* (New York: Columbia

University Press, 1963), 269–78; and Frank J. Warnke, *Versions of Baroque: European Literature in the Seventeenth Century* (New Haven: Yale University Press, 1972).

7. José Antonio Maravall, *El mundo social de* La Celestina, second edn (Madrid: Gredos, 1968), 177.

8. José Antonio Maravall, *Culture of the Baroque: Analysis of a Historical Structure*, trans. Terry Cochran (Theory and History of Literature 25, Minneapolis: University of Minnesota Press, 1986), 4.

9. Compare Ernst Robert Curtius, *European Literature and the Latin Middle Ages*, trans. Willard R. Trask (Bollingen Series 36, Princeton: Princeton University Press, 1953), 283.

10. Michael Camille, "Simulacrum," in *Critical Terms for Art History*, ed. Robert S. Nelson and Richard Schiff (Chicago: University of Chicago Press, 1996), 40.

11. Natalie Melas, "Versions of Incommensurability," *World Literature Today* 69.2 (1995): 275–80 at 277.

12. Maravall, *Culture of the Baroque*, trans. Cochran, 149–72.

13. See my "Colonial Becomes Postcolonial," *MLQ* 65 (2004): 423–41.

14. This is to forbear discussing many other aspects of *La Celestina*. The more comprehensive accounts include those by María Rosa Lida de Malkiel, *La originalidad artística de* La Celestina, second edn (Buenos Aires: Editorial Universitaria de Buenos Aires, 1970), and Stephen Gilman, *The Art of* La Celestina (Madison: University of Wisconsin Press, 1956).

15. Gilman, *The Art of* La Celestina, 3–7, gives an informative brief account of the early editions.

16. Fernando de Rojas, *La Celestina: Comedia o Tragicomedia de Calisto y Melibea*, ed. Peter E. Russell (Madrid: Castalia, 1991), 231–3. I have also used, but do not cite, the critical edition by Miguel Marciales, 2 vols. (Illinois Medieval Monographs 1, Urbana: University of Illinois Press, 1985).

17. Here as throughout, I have adapted the translation by Lesley Byrd Simpson, *The Celestina: A Fifteenth-Century Novel in Dialogue* (Berkeley and Los Angeles: University of California Press, 1955), 10–11.

18. Rojas, *La Celestina*, ed. Russell, 233–4.

19. Rojas, *The Celestina*, trans. Simpson, 11–12.

20. Rojas, *La Celestina*, ed. Russell, 238.

21. Rojas, *The Celestina*, trans. Simpson, 15.

22. A. D. Deyermond, *The Petrarchan Sources of* La Celestina (Oxford: Oxford University Press, 1961).

23. Lida de Malkiel, *La originalidad artística*, 139.

24. González Echevarría, Celestina's *Brood*, 198–9.

25. Mariano Picón-Salas, "The Baroque of the Indies," in *A Cultural History of Spanish America: From Conquest to Independence*, trans. Irving A. Leonard (Berkeley and Los Angeles: University of California Press, 1963), 86.

26. Inca Garcilaso de la Vega, *Comentarios reales de los Incas*, ed. Aurelio Miró Quesada, 2 vols. (Caracas: Biblioteca Ayacucho, 1976), vol. I, 32.

27. Rojas, *La Celestina*, ed. Russell, 243–5.

28. Rojas, *La Celestina*, trans. Simpson, 18–19.

29. Thomas Gage, *Travels in the New World*, ed. J. Eric S. Thompson (Norman: University of Oklahoma Press, 1958), 76.

30. Francis Bacon, *New Atlantis*, in *Works*, ed. James Spedding *et al.*, 14 vols. (London, 1862–76), vol. III, 158.

31. Gilman, *The Art of* La Celestina, is the definitive study in English of the style of the fiction, as Lida de Malkiel, *La originalidad artística*, is the most distinguished study in Spanish.

32. Morris W. Croll, "The Baroque Style in Prose" (1929), in his *Style, Rhetoric, and Rhythm*, ed. J. Max Patrick and Robert O. Evans *et al.* (1966; reprinted Woodbridge, CT: Ox Bow Press, 1989), 210.

33. Rojas, *La Celestina*, ed. Russell, 332.

34. Rojas, *La Celestina*, ed. Russell, 360–1.

35. Rojas, *La Celestina*, ed. Russell, 598–9.

36. Rojas, *La Celestina*, trans. Simpson, 159.

37. Compare Nelson, *Baroque Lyric Poetry*, 32–40.

38. Pedro Calderón de la Barca, *La vida es sueño*, ed. José M. Ruano de la Haza (Madrid: Castalia, 1994), 187–8, 209–10.

39. Pedro Calderón de la Barca, *Life's a Dream*, trans. Kathleen Raine and R. M. Nadal (London: Hamish Hamilton, 1968), 38, 47–8.

40. Peter N. Dunn, "Pleberio's World," *PMLA* 91 (1976): 406–19 at 417.

41. Charles S. Singleton, *An Essay on the* Vita Nuova (Baltimore: The Johns Hopkins University Press, 1949), 5.

42. Haroldo de Campos, "The Rule of Anthropophagy: Europe under the Sign of Devoration," trans. Maria Tai Wolff, *Latin American Literary Review* 14.27 (1986): 42–60 at 56.

43. Campos, "The Rule of Anthropophagy" on Matos; Severo Sarduy, "Sur Góngora," *Tel Quel* 25 (1966): 91–3; and Octavio Paz, *Sor Juana, Or, The Traps of Faith*, trans. Margaret Sayers Peden (Cambridge, MA: Belknap Press of Harvard University Press, 1988). See also Severo Sarduy, "The Baroque and the Neobaroque," in *Latin America in Its Literature*, ed. César Fernández Moreno, trans. Mary G. Berg (New York: Holmes and Meier, 1980), 114–32.

44. Campos, "The Rule of Anthropophagy," 49. The final ellipsis is in the original.

45. Stephen Gilman, *The Spain of Fernando de Rojas: The Intellectual and Social Landscape of* La Celestina (Princeton: Princeton University Press, 1972), 25.

Epilogue

11

Translations and transnationals:
pre- and postcolonial

Ato Quayson

As theories and ideas from postcolonial studies have been applied
increasingly to different disciplinary domains, both postcolonialism
and the nature of these other disciplinary domains have undergone
progressive transformation. In literary studies we now have postcolonial applications to Shakespeare and the Romantic period, as well as to
Irish, Scottish, and even Korean studies. Further afield, there are the
now-standard postcolonial inflections to anthropology, history, philosophy, and urban studies. More unexpected disciplinary areas that have
embraced postcolonial ideas are science fiction and management studies.
However, in all these cases it has become clear that postcolonialism has
traveled far from its initial basis in discussions of the relations between
the colonizer and the colonized, of the unsettled and mutually defining
interactions between the empire and its peripheries, and of the flows
and counter-flows of ideas, practices, and peoples between formerly
colonized places and the West.

Several things make these transpositions from postcolonial theory
readily comprehensible. The first, and perhaps most obvious, is that
postcolonialism is inherently about relations of hegemony and resistance in the encounter between different cultures and peoples. Even
though empire and colonialism established the parameters of this
dynamic on a large historical scale, it is also evident that such encounters persist in miniature in various other contexts. It is this essential
hegemonic/counter-hegemonic dialectic within postcolonial debates
that makes ideas from the field amenable to productive transfer into
other domains. But in such transfers there is a translation of the prelim-
inary categories into different forms of articulation. Thus in management studies, perhaps the most unexpected context for the application

of postcolonial theory, workers are cast as the postcolonial subalterns in their struggles with management. The endemic storytelling cultures within organizations are then interpreted as the means by which a representational nexus is established that allows the worker-as-subaltern to adopt and shift his or her subject positions in relation to management, now cast as the hegemonic authority.[1]

There are three main steps I take in this epilogue to *Postcolonial Approaches to the European Middle Ages*. Reading first as a postcolonial critic, I outline what I see to be some of the distinctive methodological and discursive features of the essays in this collection and discuss how these features might help to reconfigure the "postcolonial" in its varied applications. Secondly, I outline, in terms of both content and methodological features, the terms by which the postcolonial might be enriched by perspectives from medieval scholarship. As I will be suggesting later, there are various comparative possibilities that are clarified when the field of medieval studies is seen in *contrapuntal copresence* with other areas of literary studies, rather than in the form of chronological sequence that obeys a brutal logic of evolution and literary supersession or decay. Contrapuntal copresence, borrowed from Edward Said's *The World, the Text, and the Critic*, but recast for the present context, implies not just comparison but an understanding of how different levels of the medieval text (tropes, religious sensibilities, and signifiers that betray anxieties about variant sociocultural encounters) might be related dialogically to later, postcolonial texts and their varied discursive and symbolic configurations understood alongside one another.[2] My aim is to outline areas of cross-fertilization between medieval studies and postcolonialism. I conclude by musing about the implications that such a conjunctural copresence between medieval and postcolonial studies might have for conceptualizing new pedagogies.

MEANS, METHODS, AND MEANINGS

Several features of medieval scholarship bring themselves to the attention in the essays in this collection. First is the absolute centrality of material culture – cultural artifacts, paintings, maps and manuscripts, architecture, roads, and churches – and of the many skills that are called upon in discussing them and understanding their significance. From the introduction onwards, the stage is set for the centralization of material culture as a starting point for wider meditations. The discussion of the *Très riches heures* of Jean, duc de Berry and its illumination by the Limbourg brothers establishes essential features of the medievalist's approach to such material culture. Within the manuscript illumination, we are invited to take note of the multivalent layers that coalesce around the representation of the Magi and their quest for the newborn Christ. These layers include the determinations of foreground and background, the cross-layered emblems of different cityscapes, the highly suggestive sartorial details of the Magi on display and the religious sensibility that suffuses all aspects of the painting.

What is evident from this rich manuscript illustration is the degree to which the material artifact embraces various sensibilities and temporal trajectories, and indeed the uncanny simultaneity of the sacred and the mundane. This makes the artifact an object that is both an archive and a quasi-archaeological site for interpretative excavation. But to excavate its meanings properly requires a whole array of skills, from the knowledge of deep history and the grasp of languages, to the understanding of the subtle interrelations within an evolving Christian structure of feeling that had to Other what it perceived as potentially contaminating and threatening. This Othering is by no means simple or straightforward: from the *Très riches heures* emerges an ambivalent representation of the Magi as bearers of objects of desire, even as they stand slightly outside the realm of salvation. More importantly, the *Très riches heures* acts as the conjunctural site of multiple realities, not all of which are visible at the same time. For the modern medievalist, there is the need to "travel" both conceptually and imaginatively along the "code of signals," as Caravaggio puts it in Michael Ondaatje's *The English Patient*, even whilst surrendering to the incredible beauty of the illumination.[3] And, as in Caravaggio's efforts in unthreading the story from the patient, who himself has the sensibility of an encyclopedic labyrinth (symbolized by his well-thumbed and cross-referenced copy of Herodotus), the process of unraveling the past involves a mixture of wonder and loss, and of knowledge driven by an ultimately insatiable curiosity.

The chapters that follow make similar critical and discursive moves to Kabir and Williams's essay, but to strategically different effect. For Nicholas Howe, for example, the Roman *spolia* that litter the

Anglo-Saxon landscape are the architectural residue of the colonial relationship between the Romans and England. The apparent self-scrutiny
of Anglo-Saxon society with regard to its relationship to the imperial
past is by no means retrievable in its full form. Rather, by crossing from
architecture and Roman roads to texts and back again, meaning is to
be read within the whole spectrum of the available cultural ensemble,
whether the traces of this ensemble are architectural, archival, or indeed
archaeological. The distance established with the Roman past produces a
"staggered" postcolonialism. There is the self-conscious postcolonialism
that seeks to interpret the past and perhaps appropriate it for contemporary uses. This version of postcolonialism develops under the rubric of
temporal transcendence. The past is thus a different country that has to
be understood for the present to be lived. But there is another sense of
postcolonialism as the quest for models of cultural practice produced by
the conjuncture between the imperial and the colonized, and the native
and the foreign, in which "native" and "foreign" are mutually defining in
terms of what Frantz Fanon terms the "zone of occult instability where
the people dwell."[4]

The second discursive move that these essays share is the practice
of what might be termed historical emblematization. This has various
dimensions. Sometimes in the material under discussion there seems
to be a straightforward intertextual invocation of Roman or classical
models and templates. However, the term "intertextuality" does not do
full justice to the social, political, and even emotional investments that
pertain to the practice of invoking the past. For example, James Harper's
chapter on "Turks as Trojans" details the relays of signification between
different paintings and periods that allowed the Trojans to be represented
first in the rich Eastern garb and demeanor of Turks, and subsequently
in the cuirass armor of the ancient Romans. Each representation is part
of a larger discursive nexus in the relationship between Western Europe
and Turkey, which first was one of admiration and wonder, and then,
with the onset of the Ottoman threat, was succeeded by suspicion and
terror. Artistic representations of the Trojans, assumed ancestors of the
Italians, the English, the Burgundians, and the Habsburgs, are then
situated in the interstices between wonder and terror, defining in their
own way Europe's changing relationship to its various competitors in
the medieval world.

That the legacy of imperial Rome is itself being deployed for purposes of propaganda is not insignificant either, because, as Ananya Jahanara Kabir's "Analogy in translation" shows, invocations of ancient Rome enable an incredibly fertile payout of sign, symbol, and meaning. Kabir's felicitous term, "analogical calculus," captures the situated and strategic ways in which ancient Rome was invoked and reveals the second dimension of historical emblematization: depending on the desired political objectives, the English were typified in various discursive positions as Romans, Normans, or even Anglo-Saxons. The analogies were then far from idle or decorative. They were central to the calculus of power. The notion of "analogical calculus" applies also to the essays by Suzanne Akbari and Alfred Hiatt, which show how successive practices of map-making in the Middle Ages invoke the discursive past of cartographic practice to situate a new enterprise and to enable the maps to be read as symbolic ensembles. The medieval map, then, becomes an emblematic template of an entire world-view, but one that is to be seen within the traces of cartographic practices reaching back into the classical and Roman periods as well as forward to present-day cartographic representations of Palestine, allowing us, as Howe puts it, "to read images of land in terms of the histories they incorporate or erase."

The third main feature of the collection concerns a specifically situated human consciousness contemplating the legacy of the distant past and attempting to translate this directly into a personal theater of contemplation and action. In Michelle Warren's "Au commencement était l'île," Joseph Bédier's alienation is the product of an existential rupture of a colonial identity split between two homelands. At stake in his double consciousness is the concept of "homeland" itself, raising the question of whether the life-long engagement with the *Chanson* really succeeds in bridging the existential void. In Deanne Williams's "Gower's monster," John Gower appropriates the monstrous figure of Nebuchadnezzar as a channel for the production of the hybrid text of the *Confessio Amantis* and also as a means of meditating upon the mixed nature of translation itself, moving between barbarism and civility, miracle and metaphor, and man and beast. The monstrous provides further opportunity to stage a labile zodiac of textual epiphanies in Seth Lerer's "On fagne flor." Lerer attends with wonder to Heaney's own sense of wonder as conveyed in his translation of *Beowulf.* Responding to Heaney's interpellation of the history of Northern Ireland within the body of *Beowulf,* Lerer initiates a process of self-reflexivity that includes himself as medieval and postcolonial critic.

The three main discursive critical maneuvers I have outlined – the centralization of material culture, historical emblematization and the implications of an analogical calculus, and the intimate and situated personal encounters with the past – all provide productive lines of development for postcolonial studies. Interest in material culture and in popular culture more generally has vastly expanded following the burgeoning of the field of cultural studies. Evolving at first from the marxist-inspired work of Stuart Hall and others at the Birmingham Centre for Contemporary Culture in the 1960s, cultural studies has veered into current postmodernist-inflected studies of popular culture that tend to place material culture in a rather peculiar position of simultaneous privilege and peripherality. For often the study of material artifacts and of popular culture is done so as to illustrate already existing postmodernist and poststructuralist theories of the expressive totality of fragments, the instability of subject positions, and the specularization of identity that has been generated through the power of advertising and the media.[5] The lament of most critics of current versions of cultural studies is precisely the fact that there is no clear attempt to embed material objects within their contexts of production. Rather, the emphasis seems to be predominantly on consumption and interpretation, with the traces of relations of productions that are left within the material object gaining scant attention.[6]

Material and popular culture have also been of interest to postcolonial studies. One thinks of Anthony Appiah's discussion of the Yoruba man and his bicycle in *In My Father's House,* of Ashis Nandy's wide-ranging discussion of Bollywood films as signs of the formation of an Indian popular structure of feeling in his introduction to *The Secret Politics of Our Desires,* or of Achille Mbembe's discussion of political comics in Cameroon in *On the Postcolony.*[7] All these instances differ from the examples given us by medieval scholarship in at least one central respect. The sense in which medievalists take their material objects as conjunctural differs sharply from how comparable material or popular cultural domains are perceived by postcolonial scholars. For the medieval material object is layered with multiple levels of signification: one of the effects of long centuries of interpretation. The medieval material object is conjunctural because of the multivalent worlds it often brings together as well as the sedimentation of successive acts of interpretation upon its surface. The very fact that the languages in which they were encapsulated have to be studied and are not necessarily lived languages in the present day also adds to their layering. That is not to say that the material object in the postcolonial domain is not also conjunctural and layered. However, the temporal proximity of the postcolonial object to the critical universe that attempts to make sense of it implies that wonder in this context is a function of a certain experiential immediacy, thus calling for different procedures by which its conjunctural layering is to be addressed.

The notions of conjuncture and layering are themselves useful as modalities for transposition between the two disciplinary domains. Each level of the object under discussion, be it a text, a painting, a map, or an architectural site, is to be taken primarily as the conjunctural location of various vectors, with each vector being itself taken as opening out to other levels. What emerges then, in practice, is in a way a mirroring of the interactive intermeshing levels of any fertile literary or social phenomenon. With regard to the literary artifact, each of its levels is best seen as interacting rather than stable, such that the effort to isolate a single dimension for analysis must necessarily take account of the other levels that impinge upon it and that in fact allow it to become visible as an object of analysis in the first place. Thus, when we isolate characterization, metaphor and symbol, spectacle and setting, and the spatiotemporal and ethical coordinates of the literary universe, we conduct this isolation only as a heuristic surgical operation to allow us to talk about the specific literary phenomenon we are interested in. But there is no true literary criticism that then settles on the individual level of analysis as self-sufficient. Rather, in the best traditions of literary criticism there is a constant process of embedding and re-embedding into larger contexts of signification.

The critical question with regard to a reading of non-literary phenomena on the other hand, is how to isolate a particular social, political, or economic detail for analysis while managing to avoid severing it from the complex and contradictory historical processes that transect the non-literary detail in the first place. The manner in which textual levels interact is not the same as that by which different vectors of society and culture interact. The point is that each social phenomenon has a different way in which it expresses its determinative contradictions. Furthermore, the rates at which different contradictory elements alter and change historically are not the same. It is these methodological inflections, and not just the transfer of specific insights from postcolonialism, that seem to me to bear productive extrapolation for the mutual cross-illumination of the two fields. The careful work of embedding that we find in medieval scholarship has methodological resonances for postcolonial studies.

A Yoruba proverb affirms, "Aiye l'oja, orin n'ile" [the world is a market and heaven is home], showing how important the marketplace is in the culture's conception of cosmos. This proverbial encapsulation of the confluence of the physical and the spirit worlds becomes the informing matrix behind Wole Soyinka's *Death and the King's Horseman*, but is easy to miss unless we become alert to the status of material objects and the relationship they have with other levels of signification in the play. The opening of the play takes us directly into the wealth of a material domain; the set is composed of market stalls packed with cloths of resplendent colors and designs. This provides a backdrop to the tragic action that will unfold, which centers on the failed bid of the King's Horseman in committing ritual suicide as enjoined upon him by tradition following the death of the recently deceased king. Much later, and at the critical point of liminal crossing, Elesin Oba is interrupted in his trance by the white District Commissioner. But Elesin acknowledges that the interruption was not entirely to blame for his failure. He acknowledges that he has been overly tied to affairs of the flesh, having earlier persuaded the head of the market women to arrange for him to sleep with a young woman who catches his eye on his last day on earth. It is this vector of hedonistic fervor, folding simultaneously the sacred dimension to his epic task, that undermines his capacity to achieve the ritual crossing. Significantly, the liminality at the level of character consciousness is given a perfect and colorful expression in the material effusions of the marketplace and the resplendent cloths on display at the start of the play. If it is noted that the cloths that Elesin wears are themselves those lavished upon him by the market women, we see that Soyinka achieves a subtle metonymic displacement of the *sense of liminality* from the market, already stipulated by the culture as lying on the crossroads between earth and heaven, onto the person of Elesin himself. Thus we find that, following the procedures elaborated by medieval scholars, the material domain is to be taken as a conjunctural location of several interlocking vectors of significance, from the sense of a world-view, to the ritual relations between men and women as conveyed in the circuit of gift exchange, to the more metaphorical implications of material details as signifiers of the temptations of the flesh.

Something of this material alertness even helps us to gloss the canonical texts that have become such intense interpretative objects in postcolonial studies. In reading *Othello*, for example, a question that becomes pertinent is why there are various literal and metaphorical references to beds. The bed had a particular place in the Renaissance, and in Shakespeare's plays there are numerous references to it, but none more tragically significant than in *Othello*. The bed moves from the domain of innuendo, as is seen in Iago's strident "Even now, now, very now, an old black ram/ Is tupping your white ewe" (I.i.87–8) with all its implied terror of miscegenation, to a peculiarly saturated reference in Othello's moment of self-loathing:[8]

> Haply for I am black
> And have not those soft parts of conversation
> That chamberers have, or for I am declined
> Into the vale of years.
> (III.iii.268–70)

The word "chamberers" here does dual service. On the one hand, it refers to drawing-room gallants, polished Venetian men who possess the requisite cultural skills to impress and indeed win women, something in which Othello declares himself deficient. The second meaning, more pertinent to the various resonances of the bed, is that implied biblically in Romans 13.13, "Let us walk honestly . . . not in rioting and drunkenness, neither in chambering and wantonness," which E. A. J. Honigmann, the editor of the 1997 Arden edition, suggests lies behind Shakespeare's choice of word in this context. By the time Iago comes to expound on Cassio's sleep-talking about Desdemona, elaborating upon it with descriptions of how Cassio throws his thigh upon Iago's and squeezes his hand, the bed has shifted precariously into the domain of sexual anomaly. The final scene materializes what has been variously referenced in the play, bringing together with great intensity the many poignant metaphorical and other locations of the bed.

In the shifting references to this material object, we also sense the liminal position that is assigned to the many categories that radiate out of it: the sanctity of marriage, sexual identity, the relationship between the public and the private spheres, the problematic status of intimacy. And intimacy itself shifts terrain. It is odd that the play devotes so much attention to the "conduct of intimacy" between Iago and Othello – two men – progressively displacing the intimacy between man and wife that should have been central to the action. More significantly, this intimacy is structured around narratives of the Self, the discourse of self-fashioning that Greenblatt writes of and which we see here in Othello's fixation with managing his life's narrative in such a way as not to be remembered as a cuckold. His race is central to his identity, but only to the degree that he adopts this into his narrative of self-fashioning, expressing sometimes an epic sensibility, as in his address to the Senate, at others a certain peculiar self-loathing, as we have already noted. Ironically, however, it is precisely the area of self-fashioning that is his weakest link. For he imagines himself to be controlling his narrative of self-fashioning, when this is in fact progressively hijacked and controlled by Iago. And all this because the bed radiates meanings that, in being shifted symbolically between contexts, serve for the characters to transpose the question of identity onto the hermeneutical implications of the variable locations of the material object with which the self seems to be so desperately entangled. Taking a leaf directly from medieval scholarship for a postcolonial reading, then, references to material objects would be centered upon as one of the primary levels of interpretation, out of which several layers might be explored.

Often, language itself becomes such a material object, and seems to take its place within a "social life of things," as Appadurai puts it. This is particularly so when we are confronted with a language that seems designed to alienate our established assumptions of its apparent transparency.[9] Such an example can be seen in Mauritian Dev Virahsawmy's *Toufann*, which is a palimpsestic layering of languages as well as a strategic reappropriation of *The Tempest*. Though originally written in Mauritian Kreol in 1991, it was not until the summer of 1999 that it was staged in London, with an English translation of the play usefully provided in Martin Banham *et al.*'s *African Theatre: Playwrights and Politics* in 2001.[10] *Toufann* is a major reappropriation of the earlier text as a conduit for a dramatically different set of concerns. Mauritius has itself had a colorful and fascinating colonial history, including Dutch, French, and British influences. Furthermore, its strategic location had implications for contests between the French and the British elsewhere within their respective empires.[11] The fact that the play was originally in Kreol suggests a confluence of vectors. Kreol, the primarily spoken lingua franca of Mauritius, is a mixture of French, Hindi, and various other local languages. Like all Creoles, it evolved as the common language between colonizers and slaves. For Mauritius, the slave population was primarily African and Madagascan, with smaller numbers of Indian and Malaysian slaves. For educated elites of Mauritius, it is a language to be shunned. However, its popularity as the main language of dialogue and exchange cuts across all classes. With *Toufann*, and the various other plays he has written in Kreol, Virahsawmy's aim is to place the language firmly as one of a rising popular consciousness. Given also that various characters such as Kordelia, Kalibann, Ferdijnan, Aryel, Kaspalto and Damarro (Kreol for Trinculo and Stephano), and even Yago refuse to accept their allotted roles, either within the framework of the play itself or in terms of the implicit intertextual relations they are meant to invoke with other Shakespearean characters, the play lays out the means by which a counter-discourse to dominant history is to be imagined. The play stages a dialogical movement of transition in which the Kreol language, itself already an interface of various languages, is used to outline the parameters of a variegated imaginary, the language itself acquiring a social life among various spoken and literary languages, all of which have local and not-so-local implications for interpretation.

The implications of the notion of historical emblematization, one of the discursive elements of the medieval essays we noted earlier, can also be seen to have direct relevance to postcolonial literature. When, in Raja Rao's *Kanthapura*, Moorthy translates Gandhi's ideology into the life and mores of the villagers, he does this by way of a form of historical emblematization. It is the only way in which the villagers will understand the nature of the decolonization struggle and convert it into their own uses. The entire novel itself, as it is told by the old lady narrator, takes the form of a secularized Indian epic. The foreground teems with characters, all marked out by either their occupation, their location in the village, or some personal foible that becomes a defining mark: Corner-House Moorthy, Temple Kakshamma, Front-House Akkamma, Coffee-Planter Ramayya, Beadle Timmayya, and many, many more. Rao weaves a tapestry of fleeting and not-so-fleeting human interactions whose consequences, as connected to the translated forms of Gandhi's ideology, define the villagers as characters in an epic narrative. This is something already detailed in the work of Subaltern Studies historians who have argued persuasively for seeing the Indian nationalist struggle as undergoing a series of translations from "below," among the workers and peasants.[12] The process of adopting tropological models from an indigenous domain for historical transposition into a new, incipiently post-colonial context is not limited to *Kanthapura*. We can see it operating in texts as varied as Amadou Hampâté Bâ's *The Fortunes of Wangrin*, Miguel Angel Asturias's *Men of Maize*, Ama Atta Aidoo's *Anowa*, and Robert Kroetsch's *What the Crow Said*, among others that both are generically different and come from different parts of the postcolonial world.

When the characters in Brian Friel's *Translations* persistently invoke the classical past in trying to cope with the present realities of British cartography and colonization, they bring together the aspects of historical emblematization and the situated personal encounters with the past we noted as being pertinent to the medieval realm. The act of changing Irish names to English ones is contested not by any blatant acts of subversion by the locals, but by the reaching beyond the English for a mode of epic sensibility drawn from the classical past. That this may well be a form of escapism does not detract from the epic nature of the gesture. There is even the possibility of a productive comparison to Salman Rushdie's *The Moor's Last Sigh* on the question of the identity of maps: Moraes Zogoiby's self-conception needs to be constantly negotiated as he changes geographical locations, almost as if to suggest that the geographical location contaminates his consciousness with its inherent structure of feeling. And in terms of a situated encounter with the past, does Walcott not stand in the same relationship to the canonical corpus as Heaney does to *Beowulf*? And what are we to make of Du Bois's statement in *Souls of Black Folk*: "I sit with Shakespeare and he winces not. Across the color line I move arm in arm with Balzac and Dumas, where smiling men and welcoming women glide in gilded halls. From out the caves of evening that swing between the strong-limbed earth and the tracery of the stars, I summon Aristotle and Aurelius and what soul I will, and they come all graciously with no scorn or condescension" (665)? Does Bédier, admittedly from a completely different racial and structural location, not echo the same sentiment of being welcome among the elect of Culture in his engagement with the *Chanson*? Are both these writers not attempting to negotiate their double consciousness through this form of elevated engagement? And when C. L. R. James writes in *The Black Jacobins* (1938) of the incredible rhetorical power of Toussaint L'Ouverture in whipping up the fervor of the slaves of San Domingo for freedom and leading them to fight against the French, is there not a whiff of the classical Roman general as described by Tacitus and Thucydides in his demeanor and carriage?[13]

CROSS-DISCIPLINARY CONVERSATIONS AND THE QUESTION OF PEDAGOGY

Reading this collection of essays, it struck me quite forcefully that my disciplinary training seemed to have been designed precisely to prevent the kinds of dialogue I was having with these medieval scholars. And the same would count for the other side. And yet it became rapidly clear that several debates in medieval studies anticipate many of the questions that engage the attention of postcolonial scholars, even if from a completely different disciplinary purview.

It is in Roland Greene's chapter, which I have left off discussing till now, that the anticipation of many issues in postcolonial studies comes to the foreground. His discussion of Rojas's *La Celestina* as a protobaroque fiction that is defined as "the eruption of artifice – in the service of incongruity, disproportion, and anachronism – against a background of orthodoxy" is applicable to the genre of magical realism, taken by many people as the signature of the postcolonial literary imaginary. For it is precisely in this that magical realism is distinctive; not because of its sharp difference from established protocols of realism, but in the varied degree in which it highlights the apparent incommensurability between the fantastic and the real and converts it into a mode of equivalence in which neither is allowed to supersede the other. From Greene's account, *La Celestina* stands in a simultaneous relationship of residuality and emergence (following Raymond Williams), both looking back at the late medieval world and anticipating impulses within the Renaissance world. This makes of *La Celestina* a conjunctural hybrid, conjunctural in that the titular protagonist is composed of variant signifiers of desire and set against a backdrop of medieval romance, and, at the same time, representative of a mode of figuration that would become absolutely normalized. Its conjuncturalness is then the holding together of apparently contrastive structures of feeling that reside within different historical configurations. *La Celestina's* conjunctural status is similar to Gower's Nebuchadnezzar and yet may be differentiated in one important respect: the protocol for figuring Nebuchadnezzar does not necessarily anticipate any later forms of textual hybridity but rather resides at the level of a register of moral panic and the question of transcendence. It is this vector of its otherness that gets replicated in later accounts of metamorphosis, and not its precise form of textual hybridity.

And yet, reading the two together from the perspective of magical realism reveals ways in which a typology of magical realism might benefit from establishing a deep history that would go as far back as the medieval realm. For what is quickly discernible is that magical realism soon breaks down into plural forms – magical realisms – which are defined in terms of an opposition between a hybrid discourse and a focus on metamorphosis and the many implications of translation that derive from this. Thus we see that magical realist texts such as Marquez's *One Hundred Years of Solitude*, Salman Rushdie's *Midnight's Children*, Laura Esquivel's *Like Water for Chocolate*, and Juan Rulfo's *Pedro Paramo* would fall roughly into the first category, with Miguel Angel Asturias's *Men of Maize*, Ben Okri's *The Famished Road*, and Robert Kroetsch's *What the Crow Said* falling into the second. This is not to suggest rigorous dichotomies or indeed that all magical realist texts can be so easily slotted into such categories, but to show how critically accounting for literary texts in the postcolonial world can be enriched with reference to the medieval world.

This goes beyond the call for a fresh understanding of literary history. Rather it calls for a contrapuntal form of reading between the two domains that is foundational to the kinds of training that are provided in the two domains in the first place. In other words, it should be possible to design a pedagogy that would take the contrapuntal reading of postcolonialism with other domains and disciplines that exhibit similar configurations of vectors (conquest, resistance, hybridity, the self/other dialectic, the formation of a variegated social imaginary in the face of empire, etc.) as part of the thinking in the field in the first place. From the evidence of the chapters in this collection, it is clear that medieval studies would find the contrapuntal encounter highly productive. It is only in this way that we would achieve what we can take to be the true impulse of any progressive pedagogy: to integrate a skeptical interlocutor into the very processes by which we establish our conceptual categories and to transcend the limitations of our own thought shaped by the disciplinary boundaries within which we are trained and gain professional validation.

NOTES

1. See for example, Yiannis Gabriel, *Storytelling in Organizations: Facts, Fictions, and Fantasies* (Oxford: Oxford University Press, 2000), and more directly engaging with postcolonialism, *Postcolonial Theory and Organizational Analysis: A Critical Engagement*, ed. Anshuman Prasad (London: Palgrave Macmillan, 2003).
2. Edward Said, *The World, the Text, and the Critic* (Cambridge, MA: Harvard University Press, 1984; reprinted London: Vintage, 1991).
3. Michael Ondaatje, *The English Patient* (London: Picador, 1992), 248–9.
4. Frantz Fanon, "The Pitfalls of National Culture," in *Wretched of the Earth*, trans. Constance Farrington (New York: Grove Press, 1963; reprinted London: Harmondsworth, 2001), 183.
5. On the specularity of identity, see Jean Baudrillard, *The Orders of Simulacra: Simulations*, trans. Paul Foss, Paul Patton, and Philip Bleitchman (New York: Semiotext(e), 1983). On the instability of subject positions, see Slavoj Zizek, *The Sublime Object of Ideology* (London: Verso, 1989) and Judith Butler, *The Psychic Life of Power* (Stanford: Stanford University Press, 1997); and on the expressive nature of the postmodern fragment, see Robert C. Holub, "Fragmentary Totalities and Totalized Fragments: On the Politics of Anti-systemic Thought," in *Postmodern Pluralism and Concepts of Totality*, ed. J. Hermand (New York: Peter Lang, 1995), 83–104.
6. See, for example, Terry Eagleton, *The Illusions of Postmodernism* (Oxford: Blackwell, 1996) and Neil Lazarus, *Nationalism and Cultural Practice in the Postcolonial World* (Cambridge: Cambridge University Press, 1999).

7. Anthony K. Appiah, *In My Father's House: Africa in the Philosophy of Culture* (London: Methuen, 1992), 224–40; Achille Mbembe, *On the Postcolony* (Berkeley: University of California Press, 2002); *The Secret Politics of Our Desires: Innocence, Culpability and Indian Popular Cinema,* ed. Ashis Nandy (London: Zed Books, 1998).
8. William Shakespeare, *Othello* ed. E. A. J. Honigmann, The Arden Shakespeare (Surrey: Thomas Nelson and Sons Ltd., 1997).
9. There are many such linguistic alienation effects to be seen in postcolonial literature. Often this is connected to challenging the centrality of the colonially imposed language. Examples range from Chinua Achebe's proverbially saturated discourse in *Things Fall Apart* and *Arrow of God,* to Ken Saro-Wiwa's pidgin-inflected "rotten English" in *Sozaboy: A Novel in Rotten English,* to the adventurous creolized forms in Benjamin Zephaniah and Lorna Goodison's poetry among others.
10. Dev Virahsawmy, *Touffan,* in *African Theatre: Playwrights and Politics,* ed. Martin Banham *et al.* (Oxford: James Currey, 2001).
11. I wish to thank Anjali Prabhu for sharing with me her work on the theory of hybridity and its application to Mauritius and La Réunion, which provides the historical background to this section.
12. Particularly productive in linking peasant consciousness to the unfolding nationalist struggle is Shahid Amin's classic essay, "Gandhi as Mahatma," in *Selected Subaltern Studies,* ed. Ranjit Guha and Gayatri Spivak (Oxford: Oxford University Press, 1988), 288–348. For a discussion of the work of Subaltern Studies historians and their implications for postcolonial studies, see my "Postcolonial Historiography and the Problem of Local Knowledge," in *Postcolonialism: Theory, Practice or Process?* (Cambridge: Polity, 2000).
13. C. L. R. James explicitly distances himself from the Roman historians in his Preface to the 1994 edition of *The Black Jacobins* (London: Alison and Busby, 1963). And yet, it is also clear that he is relying on certain models of military speeches for the addresses of Toussaint to his followers. Given James's thorough classical education, it is not far-fetched to speculate that the speeches were modeled on Greek and Roman examples.

Bibliography

Aarsleff, Hans. "Scholarship and Ideology: Joseph Bédier's Critique of Romantic Medievalism," in *Historical Studies and Literary Criticism*, ed. Jerome J. McGann. Madison: University of Wisconsin Press, 1985, 93–113.

——— *The Study of Language in England, 1780–1860*. Minneapolis: University of Minnesota Press and London: Athlone, 1983.

Aebischer, Paul, ed. *Le Voyage de Charlemagne à Jerusalem et à Constantinople*. Geneva: Droz, 1965.

Ahmed, Aijaz. *In Theory: Classes, Nations, Literature*. New York: Verso, 1992.

Akbari, Suzanne Conklin. "Imagining Islam: The Role of Images in Medieval Depictions of Muslims," *Scripta Mediterranea* 19–20 (1998–99): 9–27.

——— *Idols in the East: European Representations of Islam and the Orient 1100–1450*. Philadelphia: University of Pennsylvania Press, forthcoming.

Alexander, David. "Two Aspects of Islamic Arms and Armor: Part I. Turban Helmets," *Metropolitan Museum of Art Journal* 18 (1984): 97–104.

Almagià, Roberto. *Monumenta cartographica Vaticana*, 4 vols. Vatican City: Biblioteca Apostolica Vaticana, 1944–55.

Amin, Shahid. "Gandhi as Mahatma," in *Selected Subaltern Studies*, ed. Ranjit Guha and Gayatri Spivak. Oxford: Oxford University Press, 1988, 288–348.

Anderson, Andrew Runni. *Alexander's Gate, Gog and Magog and the Inclosed Nations*. Cambridge, MA: Medieval Academy of America, 1932.

Anderson, Benedict. *Imagined Communities*. London: Verso, 1983.

Andrew, Malcolm and Ronald Waldron, eds. *The Poems of the Pearl Manuscript* (London: Edward Arnold, 1978).

Anonymous. *An Historical Essay on the English Constitution*. London: Edward and Charles Dilly, 1771.

Anonymous. "Les amis de Joseph Bédier," *Aux Ecoutes*, September 3, 1938.

Anonymous. "Of Government Education in Bengal," *Calcutta Review* 5 (1845): 211–63.

Appadurai, Arjun, ed. *The Social Life of Things: Commodities in Cultural Practice*. Cambridge: Cambridge University Press, 1986.

Appiah, Anthony K. *In My Father's House: Africa in the Philosophy of Culture*. London: Methuen, 1992.

Armstrong, Edward C., ed. *The Medieval French Roman d'Alexandre*, vol. VI: *The Version of Alexandre de Paris*. Princeton: Princeton University Press, 1976.

Bibliography

Arnold, C. J. *Roman Britain to Saxon England*. Bloomington: Indiana University Press, 1984.

Ashby, George. *Active Policy of a Prince*, ed. M. Bateson. EETS ES 76. London: Oxford University Press, 1899.

Ashcroft, Bill. *Post-Colonial Transformation*. London: Routledge, 2001.

Asselberghs, Jean-Paul. "Les tapisseries tournaisiennes de la guerre de Troie," *Revue Belge d'Archéologie et d'Histoire de l'Art* 39 (1970): 93–183.

Auerbach, Erich. "Figura," in *Scenes from the Drama of European Literature*. New York: Meridian Books, 1959, 11-71.

Bacon, Francis. *New Atlantis*, in *Works of Francis Bacon*, 14 vols., ed. James Spedding, Robert Leslie Ellis, and Douglas Denon Heath, vol. v. London: Longman, 1862–76.

Bailyn, Bernard. *The Ideological Origins of the American Revolution*. Cambridge, MA: Harvard University Press, 1971.

Ballantyne, Tony. *Orientalism and Race: Aryanism in the British Empire*. Basingstoke: Palgrave, 2001.

Barczewski, Stephanie. *Myth and National Identity in Nineteenth Century Britain: The Legends of King Arthur and Robin Hood*. Oxford: Oxford University Press, 2000.

Barquissau, Raphaël. "Joseph Bédier," in *Une Colonie colonisatrice*. Saint-Denis: E. Drouhet, 1922, 67–86.

Bartlett, Robert. *The Making of Europe: Conquest, Colonization and Cultural Change 950–1350*. Princeton: Princeton University Press, 1993.

Bately, Janet. *The Old English Orosius*. EETS SS 6. Oxford: Oxford University Press, 1980.

Baudrillard, Jean. *The Orders of Simulacra: Simulations*, trans. Paul Foss, Paul Patton, and Philip Bleitchman. New York: Semiotext(e), 1983.

Beadle, Richard and A. J. Piper, eds. *New Science Out of Old Books: Studies in Manuscripts and Early Printed Books in Honour of A. I. Doyle*. Aldershot: Scolar Press, 1995.

Becker, Andrew Sprague. *The Shield of Achilles and the Poetics of Ekphrasis*. Lanham, MD: Rowman and Littlefield, 1995.

Bede. *Ecclesiastical History of the English Church and People*, ed. Bertram Colgrave and R. A. B. Mynors. Oxford: Clarendon Press, 1969.

Bédier, Joseph. Collège de France, c-vIII, liasse 106. Speech given in San Francisco (n.d.).

"De l'édition princeps de la *Chanson de Roland* aux éditions les plus récentes," *Romania* 63 (1937): 433–69; 64 (1938): 145–244, 489–521.

Discours de réception à l'Académie française, prononcé le 3 novembre 1921. Paris: Champion, 1921.

ed. *La Chanson de Roland*. Paris: Piazza, 1922.

La Chanson de Roland, commentée. Paris: Piazza, 1921.

"L'art et le métier dans la *Chanson de Roland*," *Revue des Deux Mondes* 13 (1913): 292–321.

Le Lai le l'ombre. Paris: Champion, 1913.

"Le moyen âge," in *L'Encyclopédie française*. Paris: Comité de l'Encyclopédie, 1935.

Légendes épiques: recherches sur la formation des chansons de geste. 4 vols. Paris: Champion, 1908–13.

Les Fabliaux, third edn. Paris: Champion, 1911.

Bell, Tyler. "Churches on Roman Buildings: Christian Associations and Roman Masonry in Anglo-Saxon England," *Medieval Archaeology* 42 (1998): 1–18.

Benjamin, Walter. "The Task of the Translator," in *Illuminations*, trans. Harry Zohn. New York: Schochen, 1968, 69–82.

Benoît de Sainte-Maure. *Le Roman de Troie par Benoît de Sainte-Maure*, vol. 1 trans. Léopold Constans. Paris: Firmin Didot, 1904.

Le Roman de Troie en prose, version du Cod. Bodmer 147, ed. Françoise Vielliard. Series Bibliotheca Bodmeriana, Textes 4. Cologny and Geneva: Fondation Martin Bodmer, 1979.

Benson, Larry D., ed. *The Riverside Chaucer*. Boston: Houghton Mifflin, 1987.

Bhabha, Homi, ed. *Nation and Narration*. New York: Routledge, 1990.

The Location of Culture. London: Routledge, 1994.

Biddick, Kathleen. *The Shock of Medievalism*. Durham, NC and London: Duke University Press, 1998.

Billiard, Auguste. *Voyage aux colonies orientales*. Paris: Librairie Française de l'Advocat, 1822.

Birch, W. De G., ed. *Cartularium Saxonicum*. London: Phillimore and Co., 1885–93.

Bjork, Robert E. and John D. Niles, eds. *A Beowulf Handbook*. Lincoln: University of Nebraska Press, 1997.

Blair, John, ed. *Minsters and Parish Churches: The Local Church in Transition, 950–1200*, Oxford University Committee for Archaeology, Monograph 17. Oxford: Oxbow, 1988.

Blake, N. F., ed. *Caxton's Own Prose*. London: André Deutsch, 1973.

Boehmer, Elleke. *Colonial and Postcolonial Literature: Migrant Metaphysics*. Oxford: Oxford University Press, 1995.

Boissonade, Prosper. *Du Nouveau sur la Chanson de Roland*. Paris: Champion, 1923.

Boswell, Joseph, T. Northcote Toller, and Alastair Campbell, eds. *An Anglo-Saxon Dictionary*. Oxford: Oxford University Press, 1998.

Bosworth, Joseph and T. Northcote Toller, eds. *An Anglo-Saxon Dictionary*. Oxford: Oxford University Press, 1882–98.

Bouloux, Nathalie. *Culture et savoirs géographiques en Italie au XIVe siècle*. Turnhout: Brepols, 2002.

Breckenridge, Carol A. and Peter Van der Veer, eds. *Orientalism and the Postcolonial Predicament: Perspectives on South Asia*. Philadelphia: University of Pennsylvania Press, 1993.

Brotton, Jerry. *The Renaissance Bazaar: From the Silk Road to Michelangelo*. Oxford: Oxford University Press, 2002.

Brown, Elizabeth A. R. "The Trojan Origins of The French: The Commencement of a Myth's Demise 1450–1520," in *Studies in Ethnic Identity and National Perspectives in Medieval Europe*, ed. Alfred P. Smyth. New York: St. Martin's Press, 1998, 135–79.

Bibliography

Buchthal, Hugo. *Historia Troiana: Studies in the History of Mediaeval Secular Illustration.* London: Warburg Institute, 1971.

Burden, Michael, ed. *A Woman Scorn'd: Responses to the Dido Myth.* London: Faber and Faber, 1998.

Burger, Glenn, Lesley B. Cormack and Natalia Pylypiuk, eds. *Making Contact: Maps, Identity, and Travel.* Edmonton: University of Alberta Press, 2003.

Burton, Robert. *Anatomy of Melancholy.* Oxford: Henry Cripps, 1632.

Butler, Judith. *The Psychic Life of Power.* Stanford: Stanford University Press, 1997.

Bynum, Caroline Walker. *Metamorphosis and Identity.* New York: Zone Books, 2001.

"Wonder." Presidential Address to the American Historical Association. *American Historical Review* 102 (1997): 1–17.

Calvino, Italo. *Le città invisibili,* third edn. Turin: Einaudi, 1972.

Invisible Cities, trans. William Weaver. New York: Harcourt Brace Jovanovich, 1974.

Camille, Michael. "Simulacrum," in *Critical Terms for Art History,* ed. Robert S. Nelson and Richard Schiff. Chicago: University of Chicago Press, 1996, 31–43.

"*The Très Riches Heures*: An Illuminated Manuscript in an Age of Mechanical Reproduction," *Critical Inquiry* 17 (1990): 72–107.

Campbell, A., ed. and trans. *The Chronicle of Æthelweard.* London: Nelson, 1962.

Campbell, James, ed. *The Anglo-Saxons.* Oxford: Phaidon, 1982.

Campbell, Thomas. *Tapestry in the Renaissance: Art and Magnificence.* New York, Metropolitan Museum of Art, 2002.

Cardini, Franco. *La Cavalcata d'Oriente: I Magi di Benozzo a Palazzo Medici.* Rome: Tomo Edizioni, 1991.

Carter, Paul. *The Road to Botany Bay: An Essay in Spatial History.* London: Faber and Faber, 1987.

Cary, George and D. J. A. Ross. *The Medieval Alexander.* Cambridge: Cambridge University Press, 1956.

Cassidy, F. N. and R. N. Ringler, eds. *Bright's Old English Grammar and Reader,* third edn. New York: Holt, 1971.

Céard, Jean. *La Nature et les prodiges.* Traveaux d'Humanisme et Renaissance 158. Geneva: Librarie Droz, 1977.

Cheyfitz, Eric. *The Poetics of Imperialism: Translation and Colonization from the Tempest to Tarzan.* New York: Oxford University Press, 1991.

Clark, C., ed. *The Peterborough Chronicle, 1070–1154,* second edn. Oxford: Clarendon, 1970.

Cohen, Gustave. *Ceux que j'ai connus.* Montreal: Editions de l'Arbre, 1946.

Cohen, Jeffrey Jerome. "Monster Culture (Seven Theses)," in *Monster Theory: Reading Culture,* ed. Jeffrey Jerome Cohen. Minneapolis: University of Minnesota Press, 1996, 3–25.

Of Giants: Sex, Monsters and the Middle Ages. Minneapolis: University of Minnesota Press, 1999.

The Postcolonial Middle Ages. New York: St. Martin's Press, 2000.

Cohen, Jeremy, ed. *From Witness to Witchcraft: Jews and Judaism in Medieval Christian Thought.* Wolfenbütteler Mittelalter-Studien 11. Wiesbaden: Harrassowitz, 1996.

Cohn, Bernard. "The Command of Language and the Language of Command," in *Subaltern Studies IV: Writings on South Asian History and Society*, ed. Ranajit Guha. Delhi: Oxford University Press, 1985, 276–339.

Coleman, Janet. *English Literature in History, 1350–1400*. New York: Columbia University Press, 1981.

Medieval Readers and Writers. New York: Columbia University Press, 1981.

Colgrave, Bertram, ed. and trans. *Two Lives of Saint Cuthbert*. Cambridge: Cambridge University Press, 1940.

Colgrave, Bertram and R. A. B. Mynors, eds. *Bede's Ecclesiastical History of the English People*. Oxford: Clarendon Press, 1969.

Colley, Linda. *Britons: Forging the Nation, 1707–1837*. New Haven, CT and London: Yale University Press, 1992.

Copland, Rita. *Rhetoric, Hermeneutics, and Translation in the Middle Ages*. Cambridge: Cambridge University Press, 1991.

Corbellari, Alain. *Joseph Bédier: écrivain et philologue*. Geneva: Droz, 1997.

"Traduire ou ne pas traduire: le dilemme de Bédier. A propos de la traduction de la *Chanson de Roland*," *Vox Romanica* 56 (1997): 63–82.

Corner, James, ed. *Recovering Landscape: Essays in Contemporary Landscape Architecture*. Princeton: Princeton Architectural Press, 1999.

Corsini, Eugenio. *Introduzione alle Storie di Orosio*. Turin: Giappichelli, 1968.

Cramp, Rosemary J. "*Beowulf* and Archaeology," *Medieval Archaeology* 1 (1957): 57–77.

Croll, Morris W. "The Baroque Style in Prose" (1929), in his *Style, Rhetoric, and Rhythm*, ed. J. Max Patrick and Robert O. Evans *et al*. 1966. Princeton: Princeton University Press; reprinted Woodbridge, CT: Ox Bow Press, 1989, 207–33.

Curtius, Ernst Robert. *European Literature and the Latin Middle Ages*, trans. Willard R. Trask. Bollingen Series 36. Princeton: Princeton University Press, 1953.

Dalrymple, William. *White Mughals: Love and Betrayal in Eighteenth-Century India*. London: Flamingo, 2003.

Daretis Phrygii. *De Excidio Troiae Historia*, ed. Ferdinand Meister. Stuttgart and Leipzig: B. G. Teubner Verlagsgesellschaft, 1991.

d'Ascia, Luca. *Il Corona e la Tiara: L'Epistola a Maometto II di Enea Silvio Piccolomini (Papa Pio II)*. Bologna: Edizioni Pendragon, 2001.

Davis, Kathleen. "National Writing in the Ninth Century: A Reminder for Postcolonial Thinking about the Nation," *Journal of Medieval and Early Modern Studies* 28 (1998): 611–37.

Davis, Leigh. *Acts of Union: Scotland and the Literary Negotiation of the British Nation, 1707–1803*. Stanford: Stanford University Press, 1999.

de Campos, Haroldo. "The Rule of Anthropophagy: Europe under the Sign of Devoration," trans. Maria Tai Wolff, *Latin American Literary Review* 1427 (1986): 42–60.

de la Barca, Pedro Calderón. *La vida es sueño*, ed. José M. Ruano de la Haza. Madrid: Castalia, 1994.

Life's a Dream, trans. Kathleen Raine and R. M. Nadal. London: Hamish Hamilton, 1968.

de la Roncière, M. and M. Mollat du Jourdin. *Les Portulans: cartes marines du XIIIe au XVIIe siècle*. Fribourg: Office du Livre, 1984.

de la Vega, Garcilaso, the Inca. *Comentarios reales de los Incas*, ed. Aurelio Miró Quesada, 2 vols. Caracas: Biblioteca Ayacucho, 1976.

de Mandach, André. *Chanson de Roland: transferts de mythe dans le monde occidental et oriental*. Geneva: Droz, 1993.

Degenhart, Bernhard and Annegrit Schmitt. *Marino Sanudo und Paolino Veneto: Zwei Literaten des 14. Jahrhunderts in ihrer Wirkung auf Buchillustrierung und Kartographie in Venedig, Avignon und Neapel*. Tübingen: Ernst Wasmuth, 1973.

delle Colonne, Guido. *Historia Destructionis Troiae: Guido delle Colonne*, trans. Mary Elizabeth Meek. Bloomington: Indiana University Press, 1974.

Desmond, Marilynn. *Reading Dido: Gender, Textuality, and the Medieval Aeneid*. Minneapolis: University of Minnesota Press, 1994.

Deyermond, A. D. *The Petrarchan Sources of* La Celestina. Oxford: Oxford University Press, 1961.

Dictys Cretensis. *Ephemeridos Belli Troiani Libri*, ed. Werner Eisenhut. Leipzig: B. G. Teubner, 1958.

Dingwaney, A. and L. Maier. *Between Languages and Cultures: Translation and Cross-cultural Texts*. Philadelphia and London: University of Pennsylvania Press 1995.

Dinshaw, Carolyn. *Getting Medieval: Sexualities and Communities, Pre- and Postmodern*. Durham, NC: Duke University Press, 1999.

Disraeli, Isaac. *Amenities of Literature*, 3 vols. London: Edward Moxson, 1841.

Dobbie, E. V. K. *The Anglo-Saxon Minor Poems*. Anglo-Saxon Poetic Records, vol. 6. New York: Columbia University Press, 1942.

Doob, Penelope Reed. *Nebuchadnezzar's Children: Conventions of Madness in Middle English Literature*. New Haven: Yale University Press, 1973.

Douglas, Mary. "The Forbidden Animals in Leviticus," *Journal for the Study of the Old Testament* 59 (1993): 3–23.

Duff, Alexander. *Missionary Addresses, 1835–1839*. Edinburgh: Johnstone and Hunt, 1850.

Dumville, David N. "Sub-Roman Britain: History and Legend," *History* 62 (1977): 173–92.

Dunn, Peter N. "Pleberio's World," *PMLA* 91 (1976): 406–19.

Eagleton, Terry. *The Illusions of Postmodernism*. Oxford: Blackwell, 1996.

Eaton, Tim. *Plundering the Past: Roman Stonework in Medieval Britain*. Stroud: Tempus, 2000.

Echard, Siân and Clare Fanger, trans. *The Latin Verses in Gower's Confessio Amantis: An Annotated Translation*. East Lansing: Colleagues Press, 1991.

Echhardt, Alexandre. "La légende de l'origine troyenne des Turc," *Kőrösi Csoma-Archivum* 2 (1967): 422–33.

Edson, Evelyn. *Mapping Time and Space: How Medieval Mapmakers Viewed Their World*. London: British Library, 1997.

Erskine, Andrew. *Troy between Greece and Rome: Local Tradition and Imperial Power*. Oxford: Oxford University Press, 2001.

Eto, Yasuharu. "*Andreas* lines 1229–52," *Explicator* 52 (1994): 195–6.

Evans, Ruth. "Historicizing Postcolonial Criticism: Cultural Difference and the Vernacular," in *The Idea of the Vernacular: An Anthology of Medieval Literary Theory 1280–1520*, ed. Jocelyn Wogan-Brown, Nicholas Watson, Andrew Taylor, and Ruth Evans. University Park, PA: Penn State Press, 1999, 366–70.

Fabbrini, Fabbrizio. *Paulo Orosio: uno storico*. Rome: Edizioni di Storia e Letteratura, 1979.

Fanon, Frantz. "The Pitfalls of National Culture," in *Wretched of the Earth*, trans. Constance Farrington. New York: Grove Press, 1963; reprinted London: Harmondsworth, 2001, 148–205.

Finberg, H. P. R. *Gloucestershire*. London: Hodder and Stoughton, 1955.

Fisher, John Hurt. *John Gower: Moral Philosopher and Friend of Chaucer*. New York: New York University Press, 1964.

Fitzgerald, F. Scott. *The Crack-Up*. New York: New Directions, 1945.

Flint, Valerie I. J. "The Hereford Map: Its Author(s), Two Scenes and a Border," *Transactions of the Royal Historical Society*, sixth series 8 (1998): 19–44.

Floyd-Wilson, Mary. *English Ethnicity and Early Modern Drama*. Cambridge: Cambridge University Press, 2003.

Fontaine, Jacques. *Isidore de Seville et la culture classique dans l'Espagne wisigothique*, 3 vols. Paris: Etudes Augustiniennes, 1959-83.

Foster, Brian and Ian Short, eds. *The Anglo-Norman Alexander (Le Roman de toute chevalerie) by Thomas of Kent*, 2 vols. Anglo-Norman Text Society 29–33. London: Anglo-Norman Text Society, 1976–77.

Foucque, Hippolyte. "Joseph Bédier: l'homme; le médiéviste," *Académie de l'Ile de la Réunion: Bulletin* 21 (1963–64): 119–31.

Frantzen, Allen J. *The Desire for Origins: New Language, Old English and Teaching the Tradition*. New Brunswick and London: Rutgers University Press, 1990.

"The Disclosure of Sodomy in *Cleanness*," *PMLA* 111 (1996): 451–64.

Frazer, R. M., Jr, trans. *The Trojan War: The Chronicles of Dictys of Crete and Dares the Phrygian*. Bloomington: Indiana University Press, 1966.

Freeman, E. A. *Comparative Politics: Six Lectures*. London: Macmillan, 1873.

Historical Essays. London: Macmillan, 1871.

The History of the Norman Conquest and Its Results, 6 vols. Oxford: Clarendon, 1867–79.

Friedman, John Block. *The Monstrous Races in Medieval Art and Thought*. Cambridge, MA: Harvard University Press, 1981.

Fulcher of Chartres. *Historia Hierosolymitana (1095–1127)*, ed. Heinrich Hagenmeyer. Heidelberg: Carl Winter, 1913.

Gabriel, Yiannis. *Storytelling in Organizations: Facts, Fictions, and Fantasies*. Oxford: Oxford University Press, 2000.

Gage, Thomas. *Travels in the New World*, ed. J. Eric S. Thompson. Norman: University of Oklahoma Press, 1958.

Garaud, Christian and Janine Irigoin, eds. *Une Amitié de jeunesse: 148 lettres inédites (1886–1900). Joseph Bédier, Emile Mâle, Joseph Texte*. New York: Peter Lang, 1999.

Bibliography

Garland, Cannon and Kevin R. Brine, eds. *Objects of Enquiry: The Life, Contributions and Influence of Sir William Jones, 1746–1794*. New York and London: New York University Press, 1995.

Gautier Dalché, Patrick. "De la glose à la contemplation. Place et fonction de la carte dans les manuscrits du haut moyen âge," *Settimane di Studio del Centro Italiano di Studi sull'Alto Medioevo* 41 (1994): 749.

Carte marine et portulan au XIIe siècle: le "Liber de existencia riveriarum et forma maris nostri Mediterranei" (Pise, circa 1200). Rome: Ecole Française de Rome, 1995.

"Décrire le monde et situer les lieux au XIIe siècle: l'*Expositio mappe mundi* et la généalogie de la mappemonde de Hereford," *Mélanges de l'Ecole Française de Rome. Moyen Age* 112 (2001): 343–409.

ed. *La "Descriptio Mappae Mundi" de Hugues de Saint-Victor: texte inédit avec introduction et commentaire*. Paris: Etudes Augustiniennes, 1988, 89–95.

Gilchrist, J. B. *Dictionary English and Hindostanee*. Calcutta: Stuart and Cooper, 1787.

Gilman, Stephen. *The Art of* La Celestina. Madison: University of Wisconsin Press, 1956.

The Spain of Fernando de Rojas: The Intellectual and Social Landscape of La Celestina. Princeton: Princeton University Press, 1972.

Gilroy-Scott, N. W. "John Gower's Reputation: Literary Allusions from the Early Fifteenth Century to the Time of *Pericles*," *Yearbook of English Studies* 1 (1971): 30–47.

Glare, P. G. W., ed. *Oxford Latin Dictionary*. Oxford: Clarendon Press, 1968.

Godman, Peter, ed. and trans. *Alcuin: The Bishops, Kings, and Saints of York*. Oxford: Clarendon Press, 1982.

González Echevarría, Roberto. Celestina's *Brood: Continuities of the Baroque in Spanish and Latin American Literature*. Durham, NC: Duke University Press, 1993.

Gosman, Martin. *La Légende d'Alexandre le Grand dans la littérature française du 12e siècle: une réécriture permanente*. Faux titre 133. Amsterdam and Atlanta: Rodopi, 1997.

Gossman, Lionel. "Augustin Thierry and Liberal Historiography," in *Between History and Literature*. Cambridge, MA and London: Harvard University Press, 1990, 83–151.

Gow, Andrew. "Gog and Magog on *Mappaemundi* and Early Printed World Maps: Orientalizing Ethnography in the Apocalyptic Tradition," *Journal of Early Modern History* 2 (1998): 61–88.

The Red Jews: Antisemitism in an Apocalyptic Age, 1200–1600. Leiden: E. J. Brill, 1995.

Greenblatt, Stephen. *Marvelous Possessions: The Wonder of the New World*. Chicago: Chicago University Press, 1991.

"Resonance and Wonder," in *Exhibiting Cultures: The Politics and Poetics of Museum Display*, ed. Ivan Karp and Steven D. Lavine. Washington and London: Smithsonian Institution Press, 1991, 42–57.

Greene, Roland. "Colonial Becomes Postcolonial," *MLQ* 65 (2004): 423–41.

Greer, Margaret R. and John Dagenais, eds. *Decolonizing the Middle Ages. Journal of Medieval and Early Modern Studies* 30 (2000).

Gregory the Great. *Moralia in Job*, ed. Marci Adraien. Turnhout: Brepols, 1979.

Grosjean, Georges, ed. *Mapamundi: The Catalan Atlas of the Year 1375*. Dietikon and Zurich: Graf, 1977.

Guha, Ranajit and Gayatri Chakravorty Spivak, eds. *Selected Subaltern Studies*. Oxford and New York: Oxford University Press, 1988.

Hadfield, Andrew. *Literature, Travel and Colonial Writing in the English Renaissance: 1545–1625*. Oxford: Clarendon Press, 1999.

Hahn, Thomas. "The Difference the Middle Ages Makes: Color and Race before the Modern World," *Journal of Medieval and Early Modern Studies* 31 (Winter 2001): 1–37.

Hanning, Robert W. *The Vision of History in Early Britain from Gildas to Geoffrey of Monmouth*. New York: Columbia University Press, 1966.

Hardison, Robert. *Eccentric Spaces*. Cambridge, MA: MIT Press, 2000.

Hardt, Michael and Antonio Negri. *Empire*. Cambridge, MA: Harvard University Press, 2000.

Harley, J. B. and David Woodward. *The History of Cartography*, vol. 1. Chicago: University of Chicago Press, 1987.

Harper, James. "The Barberini Tapestries of the Life of the Urban VIII: Program, Politics and Perfect History for the Post-Exile Era," PhD dissertation, University of Pennsylvania, 1998.

Harvey, P. D. A. *The History of Topographical Maps: Symbols, Pictures and Surveys*. London: Thames and Hudson, 1980.

Hawkes, Sonia Chadwick and G. C. Dunning. "Soldiers and Settlers in Britain, Fourth to Fifth Century," *Medieval Archaeology* 5 (1965): 1–70.

Heaney, Seamus, trans. *Beowulf*. New York: Farrar, Straus, Giroux, 2000.

Poems, 1965–1975. New York: Farrar, Straus, Giroux, 1980.

Heather, Peter, ed. *The Visigoths: From the Migration Period to the Seventh Century. An Ethnographic Perspective*. Woodbridge: Boydell, 1999.

Heber, Reginald. "Morte D'Arthur," in *The Poetical Works of Reginald Heber*. London: John Murray, 1841.

Higgitt, J. C. "The Roman Background to Medieval England," *Journal of the British Archaeological Association*, third series 36 (1973): 1–15.

Hill, Christopher. "The Norman Yoke," in *Puritanism and Revolution: Studies in Interpretation of the English Revolution of the Seventeenth Century*. London: Secker and Hudson, 1958: 50-122.

Hingley, Richard and David Miles. "The Human Impact on the Landscape: Agriculture, Settlement, Industry, Infrastructure," in *The Roman Era: The British Isles, 55 BC–AD 410*, ed. Peter Salway. Oxford: Oxford University Press, 2002, 141–71.

Hoccleve, Thomas. *Regement of Princes, and Fourteen Poems*, ed. F. J. Furnivall. EETS ES 72. London: Oxford University Press, 1887.

Holsinger, Bruce. "Medieval Studies, Postcolonial Studies and the Genealogies of Critique," *Speculum* 77 (2002): 1195–227.

Bibliography

Holub, Robert C. "Fragmentary Totalities and Totalized Fragments: On the Politics of Anti-systemic Thought," in *Postmodern Pluralism and Concepts of Totality*, ed. J. Hermand. New York: Peter Lang, 1995, 83–103.

Hooke, Della. *The Landscape of Anglo-Saxon England*. London: Leicester University Press, 1998.

Horsman, Reginald. *Race and Manifest Destiny*. Cambridge, MA: Harvard University Press, 1981.

Hoskins, W. G. *Local History in England*, third edn. London: Longman, 1984.

The Making of The English Landscape. London: Penguin, 1985.

Howe, Nicholas. "Rome: Capital of Anglo-Saxon England," *Journal of Medieval and Early Modern Studies* 34 (2004): 147–72.

Huggan, Graham. "Decolonizing the Map: Post-Colonialism, Post-Structuralism and the Cartographic Connection," *Ariel* 20 (1989): 115–31.

Hume, David. "Of the Academical or Sceptical Philosophy," in *An Enquiry Concerning Human Understanding*, ed. Charles W. Eliot. The Harvard Classics 37. New York: P. F. Collier and Son Co., 1909–14.

Hunter, Michael. "Germanic and Roman Antiquity and the Sense of the Past in Anglo-Saxon England," *Anglo-Saxon England* 3 (1974): 29–50.

Ingham, Patricia Clare and Michelle R. Warren. *Postcolonial Moves: Medieval to Modern*. New York: Palgrave Macmillan, 2003.

Isidore of Seville. *Etymologiarum sive originum libri xx*, ed. W. M. Lindsay, 2 vols. Oxford: Clarendon Press, 1911.

James I of Scotland. *The Kingis Quair*, ed. A. Lawson. London: Oxford University Press, 1910.

James, C. L. R. "Preface", in *The Black Jacobins*. London: Alison and Busby, 1963; reprinted 1994.

James, Mirollo V. *The Poet of the Marvelous: Giambattista Marino*. New York: Columbia University Press, 1963.

Janvier, Yves. *La Géographie d'Orose*. Paris: Société d'Edition "Les Belles Lettres," 1982.

Jardine, Lisa. *Worldly Goods: A New History of the Renaissance*. New York: Doubleday, 1996.

Jardine, Lisa and Jerry Brotton. *Global Interests: Renaissance Art between East and West*. Ithaca: Cornell University Press, 2000.

Jauss, Hans Robert. "The Alterity and Modernity of Medieval Literature," *New Literary History* 10 (1979): 181–227.

Jenkins, T. Atkinson, ed. *La Chanson de Roland: Oxford Version*. Boston: Heath, 1924.

Jones, Michael E. *The End of Roman Britain*. Ithaca: Cornell University Press, 1996.

Jones, Richard Foster. *The Triumph of the English Language: A Survey of Opinions concerning the Vernacular from the Introduction of Printing to the Restoration*. London: Oxford University Press, 1953.

Justice, Steven. *Writing and Rebellion: England in 1381*. Berkeley: University of California Press, 1994.

Kant, Immanuel. *Observations on the Feeling of the Beautiful and the Sublime*, trans. John T. Goldthwait. Berkeley: University of California Press, 2003.

Kaplan, Paul. *The Rise of the Black Magus in Western Art*. Ann Arbor: UMI Research Press, 1985.

Kemble, John Mitchell. *The Saxons in England*, 2 vols. London: Longman, 1849.

Kinoshita, Sharon. "'Pagans Are Wrong and Christians Are Right': Alterity, Gender, and Nation in the Chanson de Roland," *Journal of Medieval and Early Modern Studies* 31.1 (2001): 79–111.

Klaeber, F., ed. *Beowulf*, third edn. Boston: Heath, 1950.

Kliger, Samuel. *The Goths in England: A Study in Seventeenth and Eighteenth Century Thought*. New York: Octagon Books, 1972.

Kline, Naomi Reed. *Maps of Medieval Thought: The Hereford Paradigm*. Woodbridge: Boydell, 2001.

Koch, Guntram and Hellmut Sichtermann. *Romisches Sarkophage*. Munich: C. H. Beck, 1982.

Krapp, G. P., ed. *Andreas: The Vercelli Book*. Anglo-Saxon Poetic Records, vol. II. New York: Columbia University Press, 1932.

Krapp, G. P. and E. V. K. Dobbie, eds. *The Exeter Book*. Anglo-Saxon Poetic Records, vol. III. New York: Columbia University Press, 1936.

Kyng Alisaunder, vol. II, ed. G. V. Sneithers, EETS OS 237. London: Oxford University Press, 1957.

Lafferty, Maura K. "Mapping Human Limitations: The Tomb Ecphrases in Walter of Châtillon's *Alexandreis*," *Journal of Medieval Latin* 4 (1994): 64–81.

Lawton, David. "The Surveying Subject: The 'Whole World' of Belief: Three Case Studies," *New Medieval Literatures* 4 (2001): 9–37.

Lazarus, Neil. *Nationalism and Cultural Practice in the Postcolonial World*. Cambridge: Cambridge University Press, 1999.

Leonard, Irving A. *Baroque Times in Old Mexico: Seventeenth-Century Persons, Places, and Practices*. Ann Arbor: University of Michigan Press, 1959.

  Books of the Brave: Being an Account of Books and of Men in the Spanish Conquest and Settlement of the Sixteenth-Century New World, second edn. Berkeley and Los Angeles: University of California Press, 1992.

Leslie, R. F., ed. *Three Old English Elegies*. Manchester: Manchester University Press, 1961.

Levison, Wilhelm. *England and the Continent in the Eighth Century*. Oxford: Clarendon Press, 1946.

Lewis, Suzanne. *The Art of Matthew Paris in the* Chronica Majora. Aldershot: Scolar Press, 1987.

Lida de Malkiel, María Rosa. *La originalidad artística de* La Celestina. Second edn. Buenos Aires: Editorial Universitaria de Buenos Aires, 1970.

Longinus. *On the Sublime*, ed. and trans. W. R. Roberts. Cambridge: Cambridge University Press, 1935.

Longnon, Jean and Raymond Cazelles. *The Très riches heures of Jean, Duke of Berry*. Musée Condé, Chantilly. Preface Millard Meiss, trans. Victoria Benedict. New York: George Braziller, 1969.

Luard, John. *A History of the Dress of the British Soldier: From the Earliest Period to the Present Time*. London: William Clowes and Sons, 1852; reprinted London: Muller, 1971.

Lunt, James D. *Scarlet Lancer*. London: R. Hart-Davis, 1964.

Macaulay, G. C. *The English Works of John Gower*. EETS ES 81, 82. London: Oxford University Press, 1900; reprinted 1969.

Macaulay, Thomas Babington. *Selected Writings*, ed. John Clive and Thomas Pinney. Chicago and London: University of Chicago Press, 1972.

Mack, Rosamond E. *Bazaar to Piazza: Islamic Trade and Italian Art 1300–1600*. Berkeley: University of California Press, 2002.

McKendrick, Scott. "The Great History of Troy: A Reassessment of the Development of a Secular Theme in Late Medieval Art," *Journal of the Warburg and Courtauld Institutes* 54 (1991): 43–82.

Madar, Heather. "The Mark of the Beast: Ottoman Turks in Dürer's Apocalypse." MA thesis, University of California, Berkeley, 1999.

The Turk and Islam in the Western Eye (1453–1750), ed. James Harper, forthcoming.

Mâle, Emile. *L'Art religieux du XIIe siècle en France*. Paris: Librairie Armand Colin, 1928.

Malmstrom, Ronald E. "Note on the Architectural Setting of Federico Barocci's *Aeneas' Flight from Troy*," *Marsyas* 14 (1968/69): 43–7.

Maravall, José Antonio. *Culture of the Baroque: Analysis of a Historical Structure*, trans. Terry Cochran. Theory and History of Literature 25. Minneapolis: University of Minnesota Press, 1986.

El mundo social de La Celestina, second edn. Madrid: Gredos, 1968.

Marciales, Miguel. *La Celestina*, 2 vols. Illinois Medieval Monographs 1. Urbana: University of Illinois Press, 1985.

Margary, Ivan D. *Roman Roads in Britain*. London: John Baker, 1973.

Matar, Nabil. *Islam in Britain 1558–1685*. Cambridge: Cambridge University Press, 1998.

Turks, Moors and Englishmen in the Age of Discovery. New York: Columbia University Press, 1999.

Maurin, Henri and Jacques Lentge, eds. *Le Mémorial de la Réunion*. 7 vols. Saint-Denis: Australe, 1979–81.

Mbembe, Achille. *On the Postcolony*. Berkeley: University of California Press, 2002.

Mehrez, Samia. "Translation and the Postcolonial Experience," in *Rethinking Translation*, ed. Lawrence Venuti. New York and London: Routledge, 1995, 120–38.

Mehta, Uday Singh. *Liberalism and Empire: A Study in Nineteenth-Century British Liberal Thought*. Chicago and London: Chicago University Press, 1999.

Meinig, D. W., ed. *The Interpretation of Ordinary Landscapes*. New York: Oxford University Press, 1979.

Melas, Natalie. "Versions of Incommensurability," *World Literature Today* 69 2 (1995): 275–80.

Merrills, Andrew. *History and Geography in Late Antiquity*. Cambridge: Cambridge University Press. Forthcoming.

Merwin, W. S. *The Mays of Ventadorn*. Washington, DC: National Geographic, 2002.

Metcalf, Thomas. *The New Cambridge History of India* III.4: *Ideologies of the Raj.* Cambridge: Cambridge University Press, 1995.

Miller, Konrad. *Mappae Mundi: Die ältesten Weltkarten*, 6 vols. Stuttgart: Roth, 1895–98.

Miller, Thomas. *The Old English Version of Bede's Ecclesiastical History.* EETS OS 95. London: Oxford University Press, 1890.

Millett, Martin. *The Romanization of Britain: An Essay in Archaeological Interpretation.* Cambridge: Cambridge University Press, 1990.

Minnis, A. J. *Gower's Confessio Amantis: Responses and Reassessments.* Cambridge: D. S. Brewer, 1983.

Mirollo, James V. *The Poet of the Marvelous: Giambattista Marino.* New York: Columbia University Press, 1963.

Morris, Richard. *Churches in the Landscape.* London: Phoenix, 1997.

Mudimbe, V. Y. "The Power of the Greek Paradigm," *South Atlantic Quarterly* 92 (1993): 361–85.

Muir, Richard. *The New Reading the Landscape: Fieldwork in Landscape History.* Exeter: University of Exeter Press, 2000.

Myres, J. N. L. *Oxford History of England*, vol. IB: *The English Settlements.* Oxford: Clarendon Press, 1986.

Nandy, Ashis, ed. *The Secret Politics of Our Desires: Innocence, Culpability and Indian Popular Cinema.* London: Zed Books, 1998.

Nebenzahl, Kenneth. *Maps of the Holy Land: Images of Terra Sancta through Two Millennia.* New York: Abbeville Press, 1986.

Nelson, Lowry, Jr. *Baroque Lyric Poetry.* New Haven: Yale University Press, 1961.

Nichols, Steven. *Romanesque Signs: Early Medieval Narrative and Iconography.* New Haven: Yale University Press, 1983.

Niranjana, Tejaswini. *Siting Translation: History, Post-Structuralism and the Colonial Context.* Berkeley and Los Angeles: University of California Press, 1992.

Norman, C. B. *Colonial France.* London: W. H. Allen, 1886.

Ondaatje, Michael. *The English Patient.* London: Picador, 1992.

Orosius, Paulus. *Historiarum adversum paganos libri vii*, ed. C. Zangemeister. Leipzig: Teubner, 1889.

   The Seven Books of History against the Pagans, trans. Roy J. Deferrari. Washington, DC: Catholic University of America Press, 1964.

Osborn, Marijane. "Laying the Roman Ghost of *Beowulf* 320 and 725," *Neuphilologische Mitteilungen* 70 (1969): 246–55.

Paine, Thomas. *Political and Miscellaneous Works*, ed. R. Carlile. London: J. Ridgeway, 1819.

Paley, Frederick. *The Epics of Hesiod*, second edn. London, 1883.

Paris, Gaston. *La Poésie du moyen âge.* 2 vols. Paris: Hachette, 1922.

Parker, Patricia. *Shakespeare from the Margins: Language, Culture, Context.* Chicago: University of Chicago Press, 1996.

Parkes, Malcolm. *Scribes, Scripts and Readers: Studies in the Communication, Presentation and Dissemination of Medieval Texts.* London: Hambledon Press, 1991.

Parliamentary Papers, Nov. 1852–Aug. 1853, vol. 32.

Bibliography

Paz, Octavio. *Sor Juana, Or, The Traps of Faith*, trans. Margaret Sayers Peden. Cambridge, MA: Belknap Press of Harvard University Press, 1988.

Peabody, Norbert. "Tod's *Rajast'han* and the Boundaries of Imperial Rule in Eighteenth-Century India," *Modern Asian Studies* 30 (1986): 185–220.

Pellat, C. and Y. Pellat. "L'idée de Dieu chez les Sarrasins des chansons de geste," *Studia Islamica* 22 (1965): 5–42.

Peters, Edward, ed. *The First Crusade: The Chronicle of Fulcher of Chartres and Other Source Materials*, second edn. Philadelphia: University of Pennsylvania Press, 1998.

Philipp, Hans. *Die historisch-geographischen Quellen in den Etymologiae des Isidorus von Sevilla*, 2 vols. Berlin: Weidmannsche Buchhandlung, 1913.

Picón-Salas, Mariano. "The Baroque of the Indies," in *A Cultural History of Spanish America: From Conquest to Independence*, trans. Irving A. Leonard. Berkeley and Los Angeles: University of California Press, 1963.

Pius II (Aeneas Silvius Piccolomini). *Aeneae Sylvii Piccolominei Senensis, qui post adeptum pontificatum Pius eius nominis secundus appellatus est, opera quae extant omnia, nunc demum post corruptissimas aeditiones summa diligentia castigata & in unum corpus redacta, quorum elenchum versa pagella indicabit.* Basel: Henric Petrina, 1551: reprinted Frankfurt: Minerva G.M.B.H., 1967.

Pliny. *Natural History*, ed. and trans. D. E. Eichholz. Loeb Classical Library, 36. London: Heinemann, 1962.

Plummer, Charles, ed. *Two of the Saxon Chronicles Parallel*, 2 vols. Oxford: Clarendon Press, 1892, 1899.

— ed. *Venerabilis Baedae: Opera Historica*. Oxford: Clarendon Press, 1966.

Pollock, Sheldon. "Deep Orientalism: Notes on Sanskrit and Power beyond the Raj," in *Orientalism*, ed. Breckenridge and Van der Veer: 45–75.

Prasad, Anshuman, ed. *Postcolonial Theory and Organizational Analysis: A Critical Engagement*. London: Palgrave Macmillan, 2003.

Prinz, Otto, ed. *Die Kosmographie des Aethicus*, MGH, Quellen zur Geistesgeschichte des Mittelalters 14. Munich: Monumenta Germaniae Historica, 1993.

Prior, Katherine, Lance Brennan, and Robin Haines. "Bad Language: English, Persian and Other Esoteric Tongues in the Dismissal of Sir Edward Colebrooke as Resident of Delhi in 1829," *Modern Asian Studies* 35 (2001): 75–112.

Pseudo-Bede. *In Matthaei Evangelium Exposito*, ed. J. P. Migne. Patrologia Latina, vol. 91. Paris, 1844–1864.

Quayson, Ato. *Postcolonialism: Theory, Practice or Process?* Cambridge: Polity, 2000.

Quintus Smyrnaeus. ΤΩΝ ΜΕΘ ΟΜΗΡΟΝ *(The Fall of Troy)*, 11.31–2. Loeb Classical Library. London and Cambridge, MA: Harvard University Press, 1962.

Ratkowitsch, Christine. *Descriptio picturae: Die literarische Funktion der Beschreibung von Kunstwerken in der lateinischen Grossdichtung des 12. Jahrhunderts*. Vienna: Verlag des Österreichischen Academie der Wissenschaften, 1991.

Reed, Michael. *The Landscape of Britain: From the Beginnings to 1914*. London: Routledge, 1997.

Rivet, A. L. F., ed. *The Roman Villa in Britain*. London: Routledge and Kegan Paul, 1969.

Robinson, Fred C. "Retrospection in Old English and Other Early Germanic Litera-
    tures," *The Grove: Studies on Medieval English Language and Literature* 8 (2001):
    255–76.

Rocher, Rosane. *Orientalism, Poetry, and the Millennium: The Checkered Life of
    Nathaniel Brassey Halhed, 1751-1830.* Delhi: Motilal Banarsidass, 1983.

Rojas, Fernando de. *La Celestina: Comedia o Tragicomedia de Calisto y Melibea*, ed. Peta
    E. Russell. Madrid: Castalia, 1991.

Rosa, Lucia Gualdo, Isabella Nuovo, and Domenico Defilippis, eds. *Gli umanisti e la
    guerra otrantina: testi dei secoli XV e XVI.* Bari: Edizioni Dedalo, 1982.

Rubenson, Sven. *The Lion of the Tribe of Judah: Christian Symbols and/or Imperial Title.*
    Addis Ababa: Haile Sellassie I University, 1965.

Sagundino, Niccolo. *De Turcarum Origine.* Viterbo, 1531.

Said, Edward. *Orientalism.* New York: Random House, 1978.

    "Palestinians under Siege," *London Review of Books*, 14 December 2000.

    The World, the Text, and the Critic. Cambridge, MA: Harvard University Press, 1984;
        reprinted London: Vintage, 1991.

    A History of Roman Britain. Oxford: Oxford University Press, 1993.

    Roman Britain. Oxford: Oxford University Press, 1981.

Salway, Peter. *The Oxford Illustrated History of Roman Britain.* Oxford: Oxford
    University Press, 1993.

Sarduy, Severo. "The Baroque and the Neobaroque," in *Latin America in Its Literature*,
    ed. César Fernández Moreno, trans. Mary G. Berg. New York: Holmes and Meier,
    1980, 114–32.

    "Sur Góngora," *Tel Quel* 25 (1966): 91–3.

Scherer, Margaret R. *The Legends of Troy in Art and Literature.* New York and London:
    Phaidon, 1964.

Schwoebel, Robert. *The Shadow of the Crescent: The Renaissance Image of the Turk,
    1453–1517.* New York: St. Martin's Press, 1967.

Sebald, W. G. *Austerlitz*, trans. Anthea Bell. New York: Random House, 2001.

Sedgfield, W. J., ed. *King Alfred's Old English Version of Boethius De Consolatione
    Philosophiae.* Oxford: Clarendon Press, 1899.

Shakespeare, William. *A Midsummer Night's Dream*, ed. Peter Holland. Oxford: Oxford
    University Press, 1994.

    Othello ed. E. A. J. Honigmann. The Arden Shakespeare (Surrey: Thomas Nelson &
        Sons Ltd., 1997).

Shepherd, Alan, ed. *The Fall of Troy in the Renaissance Imagination.* Toronto: Center
    for Renaissance and Reformation Studies. Forthcoming.

Shippey, T. A., ed. "Maxims II," in *Poems of Wisdom and Learning in Old English.*
    Cambridge: Brewer, 1976, 76.

Simpson, James. *Sciences and the Self in Medieval Poetry: Alan of Lille's Anticlaudianus
    and John Gower's Confessio Amantis.* Cambridge: Cambridge University Press,
    1995.

    The Oxford English Literary History, vol. II: *Reform and Cultural Revolution,
    1350–1547.* Oxford: Oxford University Press, 2002.

Bibliography

Simpson, Lesley Byrd, trans, *The Celestina: A Fifteenth-Century Novel in Dialogue* Berkeley and Los Angeles: University of California Press, 1955.

Sinclair, Iain. *London Orbital: A Walk around the M25*. London: Granta, 2002.

Singleton, Charles S. *An Essay on the* Vita Nuova. Baltimore: The Johns Hopkins University Press, 1949.

Smith, A. H. *English Place-Name Elements*. English Place Name Society 25. Cambridge: English Place Name Society, 1956.

Soykut, Mustafa. *The Image of the "Turk" in Italy: A History of the "Other" in Early Modern Europe: 1453–1683*. Berlin: K. Schwarz, 2001.

Southern, R. W. *Western Views of Islam in the Middle Ages*. Cambridge, MA: Harvard University Press, 1962.

Speed, Diane. "The Saracens of *King Horn,*" *Speculum* 65 (1990): 564–95.

   A Critique of Postcolonial Reason: Toward a History of the Vanishing Present. Cambridge, MA: Harvard University Press, 1999.

   "Can the Subaltern Speak?," in *Marxism and the Interpretation of Culture*, ed. Cary Nelson and Lawrence Grossberg. Urbana: University of Illinois Press, 1988, 271–313.

Spivak, Gayatri Chakravorty. *Death of a Discipline*. New York: Columbia University Press, 2003.

   "Subaltern Studies: Deconstructing Historiography," *Subaltern Studies* 4 (1985): 330–63.

Stokes, Eric. *The English Utilitarians and India*. Oxford: Oxford University Press, 1959.

Strohm, Paul. "Form and Social Statement in *Confessio Amantis* and *The Canterbury Tales*," *Studies in the Age of Chaucer* 1 (1979): 17–41.

Suleri, Sara. *The Rhetoric of English India*. Chicago: Chicago University Press, 1992: 49–74.

Summerson, John. *Heavenly Mansions and Other Essays on Architecture*. New York: Norton, 1998.

Sutherland, A. C. "The Imagery of Gildas's *De Excidio Britanniae*," in *Gildas: New Approaches*, ed. Michael Lapidge and David Dumville. Woodbridge: Boydell, 1984, 157–68.

Talvacchia, Bette. "Homer, Greek Heroes, and Hellenism in Giulio Romano's Hall of Troy." *Journal of the Warburg and Courtauld Institutes* 51 (1988), 235–42.

Tanner, Marie. *The Last Descendent of Aeneas: The Hapsburgs and the Mythical Image of the Emperor*. New Haven: Yale University Press, 1993.

Taylor, H. M. and Joan Taylor. *Anglo-Saxon Architecture*. Cambridge: Cambridge University Press, 1965.

Tekindag, M. C. S. "Thoughts on the Letter sent by Pope Pius II to Sultan Mehmet the Conqueror," in *Lectures Delivered on the 511th Anniversary of the Conquest of Istanbul*. Istanbul: Fen Fakültesi Döner Sermaye Basimevi, 1967.

Theune-Grosskopf, Barbara. *Troia: Traum und Wirklichkeit*. Stuttgart: Verlagbüro Wais and Partner, 2001.

Thierry, Augustin. *The History of the Conquest of England by the Normans*, trans. William Hazlitt, 2 vols. London: David Bogue, 1771.

Bibliography

Tolkien, J. R. R. "*Beowulf*: The Monsters and the Critics," in *Interpretations of Beowulf: A Critical Anthology*, ed. R. D. Fulk. Bloomington: University of Indiana Press, 1991, 14–44.

Tomasch, Sylvia and Sealy Gilles, eds. *Text and Territory: Geographical Imagination in the European Middle Ages*. Philadelphia: University of Pennsylvania Press, 1998, 79–96.

Tomaselli, Sylvia. "The Enlightenment Debate on Women," *History Workshop* 20 (1985): 101–24.

Townsend, David, trans. *The Alexandreis of Walter of Châtillon: A Twelfth-Century Epic*. Philadelphia: University of Pennsylvania Press, 1996, 126–7.

Trautmann, Thomas R. *Aryans and British India*. Berkeley: University of California Press, 1997.

Treptow, Kurt W. "Albania and the Ottoman Invasion of Italy, 1480–1481," *Studia Albanica* 27 (1990): 81–106.

Trevelyan, C. E. *Treatise on the Education of the People of India*. London: Longman *et al.*, 1838.

Turner, Nicholas. *Federigo Barocci*. Paris: Vilo, 2000.

Tymoczko, Maria. *Early Irish Literature in English Translation*. Manchester: St Jerome, 1999.

  "Postcolonial Writing and Literary Translation," in *Post-Colonial Translation: Theory and Practice*, ed. Harish Trivedi and Susan Bassnett. London: Routledge, 1999, 19–40.

Vance, Norman. *The Victorians and Ancient Rome*. Oxford: Blackwell, 1997.

Vaughan, Richard. *Matthew Paris*. Cambridge: Cambridge University Press, 1958.

Venturi, Franco. "Oriental Despotism," *Journal of the History of Ideas* 24 (1963): 133–42.

Vergès, Françoise. *Monsters and Revolutionaries: Colonial Family Romance and Métissage*. Durham, NC: Duke University Press, 1999.

Verlinden, Charles. "Le présence turque à Otrante (1480–1481) et l'esclavage," *Bulletin de l'Institut Historique Belge de Rome* 53–4 (1983–84): 165–76.

Virahsawmy, Dev. *Touffan, in African Theatre: Playwrights and Politics*, ed. Martin Banham *et al*. Oxford: James Currey, 2001.

Vishwanathan, Gauri. *Masks of Conquest: Literary Study and British Rule in India*. Oxford: Oxford University Press, 1989.

  ed. *Piracy, Slavery and Redemption: Barbary Captivity Narratives from Early Modern England*. New York: Columbia University Press, 2001.

  ed. *Three Turk Plays from Early Modern England*. New York: Columbia University Press, 2000.

Vitkus, Daniel. "Turning Turk in *Othello*: The Conversion and Damnation of the Moor," *Shakespeare Quarterly* 48.2 (1997): 145–76.

Vitkus, Daniel and Jyotsna Singh, eds. *Rethinking Postcoloniality. Journal X*, 6 (2001).

von den Brincken, Anna-Dorothee. *Fines Terrae: Die Enden der Erde und der vierte Kontinent auf mittelalterlichen Weltkarten*. MGH, Schriften 36. Hanover: Hansche, 1992.

Walker, Roger M. "'Tere major' in the *Chanson de Roland*," *Olifant* 7 (1979): 123–30.

Wallace, David, ed. *The Cambridge History of Medieval English Literature*. Cambridge: Cambridge University Press, 1999.

Walter of Châtillon. *Alexandreis*, ed. Marvin Colker, *Galteri de castellione Alexandreis*. Padua: Antenore, 1978.

Warnke, Frank J. *Versions of Baroque: European Literature in the Seventeenth Century*. New Haven: Yale University Press, 1972.

Warton, Thomas. *The History of English Poetry*, 2 vols. London: Thomas Tegg, 1824.

Webb, J. F. and D. H. Farmer. *The Age of Bede*. Harmondsworth: Penguin, 1983.

Wellek, René. "The Concept of Baroque in Literary Scholarship," *Journal of Aesthetics and Art Criticism* 5 (1946): 70–109.

Wells, Peter S. *The Barbarians Speak: How the Conquered Peoples Shaped Roman Europe*. Princeton: Princeton University Press, 1999.

Westphalen, Tilman. *Beowulf 3150–55: Textkritik und Editionsgeschichte*, 2 vols. Munich: Fink, 1967.

Westrem, Scott D., ed. *The Hereford Map: A Transcription and Translation of the Legends with Commentary*. Turnhout: Brepols, 2001.

Weynand, Johanna. *Der Roman de toute chevalerie des Thomas von Kent in seinem Verhältnis zu seinen Quellen*. Bonn: Carl Georgi, 1911.

Whitbread, Leslie. "*Beowulf* and Archaeology," *Neuphilologische Mitteilungen* 69 (1968): 63–72.

Wiley, Raymond A., ed. and trans. *John Mitchell Kemble and Jakob Grimm: A Correspondence 1832–1852*. Leiden: Brill, 1971.

Williams, Deanne. *The French Fetish from Chaucer to Shakespeare*. Cambridge: Cambridge University Press. 2004.

  "Papa Don't Preach: The Power of Prolixity in *Pericles*," *University of Toronto Quarterly* 71 (2002): 595–622.

Williams, Howard. "Ancient Landscapes and the Dead: The Reuse of Prehistorical and Roman Monuments as Early Anglo-Saxon Burial Sites," *Medieval Archaeology* 41 (1997): 1–32.

Williams, John. "Isidore, Orosius and the Beatus Map," *Imago Mundi* 49 (1997): 7–32.

Wilson, Bronwen. "Reflecting on the Turk in Late Sixteenth-Century Venetian Portrait Books," *Word and Image* 19 (2001): 1–37.

Winterbottom, Michael, ed. and trans. *Gildas: The Ruin of Britain and Other Works*. London: Phillimore, 1978.

Wogan-Browne, Jocelyn, Nicholas Watson, Andrew Taylor, and Ruth Evans. *The Idea of the Vernacular: An Anthology of Medieval Literary Theory, 1280–1520*. University Park, PA: Penn state Press, 1999.

Wolfe, M. and J. Howe, eds. *Inventing Medieval Landscapes*. Gainesville: University Press of Florida, 2002.

Woodward, Christopher. *In Ruins*. New York: Pantheon, 2002.

Wrenn, C. L. *A Study of Old English Literature*. New York: Norton, 1966.

Wrenn, C. L. and W. F. Bolton, eds. *Beowulf*, third edn. London: Harrap, 1973.

Yeager, R. F., ed. *Chaucer and Gower: Difference, Mutuality, Exchange*. Victoria, BC: University of Victoria, 1991.

   ed. *Revisioning Gower*. Asheville, NC: Pegasus Press, 1998.

Young, Brian. "'The Lust of Empire and Religious Hate': Christianity, History and India, 1790–1820," in *History, Religion and Culture: British Intellectual History 1750–1950*, ed. Stefan Collini, Richard Whatmore and Brian Young. Cambridge: Cambridge University Press, 2000, 91–111.

Young, Robert. *Colonial Desire: Hybridity in Theory, Culture, and Race*. London and New York: Routledge, 1995.

Zeeman, Nicolette. "The Verse of Courtly Love in the Framing Narrative of the *Confessio Amantis*," *Medium Aevum* 60 (1991): 222–40.

Zizek, Slavoj. *The Sublime Object of Ideology*. London: Verso, 1989.

   Welcome to the Desert of the Real: 5 Essays on September 11 and Related Dates. London: Verso, 2002.

Zupitzta, Julius, ed. *Aelfric's Grammatik und Glossar*. Berlin: Weidmann, 1880.

Index

Index

floors
Beowulf, descriptions in, 82–4
mosaic, 82–4, 85
Roman, 77, 78
Littlecote Villa, 85
Woodchester Great Pavement, 85
tessellated, 82–4, 85
Foucque, Hippolyte, 216
France, 211, 212, 216, 219, 220
Ottoman Empire and, 172
Frantzen, Allen, 17, 134
Freeman, Edward Augustus, 197–8
Comparative Politics, 199–200
French, 129, 138, 221
British colonial discourse and, 186, 188, 189, 192
medieval England and, 16, 129
Friel, Brian, *Translations*, 264
Froissart, Jean, 127, 128

Gaelic, 197
Gage, Thomas, 240
Gascony, 57
Gautier, Léon, 205, 217
geography
late antique, 15
medieval, 106, 117, 123
colonizing process, 48–9, 60
crusading maps and, 61
postcolonial process, 48, 52, 60
see also Isidore of Seville, *Etymologiae*
Gilchrist, John Borthwick, *Dictionary English and Hindostanee*, 186, 187, 189, 190, 192
Gildas, 184
The Ruin of Britain, 27–8
Gilman, Stephen, 247
Giulio Romano, "Hall of Troy" frescoes, 171–2
Gladiator, 11
Gog and Magog, 109, 110, 113, 115, 116–17
González Echevarría, Roberto, 228, 229, 235, 246
Gothic, 198
Gower, John, 15–16
and literary hybridity, 142
as political conservative, 127–9
Confessio Amantis, see Confessio Amantis
criticism on, 127–9
Mirour de l'omme, 129, 132
postcolonial approaches to, 144, 145–6
Vox Clamantis, 129, 132
Greece, 111
Greek culture, 54, 55, 83–4, 157
Greek language, 131, 141
British colonial discourse and, 186, 188, 189, 192, 199

letter from Alexander to Aristotle, 121
Greeks
as medieval Europeans, 155, 165
distinct from Trojans, 152, 153, 165
Greenblatt, Stephen, 2, 6, 262
Greer, Margaret R., 9
Gregory the Great, n. 33, 46, 133, 134
Grendel, 77, 87, 91, 95, 97
Guido delle Colonne, *Historia destructionis Troiae*, 153, 165

Hadfield, Andrew, 14
Hadrian's Wall, 36, 37–8
Halhed, Sir Nathaniel, 186, 190, 192
Hardison, Robert, 29
Hardt, Michael, 11
Hastings, Warren, 183, 191
Heaney, Seamus, 13, 265
as postcolonial poet, 89–90, 98
Freedman, 89–90
No Sanctuary, 91
translator of *Beowulf*, 77, 78, 86, 88–9, 91, 96
see also Beowulf, postcolonial artifact
Heart of Darkness, 26
Heber, Bishop Reginald, "Morte D'Arthur," 200–1
Hector, 156
Hengest, 197
Heorot, 77, 83, 87, 97, 98
Hercules, 135
Pillars of, 109, 116
Highlands, 190
Hindustani, 185, 187
see also Gilchrist, John Borthwick
Historical Essay on the English Constitution, 188–9
history, Christian, 30, 31, 106–8
Anglo-Saxon conversion and, 30, 31
French, 222
Hereford *mappa mundi* and, 57–60
Holsinger, Bruce, 10, 19
Holy Land, 13, 114
see also Jerusalem; maps, medieval, Holy Land and
Homer, 152
Horace, 211
Hoskins, W. G., 35
Hrothgar, 87–8, 97
"Sermon" of, 80–97
humanism, 230, 231, 236, 237
Hume, David, 7, 8
hybridity
baroque and, 237
conjunctural, 266
Gower and, 142
Heorot and, 13

CAMBRIDGE STUDIES IN MEDIEVAL LITERATURE

CPSIA information can be obtained
at www.ICGtesting.com
Printed in the USA
LVHW091953121119
637140LV00007B/101/P

9 780521 827317